Downtown

Downtown

A History of Downtown Minneapolis and Saint Paul
in the Words of the People Who Lived It

Edited by David Anderson

NODIN PRESS

ISBN: 0-931714-83-4

First Edition

Library of Congress Number: 99-068392

Nodin Press, a division of Micawber's, Inc.
525 North Third Street
Minneapolis, MN 55401

Printed by Printing Enterprises

To my wife Ellen
and in memory of Dave Moore

Acknowledgments

This book has been over seven years in the making and the time has come to recognize the many people who have been so helpful and supportive along the way.

Special thanks to:

Norton Stillman, who has once again been so kind as to take me up on one of my ideas, and who has so graciously agreed to publish *Downtown*.

Russ Fridley, whose encouragement, expertise and unflagging editorial assistance have been invaluable to its completion.

Patrick Ring and Randy Jeans, those good friends and boon companions who accompanied me on walking tours of the two downtowns.

Wendy Chisholm Olson, Donna Lagato and computer ace Arthur Brady, those three intrepid typists who took on the always challenging job of deciphering my handwriting.

Larry Millett, whom I've never met, but whose wonderful book, *Lost Twin Cities*, proved to be an infinitely valuable resource.

The Minnesota Historical Society, the St. Paul Public Library, the Minneapolis Public Library (especially those always helpful folks who care for the Minneapolis Collection), the Ramsey County Historical Society and the Hennepin County Historical Society.

Finally, special thanks to my family (especially wife Ellen, father Clarence, mother Kitty, sister Peggy and brother Michael), their love and encouragement has known no end.

And last, but certainly not least, a *very* special thanks to *Downtown*'s many contributors (especially to the late Dave Moore, who, though ill, took the time to write a wonderful foreword for me). Obviously, there could have been no book without them.

CONTENTS

PART TWO
DOWNTOWN SAINT PAUL

Foreword

by Dave Moore

I cherish the memory of my downtown Minneapolis. Never has my affection for that remembrance been stronger than it is now—now that it has become hollow and soulless.

Today, as it struggles to become a seductive shopping haven for the rich, out of reach of the middle citizen, the fervent quality of a downtown Minneapolis of fifty and sixty years ago is as vivid in my mind's eye as it was then.

Almost haunting in its clarity is the bustle of Hennepin Avenue, glistening with what seemed a thousand movie theaters, quirky novelty stores, sawdust-floored meat markets (Great Northern on the west side of Hennepin, Witt's on the east) coffee and donut niches nestled between candy and card emporiums which, in turn, flanked barber shops, beauty salons, dry cleaning parlors and a cobbler's shop. All expressions of hundreds of small human initiatives. The memory begs, particularly when contrasted with the Hennepin of today and its avenue-stretching walls of windowless structures showing off a corporate power indifferent to the human spirit. They seem almost to be standing watch over Hennepin, in case some positive human endeavor should suddenly break out.

How I savor the memory of Nicollet Avenue's city life, with its two-way automobile traffic co-mingling with its people on the sidewalks, the random coming together of citizens in great mass. In my personal dictionary "puberty" would be defined as "that time in life when one is allowed, for the first time, to ride the streetcar downtown, by one's self."

"Soloing on the yellow banana" was the first acknowledged sign of social arrival. Such a time, for most of us, was age 11. Depending on their parents' respect for the child rearing codes of the day, some boys arrived at that point sooner than others. Bobby Finke, for instance, was allowed by this very permissive parents to make his solo trip at age nine! That put him way ahead of the rest of us on the ladder to social maturity. He extended the distance several years later when, at age 16, he was bodily ejected from a Washington Avenue house of prostitution. None of us ever really caught up with Bobby.

My allowance at age 11 was one buck. A dollar a week could take an 11-year-old quite a way in those days. A dime (or token) was the streetcar fare downtown. You got off at Seventh and Hennepin, walked a block east to the Greyhound Bus Station where you wormed your way onto a stool at the teeming lunch counter. For 55 cents you ordered a hot roast beef sandwich with mashed potatoes and gravy and a glass of milk. Pie was a quarter, but if all you had was your one dollar allowance you sacrificed the pie because you needed a quarter to get into the State Theater (*Night Must Fall* with Robert Montgomery, Rosalind Russell and Dame May Whitty) and a dime to get home on the Bryant-to-50th streetcar.

The movie notwithstanding, the highlight of the adventure was the lunch at the Greyhound Bus counter, where you squeezed yourself onto a stool between travelers. I'm not sure I can recreate this; you really had to be there: the bread sits in the center of the plate, right smack in the middle is a mountain-like scoop of the whitest white mashed potatoes you've ever seen; streaming down all its sides is thick, brown gravy that pools to cover every inch of the plate. If you asked you could get an extra piece of bread for mopping up the leftover gravy. Once, Jack Garske even asked for extra gravy. And got it! I'll never forget that. Nor this conversation, which I remember word for word:

WAITRESS: (clearing dishes of man to my right) Well, you sure must have liked the potatoes and gravy.
MAN TO MY RIGHT: Yep, as good as the Granger's in Duluth.
WAITRESS: Thank you, glad you liked it.
MAN TO MY RIGHT: (turning to me). I didn't want _tell her, but the gravy's better at Granger's.
ME: Oh.

But I really didn't see how it could be.

More often than not, taking the streetcar downtown was done with friends. At least one, perhaps two Fridays in the summer. Saturdays in the winter were good days because on Friday the movies changed and very often the goal of the trip was . . . hold on, folks, it gets pretty darned exciting here . . . are you ready? The goal was to check out the pictures of the scenes from the movie which were on display in front of the theater. Maybe a dozen at each theater. That's why you went with a friend: it was almost too much for one kid to handle. With ten movie theaters—count them, ten!—that kind of action would take a good portion of the afternoon. Make that ten including the uhh, well, the ALVIN. The last and only burlesque house in town, right there on Seventh Street, off Hennepin. For 11-year-olds, checking the pictures at the Alvin required a bit more time. There seemed to have been more photographic artistry involved than in the pictures, say, at the Gopher or Lyric or Aster. Particularly since none of us could get into the Alvin. Except, of course, Bobby Finke.

I'm sure it was my father's furniture store, founded at the turn of the century by his father, that opened my way to the joys of downtown. The last one of hundreds of small and mid-sized businesses that reflected the merchant's staying power of those days, before the bullying encroachment of the ravenous corporate axis. Moore & Scriver's residency in the elegant Young-Quinlan building on the corner of Ninth Street and Nicollet Avenue, was a four-floor display of fine furniture and tasteful objects of design. Its neighbors there on Nicollet Avenue were smallish shops that suggested patronage of good breeding: Ivey's Chocolate Shop, where small mints were served with mid-afternoon tea; Stendahl, the Shoeist; Bjorkman's and Raleigh's furs and women's finery; and the Silver Latch, a mite of a restaurant on Tenth Street, so impeccable that fresh napkins were brought with the dessert.

On those early teen occasions when a dental appointment or study at the library brought me downtown after school, I generally managed to get to the store an hour or so before its 5:30 closing to catch a ride home with my father. There, on the first floor, sunk deep in an overstuffed chair, out of sight, I could pick up muted tones of my father's conversation with a customer, who, often as not, turned out to be a niece or a granddaughter of a customer of his father decades ago.

In the early forties my father bought out the last of his partners and moved Moore & Scrivner Fine Furniture, to a barely visible little niche at 1114 Nicollet Avenue. As my father's step slowed, so too did his willingness to compete and market against the larger stores and the growing suburban centers. In those last years, with diminishing clientele, the store served him, primarily, as a creative writing sanctuary. Nearly every hour of the day he could be found seated on a worn davenport in the rear of the store, jotting into little notebooks verse and short fiction, much of it do with the complexities of nature and man.

Years later, my brother and I arranged for a thin volume of those writings to be published, entitled *My Soul Walked Naked in the Street*. Like the store, it did not do a brisk business. But unlike the store, it gave my father great satisfaction in his last years. More than once I have wondered what kind of weirdo little kid I must have been to have relished those occasional Sundays when my father packed the family—mother, older sister, older brother—into the Ford for the trip downtown and lunch with Grandma Moore at the Hampshire Arms Hotel where she had kept an apartment for many years.

In those days, conspicuous on the eastern boundary of the downtown shopping district, were the residential hotels. Before the Leamington was bought by Robert Short it stood for many years as a not inexpensive residency for older people of some means. Across the street, on Third Avenue, between Tenth and Eleventh streets, was the rather stately Curtis Hotel, owned by the Melony Family which they maintained as both a hotel and residential address for aging tenants, more for singles than couples.

One block over and one block down, on the corner of Fourth Avenue and Ninth Street, stood the venerable Hampshire Arms, a six-story, red stone monument to old money and even older fashion. The general ambiance of the hotel's lobby was a study in austerity that would have made Queen Victoria nervous. But Grandma Moore, stately and serene, was comfortable there. In the movies she would have been played first by Ethel Barrymore, and later, by Gladys Cooper.

Yet I must have enjoyed my Sundays there, for my memory of them is so precise. Particularly that lobby where the only sound to break the funereal gloom was the stammering clackety of the iron-gated doors of the creaking elevator. Stacks of railroad timetables covered the ledge of a window that looked into a darkened sitting room where there was seldom more evidence of life than a vase of wistful flowers.

Considerably cheerier and just as crisp in memory is the elegantly appointed dining room. To describe it as "old world" misses the mark—by a couple of worlds. Always, at lunch or dinner, a string trio was within dissonant reach of all diners.

Looking back, I'm sure what salvaged those Sundays for me was the Hampshire Arms' cream of tomato soup. I have not since found, nor do I ever expect to find, a match for it . It was creamed in such a way as to be nearly white, but without a loss of, as I remember it, tomato taste. I enjoyed it particularly when it was served by Floyd, a waiter who may have been only a bit older than the hotel itself, and who was not above chiding his own shakiness. It was always a matter of tense anticipation as Floyd wobbled the soup to the table. "Ah," he would say to my father. "Kept most of it in the cup that time, all right." Floyd was not without his pride.

He was one of whom I remember to be among a half dozen or so antique waiters, each managing to hang on to some semblance of fading dignity. There they are, standing in a distant corner of the Victorian dining room, properly tuxedoed, and looking for all the world like servants who, obediently, have arrived early to pose for a group picture.

The memories of those sweet and innocent times are pleasing, to be sure. But even I, notorious sentimentalist that I am, have no wish to return to their antiquity.

But, surely, don't all of us feel the need for a restoration of community to downtown Minneapolis? Recently Charles Leer, a bright young urban development consultant outlined in the *Minneapolis Star Tribune,* a proposal to convert the commercially blighted section of Hennepin Avenue known as "Block E" into an open space, "a town square or central park that would . . . bring together many different people, young and old, rich and poor, a full rainbow of colors on common ground in the core of downtown."

Mr. Leer goes on to explain a space that could feature "sitting areas with clusters of trees, fountains and soft, gravel pathways. Perhaps a skating rink in the winter, an amphitheater in the summer. Vendors of food and wares could market on the periphery. "The block," he wrote, "could be a true 'slice of life.'"

That would include, I hope, a hot roast beef sandwich with mashed potatoes and gravy.*

---

* This foreword was written by Dave Moore shortly before his death in January 1998. His enthusiasm for this project was greatly appreciated, and we are saddened that he is not here to see its completion.

What is the city but the people!
William Shakespeare

I must go and find out, I said, What is the voice of the city . . .

O. Henry

Introduction

BY DAVID ANDERSON

Downtown! Has there ever been a word that evokes a greater sense of excitement and adventure? Downtown . . . a simple word, but one which has the power to conjure up a whole world of images in our minds. Once we couple the word with the name of our two great cities those images become even more evocative and more specific. The moment we've uttered the words DOWNTOWN MINNEAPOLIS and DOWNTOWN SAINT PAUL, there are literally a million images—Seventh and Wabasha, Mickey's Diner, the Forum Cafeteria, the Foshay Tower, the 620 Club, the "Yellow Bananas," the First National Bank Building, the IDS Tower, Nicollet Mall, Dayton's, Donaldson's, Bridgeman's, Woolworth's, the Emporium, the Golden Rule, the Paramount, the World, the Orpheum, the Alvin, the West, the Ryan, the World Series Celebrations, VE Day, the Aquatennial and Winter Carnival Parades—which are brought immediately (and wonderfully) to mind.

Though the Golden Age of the two downtowns lasted less than three quarters of a century (the heyday of both downtown St. Paul and downtown Minneapolis, just like the downtowns of most of America's great cities, lasted only from the 1880s until the end of World War II), both cities grew rapidly in their early days and both were sprouting remarkably vibrant and exciting downtowns only a few short years after they had been carved out of the wilderness. J. Fletcher Williams, St. Paul's first historian, captured the essence of the soon-to-be capital city's early downtown when in his book, *A History of St. Paul to 1875,* he described the excitement and frenzy which characterized downtown St. Paul during the boomtown summer of 1857:

> St. Paul was said by travelers to be the fastest and liveliest town on the Mississippi River. The hotels and boarding houses were crowded to overflowing. The principle business streets fairly hummed with the rush of busy life. Building was never so brisk. Saloons, of course, throve as they always do, be times flush or hard. That season they coined money; so, also, did the livery stables. The city was continually full of tourists, spectators, sporting men, and even worse characters—all spending gold as though it were dross.

By the 1880s, both downtown St. Paul and downtown Minneapolis were growing at a phenomenal rate, a rate so rapid, in fact, that the two cities spent $17.8 million on construction in 1883 alone! By the 1890s both downtowns were densely built up along most of their core streets (most especially along Fourth and Jackson in St. Paul and along Nicollet Avenue in Minneapolis) as dozens of new "skyscrapers" and fancy retail emporiums took up residence among the wooden buildings and tumble-down shanties still much in evidence on downtown's muddy and manure-choked streets. "There was an almost solid wall of buildings in these places, and the result was urban congestion at it's best," wrote St. Paul architectural critic Larry Millett in his book, *Lost Twin Cities,* that incomparable study of lost Twin Cities architecture in which he further characterizes this period in the two downtowns' history as one which had attained "a kind of rambunctious grandeur," and also one in which "an amazing amount of visual clutter" was the hallmark of downtown's streets:

> Sidewalks were carnivals of boisterous capitalism, a chaotic medley of sights, sounds and smells. They were crowded not only with people but also with a wide assortment of freestanding and overhanging signs, numerous clocks (almost every jeweler had one in front of his shop), rows of huge multi-masted utility poles, plus a generally mismatched array of lamps, benches, water fountains and trashbins.

The downtown St. Paul and Minneapolis of this era—the so-called "Golden Age" of Midwest cities—were thus forged in a far different time than our own—a time which had not yet discovered zoning laws and city planning, a time in which it had not yet occurred to anyone to try to homogenize, standardize or sanitize downtown's streets. Lewis Mumford, that foremost scholar of the city, could just as well have been describing the "rambunctious" and up-and-coming downtowns of the "Golden Age" as he could the emerging Greek city-states of the fifth century B. C., when in his classic study, *The City in History,* he described Athens and its neighbors as having achieved something "deeply organic, something close to the quick core of human existence . . . a wild union of opposites, restriction and exuberance, Apollonian discipline and Dionysian delirium, rational intelligence and blind intuition, muddy tumble and skyward flight."

During the first three decades of the twentieth century the population of both cities soared (in Minneapolis it more than doubled from 203,000 in 1900 to 460,000 in 1930; and in St. Paul it increased from 163,000 to 270,000 during the same period) as both downtowns reached their historic highs in street-level density, and both took on the wonderfully familiar shapes and personalities that would for so many years be so inextricably woven into the very fabric of our lives. This was the heyday of the "brawny, brawling, muscular city,"* the last great era of downtown growth (the depression and then the war would put a halt to most construction beginning in the early thirties), the last time in history when the two downtowns could be said to be at the absolute center of their respective community's lives.

Though the great wave of post-war prosperity would temporarily mask the worst of downtown's problems, it was clear by the late forties and the early fifties that both had entered upon a period of significant decline. Suburban flight was sucking money, jobs and industry out of their old commercial cores at an alarming rate (between 1948 and 1954 retail sales plummeted by some $15 million in downtown St. Paul, and in downtown Minneapolis

things were almost as bleak), while the twin scourges of urban renewal and the federal highway program were wreaking their havoc on the buildings and neighborhoods that had been left behind.

In 1955 General Mills announced that it was abandoning downtown Minneapolis and that it would establish its new headquarters in Golden Valley. In 1956, Southdale, the world's first enclosed, climate-controlled shopping mall, opened for business in Edina. It was clear from that point on that the suburbs were where the action would be at. Downtown Minneapolis and downtown St. Paul—just like downtowns everywhere—would now be in a fight for their very lives.

Downtown is essentially an anecdotal—as opposed to a narrative—history of downtown St. Paul and downtown Minneapolis. While both of it's sections begin with a brief overview of the history and development of one of the two downtowns, and while both sections contain a number of articles *about* some aspect or other of each, the reader will soon discover that the heart and soul of this book are the stories of each of it's many contributors—the individual, the unique, and the personal reminiscences of just a few of the many millions of people who made downtown St. Paul and downtown Minneapolis the living, breathing, hustling, bustling, vibrant and eternally exciting centers of community life that we all once knew them to be.

I have gathered these accounts from many sources (books, magazines, interviews, newspapers, diaries, journals), from many different historical periods (the earliest is from 1850, the latest from the 1990s), and from many different kinds of people (there are accounts here from the most "respectable" and well-known of local residents and visitors to the two cities, as well as those gathered from the ranks of so-called "ordinary" people, even some by guys who have lived on downtown's streets).

It is important to emphasize that *Downtown* does not pretend to be a complete or a comprehensive history of either downtown Minneapolis or downtown St. Paul. It is, rather, something more closely resembling a social history of the two downtowns—a book not so much *about* downtown as one

---

* Joel Garreau, *Edge City*

about people and about their experiences of *being* downtown; about what it actually felt like to live, work, shop, play, eat, drink and celebrate in downtown St. Paul and Minneapolis from the earliest times down until the present day.

From the beginning of the first section of *Downtown* (the *Minneapolis Tribune's* account of the Great Mill Explosion of May 2, 1878), until the end of the last (Greg Horan's powerfully evocative piece about a night spent on downtown St. Paul's streets), it has been my goal to present the reader with as varied and wide-ranging an assortment of stories and perspectives as possible, it being my firmly held belief that these stories, both when read individually and when taken together as a whole, will provide the reader with a deeper and far more richly textured understanding of the worlds of downtown St. Paul and downtown Minneapolis than any amount of analysis or explication on the part of the editor (or on the part of any single individual) would ever be able to provide. Whether it's Alice Montfort Dunn's charming and variegated description of life in downtown St. Paul as seen from her strategic perch at the old Windsor Hotel of the 1880s ("People and Places in Old St. Paul"), A. J. Russell's poetic and unabashedly sentimental evocation of Minneapolis' old Newspaper Row ("Fourth Street"), or Charles Rumford Walker's blow-by-blow description of the Great Trucker's Strike of 1934, and of the decidedly unsentimental events of the Battle of Deputies Run ("Battle in the Streets"), each of these pieces—and the some three dozen which accompany them—has been chosen not only because it adds greatly to our understanding of the many (and often sadly lost) worlds of downtown St. Paul and Minneapolis, but also because it has the power to do so in it's own very particular and personal way.

Believe it or not there has never been a book written about either downtown Minneapolis or St. Paul.* Of the countless volumes that have been published on some aspect or other of the history of the state of Minnesota in the last century-and-a-half, not a single one has been devoted, either in whole or in any significant part, to the history of either or both of the two downtowns—a stunning and really quite unfathomable oversight given their status as the twin hubs of the state's two greatest cities, the once absolute and unchallenged centers of its social, political and economic life.

Of course neither downtown St. Paul nor downtown Minneapolis will ever come close to occupying the positions of absolute dominance that they once did. The best that their partisans can hope for is that they will be able to share a place in the spotlight with the now innumerable suburban shopping centers, most especially, of course, the Mall of America. It's important to remember, however, that much was lost when we abandoned our cities and downtowns for those shopping malls. It's important to remember that we paid a terrible price when we left our streets and downtowns behind. In *The City in History*, Lewis Mumford warns us of the folly of turning our backs on the streets of our cities and downtowns, reminding us that Plato, that most notable of all city planners, made that very mistake when he designed his famous Utopia almost 2,500 years ago.

> When Plato turned his back on the disorder and confusion of Athens to rearrange the social functions of the city. . . he also turned his back, unfortunately, on the essential life of the city itself, with its power to crossbreed, to intermingle, to reconcile opposites, to create new synthesis, to elicit new purposes not predetermined by the petrified structure itself. In short, he rejected the potentiality of transcending race and caste . . . What he did not expect, apparently, was that this geometric heaven might, in terms of man's suppressed potentialities, turn out to be a living hell.

The city that Plato proposed to create in that distant world of ancient Greece was not, of course, all that different from the world that we created in the typical American suburb of the last half of the twentieth century. Plato, just like his modern suburban counterpart, had sought refuge in a sterile, planned, and utterly homogenous environment, rejecting above all else the messiness and the unpredictability (i.e. the "undesirable" people) that were so inevitably (and inconveniently) to be found upon a city's streets. "Plato's polis might be described as a walled prison without room for the true activities of the city within it's prison yard," said Mumford, pointing out that Plato's whole concept of the ideal polis was a

---

*At least not one the editor could find. If the reader knows of any such book the editor would greatly appreciate hearing about it.

"self-isolating one," a place "meant for upper class use alone," one in which Plato, eerily anticipating the enclosed shopping mall of the latter half of the twentieth century, even went so far as to propose an ideal habitat for his utopia's wealthy inhabitants, one in which, says Mumford, "he had no use for fresh air from outdoors, instead contriving a windowless chamber into which he could pump artificially purified air, anticipating the absurdities of a certain type of modern mind by twenty-four hundred years."

The history of downtown Minneapolis and St. Paul is a large subject, larger, certainly, than could ever be adequately covered in a volume of this size. It's my hope, therefore, that the reader of *Downtown* might be able to find it in his or her heart to forgive its inevitable failings and omissions, especially its failure to discuss any of the countless people, places and events that could (and undoubtedly *should*) have been covered in its pages, but which have been so unfortunately omitted, either due to ignorance on the part of its editor, or to the inevitable constraints imposed upon him by limited space and time.

It's my hope that *Downtown*, no matter what its failings and limitations, will have succeeded in at least one respect. That it will have succeeded in capturing something of the *essence* of the two downtowns. Downtown Minneapolis and St. Paul were both unique and wonderful places, each with its own particular history and ambience, each having proudly occupied a place at the very heart of its community's life. If *Downtown* has succeeded at nothing else, I hope that it has succeeded in capturing both places in at least some of their richness and depth of character, that it has, through the medium of its many and various voices, brought us close to the heart and soul of the two downtowns.

"A city begins with a place and ends with people," wrote B. A. Botkin in his book, *Sidewalks of America*. Here, then, are the stories of the people who have made the places we call downtown Minneapolis and St. Paul.

Part One
Downtown Minneapolis

History has permitted the average city in Europe a thousand years in which to make the transition from barbarism to maturity. Minneapolis, through a skipping and compression of historic stages from backwoods to civic maturity, achieved "civilization" in little more than forty.

Charles Rumford Walker

Chapter One

A Brief History of Downtown Minneapolis

by David Anderson

One of the earliest photographs of the area of downtown Minneapolis. Note the Stevens House behind teepee at right. *Minneapolis Public Library.* **Mpls. Collection.**

The Early Days

The first white person to formally lay claim to lands that would one day be a part of the city of Minneapolis was Franklin Steele, a transplanted New Englander (and Fort Snelling's enterprising young sutler), who in July of 1838 became the first claimant to the east bank section of St. Anthony Falls that had been separated from the Fort Snelling reservation by the treaties of 1837.

The settlement which grew up on and around Franklin Steele's claim was not originally a part of the city of Minneapolis. It was instead a prosperous village called St. Anthony, whose population grew spectacularly from some 248 souls in 1848 to 4,689 in 1857, largely due to the success of the flour and saw mills constructed by Steele and his associates following the damming of the river's eastern channel in 1848.

Although at first glance (and at least from a distance) the budding little settlement "looked much like a New England village," wrote Lucille M. Kane in her book, *The Falls of St Anthony,* a second and closer look apparently revealed a rather different picture, a somewhat less idyllic (though probably quite typical) frontier scene, "in which houses built of green lumber cured [while] on their foundations, to the annoyance of housewives who mopped up the oozing moisture. Nasty, piratical pigs roamed at will, and the streets were filled with stumps. Stagecoaches, carts and wagons rumbling in from St. Paul spilled out passengers with mountains of baggage and freight. Indians wandered through the town, strangers to the noise and bustle around them. Piles of logs and lumber from the sawmills dotted the landscape, and the whine of the saws could be heard above the roar of the falls."

Despite its early success, St. Anthony's dominance at the falls was not to last for long. By 1865 its population had dropped to 3,499 and its fortunes had sunk so low that one observer went so far as to call it "the city of the unburied dead." Almost overnight, it seems, the panic of 1857 and the chronic financial problems of St. Anthony Falls Water Power Company, had caused the city to fall well behind Minneapolis, its vigorous and thriving neighbor across the river.

The village of Minneapolis (its name was first proposed by one Charles Hoag, who had derived it from "Minnehaha," the Dakota word for "laughing waters," and "polis," the Greek word for "city") got its legal start in 1852 when Congress passed a long-awaited bill severing over 26,000 acres from the Fort Snelling reservation, finally allowing Colonel John H. Stevens (Franklin Steele's bookkeeper) and other early squatters to legally get their hands on the much coveted real estate which abutted St. Anthony Falls' west bank. Stevens' claim of 160 acres included a major portion of what would now be considered "the loop," and encompassed the land from Second Avenue South to Bassetts Creek and from the river bank back to the area around present day Seventh Street. Exhibiting admirable foresight,

Stevens gave away lots from his own claim in order to encourage development, wisely platting wide streets and good-sized-lots. He also built a small white frame house (the first in Minneapolis and probably the only frame dwelling from there to the Rockies) on the river bank near the ferry landing, and he lived there with his family on what soon came to be known as "Ferry Farm." "In a very true sense [Stevens'] white house was the embryo of the city," wrote Calvin Schmid in his book, *Social Saga of Two Cities*. "The first child in Minneapolis was born there; land was bought and sold; religious services were held; federal judges sat in court there; and political parties met there to choose candidates; travelers stayed the night, and musicals were given. It was a bank, real estate office, theater, church, court, hospital and hotel. Even in the first house in the old city, all embryonic institutions of the present metropolis functioned in the service of the people."

With the opening of the west bank land for private ownership, settlers poured in rapidly. In 1854 there were a dozen houses on the Minneapolis side; by autumn of the next year over one hundred had been built and the settlement's population had increased to almost one thousand. By 1855 the various west bank saw mills had been consolidated into a partnership holding of twelve men (among them were such prominent early settlers as Dorelius Morrison and William D. and Cadwallader C. Washburn), and by 1856 the settlement featured a full compliment of schools, churches, cultural organizations and stores. By 1857 Minneapolis had become a bustling business center, a fact made clear by the following description of it and of St. Anthony in the May 7, 1857 issue of the *St. Anthony Republican:*

Business. Never before have the streets of this dual city seen such business activity. Steamboat whistles sound at both ends of the city. An unending number of goods laden wagons and carriages . . . All of the ladies are out to get first choice . . . Continued rattle of machines. New buildings shooting up right and left. Everyone in a hurry. Such is the life of St. Anthony and Minneapolis.

Minneapolis as it looked from the corner of Second Avenue and Washington, 1857. This picture was taken from the roof of the St. James Hotel. *Minneapolis Public Library.* **Mpls. Collection.**

MINNEAPOLIS IN 1870.
FROM ROOF OF WINSLOW HOUSE.

Published by E. A. Bromley, Minneapolis
from the original Upton negatives.

The sawmills of St. Anthony, 1870. *Minneapolis Public Library.* Mpls. Collection.

Consolidation, and Rivalry With St. Paul

By 1856 Minneapolis' population was 4,607, and its well managed and prosperous Minneapolis Mill Company had seen to it that the city was turning out five times as much flour and twice as much lumber as its eastern neighbor, making it clearly the dominant of the two cities. Gradually, it became clear to the people on both sides of the river that it made no sense to maintain two separate municipal organizations, and in 1872 the east and west bank settlements were consolidated into the single city of Minneapolis.

Once united into a single powerful manufacturing center, the newly unified young city set about the great task of gaining supremacy over St. Paul, its neighbor and longtime competitor downriver. One can get some sense of the tone of this competition—and of the genuine seriousness with which it had always been fought—when one encounters in an article in the *St. Anthony Express* of July 5, 1851, the rather ungenerous hope of its author that the city of St Paul would, upon losing out in the then raging battle over which city would become the "true head" of navigation of the Mississippi," retrograde into a modest little village [where] the grass will grow in the now crowded and busy exchange [and where] the owls will build their nests in the City Hall, grand even in ruins."

The battle between the two cities would be fought on many other fronts over the years (politics, population, economic supremacy, even baseball), with Minneapolis proving to be the winner more often than not. By 1880 it had passed St. Paul in population (46,887 to 41,473), as thousands of new immigrants (Swedes, Norwegians and British predominated) poured into the city, many finding employment in the 24 mills that were crowded into the small industrial area by the falls. By 1880 the milling district had become the most productive in the country, producing some two million barrels of flour annually. Lumbering was still the city's biggest claim to fame, however, as by 1901 its mills were finishing off the last of the regions white pine at the world-record rate of 552 million board feet per year! "As the settlers exploited the forests and other natural resources," said the *WPA Guide to Minnesota*, "[they] shared the powers of ruthlessness and vision that characterize all conquerors, making it possible for them to build a great city in a phenomenally short time; a city that carried two infant industries to world records in little more than a single generation."

Bridge Square

When the first suspension bridge between Minneapolis and St. Anthony was completed in 1855 (it was also the first permanent span of any kind built across the Mississippi) the so-called "Bridge Square" district, which developed around the bridge on the Minneapolis side of the river, became the center of activity in the newly developing downtown Minneapolis. The bridge was crucial to the establishment of Bridge Square as Minneapolis' early central business district. Its importance in establishing the nexus of Hennepin and Nicollet Avenues (at Washington Avenue) as the two most important downtown business streets was explained by Isaac Atwater in his book, *The History of Minneapolis*:

> The building of the suspension bridge was a far more important factor in determining the future center of business and indeed was decisive in favor of Hennepin and Nicollet . . . The opening of . . . the bridge had the natural effect of stimulating the

building up of streets leading to it on the west side of the river. From its western terminal the territorial road, now Hennepin Avenue, led to the lakes and thence to the fine farming country beyond them. Stores and shops rapidly concentrated about this central part of town. Land owners at the upper and lower parts of the town realized that other avenues must be opened across the river to maintain the prestige of those sections. For the next thirteen years, the Suspension Bridge was the only avenue connecting the two cities facing each other across the river.

Hay Market at Bridge Square, 1873. *Minnesota Historical Society.*

The Rise of Downtown

Downtown Minneapolis grew rapidly after the Civil War, and by the 1870s had begun to sprout such notable brick and Platteville limestone structures as the Brackett Block, at what is now Marquette and Second Street (1871), the City Hall at Bridge Square (1873), Jefferson School, at Seventh Street and First Avenue North (1871), Central High School, at Eleventh Street and Fourth Avenue South (1878), and the City Market House, at Hennepin Avenue and First Street (1876). Two prominent theaters also

The Minneapolis City Hall—Hennepin County Courthouse as it appeared from Third Avenue South looking toward Fifth Avenue. Note that the courthouse was built at a time (it was completed in 1906) when this was still a residential area. *Minnesota Historical Society.*

opened in the years after the war, the Pence Opera House (1867), and the Academy of Music (1872), both on lower Hennepin Avenue. Not all forms of downtown entertainment were always quite so "cultural," however, as was shown by the census of 1880 which revealed that downtown Minneapolis was also home to four brothels and 176 saloons!

The population of Minneapolis grew rapidly during the 1880s, and by 1895 had reached 192,823, eighteenth largest of any city in the country. By this time the city had also begun to develop a full-blown "downtown," a downtown which according to Lucille M. Kane and Alan Ominsky in their book, *Twin Cities*, had by that time taken on "the texture of big cities during the golden age."

Downtown buildings—massive, vaulted, arched, towered, and profusely ornamented reflected the city's prosperity, civic pride, and exuberance, as well as new architectural styles. Visitors could enjoy the cities growing maturity. [They] might drop in at the new public library, shop at Donaldson's Glass Block Store, and ascend on "fantastic birdcage elevators" to the twelfth floor of the Guaranty Building (later the Metropolitan) for dining in the "skyroom" restaurant, a stroll through the roof garden, and a climb to the look-out tower. From the tower they could watch workmen putting up the new city hall-courthouse known as the municipal building, a massive red granite "stone pile" completed in 1905.

Bridge Square c. 1891. *Hennepin County Historical Society.*

The 1880s and 1890s were a period when both public and private buildings were going up at an unprecedented rate in downtown Minneapolis, a rate so impressive, in fact, that upon his visit to the city in 1891 the distinguished architectural critic Montgomery Schuyler expressed his astonishment at the explosive growth of downtown Minneapolis, pointing out when asked to compare it to downtown St. Paul, that "whereas St. Paul has been developed from the frontier trading posts of the earlier days by an evolution, the successive stages of which have left their several records, Minneapolis has risen like an exhaltation . . . sprung from the heads of its progenitors full panoplied in brick and mortar."

Among the most significant new structures that Schuyler would have seen during his 1891 visit

were: The Lumber Exchange, at Fifth and Hennepin (1886), Temple Court, at Washington and Hennepin (1886), the Bank of Minneapolis, at Third and Nicollet (1887), the Globe Building, at Fourth and Hennepin (1889), and the Western Guaranty Loan (Metropolitan) Building (1890), which at 12 stories in height began a reign over the Minneapolis skyline that would last for the next 24 years. The Industrial Exposition Building (1886), which was over one square block in size, and located on the east bank near St. Anthony Falls, and the Syndicate Block (1883), which covered over five acres of floor space at Nicollet, between Fifth and Sixth, were the two most capacious buildings of the day.

The 1880s also saw a decided shift in downtown's center of gravity, a shift away from the old Bridge

Square District, and one in which the city's important buildings gradually began to migrate south along Hennepin and Nicollet avenues, with Nicollet becoming the city's most important retail street. In 1884 the opening of the magnificent West Hotel, at Fifth and Hennepin, gave a boost to that avenue, which gradually developed into the city's major entertainment strip. Bank and office buildings spread out along Nicollet, Marquette and Second Avenue South, while the wholesale district developed north

The Rise of Nicollet Avenue

Nicollet Avenue was named after Joseph N. Nicollet, a French scientist and explorer who visited and mapped the upper sources of the Mississippi in 1836. The name "Nicollet" was given to the avenue (actually, it was called Nicollet Street until 1887) by Colonel John H. Stevens shortly after his farm was platted into city lots in 1854.

Nicollet Avenue got its start because there hap-

The West Hotel, at right, and the Masonic Temple under construction, c. 1887. *Hennepin County Historical Society.*

of Hennepin. Property values were rising so rapidly during this time that most churches and homes were forced out of the downtown area. By 1884, virtually no private residences remained.

pened to be a small body of water called Goose Pond located in the middle of Bridge Square. When people crossed over to Minneapolis from the St. Anthony side of the river they ran straight into Goose Pond, and when doing so had to decide whether they wanted to go around it to the right or to the left. The trail to the left of the pond went to Fort Snelling and became what is now Nicollet Avenue. The trail to the right headed toward the northern settlements and became Hennepin Avenue. The "Bridge Square" district which grew up at the junction of Hennepin and Nicollet soon became the retail center of the city, with its motley collection of general stores, impermanently housed in rude structures, providing city residents with as wide a variety of merchandise as was then generally available. Barter was as common as were cash transactions in those early days, as white fur traders would come in from the west and the northwest with furs and pelts obtained from the Indians and would exchange them for a variety of goods which they would then use to carry on further transactions.

The era of "general merchandise" prevailed in Minneapolis until several years after the close of the Civil War, when because of increasing demand it became necessary for the city's retail merchants to carry larger stocks and a wider assortment of goods.

The first city business to branch out in this manner was the dry goods establishment of G. W. Hale & Co., which opened for business in 1867 in a cheap little balloon frame building on Washington Avenue near Nicollet, and moved five years later to a brick structure on Third and Nicollet. In 1873 it merged with Jefferson Hale's store at 250 Nicollet, and soon became the principle mercantile establishment in the city. G. W. Hale expanded again in 1884 and again in 1905, at that point under the name J. W. Thomas and Company. "I was very impressed with Hale and Thomas," said 90-year-old Mrs. Clarkson Lindley (the daughter of prominent early settler, Samuel Gale) when recalling the early days of downtown Minneapolis for Barbara Flanagan and the *Minneapolis Tribune* in 1958. "Remember we had wooden sidewalks and streets of mud then. And in the rainy weather the mud flowed like a river down Nicollet. The store employed a man to stand at the corner of Fifth and Nicollet and sweep mud off the crossing so the ladies wouldn't dirty their long skirts. He worked so hard and whenever he stopped sweeping the mud oozed back. I always wore long skirts—all the young teenagers did—and I remember how our

skirts were simply caked with mud. We'd go home and hang them out to dry, then scrape off the mud."

The first genuine "department store" in Minneapolis was opened by S. G. See at Ninth and Nicollet in 1875. This location was considered at that time to be "away out on the prairie," and See, in order to try to get people to this "remote location" was forced to advertise heavily and offer free trolley rides to and from the store for all female shoppers. The store never caught on, however, and See was forced to close it and return to Chicago, the location of his first department store.

In 1902 Worthington banker and real estate investor George D. Dayton, owner of a number of valuable pieces of downtown real estate (including the site of the old Westminster Presbyterian Church, which had burned down at its location at Seventh and Nicollet in 1897), made his entry into the downtown retail scene when, as a silent partner with the owners of R. S. Goodfellow and Company, he built his famous store on the corner of Seventh and Nicollet. (Fire destroyed the original store in 1917; the present 12-story building was put up in its place.) This store, which originally was stocked with merchandise from Goodfellows and bore that company's name, was not a financial success, however, and Dayton soon found it necessary to change its name to Dayton's and to buy his partners out. Soon he and his son Draper would have the store on a sound financial footing, and would dramatically turn its fortunes around.

Among the other early retailers on Nicollet Avenue was the firm of Ingram, Olson and Company, which opened for business between Washington Avenue and Second Street in 1886. In 1893 Ingram, Olson moved to the corner of Fifth and Marquette where, known as the S. E. Olson Company, it advertised itself as "The Big Store." When Alonzo J. Powers became president under new ownership in 1901 the firms name was changed to Powers Mercantile Company. Under Power's stewardship a Nicollet Avenue corner was added to the store in 1906 (the company had acquired the Arcade which led through its building to Nicollet Avenue some years earlier), and the first "moving stairway" (or escalator) ever seen in the city of Minneapolis was installed. The company continued to be known as Powers until it closed its doors in 1985.

Powers department store as it appeared at its Fifth and Nicollet location in 1908. *Hennepin County Historical Society.*

Powers as it appeared in 1951 from the almost exact place that the above photo was taken. *Hennepin County Historical Society.*

Meanwhile, a large new store had been opened at Sixth and Nicollet by Colton & Company, in a one-story wood-frame building which featured as its principle attraction more windows than any other store in the city. (This corner had been previously occupied by a large residence surrounded by shade trees and a lawn.) William Donaldson, who had opened a men's furnishing shop at Third and Nicollet in 1881, so admired "The Glass Block" that he and his brother Lawrence bought the building and in 1884 reopened it as Donaldson's Glass Block Store. By 1888 the brothers had built a new five-story building that was composed almost entirely of glass and iron. It featured a total of 14 departments devoted to such categories of goods as upholstery, boots and shoes,

carpets, millinery, cookery, glassware and house-keeping goods, as well as a complete lunchroom, an innovation which prior to that time had been attempted only by the biggest department stores out east. After the death of William Donaldson in 1907, the store became the L. S. Donaldson Company and expanded its building to the corner of Seventh and Nicollet, where it remained until 1982 when the store was moved into new and smaller quarters across the Nicollet Mall. The Donaldson name vanished from the Twin Cities retail scene in 1987 when Carson, Pirie, Scott of Chicago acquired all of Donaldson's Twin Cities stores. Carson, Pirie, Scott closed these stores in the early 1990s, however, due to chronically inadequate sales.

Donaldson's Glass Block, at Sixth and Nicollet, c. 1925. *Minneapolis Public Library.* Mpls. Collection.

Donaldson's shoe department, 1910. *Minnesota Historical Society.* Photo by C. J. Hibbard & Co.

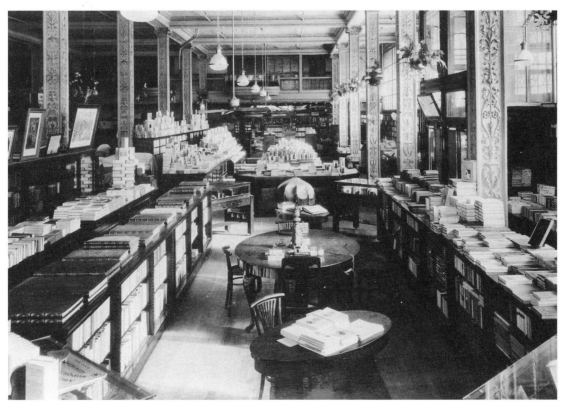

Powers book department, 1915. *Minnesota Historical Society.*

Interior of Young, Quinlan Co., October 18, 1944. *Minnesota Historical Society.* **Photo by Norton & Peel.**

By 1894 the population of Minneapolis had risen to 190,000 and Nicollet Avenue was paved, lit by gaslight, and bustling with people, most of whom had come there to shop in its department stores and specialty shops. Amazingly, none of the stores of that era had as yet thought to sell ready-to-wear clothing (Minneapolis residents had to go to New York to buy such fashions; otherwise, the city's women cultivated their favorite dressmaker, millinery shop and dry goods store, and men had their suits and shirts made to order) until Elizabeth Quinlan, then a star saleswoman at Goodfellow's, and her partner Fred Young, opened a fashionable women's ready-to-wear specialty shop called the Young Quinlan Company in a small back room at 513 Nicollet in 1894.

Elizabeth Quinlan was the first and only female clothing buyer in the country at that time, and her shop only the second ready-to-wear woman's clothing store in the country. In 1926, with the financial backing of the Rothschilds, she built an elegant new Italian Renaissance-style building at Ninth and Nicollet, a Mall landmark (now occupied by Polo, Ralph Lauren; the Young Quinlan Company went out of business in 1985) that remains to this day. Before her death in 1947 Elizabeth Quinlan won recognition for her retailing innovations from both *Time* and *Fortune* magazines. During the Great Depression Franklin Roosevelt appointed her to the national board of the N. R. A.

By 1910 the center of downtown had moved to the southeast corner of Fourth and Nicollet, with Nicollet Avenue being broad, well paved, handsomely lighted, and filled with retail stores that ranged in size from the great buildings which occupied the better part of a block, down to those filling recesses of the smallest kind. "Nicollet Avenue's handsome stores are so successfully decorated that the sidewalks in front of them are consistently thronged with eager shoppers and sightseers," said the *Minneapolis Journal* in 1911. "It shares with Fifth Avenue in New York the unique feature of freedom from streetcar tracks, and this makes it a great resort for pedestrians, of whom there is during the daylight hours a constant parade to and fro, which becomes at times, at the holiday season for example, or on a Saturday, a dense crowd." This freedom from the trolley lines (the business interests of the city had deliberately chosen to have the streetcars run on Hennepin and Marquette, but not Nicollet) enabled Nicollet Avenue to promote itself on the basis of its convenience and its safety for children and was yet another reason why it was able to secure its dominance as the city's primary retail street.

Christmas decorations at Nicollet Avenue and Seventh Street, c. 1935. *Minnesota Historical Society.*

Hennepin Avenue, c. 1915. *Hennepin County Historical Society.*

Early Hennepin Avenue

By the mid 1860s the west bank settlement of Minneapolis was firmly established, and Hennepin Avenue had become its undisputed commercial center. This period marked what soon came to be known as Hennepin Avenue's "boom and bloom" years, as in addition to the impressive array of businesses which occupied the two-story wooden structures that lined both sides of the street (among them were a mill, a bookstore, a farmer's supply store, a molding and picture frame factory and hardware and furniture stores) it featured the magnificent Pence Opera House, the city's first theater, and also one of the few survivors of an 1866 fire that destroyed most of the first generation of buildings that comprised the city's early business district.

Bridge Square, at the foot of Hennepin, emerged during this period as the city's banking and commercial center, becoming with the completion of the new city hall in 1873 its civic center as well. The City Hall building, a rather curious wedge shaped structure that was 160 feet long, but only twenty feet wide at its narrow end on First Street (Nicollet Avenue ran along its east side; Hennepin on its west side) housed such essential city institutions as the *Minneapolis Tribune*, the Post Office and the Northwestern Telegraph Company. The building proved to be a firetrap, however (it was also poorly ventilated; sewage fumes were said to have regularly sickened postal workers on its first floor), and by 1889 the city was already planning a new (and the still extant) City Hall to take its place.

By the 1880s Minneapolis had become a wealthy city, and the new buildings constructed on Hennepin Avenue during that period were a dramatic demonstration of that fact. The seven-story Boston Block (1881), at Third and Hennepin and the Kasota Block (1884), near Bridge Square, were two of the city's first "skyscrapers" and were, along with the eleven-story Lumber Exchange Building (1886), the Masonic Temple, the Globe Building and the Sykes and Wright Blocks (all 1889) among the most prominent structures in the city during that decade. By the 1890s, however, this great building boom had come to an end (the depression of 1893 and building codes which discouraged the construction of skyscrapers

had seen to that), and by the end of the century the fashion and retail center of town had begun to shift from Hennepin Avenue to Nicollet, causing Hennepin to slip into its first period of decline.

The Avenue was soon on the rebound, however, as the great age of Vaudeville was to come to its rescue, bringing with it the many great theaters which would shape its character for the next fifty years. By the 1920s such theaters as the Astor, the Grand, the Blue Mouse (later the Lyric), the New Garden, the Pantages, the Palace, the State (the first on the Avenue designed primarily for movies), and the Hennepin Orpheum (an opulent 2200 seat Italian Renaissance palace which cost a million dollars to build in 1921, and was said to be the biggest Vaudeville house outside of New York) were the main focus of life on the street. By 1917 Vaudeville had become so dominant that the Majestic Hotel, at Seventh and Hennepin, could make the rather amazing boast that it was the only modern popularly-priced hotel within one block of ten theaters.

The Majestic Hotel, c. 1904. *Minneapolis Public Library. Mpls. Collection*

The first Orpheum Theater, at 25 Seventh Street South, was an eighteen-hundred seat vaudeville house, and was built in 1904.
Minneapolis Public Library. Mpls. Collection.

A major slump hit the Vaudeville theaters in the early 1920s, however, as the movies and the desertion of the major stars to Hollywood (such headliners as Al Jolson, George Jessel, Burns and Allen, the Marx Brothers, Sophie Tucker and Gypsy Rose Lee had all played the Hennepin Avenue theaters, and all, of course, went on to movie careers) brought about vaudevilles decline. Soon the depression would seal live theater's doom, and Hennepin Avenue would once again find itself in for hard times.

The bars (and, during prohibition, the upstairs speakeasies) kept Hennepin's nightlife hopping during the depression years, though the Avenue—especially the lower Avenue—was in obvious trouble when viewed in the cold light of day. During those years vacant buildings and bankrupt businesses proliferated, as the once prosperous business section on lower Hennepin had deteriorated to such an extent that one observer described it as being little more than "a tumble down collection of cheap movie houses and restaurants, squalid flop houses, pawn shops and penny arcades."

During the next three decades many of Hennepin Avenues landmark structures were torn down, as economic "necessity" and the mania for urban renewal claimed the West, the Phoenix, the St. James and the Hans European hotels, the Astor and Grand theaters, the Boston Block office building, the Loeb Arcade, the former Pence Opera House (the Union City Mission from 1915 on) and the Gateway Pavilion and Park. Today, of course, Hennepin Avenue is still a street in transition (its infamous Block "E," between Sixth and Seventh streets, remains a parking lot as of this writing, with no firm development plans in place), though it remains with its theaters (the Hennepin Center for the Arts, the Orpheum, the State, the Hey City Theater) as well as its "lower-end "entertainment venues (Augie's, The Gay '90s, Dream Girls) downtown Minneapolis' principle entertainment street.

Tom Mix and his boys in front of the State Theater, May 7, 1929. *Minneapolis Public Library.* Mpls. Collection.

Delivery wagons lined up in front of Yerxa Bros. Grocery, at Fifth and Nicollet, 1896. That's Olson's Department Store next to it on the right. Olson's was later to become Powers. *Minnesota Historical Society.*

The Turn of the Century

By the turn of the century Minneapolis' population had reached 203,000, and it could safely be said that it had achieved the status of being a full-fledged modern city. Though it could boast many distinctions by this time (its flour and saw milling, of course, and its public parks system) it was felt by most observers that architectural distinction and imaginative and forward-looking city planning could not be counted among them. The consensus of opinion was probably more or less summed up by the *Minneapolis Journal*, when in an article of May, 1904, it commented on the sad state of the city's architecture, both at that time and during the earliest days of its history.

> Few good buildings were put up in the early days, but in the excusable haste to house a population which was growing most extraordinarily and to care for the commercial needs of both city and country, architectural principles were very commonly forgotten and thrust aside. Later this condition was aggravated by the operations of the speculators who built solely for profit and without any notion of present honor or of permanently benefiting the community. To them Minneapolis is indebted for sundry rows of tawdry tenements and a few shaky business structures which still dot the city.

The Journal's views were echoed a few years later by the city's historian Horace B. Hudson, when, in 1908, he put forward similar views, expressing particular dismay at the city's failure to create public spaces or to build and group public buildings in any coherent way. "Additions were laid out and joined to the city with no consideration for the public interest or the future," said Hudson, who went on to express particular unhappiness with Minneapolis' negligence during the great building boom of the 1880s, putting forward the opinion that the city had missed a particularly "great opportunity" during that decade "when a large number of public buildings being under consideration the city failed to group them around a common civic center or at the very least to provide some suitable setting for each."

Finally, in 1910, at the height of the so-called "City Beautiful" era, a commission, headed by William H. Dunwoody, was formed to address this and the city's other related problems (the city council was especially concerned at this time with dangerous railroad crossings and with establishing an overall traffic program). Though this commission came out with a report that proposed massive redesigning of the city around what architectural critic Larry Millett described as "a new system of diagonal boulevards lined with neoclassical buildings," its proposal was for the most part never put into effect, deemed too costly and impractical by most people at that time, and as a "grandiose and seductive hallucination" by Millett. None of the new streets it called for were ever built, though four projects which had been integrated into the plan, the new Post Office, the Minneapolis Institute of Arts, the Gateway Pavilion, and the Union Station were completed during the course of the commission's work.

The first two decades of the twentieth century were, if they were nothing else, a great era for downtown department stores, hotels and theaters. In 1902, George Dayton opened his famous department store at Seventh and Nicollet. It would eventually become the city's largest, and, of course, its best known. E. E. Atkinson opened a new store across the street from Dayton's in 1903, and in the next few years Donaldson's and Olson's (later Powers) significantly expanded their stores. Hennepin Avenue, especially at Seventh Street, emerged as the city's main entertainment street during these years, when many of the grandest and most famous theaters were built. Among them were the first Orpheum (1904), at 25 Seventh Street South; the New Garrick (1907), at 40 Seventh Street South; the Gayety (1909), at 101 Washington Avenue North; the Crystal (1909), at 305 Hennepin; the Schubert (1910), at 20 Seventh Street North; the New Palace (1914), at 414 Hennepin; and the Strand (1915), at 36 Seventh Street South. (In 1930 the Strand was remodeled and transformed into the Forum Cafeteria, one of the city's great Art Deco treasures.) Many new hotels were also built during this era. They included: the Plaza (1906), at Hennepin and Kenwood Parkway; the Radisson (1909), on Seventh Street between Nicollet and Hennepin; the Andrews (1911), at Fourth and Hennepin; the Curtis (1905, 1911), at Tenth Street and Third Avenue South; the Leamington (1912), across the street from the Curtis; the Pick-Nicollet (1924), at Hennepin and Washington; and the Ritz (1924), at Washington and Second Avenue South. During this era commerce and manufacturing spread west toward Loring Park and began to displace many old houses. The Warehouse District continued its growth north of Hennepin, with many new warehouses being built, including Butler Brothers (later Butler Square).

Looking west on Fourth Street from Hennepin in downtown Minneapolis' Wholesale District, 1912. *Minnesota Historical Society.* **Photo by Sweet.**

Many important public buildings were also completed around his time. They included: The City Hall-Hennepin County Courthouse (1906), occupying the entire block bounded by Third and Fourth Avenues South and Fourth and Fifth streets; the first Minneapolis Auditorium (1905), at Seventh and Nicollet; the Minneapolis Armory (1907), at Lyndale and Kenwood Parkway; the U.S. Post Office (1915), on Washington Avenue South; Gateway Park and Pavilion (1915); the Great Northern Station (1914), on Hennepin Avenue at the Mississippi River; and the Federal Reserve Bank (1921), at Fifth and Marquette. The nineteen-story Soo Line Building (1914) dominated the Minneapolis skyline for the next fifteen years, until it was eclipsed by the twenty-seven story Rand Tower and the thirty-two story Foshay Tower which were completed in 1929.

Looking southwest over downtown Minneapolis from the roof of the St. James Hotel, May, 1923. The Gateway Pavilion is pictured in the foreground. The tallest building at the center of this photo is the Soo Line Building. *Minneapolis Public Library*. Mpls. Collection.

This wonderful photo provides the viewer with a real sense of the bustle and excitement of downtown Minneapolis at the corner of Nicollet and Sixth Street in 1905. Note the varieties of locomotion represented (bicycles, pedestrians, automobiles, horsecarts, streetcars), and note the seeming absence of traffic signals or a traffic cop. *Hennepin County Historical Society.*

The Depression, World War II, and Urban Renewal

By 1930 the business center of the city had migrated to the corner of Seventh and Nicollet, as the most exclusive shops led the march toward the prestigious residential areas around the lakes, and their former sites became centers for humbler, more middle class shops. Meanwhile, however, lower Nicollet had been steadily deteriorating (along with the rest of the lower loop) as none of the rehabilitative efforts of that period (i.e. such projects as Maurice Rothschild's "Nicollet Plan," which proposed to rehabilitate Nicollet Avenue storefronts from Third to Fifth streets) was able to overcome the devastating impact that the Great Depression and World War II were to have on the fortunes of downtown.

By the early 1930s the depression had brought new downtown construction to a virtual halt (a notable exception was the twenty-six story Bell Telephone Building, built in 1931), with World War II ensuring that little money would be available for maintenance, remodeling or new construction during the forties (the most notable exception in that decade was the Northwestern National Bank and its famed seventy-eight ton weatherball). By the beginning of that decade the situation in downtown had become so bleak that Sinclair Lewis was undoubtedly reflecting a widely held opinion when upon his visit to the city in 1942 he expressed amazement at how "ugly" Minneapolis had become, finding its "parking lots like scars. Most buildings . . . narrow, drab, dirty, flimsy, irregular in relationship to one another—a set of bad teeth."

After World War II the automobile (and the freeways which inevitably followed it) would hasten the decline of the cities, as people and commerce deserted them en-mass, heading for the suburbs and leaving their downtowns behind. Though many of downtown Minneapolis' problems would be temporarily masked by the great period of prosperity that was to follow the war, by the 1950s it was impossible to deny that it, like many of America's great downtowns, was dying. Faced with an aging inventory of buildings, fierce suburban competition (Southdale Shopping Center, the world's first enclosed shopping mall, was built in Edina in 1956), and a drastic drop in downtown retail sales, Minneapolis' response, like that of virtually every other city in the country, was to unleash upon itself the twin forces of the Interstate Highway Program and federally financed urban renewal, trusting blindly to the then almost universally held belief that by wiping out whole city neighborhoods (and in Minneapolis' case, fully one third of its entire downtown), that a city could somehow miraculously cause the most chronic of its economic and social problems to go away.

The first residential section of the city to bite the dust was the Glenwood neighborhood, a 180-acre tract between Glenwood Avenue and Olson Highway which, beginning in 1954, saw more than 660 buildings torn down. Most of the dwellings in the Grant neighborhood were similarly destroyed in the 1960s, and public housing and high rise apartment buildings (all design disasters, many already gone) put up in their place. One can get some sense of the traumatic effect that these urban renewal programs had upon the affected communities and upon the lives of the thousands of people that they displaced when one listens to the forlorn words of one resident of the by then extinct Beltrami neighborhood (also once known as "Dog Town"), when he recalled for *Common Ground* in the spring of 1974, "that the freeway took all the old-timers, all the old people who had been here for years. I had a brother lived on Lincoln Street, they took the house six years ago and now they still ain't doing nothing with it. They ruined this neighborhood as far as that goes—the freeways ruined this neighborhood. All the people have to go—they kicked them all out of here."

In 1957 the city unleashed the wrecking ball upon its historic Gateway district, knocking down some 180 buildings and displacing over 3,000 residents and nearly 450 businesses by the time the process was completed in 1965. The most notable—and certainly least defensible—of all these casualties was, of course, the Metropolitan Building (it was historic, architecturally significant, structurally sound and almost fully occupied at the time of its razing), though many other notable structures, such as the Old Federal Courthouse, the Kasota Block, the Globe Building and the Janny Simple Hill Warehouse were lost as well. While many of the buildings that were razed during this period were badly in need of repair (dozens were nothing but rat infested slum dwellings, and certainly no loss to anyone) the city's mindless and indiscriminate slaughter of virtually every last structure in the Gateway robbed downtown not only of some of its finest nineteenth-century commercial architecture, but also of much of what Larry Millett called its "urban soul." While the Gateway was undoubtedly badly in need of development, the city of Minneapolis' decision to obliterate nearly two hundred buildings and seventeen square blocks in order to accomplish that end (the city tore down fully one third of downtown's buildings, and 40 percent of its historic central business district) can only be called mindless in the extreme. Wally Marotzke, the long-time engineer of the Metropolitan Building, probably summed up the judgement of posterity best when he told the *Minneapolis Tribune* on the day before the destruction of the Metropolitan Building was to begin: "I'm not gonna watch 'em rip it down. I don't think I could. But I'll tell you one thing: the future generations are gonna read about this building and they'll see some of the buildings they're putting up there and they'll damn us, they will, for tearing down the Met."

Demolition of the Metropolitan Building. *Minneapolis Public Library.* Mpls. Collection.

Skid Row

Though the Minneapolis skid row was not as large as those in many other cities (it was centered, of course, on Washington Avenue, and included 29 square blocks if you counted Nicollet Island, running basically from First Avenue North to Fifth Avenue South and from Fourth Street to First Street) it featured all the usual skid row institutions (cheap hotels, lodging houses, flops, hamburger joints, employment agencies, missions, welfare agencies, bloodbanks, pawnshops, liquor stores, whorehouses, "blind pigs" and "bloody bucket" saloons), and was in kind, if not in size and population (roughly 3,000 residents at the turn of the century) little different from the country's biggest and more famous skid rows, such as the Bowery in New York, the French Quarter in New Orleans, or the Barbary Coast in San Francisco.

The Minneapolis' skid row was otherwise known, of course, as the Gateway, that area of the city which began as its business and civic center in the 1880s and whose Bridge Square district served until the turn of the century as the greatest labor center in the Northwest. "Men came from northern Europe, thousands upon thousands of them," said the *WPA Guide to Minnesota*, "and for thirty years poured into this square to sit shoulder to shoulder on the curbs all day, by night to sleep shoulder to shoulder in the dreary flophouses that topped the employment offices, while they waited to be sent to the timber, and to the wheat fields, to the railroad camps, or to the mines . . . In those hey-days of expansion there was a job for every man, and Bridge Square, while admittedly ugly and perhaps not very fragrant, was generally regarded as an inevitable symptom of the city's youth and vigor."

By the turn of the century, however, the Gateway had entered into a period of precipitous decline and had, with its 109 liquor stores, bars and saloons and 130 flophouses and hotels, come to be widely regarded by the citizens of Minneapolis as the city's "skid row." (The term "skid row" had around that time come to be used in conjunction with the lower end of Seattle's waterfront, where longshoremen, unskilled workers and loggers, who had lost their jobs when the "skidding" method of logging was re-

Habitué of Gateway Park, February 22, 1946. *Minneapolis Public Library.* Mpls. Collection.

placed by the "high lead" method, would come to gather. These displaced men needed a place to live, of course, and the places where they settled became known, first in Seattle, and eventually all over the country, as "skid rows.")

By 1914 lumber production in the state had dropped to half of what it had been a decade earlier, causing more and more men to lose their jobs and to settle in Minneapolis' skid row. With them came the rowdies (many late of such sections of the city as "Hells Half Acre" and "Fish Alley"), the migratory workers, harvest hands, railroaders, prostitutes and other undesirables who would define the character of the Gateway for the next sixty years. "Proper

Minneapolitans were now growing very conscious of the rough, idle, and profane men hitting the streets of the lower loop," wrote Gateway historian David Rosheim in his book, *The Other City,* pointing out that these men were often great in number (in one particularly bad year there were so many of them sitting so close together on the curb that one ob-server expressed doubt as to whether you could have gotten a newspaper between their elbows), and almost always lacking in manners—a lack that could hardly be overstated, at least if one can judge by the following description which he quotes of a typical Gateway scene:

Christmas service at the Gateway Mission, 111 Nicollet, 1947. *Minneapolis Public Library.* Mpls. Collection.

In front of any of the saloons [on Washington Avenue] for four or five blocks the loafers congregate and vie with one another in spitting contests. As a rule, they spit toward the curb, but it is usually too far off and the sidewalk is stained in deep brown with tobacco juice, which doesn't disappear very readily in dry weather . . . Two or three refectories bunched on Washington just north of Hennepin also contribute their contingent of spitters, who befoul the flagging in a way that makes the women who pass that way have more of a care to their skirts than on a wet day.

Unfortunately, of course, spitting was the very *least* of the vices practiced by the habitues of the old Gateway, a fact made clear by Rosheim when in his introduction to *The Other City* he refers us to the following description of San Francisco's notorious Barbary Coast in order to give us a better idea of the nature of life on Minneapolis' skid row:

The Barbary Coast is the haunt of the low and the vile of every kind. The petty thief, the house burglar, the whore-monger, lewd women, cutthroats, murderers, all are found here. Dance halls and concert saloons where bleary-eyed men and faded women drink vile liquor, smoke offensive tobacco, sing obscene songs and do everything to heap upon themselves more degradation, are numerous.

The gambling house, thronged with riot-loving rowdies, in all stages of intoxication, are there. Opium dens, where heathen Chinese and God-forsaken men and women are sprawled in miscellaneous confusion . . . are there. Licentiousness, debauchery, pollution, loathsome disease, insanity from dissipation, misery, poverty, wealth, profanity, blasphemy and death are there. And hell, yearning to receive the putrid mass, is there also.

Lest the reader think that this description must surely be exaggeration—that this *was* the Barbary Coast he was talking about, after all, not a section of *our* downtown Minneapolis!—I will close by relating for his or her edification the following two statistically unassailable facts: 1) The Gateway was home

Habitués of Gateway Pavilion, June 7, 1950. *Minneapolis Public Library.* Mpls. Collection.

to an incredible amount of prostitution (during the 1920s, a Grand Jury investigation found that there were 30 whorehouses employing 300 inmates within a radius of 600 feet from Marquette Avenue and First Street South). 2) The Gateway was home to a truly staggering number of saloons (at the turn of the century there was an area of the New York slums inhabited by approximately half-a-million tenants who were served by 4,065 saloons. If that same tenement section had had the same ratio of drinking establishments to residents—110 for 3,000 people—that was to be found in the Gateway during roughly the same period of time, it would have been home to 18,260 saloons!).

The Union City Mission

In April, 1935, my money was exhausted, and when I was not in the General Hospital, I stayed at the Union City Mission at the corner of Hennepin Avenue and Second Street. I had become a public charge on the State of Minnesota and the City of Minneapolis.

The Union City Mission is a dilapidated old building, an eyesore to the city. I slept in a dormitory, which held about 50 beds. Altogether there must have been 200 or 300 beds in the different rooms or dormitories. It was an awful place at night; bums coming in at all hours; sometimes they would fall over your bed. There were whites, blacks, Mexicans and Indians. As there were no lockers to keep your clothes in, you had to lay them under your pillow. Otherwise, they might be stolen before morning.

Some of these men were de-horners. A "de-horner" is a denatured alcohol drinker. This stuff retails at some of the hardware stores and at some drug stores at 60 cents a gallon. It is intended to be used as a body rub, or to be put in the radiator of your car if you have one, in the wintertime, to keep the water from freezing. It Is also supposed to he poisonous, but many of these poor bums, both young and old, drank it because it was cheap, as they could always go out on the "stem," that means the street, and bum a dime or fifteen cents, or maybe a quarter, and then buy a bottle or this stuff. It is sure to set a man crazy after continued use, and death is nearly certain after drinking it a few years.

Now at the Union City Mission they never gave anybody anything for nothing that I ever heard of. If you did not have money, you couldn't sleep or eat there, unless you had a meal book and bed book from the Division of Public Relief. But if you had money you could sleep there by paying 15 cents a night for your flop.

Paul Ferrell

Nicollet Mall under construction, July 20, 1967. *Minnesota Historical Society.* Photo by Seibert of *Minneapolis Star-Tribune.*

Nicollet Mall

During the years from 1947 to 1958 office space in downtown Minneapolis was growing at an annual rate of only one percent per year; retail sales were stagnant; at least half of downtown's retail buildings (especially those on lower Nicollet and Hennepin avenues) were in substandard condition; no new hotels had been built since the 1920s; traditional industries were no longer creating jobs; there were no cultural facilities, and traffic congestion and parking problems were getting worse with each passing year. By 1955 the situation had become so bleak (General Mills had announced that it was moving its offices and 800 em-

ployees to Golden Valley, and Southdale Shopping Center was scheduled to open in Edina the following year) that the downtown business community, fearing for its very survival, formed the Downtown Council, and began to look for ways to revitalize the city's downtown core.

In 1959 the Downtown Council, in conjunction with the city Planning Commission, released the "Central Minneapolis Plan," which among its many recommendations, called for the improvement of Nicollet Avenue. This recommendation resulted in the hiring of the firm of Barton-Aschman Associates, Inc., who called for the closing of Nicollet's eight

Nicollet Mall, looking south from Fourth Street, 1973. The just completed IDS Tower is at center. The Northwest weather ball is at left. *Minneapolis Public Library.* **Mpls. Collection.**

primary retail blocks to private cars and trucks, while leaving open a narrow winding roadway for emergency vehicles, taxis and busses. To design this urbane, elegant shopping street and pedestrian mall, the city hired the landscape architectural firm of Lawrence Halprin and Associates which was responsible for providing Nicollet Mall with its variety in sidewalk uses and looks. Halprin also designed or commissioned the mall's street furniture and "micro-architecture" (a four-sided clock, the Calder Mobile, the granite fountain), included heated bus shelters, and found ways to give each block its own character.

Construction on Nicollet Mall began in April of 1966 and ended in November of 1967. It cost $3.8 million. On September 20, 1967, First Lady Lady Bird Johnson visited the new mall and while there dedicated the Richardson Fountain, between Fourth and Fifth Streets. She was accompanied by Mrs. Hubert Humphrey and Mrs. Harold Levander and declared the mall to be "fluid and graceful." Jim Klobuchar, writing for the *Minneapolis Star* on November 22, 1967, was not so favorably impressed, saying, "There is some question of course as we view affectionately this exciting new shopping thoroughfare whether it more closely resembles a dream or a hangover."

It's safe to say, however, that the great majority of people were quite favorably impressed by the new mall as after its inception retail sales went up dramatically and millions of dollars in new construction was generated. From the day of its opening Nicollet Mall became the focal point for metro area shopping, regaining significant "market share" from its suburban competitors and claiming at its peak in 1972 an 11.3 percent share of the metro retail market.

In January of 1969 the S. S. Kresge Company sold its property at Seventh and Nicollet to IDS Properties, who in March of that year proposed that four skyways be built to lead into the 57-story skyscraper that they proposed to build on the Mall between Seventh and Eighth streets. Designed by Phillip Johnson, the IDS Center featured a nine-story glass-roofed courtyard (the Crystal Court) which was intended to serve as a "town square" and central meeting place for the city. The Crystal Court has served that function admirably, as it is used as a site for concerts, charity balls and shows, as well as for the more yeoman duty of serving as a bustling intersection and shopping place for workers and shoppers throughout each day. Since it was completed in 1973, the IDS Center has been widely acclaimed as a great innovation in the art of skyscraper design, and declared by one critic to be a "nervy and exciting place . . . the single finest enclosed space in any city in the U.S."

Downtown Minneapolis Today

As downtown Minneapolis' primary retail artery, Nicollet Mall is, of course, home to the city's major shopping complexes and malls. (In 1989 it ranked as having the highest concentration of retail space in North America, with 2.1 million square feet crammed into its busiest three blocks.) On its east side, located between Seventh and Eighth streets stands the aforementioned IDS Crystal Court, home to numerous pricey shops in Phillip Johnson's 57-story IDS Center (1973), which was long the focal point of Minneapolis' skyline (the Norwest Center, 57 stories, and First Bank Place, 59 stories, were added later), and the city's first world-class skyscraper. Located across the street from the IDS Center is, of course, Dayton's, which has been at that same location since 1902, and is the city's oldest and best-known department store. North of Dayton's is the space formerly occupied by Wards Department Store (Carson Pirie Scott, formerly Donaldson's, abandoned this location in 1993 after being at Sixth and Nicollet since 1883), and City Center, at the base of the International Multifoods Tower. Another new retail complex, the ultra-upscale Gavidae Common, home to Saks Fifth Avenue, and located between Fifth and Sixth streets, shares the next block with Caesar Pelli's Norwest Center (1988), an elegant skyscraper which serves as headquarters for the Norwest Bank Corporation, which lost its old headquarters, the Northwestern National Bank Building, to one of downtowns most spectacular fires on Thanksgiving Day, 1982. Yet another Mall landmark, the old Young Quinlan Building, at Eighth on the Mall, has been beautifully renovated and converted into shops and office space.

In 1990 Nicollet Mall was extensively remodeled for the second time, though it was not domed between Ninth and Eleventh streets, as was originally proposed by the city's initial Mall developer, the French firm, LSGI. As of this writing a Target store and a 14-story office tower on the block bounded by South Ninth and Tenth Streets and Nicollet Mall and La Salle Avenue, is scheduled to be constructed on the south end of the Mall and to open in 1999. In addition to this controversial Target plan (there has been considerable opposition to the leveling of two city blocks and the consequent loss of many small south Mall businesses), a K-12 magnet school and a graduate school of education building for the University of St. Thomas will be built on the block at Tenth Street between La Salle and Hennepin Avenues. The school project opened in the fall of 1998 and received $13 million in aid from the city.

Hennepin Avenue, downtown Minneapolis' other great retail street, has also experienced great changes in recent years, including, of course, the demolition of its old porno district, the notorious Block "E." Block "E" (located between Sixth and Seventh streets) is still a parking lot as of this writing, though its proposed developers (Brookfield Properties and McCaffery Interests) plan to turn it into a $101 million retail and entertainment complex. Their proposal would include a hotel, a 18-screen Cineplex and two floors of retail shops. The city is said to be willing to put up $38 million as its share of the project.

Opposite Block "E" is the Hennepin Avenue entrance to City Center, quite rightfully criticized from many quarters for having "turned its back" not only on Hennepin Avenue, but on Nicollet Mall as well. Though its recent remodeling and neon signage have certainly been an improvement over its old, extraordinarily dull exterior, City Center is still a prime example of the kind of "blank wall" architecture that has, along with the city's extensive system of skyways, done so much to diminish the vitality of downtown Minneapolis streets.

The Hennepin Center for the Arts (the renovated Masonic Temple, now containing theaters, restaurants, and space for various arts organizations), at Fifth and Hennepin, now serves as something of a gateway to the Warehouse District, currently one of the most vital and lively sections of downtown. The Warehouse District features a mix of renovated buildings (its first and most well known, of course, was Butler Square, one of the early exposed-beam and brick, fern-bar restorations of the seventies) which contain the by now standard array of restaurants, art galleries, antique shops and pubs. When the area became trendy in the late seventies, rent skyrocketed and many artists were forced to leave and to seek space elsewhere. Many galleries still remain, however, and the now famous "Gallery Crawls," when many galleries stage simultaneous openings, are now a Warehouse District institution. The addition in 1990 of the Target Center (home of the Timberwolves professional basketball team) to the district's already lively nightlife (it is home to some thirty bars and such chic music clubs as First Avenue and the Fine Line Music Cafe) have made the Warehouse District downtown's "happening place." It used to be textiles, now its bars," wrote Sari Gordon of the *Twin Cities Reader*, in her recent article "A Fish Story On First Avenue." "It became the Warehouse District sometime after the primary activity switched from storing to staring."

The Future

Like the Warehouse District, the rest of the downtown Minneapolis grew spectacularly during the 1980s. During that decade nearly four billion dollars was spent on downtown office construction, and downtown's share of the city's property tax base increased from 21 percent in 1980 to 41 percent in 1991. Almost daily during the eighties it seemed that the city was contemplating some huge project or other, shelling out $55 million in tax exempt bonds for Riverplace, and another $22 million on the Nicollet Mall renovation, the New Convention Center and the Hilton Hotel. One new project in particular, Gavidae Common, epitomized the glamour and the extravagance of that decade, making downtown a haven for trendy, upscale retailers such as Nieman Marcus and Saks Fifth Avenue, and leaving such faded old middle and low-brow relics as J.C. Penney and Woolworth's to close their doors.

This great boom was not without its price, of course, as the city, in its headlong rush to steel-and-

Nicollet Mall, at Seventh Street, as Mary Tyler Moore would have seen it in 1970. (Note the Mary Tyler Moore dress and hairstyle worn by the woman at bottom left). The editor of this book worked at Donaldson's at the time of the filming of Mary Tyler Moore's hat-throwing scene and can distinctly remember seeing her and Valerie Harper during one of the days when they were filming the famous opening scenes of the *Mary Tyler Moore Show*. He did not actually see Mary throw her hat, but can distinctly remember her and Valerie Harper in their almost clownish-looking makeup looking very hot and "put out" on a steamy Nicollet Mall day. *Minnesota Historical Society.*

glass glory, lost much of its innocence and its once-vaunted small town charm. While its glittering new "world class" skyline became emblematic of Minneapolis' leap into genuine "big league" status, it also became a symbol of the fact that the city is no longer a mid-sized Midwestern oasis, but rather a major metropolitan area with an exploding population of poor people (33,000 in 1980 vs. 66,000 a decade later) and all the problems (white flight, gangs, violent crime, homelessness, racial tensions, drug and domestic abuse) that that unfortunate demographic reality was inevitably to bring.

Despite the growing and increasingly intractable problems of the greater city, it seems clear that Minneapolis' downtown area is in infinitely better condition than is downtown St. Paul (or many other downtowns around the country) and seems well positioned to hold its own against the Mall of America and its many other suburban competitors. The downtown workforce (currently 140,000, up from 97,000 in 1978) when combined with an ever-increasing downtown residential population (currently 25,000, up from 15,000 in 1980) would seem to ensure the continued viability of downtown Minneapolis, providing its retailers and landlords a more than adequate base of customers for the rest of the nineties and beyond.

Chapter Two

Downtown Minneapolis:
The Nineteenth Century

The aftermath of the **Great Mill Explosion of May 2, 1878.** *Minneapolis Public Library.* Mpls. Collection.

On the evening of May 2, 1878 the Washburn "A" Mill (one of 20 mills clustered about the waterfalls of Minneapolis) exploded, causing what the headline which ran over the following story declared to be "The Most Dreadful Calamity Which Has Ever Befallen the City of Minneapolis." Nothing like it had happened before and nothing like it has happened since. Historians tell us that 18 people died that night (other figures are listed in the story) and that half the city's milling capacity was destroyed.

The Great Mill Explosion

From the Minneapolis Tribune, *May 3, 1878*

The city was startled at twenty minutes past seven last evening by a concussion which shook every building for miles from the scene of the terrible disaster, the smoke of which has not yet cleared away, and the terrible realization of which has but begun to dawn on the community. The shock was distinctly felt in the very suburbs of the city. In the business part of the city solid business blocks were shaken, and the massive plate glass windows in many of them utterly destroyed. No adequate idea can be given of the terrible force of the shock which startled the community into the belief that a terrible earthquake had occurred, marking its work of destruction. The shock had hardly subsided before the whole population were in the street. Men, women and children flocked to doors and windows with terrified faces and consternation in every movement. An ominous flame from the center of the milling district told the first story of a disaster the like of which Minnesota has not before known, and the full extent of which it is not possible to estimate. The fact that an explosion had occurred dawned on the community after the first confusion of surprise had passed away. But not until the excited crowd had surged down to the scene of the disaster was the full extent of the work of devastation in any measure realized.

It was found that the explosion had occurred in the big Washburn Mill, that it had been followed by the demolition of the Humboldt and Diamond Mills situated in the rear thereof; that one wall and the roof of the Washburn B Mill had been carried away, the solid stone wall carried from the side of the Galaxy mill, the Milwaukee & St. Paul round house more or less damaged and the stone planing mill of Smith & Parker destroyed. The explosion was followed in less time than it takes to tell it by flames which enveloped the ruins of all the buildings, communicating to the mill of Pettit, Robinson & Co., the Zenith and Galaxy mills opposite, and threatened the entire milling district and the extensive lumber yards situated further down the river.

Every imaginable theory was advanced as to the cause of the explosion. The first report noised about was to the effect that the big mill used gas manufactured within its walls. It was found that this was false, the city gas being used in the mill exclusively. Then it was charged upon the boiler, but the engine room is situated outside of the mill, and there was but about twenty pounds of steam on at the time. The excited crowd meantime clamored for an explanation, and every theory that was in any measure tenable was advanced. . . . The latest and probably the most current theory is that the explosion was the result of natural causes, not unknown to the milling business, which may be stated as being spontaneous combustion.

It is the theory of Mr. J. A. Christian, the head of the firm operating the big mill, that the fire originated in the [grinding] stones from flour dust; that a gas was created that filled the elevators and every pan of the mill, and the explosion followed. . . . without a moment's warning. The realization of the destruction of life, comparatively small though it be to what might have been the case had the explosion occurred during the day, has fallen like a pall upon the entire community.

The night force here usually consists of fifteen men. By fortuitous circumstances two of this number were absent at the time of the disaster and thirteen men suffered death. It is reported that one of the thirteen managed to escape, but the story seems improbable, and the more so since he has not been discovered up to the hour that this is penned. . . . In the Zenith mill there were two men, one of whom escaped badly burned and the other went to a horrible death, while the watchman, who was the only occupant of the Galaxy mill, miraculously escaped by jumping from the third story window into the canal below, borne down by the additional weight of a Babcock fire extinguisher which he bore upon his back.

The scenes about the fire beggar description. One poor fellow, believed to be John Boyer, employed in the Diamond mill, was seen to struggle with all the desperation of love of life out from the ruins of the Diamond mill, through flame and smoke, to the very edge of the pile of rubbish and almost out from the hungry flames. Burned and blackened was he, bleeding, too, from wounds upon his body and head, but he struggled on with all the delirious desperation of a battle for life. Human endurance was not sufficient, and when almost released from the seething cauldron he fell dead. A rope had been thrown to him by the excited crowd, but it came too late and he could not reach it. An attempt was made to reach his mangled remains, but the flames for three hours relentlessly held back the crowd. [His body] was taken out of the ruins last night, and was the only body so rescued. In the crowd were the distracted wives and mothers of some of the missing men, whose shrieks mingled with the cries of firemen, noise of the crowd and the crackling of flames. One distracted woman would have thrown herself into the flames but for the restraining power of the arms of two strong men. The majority of the employees in the mills were married men, who had an hour before gone forth from happy homes, leaving loving wives who had no thought of the horrible disaster that was to usher their loved ones into eternity.

All night long did the firemen battle the flames, the crowd watching the lapping work of destruction and the grief stricken friends of the dead men haunt the scene of the disaster and conflagration. The whole affair is so horrible, so sickening of contemplation that it makes the heart sick. Those who went to their homes last night went there with the realization that sixteen mortals had met a sudden and terrible death, and that more than one-third of the milling capacity of Minneapolis had been swept out of existence almost before it was possible to realize it, and that a loss had been entailed thereby which will not aggregate far from a million and a half of money.

As its title implies, Brenda Ueland's autobiography, Me, *is an intensely personal story, the story of her "inner life," a subject which she unabashedly declares to be "interesting," just like "everybody's in the world is interesting."*

In Me, *Brenda Ueland writes about her childhood (she grew up in a house on Lake Calhoun, at a time when that was still "out in the country"), her family and friends, her college career, her marriage and divorce, her work as a writer and journalist, and even, as the reader will be delighted to discover, about two very different experiences that she had downtown. Both of the following excerpts from* Me *(the first about her family's shopping trips to downtown Minneapolis; the second about her dreaded dance lessons at Mrs. Kingsley's Dance Studio in the old West Hotel) add immeasurably to our understanding of late-nineteenth century Minneapolis. Each is an invaluable addition to this volume.*

The Difference Between Then and Now

BY BRENDA UELAND

Photo by Bruce Carlson.
Schubert Club

Perhaps the best way to show the difference between then and now is to tell of a trip downtown. It was only four miles, but it was a slowly unfolding, fascinating adventure, a journey, a voyage.

There was no boulevard in front then. The lake came just to the edge of our wooded bank, and sometimes in rainy years our green-painted steps led right down into the water. But when we drove downtown, we went down our long dirt driveway to Richfield Road and then turned into the pretty boulevard that led around the lake. Our horse was Lady Mane, such a darling horse, such a person! She was a huge dark bay and she had been in races, I was able to boast, "Yes, sir, Lady could run a mile in a minute or something." And indeed, when trotting along and when our carriage would come up even with some other equipage, her head would go up and her velvet ears turn back and she would so nobly want to race, although her steps were getting a little jerky and short.

"Yes," Mother would say on a summer morning, "we will go downtown, dear. You and Sigurd can go."

We were brushed and dressed by Betty. I wore my boy's cap. The hired man hitched up Lady in the barn and I hastened out to help him. Even now I could twist all those straps in their various ways, in the dark. The hired man's name was Gus, but Mother always called him "August." She did not like Gus as a name. It was just as for many years she called Pete, a kind of sinister ruffianly Swede who worked around here, "Mr. Gunderson." I see now that she did it to build up his self-respect, not because she objected to saying the word "Pete," although that too was hard for her, as it would be hard for her to say "Gosh."

Interior of Donaldson's Glass Block, c. 1900. *Minnesota Historical Society.*

Then Gus—no, I guess then it was Alfred, a big young man with a red face like the Duchess's in *Alice in Wonderland,* who was eager to weigh two hundred pounds so that he could be a policeman—drove out of the barn with Lady and the carriage. It was a big strong graceful family carriage. There was a whip-socket and a whip in it. There were two adorable, be-gemmed, polished lamps with kerosene in them, to be lighted at night. I can still feel those lamps under my fingers, with a big ruby in each. The top of the carriage was down. On the high front seat Alfred and two small children could sit. On the back seat there was plenty of room for three people.

Mother was all dressed up. But she was always beautifully dressed. I never saw her in anything homely, or in a hurriedly-put on housedress. I never saw her in an apron or a casual sweater. No, she always dressed like a lovely dignified lady. She wore now her summer straw hat with a veil floating about it and she wore brightly clean white shoes and a white linen dress with a jacket. The jacket had much elaborate sewn braid and heavy lace on it.

We went out to the carriage. Sigurd with his long blond hair, ruffled blouse and tight knee pants, sat in the back seat with Mother, throwing horse chestnuts. But I sat in front with Alfred. I wanted to see to it that Alfred did not use the whip *as a whip.* It was all right perhaps for him to gently flick the flies off Lady with the whip, but he couldn't flick it at *her.* No, I couldn't stand that. I couldn't stand it even if a hired man spoke gruffly to Lady. No, he must he very polite to her, pleasant-voiced and conciliatory.

We wheeled slowly down the drive. Mother had to tell me again to be careful not to stick my legs out and touch the wheel, because it was not safe. Now there was the boulevard curving all around the lake toward the far-away courthouse tower. We could just barely see the tower, red and dim and four-cornered above the trees. It was a soft, dirt, hoof-thudding boulevard, and between the scallops of willows we could see the still glass lake and smell it.

Now just where the boulevard came to our land and had to turn off toward Lake Harriet, there was the Big Rock—that is, it was about as big as a trunk—and here there was an open sandy beach with yellow sunbeams moving in dancing network under the water.

We would drive Lady and the carriage right into the water, and she would put her head down and dawdlingly drink, or pretend to drink, looking up at the horizon after soaking her nose in it, the water sluicing out around the bit. "Oh, she has had enough. She is just fooling," we would say tenderly, and wheel in the water (look! it comes way up to the hubs!) and drive out and on our way again.

And so we trotted noiselessly along the boulevard and after what seemed like a long, long dreamy time we came to the Iron Bridge. Actually it was about three blocks from home. And then we would say: "Do you suppose she wants another drink?" for here there was a horse fountain. I would jump down and unloose her check-rein. I liked this. I was always thinking about check-reins and whether they were too tight or not. We looked at other horses and examined their check-reins and were distressed about them often.

"Well, that is enough. She is just fooling again," we said, and on we drove, dreamily clopping along on a bright Minnesota day. There is nothing so beautiful. The air is so clear that sky and grass and flowers are almost like colored glass, lighted from behind. Far away the yellow and red wheels of carriages flashed blazing white lights from their spokes.

When the carriage spokes flashed white that was always a sign of a bright, joyful, jolly summer day.

Mother went shopping in Goodfellow's Drygoods Store and at The Glass Block. It was an intermittently heart-sinking experience, because I would look around and she would be lost among all the people. Or Sigurd would he lost. But then I saw her again. I liked the baskets that ran overhead on whirring wires and came to a clicking stop at the cash girl's high desk.

Then we drove over to Hennepin Avenue. There was no pavement there, though it was the center of town, but just a broad dirty road with deep bumps and pits in it. We went to Mr. Dassett the Meat Man's and to Mr. H. A. Child the Groceryman's.

Mother bought many things to which we paid no attention. And also she got crackers, which we ate in the carriage on the long drive home. As she did not believe in shortening, in lard, the crackers we ate on the way home were water crackers, thin, round, water crackers perforated with many pinpricks; or Educator crackers, square, hard and tasteless; or Benz crackers as hard as rock. Or else we were allowed to have absurd inedible things known as "egg biscuits." These were fat with petals and thinly covered with a glazed skin, and inside there was a tasteless dry powder. It is astonishing to think we could get them down, but we ate these by the dozen and thought they were delicious. I was always deeply interested in eating, and presently I began to be a little fat. Francesca has told me since that I was really not fat then, but just sturdy. The genuine fatness did not come until fourteen or so. But they teased me and I was anxious about it inwardly.

Of course the very nicest trips downtown in the carriage were to see circus parades. Then we always hitched Lady blocks away, with her back turned to the parade, "because of the elephants." We lifted out of the carriage the iron weight on its long strap, and snapped it to her bridle, hoping anxiously that she would not turn her head and catch a glimpse over her blinders.

We always contrived to see the parade, if possible, coming and going, cutting across town in nervous excitement to intercept it. I can remember the excitement of hearing Mother read from the morning paper:

"Parade leaves Nicollet and Tenth Street at 10:15, crosses to 5th and then down Hennepin at . . . returning to the circus grounds, etc., etc." These words still shoot excitement into me.

Driving home from the parade, Lady would clop-clop heavily and peacefully along, and going down hill was always fun, for at the bottom of each hill there was over the culvert a bridge of wooden planks. We waited joyfully for the carriage to bounce over these, helping with our united weight. Fun!

Circus parade on Hennepin Avenue. This picture was taken from just north of the Masonic Temple and the West Hotel (pictured at right) and looks south down Hennepin. *Minneapolis Public Library.* Mpls. Collection.

West Hotel ballroom. *Minneapolis Public Library.* Mpls. Collection.

My mother began thinking that I should know some of the children of her nicest friends, cultivated people who lived downtown in red stone houses with porte-cocheres. There was to be a dancing school started, and I was to go to it, Mother told me. I think I rather looked forward to it.

But that was a terrible evening. It was downtown in a bleak ballroom of the West Hotel. I wore my eighth grade graduation dress, a thin white dress with much lace insertion in it, and I disliked it and felt stout and dumpy in it. Mother took me down there and we went on the street car. Of course there was nothing so hopelessly plebeian about that, because in those days, men in top hats and ladies in ermine often went to the theater on the street car.

Nobody danced with me, unless led up forcibly by Mrs. Kingsley, the teacher, a large colorless woman with huge well-placed feet and a stentorian voice. We stood in a row behind her and copied stiffly and flat-footedly her steps. Then the boys went to one side and the girls to the other, sitting in chairs along the ballroom wall. The whistle blew: "Boys choose partners." No one chose me. They streamed across to this side and that of me. None looked at me and came straight up. I was left in that row of chairs and perhaps, far along, some other unattractive girl, some uneasy homely child with braces on her teeth. What made it worse was that my mother was there. It always makes it much worse to have your family see things like that.

This dancing school suffering was to last two or three years, and sometimes I think it accounts for a whole train of things in my life, like my bad judgment in marrying and my broken, truncated emotional life thereafter. There may have been a purpose in suffering that way, a final good. The only one I can think of is that because of this book, some parent may forego forcing children.

Mother was so very kind too and not in the least domineering, and I do not know how she could have persisted in doing this to me. She did though. The only explanation I can give is that I just didn't tell her how hard it was for me. I didn't let on. She never knew how I felt.

Dancing school shifted from the West Hotel to another ballroom. And it was some place else the next year. I remember that once a boy actually asked me to dance, but it was little Sammy Sewall and he was a head shorter. I remember that in my anxious fright before dancing school, I would plan, talk to myself in imagination, make up conversations with boys, hoping to charm them. I would say this witty thing and that. It was extraordinary how it never worked, how planned conversation always seemed so extra-false and fell so flat.

There was Louise Lamb, a rather plain girl but, I guess, very rich and with an inner fierceness and dash. I remember her fur-lined carriage slippers; her energetic coldness to me in the dressing room. (The girls put powder on. I have never been able to put powder on. It seemed such dusty foolishness, and what was the point of it? But I envied how they could sit down and dab at it, just the same.) She came in an especially beautiful brougham with spidery wheels, shining horses clattering with their tiny hoofs under the porte-cochère. I came on the street car with our hired girl Marie, carrying my slippers in a bag. I think it was this ride downtown into the dark night, the street car smelling of electricity and lined with bulbs and their fiery filaments—this going to humiliation, to doom, that gave me an uneasiness about night coming on and lights appearing that lasted many, many years. I still have

this melancholy. I think it is just habit, going back to that time.

Sometimes when it got too trying I would stay in the dressing room. No, not there, because the social swells were there and chattering happily. So I would go even farther, into the toilet and rest there for a while. I don't think I looked externally pathetic or unhappy. I probably looked solid, scowling and scornful. To thunder with them! But I can't be sure.

There was to be a cotillion, a special party and we were allowed to ask a guest, each. Well, by some unlucky slip of impulsive generosity, I asked Blanche Lane. And Blanche, equally unfortunate and foolish, told her mother I had invited her. And Blanche's mother, in the private and inward horror of us both, insisted that Blanche go.

We did. It was just as bad as always and then doubled in uncomfortableness because nobody danced with Blanche—of course not. She was fatter than I. I was extra-humiliated by having as a friend one with such a funny name and a fatty, and moreover my heart absolutely bled for Blanche. But do you know what we did? And there was solace in it, a kind of revenge on our parents. Long before the party was over (we had come alone and I was to stay all night with Blanche) we sneaked away. And what did we do? Oh the wonderful nerve and gall of it (we thought!). We walked down Hennepin Avenue and there was the Lyceum Theatre. We had no money, only carfare, but somehow we teased our way to free seats in the gallery. The gallery was supposed to be at night full of tough people. Also there was a general feeling in those days that it was very dangerous, bad for young girls ("young girls" always meant something special) to be out alone late at night, and worst of all at a theatre.

After the show we went home on the street car. We felt pleased with ourselves and not one bit frightened at being discovered. To hell with parents. We giggled with delight at ourselves on the street car. And when we got to Lanes' house and were getting ready for bed, we locked ourselves in the bathroom and smoked cigarettes. For years I was proud of this escapade. It is fine to be a desperado.

The Masonic Temple (left) and the West Hotel, at the corner of Sixth and Hennepin, looking toward the river, 1904. *Minnesota Historical Society.* Photo by Sweet.

Bridge Square decorated for the G.A.R. convention, c. 1906. Nicollet Avenue is at left. Hennepin Avenue is at right. The Metropolitan Building can be seen at upper left. *Hennepin County Historical Society.*

In 1961 Joseph W. Zalusky, the editor of Hennepin County History, *wrote an article for that publication entitled "Bridge Square, Going, Going, Gone." Few people were more qualified to tell the story of Bridge Square than was Mr. Zalusky, a man who was not only an avid student of Minneapolis' history, but also one who was old enough to personally remember its heyday as the heart of the city's early downtown. The reader will note that Mr. Zalusky's article was written during the darkest days of urban renewal, that period of time when so much of the Bridge Square District was so unfortunately being torn down.*

Bridge Square

BY JOSEPH W. ZALUSKY

How many living today can remember Bridge Square when it was in its heyday? Not many! The writer of this article vividly remembers the old City Hall, Pence Opera House, the second suspension bridge, Fish Jones' Zoo, Vanstrum's Clothing, S. E. Olson Dry Goods, Union Depot, Exposition Building, Horse Cars, the Electric Light Mast, T. K. Gray's Drug Store and Mendenhall's Bank. The last two mentioned are still standing. Most of the others are but a memory now.

How did it happen to be called Bridge Square?

One who has studied the course of the Mississippi River knows that nearly all of the early traffic in the Northwest during the open water season was done by river, and understands why the first business houses in Minneapolis were located on Bridge Square. It was at this place, now Bridge Square, that the canoeists made a portage around the falls, resuming their journey near the point now occupied by the Old Milling District. Many early explorers followed this route on their return to the headwaters of the Mississippi River.

The traffic which paved the trail on the west side of the river influenced the traffic on the east side. As soon as improvements began at the falls, it naturally followed that a ferry was established across the west channel, terminating at Bridge Square.

As early as 1851, Franklin Steele realized the value of this primitive ferry and obtained a charter giving him the right to maintain it there for 10 years, provided there would be no crossing charge for Fort Snelling soldiers and supplies. William Dubay and Edgar Folsom were the first ferrymen. They were succeeded by Captain John Tapper, who was also the toll master for the first suspension bridge built in 1855.

It was natural that two trails should lead from Bridge Square, one to the north and one to the south. Southward lay Fort Snelling; Northward the frontier forts of the fur traders and early settlers. The river at this time was at least 30 feet lower than the hotel. When the first suspension bridge was built, the structure was so low that a person lying flat on his stomach could, with the aid of a four-foot lath, reach the water.

About halfway from the bridge to the hotel was a small lake which was known as "The Goose Pond." This lake was quite a barrier to vehicles and pedestrians leaving the bridge. Those en-route to the Fort went to the left; those going north traveled on the right hand side of the lake. It seems like both Nicollet and Hennepin Avenues have resulted from the divergence.

The first suspension bridge, looking toward Minneapolis, 1855. *Minneapolis Public Library.* Mpls. Collection.

The completion of the first suspension bridge in 1855 established the early supremacy of Bridge Square as a business center. The construction of the Union Depot many years later fixed its status as a railroad center. Naturally it became the principal avenue through which the great volume of traffic flowed between the two sides of the river from and to Minneapolis and St. Anthony. This resulted in the two fine retail business avenues, Hennepin and Nicollet.

The First National Bank did business on the Square. Similarly the city fathers located for some time in the old Pence Opera House, now the site of the Union City Mission. They later moved to the City Hall which was erected at the convergence of Hennepin and Nicollet. The drinking fountain (for horses) was located close to the City Hall and marked the location of the Old Time Well which supplied water to the community until, due to the prevalence of typhoid fever, it was condemned. At first it was surrounded by a copse of hazel brush; later it was enclosed by an iron fence. In the ante-bellum days, Bridge Square rang with the eloquence of political speeches and some of the most notable gatherings which resulted in the enlistment of Minnesota's sons for the Civil War were held here.

After the City Hall was finished in 1873 the authorities rented parts of the building to land corporations. Several newspapers located there; the Board of Trade once occupied a part of the space as did the Western Union Telegraph Company. The Post Office at one time was comfortably housed in the west end of the building. The first home of the Pioneer Telephone Company was also in this building.

View of Bridge Square showing the second suspension bridge, at left, the Union Station, at center, and the Exposition Building in the distance, c. 1888. *Minnesota Historical Society.* Photo by Jacoby.

Light tower at Bridge Square, c. 1882. *Minneapolis Public Library*. Mpls. Collection.

In 1882, Minneapolis claimed to have the world's tallest light fixture. It was a huge tower, 275 feet high, and was erected at the intersection of Nicollet and Hennepin avenues to light the entire city. Sad to say, when the lamps were raised to the very top, the light was so dissipated that it was ineffective. They worked best at about 100 feet above the street. The tower was made of tubular boiler plate and tapered to the top. The arc lights were on a crown or collar that was lowered by a cable and pulley each day to trim the lights, then raised again. After ten years, this method of lighting the city was finally abandoned. When it was dismantled it was weakened with cold chisels, much as a tree is cut and felled towards the bridge. Precautions were taken; the surrounding buildings were emptied and luckily no one was injured. The copper ball from the top of the mast was about 18 feet in diameter and rested in a window of a nearby store for several years. The present flagpole at the same location is 90 feet tall.

The old Athenaeum building was located on the east side of Hennepin Avenue between Second Street and Washington Avenue. It was a two-story building that underwent many changes until it was demolished in October 1913 to make way for our Gateway Park. When the Athenaeum first started it occupied a prominent place in the cultural center of Minneapolis, surrounded by banks, and the best stores. About a decade before the Athenaeum was razed many of the better things in life had deserted the area. Banks moved out, merchants found better locations elsewhere. Cheap lodging houses, eating houses, saloons, pawn shops crept in everywhere and the "down-and-outers" seemed at last to have found a haven which existed until recently. Now we are in the midst of a gigantic renovation program which is demolishing nearly all of the area now known as "Skid Row" to make room for fine industrial buildings and hotels.

The Gateway Park and Pavilion was located on the two blocks bounded by First Street, Washington, Nicollet and Hennepin Avenues. Here it is as it appeared c. 1920. *Minneapolis Public Library.* Mpls. Collection.

Henry L. Griffith was proud of the city of Minneapolis, proud of the "new sawdust town" in which he had grown up. Born on March 27, 1882, in a house on the North Side on Fifth Street, he grew up in the very heart of the city during the period of its most spectacular growth, and during his long life was associated with many of the most famous and influential figures of the Minneapolis of that day.

In 1969 Mr. Griffith wrote an account of his life in the city of Minneapolis entitled, Minneapolis: The New Sawdust Town. *(He called it that, of course, because the city was to become the biggest sawmilling center in the world.) It was a charming little book, one that was chock-full not only of stories and anecdotes of growing up in early Minneapolis (baseball games in the lumber yards; bicycling to the picnic grounds at Lake Calhoun; dancing lessons at Malcolms Dancing School; selling the* Minneapolis Journal *on downtown street corners; shopping for his first pair of long pants on Nicollet Avenue; catching frogs after swimming and selling them to Schiek's Cafe on Fourth Street), but was also an insider's look at a dynamic young city as it grew and changed and became, for better or worse, the modern metropolis that it is today.*

The following article is a compilation of most of three separate chapters from Minneapolis: The New Sawdust Town, *each chosen because it related specifically to Mr. Griffith's memories of downtown. Together these chapters provide us with a wonderful sense of what it was like to grow up in the thriving young city of Minneapolis. We are indebted to Mr. Griffith for having gotten these invaluable reminiscences down.*

Minneapolis:
The New Sawdust Town

by Henry L. Griffith

A Sawmill and Lumber Town

Most of the payroll money in the '90s came from the city's two main industries, the saw mills and the flour mills For many years Minneapolis produced more lumber, and more flour than any other city in the country. As far back as 1872, when my father moved to Minneapolis from Montana, the city was known to many settlers as the "new sawdust town" because of the many sawmills that were being built and operated there at that time.

By the time I was growing up, the sawmills had become an important feature of the urban landscape. They all had huge stacks that belched smoke from the burning of sawdust and other discarded material that was then deemed waste.

My best playgrounds were the big lumberyards near the mills. One of these yards, where "green" lumber was stored for months before being placed on the market, was located only a block from our Fifth Street home.

All the neighborhood boys used this lumber yard as play space, and the mill owners, far from objecting to our trespass, silently approved. They knew that boys were alert and observant, and would quickly note any pilfering of their property. Our games were exciting, and as I look back on them, rather dangerous. We jumped from pile to pile, and the piles were some 30 feet high.

The lumber was stacked so that the ends of boards, at intervals, extended about two feet from the pile. These made high steps by which we could mount to the top in no time. The ground of the yard had a thick covering of sawdust, spread there so that the horse-drawn lumber wagons would not sink in the mud in wet weather.

We exercised ourselves in a wide repertoire of lumber yard games. Those I remember were "Run, Sheep, Run," "Hide and Go Seek," baseball and "Can-Can," the latter one of our great favorites. In our version of "Can-Can," we would take four tall tin cans and line them up in pairs some 40 feet apart. Then we'd take turns throwing a baseball at these targets. The one who knocked over 21 cans first was the winner. The game was a crude form of bowling.

Washington Avenue at Hennepin, 1869. *Minnesota Historical Society.*

75

Our baseball games in the lumber yard were memorable. Those were the days when one of my idols was Perry Werden, a professional baseball player. Another sport was ten cat baseball, or twenty cat or thirty cat, depending on how many players we could assemble for the game. I've completely forgotten the meaning of those "cat" numbers, but I do recall the intense fun we had playing that game. A boy named Appo Ende was highly popular with our crowd. We all liked him for two reasons—he furnished almost all the balls for our games, and he was ill favored physically which somehow increased our comradely feeling toward him.

I often visited the sawmills, which lined the river all the way from Hennepin Avenue northward to Camden Place. What interested me most was the way the great logs were pulled out of the river by chain runways and then cut into lumber lengths by the huge whining saws.

The C. A. Smith Company was the first Minneapolis firm to manufacture plywood, the first one also, I think, in the country. This and other sawmills were running at full capacity during this lumber boom period, and among them were the Bovey-DeLaittre, Aikley, Carpenter Lamb, E. W. Backus, Diamond and Shevlin Carpenter mills.

Most of these mills started operating around 1890 and continued till about 1912. Lumbermen were prominent citizens during this period, and among those I later got to know and remember well were Howard DeLaittre, C. A. Smith, T. B. Walker, B. F. Nelson, Tom Shevlin and E.W. Backus.

The sawmills' big year was 1899. This was when I was 17 years old. But on many a year before this, when the spring thaws came, my mother used to load us into her one-horse buggy, tuck us under bearskin robes and take us to see the log jam upriver. We drove along the banks of the Mississippi until we reached a vantage point a little above Camden Place.

Here we drew up to watch the logjam, a great spectacle which I enjoyed as much as a circus. The logs, no longer floating calmly down the current, seemed to have fought furiously with one another as if each were trying to get downstream first. They were jammed and pushed at every possible angle in a tight-packed topsy-turvy jumble.

Later, when all the river ice had melted, mother would give us another grand treat by driving us to the lower end of the jam to watch the lumberjacks. These sturdy fellows balanced themselves on the logs with the aid of their pegged shoes and, wielding their pikes, started dislodging the logs to loosen the jam and move it downstream. A byproduct of this endeavor, which I never tired of watching, was the log-rolling contests held on the river. This was certainly no game for amateurs. The log rollers had plenty of practice behind them in their daily work, and they were practically unbeatable.

The so-called lumberjack restaurants were located in the Hennepin-Washington Avenue area, which was the center of Minneapolis' traffic and the nucleus of its commercial life. At this crossing, where the Temple Court Building stood, all streetcars had to be checked. Pavements here were of granite cobblestone. The old Nicollet House was across Hennepin Avenue where the Hotel Nicollet was later to be erected. The City Hall, built of native stone, occupied a triangle between Nicollet House and the river.

The City Market House, in the days before T. B. Walker persuaded farmers to sell their produce on his property near Sixth Street and Third Avenue North, was situated just north of Hennepin Avenue between Washington and First Street. (The old City Hay Market was located at some distance, at Lyndale and Eleventh Avenue North, where farmers, covered with their coonskin coats, used to sleep overnight on the top of their hay loads, waiting for the market to open in the morning.)

In the City Market District were the restaurants patronized mostly by lumberjacks. These rather rough eating places all served soup. One of them devised a unique method of handling reluctant payers. When a lumberjack came in and asked for soup, the waiter filled his bowl from a large syringe and then said: "Five cents please." If the customer showed signs of not paying, the waiter sucked the soup back into the syringe and told him to pay or get out.

Along Old Nicollet

In the winter of 1898—I was growing old and assuming family responsibilities—I remember taking Mother shopping on Nicollet Avenue in our horse-drawn cutter. When it looked as if she'd be shopping for a long time, I would tie the horse to a hitching ring in front of the store and cover him with a blanket. Then I'd slip into the store's entry to get out of the cold, meanwhile keeping an eye on the horse so that he wouldn't shake off his blanket. At other times I'd wrap myself up tight in a buffalo robe and try to keep my feet warm. Buffalo robes and coats, incidentally, were common winter apparel among the old-timers and my father's robe, like the others, was brought from out west.

Waiting for my mother, even in frigid temperatures, was better than following her. She loved to shop, and like most boys, I found it boring to tag along with elders as they inspected and pondered at great length the articles that they were buying—or not buying. Mother generally wasn't shopping for readymades for us. Usually she'd be seeking bargains in cloth goods which she used later in making garments for her children and she would stock upon such material for months ahead.

I never heard of her charging anything and I don't recall that charge accounts were widely used. Mother always carried an ample supply of gold coins on her person, and she paid cash for everything. Father was making plenty of money and always saw that Mother and the family were well provided for.

I wouldn't shop with my Mother, but the day I had

Interior of R. M. Chapman Grocery, c. 1891. *Minnesota Historical Society.*

to shop for myself—I was about 14—was a milestone. My mission was the fitting and purchase of my first pair of long pants, which I paid for with my own money. I went to the old Plymouth Clothing House in a mood of part elation and part fright, and got myself togged out in adult apparel. I was going to a dancing party and wanted to show my girl that I was grown up. Until that time I had always worn short pants, as did all the other boys my age—long trousers for youngsters were still in the far future. The short pants we wore till the age often were the loose type. After ten, we wore knickerbockers buckled below the knee (never above) till about 14 or 15, when we entered high school and graduated to long pants. Mothers usually hated to see their sons grow up and move away from their influences—this may have delayed for many of us, the manly thrill of owning that first pair of long pants.

Minneapolis' downtown shopping area was to move up Nicollet over the years, and many a store name was to disappear. In the '90s, you could start at Nicollet and Second Street, at the Home Trade Shoe Store, and proceed southward to Barnby's Men's Clothing Store at 234 Nicollet and on to Goodfellow's Dry Goods at 247-51.

The Palace Clothing House (Rothchild's) was at 315, and the A.D.T. messenger boy service was on the corner of Nicollet and Fourth; Witt's Meat Market was located at 411 and Yerxa Brothers grocery store at the Fifth Street corner, across from the Minneapolis Dry Goods Company and kitty-corner from Browning King's clothing store.

Past Fifth Street, at 523, was the Great Atlantic and Pacific Tea Company, and John W. Thomas competed with the Minneapolis Dry Goods across the street. Then came the Plymouth Clothing House at the corner of Sixth, with Donaldson's Glass Block across the way and extending from Sixth to Seventh. At 602 was Charles H. Cirkler's famous drugstore, the must popular place in town to take your girl to for ice cream and sodas.

Those ice cream sodas were the best to he found anywhere, and many were the girls I treated at Cirkler's. I never visited the place without finding it crowded with friends and acquaintances. It was "the spot" for our generation—its soda counter extended along one side of the store, and in the rear upstairs

was a balcony where sodas were served at fancy tables. The waitresses were a jolly crew, quick with the repartee, and they made going to Cirkler's sort of an entertainment. You always wanted to go again, and always did. And the prices there were truly "the good old days"—plain sodas 10 cents, fancy ones with fresh crushed fruit 15 cents.

Two well-known grocery stores were in this part of town—Chapman's at 732 Nicollet, and C. S. Brackett Company at 24 South Fifth Street. Chapman's was famous for its ice cream and catering service, and Brackett's for fancy groceries and bottled liquors. The Holmes Hotel at Ninth and Nicollet marked the southern border of the main shopping district, and from that point the residential area started.

On the corner of Hennepin and Fourth Street stood a one-story white house, long a loop landmark and the last residence to be razed in the downtown district. This was owned by the old and wealthy Deacon Stewart, and I remember how we ridiculed him (out of his sight and hearing, of course) for mowing the spacious lawn, when he could easily have hired someone else to do it. Sixty-five years later I was to mow my own lawn on Mount Curve with an electric power mower, take healthy pleasure in doing so and not mind a bit whatever disparaging noises young observers might make.

Downtown Was Always a Show

Minneapolis was small enough, in the time of which I write, for everybody to know or recognize its eccentric characters. Outstanding among these were Mrs. Williams and "Sid, the Rat Man." Crowds would often gather about Sid as he told his irrational and oft-repeated story, which always ended in a shouted declaration: "I think the Globe Building is just as good as the Guaranty Loan Building!" I forgot the reason for Sid's partisanship for the Globe Building, but his story and its climax were so loony that they always held us spellbound.

Mrs. Williams for years was a familiar, not to say spectacular sight downtown. So far as I know, she was the first woman to appear on the streets in pants. She always rode a man's bicycle, and downtown Nicollet Avenue was her usual cruising ground.

Her costumes varied, but usually one saw her in pink bloomers, a white dress and a big white hat adorned with pink roses. Her hair was reddish brown—her own tinting I daresay—and her face was almost a clownish mask of bright rouge and white ice powder liberally applied. She loved a crowd, poor soul, and whenever a crowd gathered she would stop at the curb and pose there, seemingly unconcerned, one leg straddled over the bicycle seat and crossbar, the other braced against the curb. The amused police let her go on her way and ignored whatever infractions of city ordinances she might have committed.

One of the first big events in downtown Minneapolis I remember was the 1892 Republican National Convention held at the West Hotel on Fifth and Hennepin. James G. Blaine and Benjamin Harrison were competing for the presidential nomination. I was thrilled by the Blaine torchlight parade which took place one night when seemingly the entire population of the city inundated the loop. The marchers carried kerosene torches mounted on long poles and as they paraded down the avenue. They lifted them up and down in perfect rhythm as they shouted Vote for Blaine, Blaine, James G. Blaine!"

Not enough voters acted on this suggestion, as history tells us, and Harrison won the Republican nomination but not the presidency, which went to Democrat Grover Cleveland.

The whole town was excited by the Republican convention, which was a unique occasion, but very nearly the whole town was excited by the periodical visits of the circus and the flamboyant circus parades. These made redletter days for all boys and most girls, but parents found that the obligation of taking their offspring to the big top made a fine excuse for escape from their daily duties. The truth, of course, was that they wanted to go to the circus as much as the children did

Amusements, Wet and Otherwise

I was a normal, fun-seeking boy in the far away, overgrown village that Minneapolis was before the turn of the century. One of the sources of fun was George Hoskins, a chum I had known as far back as 1887, when we each had velocipedes and raced each other up and down the sidewalks.

George was a younger brother of Dell Hoskins, who played drums with the old Metropolitan Opera House orchestra, conducted by Frank Danz, and who later became percussionist and librarian with the Minneapolis Symphony Orchestra. As we grew older and outgrew our tricycles, George and I would be taken by Dell to many of the famous comic operas that played regularly at the theater on First Avenue South. Our method of entry was unorthodox. George and I would be led by Dell into the orchestra pit just before the overture. After the show started we crept through the trap door and made our way to what empty seats we could find in the front row. The management must have looked the other way when a boy or two occupied certain seats near the orchestra, probably allowing its musicians the occasional privilege of non-paying guests. Once in a while our seats were claimed by latecomers, a crisis we handled by apologizing profusely and taking off to any other vacant seats we could find.

Those old songs and those gay and shapely chorus girls who could kick higher than their heads—what fond remembrances they stir after 70 years! It seemed to me that the leading man and leading lady always had superb voices, and their charm and magnetism were such as to make their audiences fall in love with them, and to bewitch at least one small boy in knee pants.

Knowing the brother of a theater musician and attending shows via "private" entry were glamorous enough, but there was an extra thrill in sometimes identifying in the chorus line a Minneapolis girl who had joined the road company in New York. I took pride in knowing one of them—her name was Helen Chaffie.

Boys were used as ushers at the "Met" but my mother was opposed to my applying for such a job, fearing I might be "contaminated" by the environment. Other parents, I'm sure, felt the same way. The theater was still suspect in many circles of the citizenry.

Among the popular songs we heard at the old "Met" were, "The Sidewalks of New York," "Sweet Sixteen," "The Bowery," "Just a Bird in a Gilded Cage," "After the Ball," "Ta Ra Ra Boom De Ay," and that song which was so popular during the Spanish-

Pedestrians at intersection of Sixth and Nicollet. The Syndicate Block is in the background, c. 1900. *Minnesota Historical Society.*

American War, "A Hot Time In the Old Town Tonight."

Chauncey Olcott, the Irish tenor, came back every year in a new operetta. Ethel Barrymore and Anna Held, so different, yet each alluring in her own way, were great favorites. The stage stars of that era seemed to have a magic power, a magnetism that made them a race apart.

Theater with live performances offered the major amusement to townspeople in the days before movies, while the corner saloons, dotted all over the city, offered relaxation and refreshment. They also served as public meeting places—for men only. Boys, of course, could not buy liquor, but they could "hang around" the premises without being shooed away because their fathers often happened to be good customers. The corner saloon was a forum for discussing politics and the issues of the day. It was, too, a "poor man's club" which required no membership card or fee.

All those places served tap beer, and if there was any bottled beer available, I never saw it. There was plenty of whiskey.

In the late '90s, the neighborhood saloons were in their heyday, more numerous than they were later.

I remember that at one street intersection, Fifth and Washington Avenue North, there were three of these establishments in 1898—one of them (on the late site of the Kildall Building) selling Lauritzen Beer, another on the opposite corner selling the product of Minneapolis Brewing Company, still another, next door to it, purveying Gluek's beer.

Saloons suffered a rather poor reputation among the "better class" of people, but they could at least be given credit for confining their sales to men, unlike the cocktail lounges of a later day which catered to men and women standing side by side along the bar.

Often, as a boy and non-drinking observer, I managed to slip into the nearer bars and observe the "salesmanship" of the bartenders, who were especially hospitable on weekends when the workers had their paychecks in their pockets.

These barkeepers paid cordial attention to such customers at that time of the week, offering them free drinks at first to loosen them up and then transferring bit by bit the payroll money to their cash registers. The later taverns and bars doubtless lightened many a bankroll but never with the genially ruthless technique of the corner saloonkeeper.

In 1956 a man named Henry Broderick wrote a self-published account of his life entitled I Remember Minneapolis. *In this book Mr. Broderick has much to tell us about the "gaslight era" in Minneapolis, as well as much about the city's early downtown. Mr. Broderick was a perceptive observer and a fine storyteller. We are much in his debt for the following account.*

Memories of Early Downtown Minneapolis

BY HENRY BRODERICK

Did you ever lift your face to the warm sun, close your eyes and, while the glow of the Lord's light cast its spell on you, think of something very dear to you? These reminiscences of Minneapolis in the gaslight era with its high button shoes, wooden sidewalks, tight corsets and pug dogs, are akin to that inner feeling of the spirit. The thought of those long ago scenes comes as a bright benediction.

Life is too short to make a business of reveries. So let's just wander around Minneapolis and look over our shoulder at that delightful decade called the Gay Nineties, when I was in the midst of burgeoning boyhood. If tears be shed, they will not be visible. One can be sentimental on the sly, eh?

I remember 1894. You are a farmer in Anoka, about eighteen miles above Minneapolis, a metropolis where 165,000 people are trying to combat conditions in perilous times. You hitch up the farm wagon drawn by two horses, load twenty bushels of potatoes in it, drive down to the big city, proceed to 616 Eighth Avenue South, laboriously remove the potatoes from the wagon, deposit them in the cellar of the Broderick home, collect your two dollars and be on your way home. Those potatoes were to last the Broderick family of ten for most of the long winter. I lived in this "potatoes-10¢-a-bushel" world, but since everything was relative, it was far from a drab or melancholy existence. To illustrate: When I was sent by my mother

to the butcher shop on Eighth Avenue South near Sixth Street, I would carry twenty-five cents and bring back enough meat for a family dinner, plus a bonus, not just a bone, for the dog.

I first attended the old Washington School, where the Hennepin County Court House now stands. There still lingers in my mind a most embarrassing incident which occurred on the very first day of school. The teacher propounded a kindergarten problem to the class. Looking sharply over her spectacles at all of us, she said, "Now children, I want you to put on your 'thinking caps.'" I looked about me in a dazed, red-faced sort of way, and sorely wondered why my parents had let me come away without a thinking cap. It was my first lesson in metaphors. When the old Washington School was moved to its present site on Eighth Avenue South and Sixth Street, the property boundary on the west side coincided with the east line of our old home at 616 Eighth Avenue South, so that we kids had merely to tumble out of the dining room window to be in the school yard. Incidentally, the first year we celebrated Arbor Day there the pupils planted about twelve elm trees. Fifty years afterwards, when pointing out these forty-foot trees to a friend, he inquired as to which particular one I had planted. Singling out the tallest and stateliest one, I quipped that when I planted a tree it *stayed* planted.

Pedestrians cross the street at Fourth and Nicollet, c. 1904–1906. *Minnesota Historical Society.*

When I was in the third or fourth grade, something happened which was to root itself in my young mind. The Hennepin County Jail was located a block distant at Eighth Avenue South and Fifth Street. Inside its bleak stone walls were confined the two Barrett boys—"Red" Barrett (nineteen) and his younger brother (seventeen) awaiting execution for the wanton murder of a street car conductor at the end of the Cedar Avenue horsecar line in front of the entrance to Layman's Cemetery. On the day preceding the grim event, each class was taken in turn to the jail and shown the scaffold and how it worked, with a huge bag of salt as a stand-in for the human body. Citizens opposed to capital punishment were shocked, and stamped it as a morbid exhibition totally unsuited to adolescent minds. Psychiatrists were not abroad in those days, but if they were, we would probably have been told that this sort of thing

would result in emotional disturbance, or a shifting of the ordained orbit, and perhaps leave an indelible mark on the mind of the child compelled to witness this gruesome process of the law. It certainly left a deep dent in my mind. It taught me indubitably that crime does not pay.

Now we are passing the old Oneida Block on Fourth Street and First Avenue South, or Marquette as it is now called. This structure has a story connected with it that is as much a part of it as its cornerstone. In the nineties, this office building carried passengers up and down in a hydraulic elevator. They weren't *carried.* They were *swished.* The sudden speed of the elevator was such as to give occupants a touch of squeamishness. The owner of the Oneida Block was the father of a young man who was destined to make lurid and absorbing pages of Minneapolis crime history.

The Hayward family also owned the Ozark Apartments at Thirteenth and Hennepin, where Claus Blixt, a mild-mannered Swede, worked as a janitor. Harry Hayward, in his late twenties, was a gay boulevardier. He was a bit on the chunky side, about five feet ten inches in height, sported a short cropped mustache, and affected extreme styles in smartly tailored clothes. He favored a modified Prince Albert coat with wide black silk lapels, and succeeded in magnetizing many of the fair sex. In the parlance of the day, some called him a "dude," which was a one-word epithet for any Fancy Dan who went in for advanced modes.

But Dapper Harry was not content with his idle lot in life. Among his amours was Catherine Ging, a fashionable dressmaker. Catherine thought she thought enough of Harry to take out a $10,000 life insurance policy with Mister Fashion Plate as the beneficiary. From then, the sordid plot took shape, finally climaxing in Catherine's murder. This was accomplished by Claus Blixt, who had a slight retainer as a down payment from Harry. Claus hired a horse and buggy from Goosman's Livery Stable on Grant Street near Nicollet, and on the pretext of a promised tryst with the object of her affections, drove her out to the lonely, wooded shore of Lake Calhoun and bashed in her skull with a railroad "T" iron.

At the exact time of the tragedy, Harry sat nonchalantly, witnessing a comedy at the Metropolitan Theatre on First Avenue South near Fourth Street. Although the scene of the crime was five miles distant from Grant Street, the driverless horse and buggy arrived back at the livery stable two hours after the murder, thus setting the investigation on foot.

In due course, after a sensational trial, our off-center Lothario was convicted and sentenced to be hanged. We kids would gather in the open air area between the old Court House and the jail to watch Harry emerge after a trial session, on the way back to his cell. He would come forth, fastidiously attired, manacled to a deputy sheriff, and pause to take deep breaths of fresh air on the stone steps at the entrance of the jail.

His sangfroid was a thing to behold. I did not exactly witness his execution, but saw it dimly through the barred windows from a vantage point on a small promontory next to the Episcopal Church opposite the jail on Eighth Avenue South, where several hundred people assembled at seven o'clock in the morning. Within a half hour, Harry's body was brought out and placed in a Warner Undertaking's hearse, drawn by horses. A large crowd pursued the hearse all the way to the undertaking parlors on Washington Avenue near First Avenue South. From Harry's barber, George Clements, who took care of my thick head of hair. I learned that Harry had invited him to witness the hanging. He naturally tried to make himself inconspicuous in a back row. When Harry was asked if he wanted to leave a few words for posterity, he spoke in a superlative matter-of-fact manner. His eyes roved over the throng, and he expressed grievous disappointment when he did not see his barber. In stentorian tones, he exclaimed, "I sent a special invitation to good old George Clements to see me off. I wonder why he didn't come." Whereupon, Clements was obliged to respond, "Present."

West Hotel. The thing I remember most about the fabulous West Hotel at Fifth and Hennepin was the carriage entrance on the Fifth Street side. This was a circular driveway, wide enough only for one carriage or hack, and protected overhead by a stone canopy, projecting over the sidewalk to the curb. To see a resplendent carriage discharge its opulent occupants was an awe-inspiring sight to a green kid, who viewed this glitter and splendor as just a glimpse of a storybook world. I had to cross this driveway on each visit to the ball park. I would look wistfully toward the richly furnished lobby, with its enchanting elegance, and try to imagine the Seventh Heaven within. I was yet to learn that youth itself is Seventh Heaven. Of course, later in life, there are other degrees of bliss.

Hennepin Avenue from Fifth Street looking towards the West Hotel, 1913. *Minnesota Historical Society.*

Annie Oakley Kiosk. Nearly all the horsecars, and later the electric lines, converged or crossed at Hennepin and Washington, which automatically made it a leading transfer point. In front of Temple Court stood a little kiosk, or shall we say "shanty," which housed the Transfer Man. Conductors did not issue transfers. Passengers trooped off the back end of the car and proceeded to the Transfer Man who handed out a slip entitling the bearer to continue the journey in another direction. In inclement weather, when youngsters were uptown, and had no liking for trudging home in a downpour of rain or a heavy snowstorm or when it was colder than Medicine Hat,

it was accepted practice to stealthily join the Transfer throng, and get an Annie Oakley for the trip home. Whether this was petty larceny, or just a prank, was never the subject of argument. It did not seem to be covered by any of the Ten Commandments.

Parades. Here was Nicollet Avenue, a broad, brave, business thoroughfare, one of the few major streets in American cities which carried no streetcars—ideal for parades and pageants. The asphalt street was bordered with clustered gas lamps—a glittering array of lights that dazzled the eye and formed a bright setting for marching bands and floats. When a parade was scheduled, Nicollet Avenue was a mecca for young and old. Folks locked their homes and all the family stood or squatted on Nicollet Avenue. A gala mood was extant, excitement took hold of everyone, spirits boiled over. America had not yet become blasé. Movies, automobiles, radio and television were unborn words.

Theatres. Let's look at the old theatres. The top temple of the acting art was the Grand, which faced Sixth Street just south of Nicollet. This was part of the still standing Syndicate Block. The Grand housed the best traveling troupes, and the leading people of the stage performed there. The boards of the Grand were trod by such immortals as Sarah Bernhardt, Lillian Russell, Nat Goodwin, Joseph Jefferson, Richard Mansfield, Robert Mantell, DeWolf Hopper and Mme. Modjeska. My brother Ed was flyman. It was a good five stories climb to reach the fly gallery where was centered all the pins and ropes that controlled the stage sets and drops. The proscenium curtain was operated by a windlass on the floor of the fly gallery. When the electric bell sounded, calling for the lowering of the curtain, the spool was unwound until the wooden base of the curtain hit the stage floor with a bang. Then, encores brought the rapid raising and lowering of the curtain, to the accompaniment of terrific manual labor and sweat on the part of the windlass operator. Quite a far cry to the push-button mechanism of today!

At the northeast corner of First Avenue South and Washington, stood a place of entertainment utterly unique in the amusement world. It was known as Kohl and Middleton's Dime Museum. You doled out a dime and climbed to the third floor, where freaks, or as they were called later, Strange People, were exhibited. The Fat Lady (four hundred twenty-five pounds), the Human Skeleton (seven feet tall, weight sixty pounds), Jo-Jo the Dog-Faced Man, the Siamese Twins, Tom Thumb, the Midget, the Bearded Lady, The Iron-Jawed girl and innumerable other specimens of nature's detours, appeared at the Museum. Once an hour, a lecturer regaled the customers with a brief history of the particular misfit who sat on the platform. But this was only one ring of a three-ring circus. Adjournment on the third floor was followed by a trek to the second floor where a passable vaudeville show went on for a half hour. Then, on down to

the ground floor, where a hardboiled set of troupers put on a brief playlet generally winding up in a blood-curdling climax, guaranteed to give every patron honest-to-God gooseflesh. This enterprise was based on the Woolworth idea of volume. It seems incredible that such a venture could be profitable, but it must be recorded that the Dime Museum was a consistent money-maker.

The Dewey Theatre, built in 1898, at Second Avenue North and Washington, housed traveling burlesque troupes. In a sense, it superseded the old Theatre Comique, for although it offered prudent glimpses of the female form, dialogue and patter were run through the wringer of respectability, and the place was patronized, by and large, by decent people who wanted their entertainment without straining their intellect. The customers were neither highbrows nor lowbrows—just brows.

The Lyceum (75¢, 50¢, 25¢) was located on Hennepin Avenue between Seventh and Eighth Streets. It was a legitimate theatre, housing an occasional traveling show, but catered chiefly to concerts and recitals. Millrun folks who went to the theatre for a good cry or a belly-laugh kept a safe distance from this haughty temple of Kultur. It was strictly out-of-bounds for denizens of the Bohemian Flats and Hell's Half Acre, who eschewed such scholarly stuff and effeminate fare as served in this bastion of the arts.

The Bijou (50¢, 35¢, 15¢), on Washington Avenue just north of Hennepin, was the home of popular priced thrillers like "One of the Brave" and similar lurid melodramas calculated to put the spectators in a state of deep freeze. When a show was a bit on the sour side, the astute management passed out free lemonade between the acts.

The Theatre Comique on the east side of Washington between Second and Third Avenues South was a rendezvous for rowdies of both sexes. Women in tights appeared there and that alone put it outside the pale of respectability. To be seen emerging from this den of iniquity, or to be seen coming away from a brothel on First Street, were both of a pattern. Decent girls and women wore dresses with hems meeting shoe tops. Those who brazenly lifted their skirts when crossing a muddy street were classified as daring. Apparel was made to *conceal* the female form, not to reveal it. This dictum extended to the beaches in summertime. A glimpse of the female ankle in the Nineties was a thrill. The present generation has been so exposed and conditioned to the distaff anatomy, that now a bold revelation of hips or bosoms is about as exciting to the male animal as a look at a girl's open-toed shoes.

Saloons. Saloons of the Nineties were at once a benevolent and iniquitous institution. The old wheeze defining them as the Poor Man's Club was only partly correct. Some were indeed genteel resorts—others criminal dives where murders were plotted and hatched. Nearly all had "Family Entrances"—a side door leading to a room back of the bar where women were served, with or without escorts. Of course women were not allowed in any bar room. As for the "Family Entrance," the average respectable woman would as soon do a strip tease in one of Donaldson's Department Store windows as to be seen coming out of one.

The exception to this rigid rule of exclusion of the fair sex had to do with Beer Gardens. These lovely oases were operated chiefly by staid and well-regarded Germans. I remember one on Sixth Street and Fourteenth Avenue South, enclosed by a high fence, where families gathered at tables under beautifully foliaged trees, in a sylvan atmosphere, and enjoyed pitchers of beer which cost ten cents.

The good saloons were places to pause for solid citizens. There were many, but let's peek at one of the best. That would be the one conducted by Z. Z. Rogers, known as 'Two-Z" Rogers at the southwest corner of Third Avenue South and Third Street. Its chief clientele were members of the Wheat Exchange and the Corn Exchange, both of these buildings being located one block to the South. The gleaming bar was about one hundred feet long, the back sixty feet or so being devoted to a buffet lunch counter. Here was an array of silver and copper containers, presided over by two white-capped chefs dispensing roast beef, baked ham, baked beans and many other palatable items. Whether one bought a glass of beer for five cents, a shot of whiskey for ten cents, or a bottle of champagne for two dollars, one was unreservedly welcome to move in on the menu either as a gentleman or a hog. Gentlemen must have predominantly outnumbered the fellows who wanted to

---

A Drug Store on Nicollet

As I was walking down Nicollet Avenue the other day I noticed a pair of buxom, red-cheeked ladies sitting before the fountain of a certain drug store. They were talking and laughing at a lively rate—and drinking. Just what they were drinking I do not know, but I have my suspicions. It was a sort of rich brown fluid, with a thick white foam, and looked to me very much like beer. At any rate, the ladies sat there, sipped it—and as they did so they chatted with a pretty, buxom woman who leaned, arms folded, with a careless grace, against the fountain. It afterwards occurred to me that I had heard there was a saloon in the rear of the drug store.

My curiosity was aroused. I began to make inquiries, and what do you think I found? The drug store fronts full on Nicollet Avenue. As you pass up and down the street the place looks innocent enough. Perhaps nine-tenths of the people who pass there every day do not know what the drug store conceals. I learned that this place had become a great resort for ladies when they were down town shopping. Beer can be had quietly enough in a restaurant, but it isn't just the thing to go into a restaurant—two ladies alone in the afternoon. But at this place one can drop in and sit down at the fountain. There is a pretty woman to wait on you—and she is discreet. You can sit there as quietly as you please and the good people whom you meet in society, and who think it is a positive sin to drink the rich brown fluid—will never be the wiser as they pass.

I could name you—if I would—a pretty list of ladies whose faces are familiar at this resort. "It's awfully jolly, you know," as I heard one remark the other day, just as she wiped her pretty red lips with a dainty handkerchief. "The only difficulty is that the boys next door are all 'on to the snap,' to use a vulgar expression. And they look so familiarly and even quizzically at you when you come out."

The Eye, 1890

A winter's day at Third and Nicollet, 1886. *Minnesota Historical Society.*

feast on five cents because the place made money so fast it wore out the cash registers.

L'envoi. Life in the Nineties carried an aura of simplicity. Great delights sprung from small happenings. Existence was still unmarred by complicated patterns. Neighborhood camaraderie flourished. The coming of the automobile, bringing with it the industrial age, gradually extinguished the old way of life. New ideas, new gadgets, new mechanical wonders led to new standards of human behavior, and soon, the old order passed into oblivion. It was like throwing away an old Valentine. Want to know what I think about life today? Put it this way: To anyone possessing good health, life should be lyrical. Every morning upon awakening, I murmur, "Thank God for this day."

At the time of his death at the age of 97 in 1960, Edward M. Conant was one of the oldest residents of Minneapolis. Born in Portland, Maine, he came to Minneapolis as a boy of seven, living with his family at the then out-in-the-country address of Eleventh Street and First Avenue South. In 1890 he began his career as secretary to T B. Walker at the time Walker's land investment firm had begun developing St. Louis Park, and in 1900 he worked as a purchasing agent for Thomas Lowry, when that giant of early Minneapolis was developing Columbia Heights. These experiences, as well as his memberships in the Minnesota Historical Society, the Hennepin County Historical Society, the Minnesota Territorial Pioneers and the Sons of the American Revolution, made Mr. Conant uniquely qualified to reflect on the incredible transformation of his adopted hometown, from primitive frontier settlement of the 1870s ("a motley collection of buildings on the prairie—without water, gas, sewer, pavement, sidewalks—not a bathtub in town") to the thriving modern metropolis it had become by the middle of the twentieth century.

In April of 1943 Mr. Conant gave a speech to the Rotary Club of Minneapolis entitled "A Small Boy in a Small Town," an account of his life and experiences in early Minneapolis, given on the occasion of his 80th birthday. Ten years later, in December, 1953, he was interviewed by the Minnesota Historical Society and at that time expanded upon his story, this time from the perspective of a man of 90. The following account is an edited version of the remarks that he made upon those two occasions. The transcription of the 1953 interview was edited by Lucille M. Kane.

A Century of Downtown Minneapolis

BY EDWARD CONANT

Looking west on Nicollet from First Street, 1868. *Minnesota Historical Society.*

I came to Minneapolis in 1870 when I was seven. Few people have had the opportunity of seeing a village of 13,000 grow to a city of half a million, and a community of nearly a million in the span of a single lifetime.

In the growth of the Twin Cities, people take so many things for granted. They came out of Minneapolis and St. Paul and find the busy business centers, and they seem to forget that it has not always been that way. It is very hard for me to make people understand the very small beginnings which I have seen, because at seven years of age I was old enough to take note of what was going on.

I wish I could draw you a word picture of Minneapolis on a September day of 1870. It was simply a little New England village. That's all it was. St. Anthony had started on the east side and then a few people came to the west side and commenced to develop that section. In 1872 the two villages were joined into one and that stopped the rivalry that existed between the two towns.

Downtown Minneapolis was right down close to the river—all the business was right by the river. The block between Washington and Third Street was the usual back street stuff, livery stage, blacksmith shops, print shops, and odds and ends of debris. The houses went out as far as Seventh Street, by the Radisson Hotel. That was the last respectable street. Beyond that the houses were scattered and they really didn't belong. It was Seventh Street and then Sixth Street and Fifth Street where people really lived. The richest people had built their homes of native blue limestone. Some had an entire city block; some half a block; a few were four to a block, one at each corner. Before street improvements began with attendant taxes, corner lots were much in demand. From Seventh Street to Twelfth a few scattered houses and, beyond that, farms.

Minneapolis was a kerosene-lighted village, white houses and green blinds. Everybody had a picket fence. There were no utilities, no conveniences whatever. The streets were simply dirt roads with a path. No sidewalks, just a trodden path on either side. There was no water, no sewer, and just kerosene lighting. I saw the first sewer put in and also the first distribution of water.

Of course, St. Anthony Falls was the attraction that brought people here, though in those days there was no way to distribute that power. So all the business, the lumber milk and the flour mills and things

of that kind, had to be right at the falls at the source of power—directly connected. So they put in a pump down there right in among the flour mills, and they took the water out of the river. It was raw water. We didn't use it for drinking at all. Everybody had a pump out in the back yard. But it did serve for the ordinary purposes of water. Then the sewer emptied into the river at the same place where they pumped the water out because that was the most convenient place to put it. There were no baths or toilets those days, so why worry?

After the laying of the water mains we soon acquired four small steam fire engines with hose carts. Minneapolis No. 1, at Sixth Ave. So. and Third Street, to protect the mills. Mutual No. 2, next to Sheiks on Third Street. Germania No. 3, across from Chas.

The interior of Schiek's Café, 1905. *Minnesota Historical Society.*

Jordans and next to Emil Kisehel, and Plymouth 114 on Twelfth Avenue No. and Third Street. All the companies were volunteer, with no horses. The city paid five dollars to anyone who would take the engine and the hose cart to a fire. When an alarm was sounded, every teamster with a team of horses would drive like mad to the nearest fire house, hoping to get the chance to earn five dollars. It was quite a sight to see these rigs tearing down Nicollet or Washington, and many accidents happened during these races.

The first gas came in 1872, and the horse cars in 1875. Coal began to be used in the early 70s, previous to that, pine mill wood and Oak and Maple cord wood was the only fuel. Every yard had its wood pile behind the house. Water in the winter was brought in huge cubes of ice three feet in diameter cut from the lakes, which was dumped in the back yard and reduced to water in the back of the kitchen range.

It is interesting to note the reaction of people to the modern improvements. Gas and Electric were expensive, but people soon began to realize their possibilities. The advent of the Weisbach burner gave us the first real illumination, but the old fashioned kerosene lamp, although a nuisance to clean and maintain gave a splendid reading light. The telephone was the hardest to introduce. A phone is of no value unless there is some one to telephone to, and it was hard to convince prospective customers that it could ever be useful. The railroads and the United States Post Office were the last to give in. The postmaster publicly stated that people would be calling up continually to ask if there were letters for them, and it would be a confounded nuisance. The railroad had the same excuse, saying that their telegraph instruments were sufficient, and it was only when we were able to talk clear to St. Paul that people began to be interested. The first exchange, down in Bridge Square, had four operators, but not all of them were on duty at any one time. The hours were from 8 a. m. to 11 p. m. I was particularly sweet on one of the girls, and when she had the 11 o'clock shift I used to crawl through a bedroom window, onto a shed roof and down a tree, and then downtown to take her home. Then I returned to my room by the same route. My parents never knew of these nocturnal pilgrimages.

Then the city commenced to grow larger. I remember when they put in the first sidewalk, up above Washington Avenue. There was a dry goods store started in the Nicollet house block. In those days they used wooden packing boxes (paper cartons were not heard of then; everything was in wooden boxes). So they took those boxes to pieces and made a sidewalk of them half way up the block to Washington Avenue and advertised that there was a sidewalk all the way from Washington Avenue up to that store—all of half a block!

One of the best memories that I have is knowing the men more or less intimately that made Minneapolis and St. Paul—John H. Stevens, for instance, and Franklin Steele. I knew them. Of course they were my father's generation. I was simply a boy. I was the Conant boy, as far as they were concerned. But I knew them all—knew them by name, and they knew me. There were the Christians and the Morrisons, and the Pillsburys, and the Langdons. My father had a grocery store which was sort of a meeting place. It was the best store in town, but it was very small compared to the supermarkets that they have nowadays. In those days the stores stayed open until nine o'clock at night. They didn't do very much business, but it was the custom to have the stores open in the evening.

Many people used to congregate at my father's store. They always had a barrel of crackers and cheese with a big knife there. As a boy I used to listen to those grownup men talk about things. The memory of those talks is very interesting. I remember one thing especially. They were trying to decide where the center of business was going to be in Minneapolis. There was a diversity of opinion. At that time everything was on Bridge Square, that is Hennepin and Nicollet Avenues, from Washington Avenue to the river, those three blocks. Everything was right in there. There were a few stores on Washington Avenue—that was between Marquette, or what was then Minnetonka Street and Hennepin. A good many said that the business center had been located and settled, and that was where it was going to be. On the other hand, the court house and mill were down at Eighth Avenue South and Fourth Street. Just why they went down there I do not know. People said, "Why, don't you know that a city always is right around the courthouse and city hall and jail? You never heard of a town but what they had a business center around the court house and jail and city hall." So the business would eventually go down there to Eighth Avenue South and Fourth Street where the court house was. Then there was another set of people who felt that business would go up the river because the mills were commencing to get away from the falls. They said the men who work in these mills would want to live near the mills and therefore North Minneapolis would be where the business would go. And you know, nobody ever thought of Nicollet Avenue at all. That never entered into the picture. Nicollet Avenue was simply a back street. Hennepin Avenue was the thoroughfare, the direct connection with the east side and also with the county out to the Lowry Hill. Nobody thought of Hennepin Avenue really as a business street because it was strictly residential clear down, commencing at Third Street. People had large houses and spacious grounds. It was a residential street out as far as Tenth Street. Of course you couldn't disturb the residences for stores; and nobody ever thought of Nicollet Avenue at all.

But commencing with the late 1870s and the early 1880s, there were some adventurous people who started what they called the Glass Block Store. It is now Donaldson's. The reason it was called the Glass Block Store was because the first plate glass that was brought to this section was put into that building. They had just enough of a structure to hold the glass, so it really was a big showcase. It was the first opportunity for window displays. It was a novelty to see those big panes of glass and to stand on the sidewalk and look way into the store. It was only a one story store, with a flat roof. In order to draw people down there, they had vaudeville shows out on the roof. They had fireworks and balloon ascensions, trapeze and everything. They didn't have speaking because there was no way of sending out the voice. But anything that could be worked with your hands and feet they had. Everybody came down to Sixth and Nicollet because we had no amusements in those days and if you wanted to see anybody you came down to Sixth and Nicollet after supper and your friends would all be there. That went on for a couple of years. That big store operated as a drawing card to bring people. Then the question was how to get people up to Sixth Street; the people who were naturally congregating along the stores on Washington Avenue. They settled it. A line of "herdics" was established. I never saw anything like them. They were a conveyance where the

Washington Avenue, 1866. *Minneapolis Public Library.* **Mpls. Collection.**

axle was dropped down so low that the floor of the conveyance was almost on the ground, just enough to clear the ground. But the wheels were up. It was something like the "stone boat" that they used to have. They had it as low as possible so there wouldn't be too much lifting. The idea of these herdics was that it was only one step off the ground, so if you stepped just one step up, you were in the conveyance. They ran as a shuttle service from Washington Avenue to Sixth Street and were free. They simply went up and down—up and down. People got on and rode up to Sixth Street. Then there was a man—his name has slipped me now—who had a full block between Fifth and Sixth Streets on Nicollet and what is now Marquette, where the Syndicate block and the Farmers Mechanics and the Federal Reserve building are located. He had one house in the center of the block and a big yard with his cows, horses, chickens and everything of that kind. He sold that to a syndicate, of which he was part, and they built the Syndicate Block. Then somebody else built a store on Fifth Street and somebody else on Fourth and Nicollet. Everybody wanted to get in on those corners because that's where the crowds were congregating.

One of the great events of the '80s was the paving of Nicollet Avenue with round cedar blocks. I don't know what the trouble was, but they didn't last very long. They were continually digging them up. The pavement extended from Washington Avenue to Seventh Street. That was the first time we had gotten ourselves out of the mud, which was terrific. Every time there was a rain storm or anything like that, it was ankle, almost knee deep. People used the pavement as a promenade. They would come down in great numbers and walk in the streets, parading up and down, enjoying the smooth pavement. I remember one Fourth of July some adventurous young men—I assume they had imbibed a little bit of the holiday spirit—bought a lot of sky rockets, big ones. They laid them down on the pavement at Seventh Street and they shot clear to Washington Avenue. It was a very careless thing to do, and the police stopped it. The horses were frightened, and the people were dashing about as that stream of jet planes came down the smooth pavement.

Probably the greatest group of celebrities that ever stood on the corner of Washington and Hennepin was assembled on that hot summer day in 1883 when the Northern Pacific Railroad drove the golden spike that finished the continuous line from the Twin Cities to the Pacific Coast. President Chester Arthur was there. Past president and general U. S. Grant was there, along with two other Civil War generals, Sheridan and Sherman. Great financial men of Wall Street and many senators and congressmen attended as well.

A great parade of the industries of this growing city started at noon to pass by the reviewing stand in front of the hotel. People went home to supper and came back for the horse drawn exhibit were still moving. Our guests were on the trains, and going east, long before the last exhibit passed the hotel.

I recall one exhibit vividly. Lumber was one of our great industries and figured large in the procession. Pulled by several teams of magnificent horses, a huge log, right out of the river, at least four feet in diameter, the wet bark glistening in the sun light, and water still dripping from its sides, had the place of honor. Following this was a log of equal size with a single slab out from each of its four sides. This was followed by a magnificent timber, all of its four sides equal, and ready for the gang saw. Then followed 10x10s, 8x8s, 4x4s, 2x4s, boards, shingles, laths that could come from this log, without a knot or blemish. The workmen of the competing lumber companies had vied with each other for the most perfect load of lumber. They were all true, some had the sides of the load smoothed and varnished, and all held the interest of the crowds for hours. Every industry in the city was represented.

Another exciting time we had: The Glass Block had put a display of fireworks out on the Nicollet Avenue side. The balloons were ascending. They had a sponge saturated with alcohol. Then they lighted the alcohol in a little wire basket, and that generated enough hot air to inflate the balloon. Away it went, soaring in the air. One of the sponges fell out. The blazing sponge fell down into the fireworks that were on the street. That was the biggest display of fireworks that we had ever seen. It knocked out all the windows in the Glass Block. It was a very exciting time. I happened to be there.

My father was always worried about me because he felt very proud of the family. He didn't want anything to happen that would hurt the reputation of the Conant family. When anything happened, I always seemed to be present. I wasn't the promulgator or instigator, but I always seemed to be there. The school house where I got my elementary education burned and it was a miracle that no one was injured. We had no fire drills or anything in those days. We had a three-story building. It was a cold February morning. The teachers got all the children out. They didn't save anything but what they had on at the moment. I remember the next morning—I was in high school then in another part of the city—my father, who was a very religious man, thanked God at our morning prayers that no lives were lost in the fire. And then he thanked God that his son, Edward, had a perfect alibi, since he was in another part of the city. If I had been attending school, there might have been some question as to how that fire started.

One of the interesting things, to me, a church man, was the movement of the churches. In those days, people walked or had horses and carriages, but most everybody walked. So everything had to be as near to the homes as possible. The churches were all downtown. We had only one Catholic church at that time, and that was on Third Street. St. Mark's Church was on Fourth Street and Hennepin. The Baptist Church was on Fifth Street and Hennepin. The Presbyterian and the Plymouth Congregational were on Fourth Street. When they commenced to move they didn't dare to move very far, or they would get out into the country. The Westminster Church moved from Fourth Street to Seventh Street, and the Plymouth Congregational moved to Eighth Street. There was some question as to whether that was going to be wise because that was getting out into the country a little bit. The Universalist Church also moved up to Eighth Street. St. Mark's moved up as far as Sixth Street. They were not quite as forward as the others, because they didn't feel they dared go any farther. The Baptists were on Fourth Street and they didn't move for a number of years. Then things began to move out south a little bit and they moved to Tenth Street. They are there now. That is the only downtown church left.

One of the early events in my Minneapolis life was the learning of the names of the avenues, most of which have since been changed. You are all familiar

Westminster Presbyterian Church, at left, as it appeared at its location on Seventh and Nicollet in 1896. The church burned in 1897 and its site became the future home of Dayton's. *Minneapolis Public Library*. Mpls. Collection.

with later changes, First Avenue to Marquette, Mary Place to Vine, later to La Salle. Western to Glenwood. Part of First Avenue North to Currie. Part of Central Avenue to East Hennepin. Like all river towns, the growth was up and down the river. On both sides of the river the numbered streets ran parallel to the river and there has never been any change. The avenue names were changed, however. What follows is a list of those changes.

In the early days:

1st Avenue S. was Minnetonka

2nd Avenue S. was Helen

3rd Avenue S. was Oregon

4th Avenue S. was California

4th Avenue S. was Marshall

6th Avenue S. was Cataract

7th Avenue S. was Russell

8th Avenue S. was Ames

9th Avenue S. was Rice

10th Avenue S. was Smith

11th Avenue S. was Pearl

12th Avenue S. was Huey

13th Avenue S. was Hanson

14th Avenue S. was Lake

15th Avenue S. was Vine

16th Avenue S. was Clay

17th Avenue S. was Avon

On the north side of Hennepin:

1st Avenue N. was Utah

2nd Avenue N. was Kansas

3rd Avenue N. was Itasca

4th Avenue N. was Dakota

5th Avenue N. was Nebraska

6th Avenue N. was Harrison

7th Avenue N. was Lewis

8th Avenue N. was Seward

9th Avenue N. was Marcy

10th Avenue N. was Benton

There was no 11th or 12th Avenue.

13th Avenue N. was Fremont

14th Avenue N. was Clayton

15th Avenue N. was Bingham

16th Avenue N. was Breckenridge

On the southeast side, the avenues ran to names of trees:

Central Avenue was Bay Street

1st Avenue S.E. was Mill Street

2nd Avenue S. E. was Pine Street

3rd Avenue S. E. was Cedar Street

4th Avenue S. E. was Spruce Street

5th Avenue S. E. was Spring Street

6th Avenue S. E. was Maple Street

7th Avenue S. E. was Walnut Street

8th Avenue S. E. was Aspen Street

9th Avenue S. E. was Birch Street

10th Avenue S. E. was Willow Street

11th Avenue S. E. was Elm Street

On the northeast side, they stole a couple of trees from the southeast side, then went on a new schedule:

1st Avenue N. E. was Linden Street

2nd Avenue N.E. was Oak street

3rd Avenue N.E. was Dakota Street

4th Avenue N.E. was Todd Street

5th Avenue N.E. was Dana Street

6th Avenue N.E. was Wood Street

Then the Catholics took hold with the following saints:

7th Avenue N.E. was St. Paul

8th Avenue N.E. was St. Anthony

9th Avenue N.E. was St. Peter

10th Avenue N.E. was St. Martin

11th Avenue N.E. was St. Genevieve

France, Penn, Lyndale, Portland and Cedar were county roads on section lines going out into the farm districts, but they had no names and they were very little used except by the country people. What we know as Broadway was an unnamed single way trail, winding through the scrub oaks and hazel bushes towards Crystal Lake, and the farming section to the north. Later, as the city grew, these trails became roads and then streets, and were given the names that they are now known by.

President William McKinley is welcomed to Minneapolis upon his visit to the city in 1899. McKinley (the bald-headed man at center) has come to the city to welcome Minnesota's troops back from the Phillipines. His carriage has just turned north off of Fourth Street and is heading up Nicollet. *Minneapolis Public Library*. Mpls. Collection.

The 1892 Republican National Convention

In 1892 the Republican Party selected the mill city for its convention, scheduled to run from the 7th through the 10th of June. The four year old Exposition Building, erected to spite St. Paul, had been closed for a year due to poor patronage. It was now completely rebuilt and redecorated for the occasion and twelve thousand seats were installed. Modern invention was evident with six telephones and hundreds of blazing gas jets.

Convention banners and streamers bearing the legend "The City is Yours" were hung at strategic spots from roofs and poles. Minneapolis bubbled with activity. Five thousand trunks arrived by train in one day, breaking all previous records as the ten thousand guests swarmed into town.

Reservations at the West Hotel had been made months in advance and every hotel in the city was taxed to capacity. Rooming houses and private dwellings accommodated hundreds more but many of the delegates preferred to stop at the Lake Park or St. Louis Hotel at Minnetonka when they learned that streetcars at Bridge Square took them straight to their destination in less than an hour's time.

In front of the Nicollet Hotel a welcoming band played "My Gal's a High Born Lady" and "Goodbye, Dolly Gray."

Mayor Winston, a Democrat, had set aside his political convictions to serve as chairman of a committee to raise fifty thousand dollars for convention expenses. The response was so great that the sum was doubled and the extra money permitted the city to offer an elaborate program. On opening day a concert of one thousand voices entertained the delegates in the huge auditorium before the guest speaker, Susan B. Anthony, gave an address that endeared her to them all.

The silver-tongued chairman of the convention, Chauncey Depew, charmed everyone with his wit. The party proceeded to nominate Benjamin Harrison for president and Whitelaw Reid of New York for vice-president. It was later due to Mr. Depew's praise, on his return east, that the fame of Minneapolis spread as a convention city.

Many of the eastern delegates, who expected to see Indians roaming the streets chasing their enemies with tomahawks, expressed astonishment at the grandeur of the West Hotel with its sumptuous banquets.

Beatrice Morosco,
The Restless Ones

Minneapolis began to be known as a convention city, long before we had facilities to handle big gatherings. The first big one was in 1891 and was managed almost exclusively by the younger set of business men and women.

Christian Endeavor, organized in 1881, wanted to celebrate its 10th birthday with a really great convention, and Minneapolis was chosen as its convention city. We accepted the challenge, but with many misgivings. (Hotel facilities were totally inadequate; we had no meeting place other than the churches, the largest one only holding 1600 people, with 10,000 expected.) The Exposition Building on the east side was quite new, and had been built with a great well in the center, with galleries for exhibition purposes on the four sides. We conceived the idea of using this central space as an auditorium, and before we had gotten through, we had a convention hall seating 5000, with an adequate stage and additional seating in the galleries. Electricity was very new those days, but we were bold enough to use it for lighting the entire building. We used the old style carbon arc lamps suspended from the ceiling. At one night's session with 6000 people present, a terrific electrical wind storm swept over the city. In swift succession two bolts of lightning came, one striking the tower, the other hitting the bank of transformers outside of the building, plunging the auditorium into total darkness, lighted only by the flashes of lightning through the windows, and then the crash of the following thunder.

Not a person left their seats, and for the three quarters of an hour they sang gospel songs until the lights came on. The newspapers of the entire country commented upon it the next day, as a modern miracle that an audience of that size could be held without a panic.

The Minneapolis Public Library, at Hennepin Avenue and Tenth Street. The First Baptist Church is at left. The library was built in 1889 and torn down in 1961. The First Baptist Church was built in 1888 and is still extant. *Minneapolis Public Library.* Mpls. Collection.

The Levi Stewart property at Hennepin and Fourth Street. *Minnesota Historical Society.*

Speaking of singing, that was a great part of the convention. The Street Car Company was operating open cars in the summer. The young people loaded those cars to capacity, and rode through the streets, singing the current gospel songs as well as the old church hymns. They were not going anywhere in particular, they were just riding and singing, and everyone in the city entered into the spirit of the occasion.

The fact that we now had an auditorium gave our businessmen the opportunity to invite the National Republican Convention in 1892. It was the first time that it had been held outside of the eastern cities. It took a lot of courage, but that was the way things were done in those days.

I had been in charge of the housing of the Christian Endeavor Convention of the year before, and I was chosen to head the housing of the delegates to the Republican Convention. It was quite a different crowd to handle. The young people were willing to put up with any kind of inconvenience, but the politicians, and many of our greatest men, wanted suites and rooms with bath and all the conveniences of a great eastern city. The West Hotel in Minneapolis and the Ryan Hotel in St. Paul were about 10 years old, and quite modern, although

bathrooms were generally "down the hall." Our other hotels were the "leftovers" from the early days—comfortable, but not elaborate.

However, we satisfied our visitors (how, I do not know). But we got away with it, and it was really a great convention, even if the Republican nominee was defeated by a Democrat the next fall.

From its earliest days, Minneapolis has had its share of interesting characters of the odd, eccentric, or amusing type. I could take up my whole time in telling about them. I presume that there are men in this room, who never saw "Sid the rat-man" standing on the curb, and telling the story of his life to anyone who would stop and listen. Those who never saw or heard him have missed a great experience. There was a time when I could repeat his talk word for word.

I am going to confine myself to just one character who was a personal friend of mine until the day of his death: Levi (Elder) Stewart. He was one of our early attorneys. Tall and sparse, his Prince Albert coat and tall silk hat made him look still taller and thinner. Coming from Maine, he was the son of a Baptist minister. He was one of our wealthiest men, acquiring large quantities of real estate, and never selling any, although he would lease for 99 or 9999 years. A bachelor, he lived alone in a one-story white

Levi (Elder) Stewart and friends in front of his residence at Fourth and Hennepin. *Minneapolis Public Library*. Mpls. Collection.

house, dropped carelessly at a crazy angel on an entire downtown quarter block, with an aged housekeeper his sole companion. It was a matter of pride with him to avoid anything modern; both home and office were lighted with kerosene lamps, and no telephone bell ever called it's message, or typewriter helped in his legal work. In the wintertime, it was not an unusual sight to see him in linen duster and straw hat, shoveling snow. Although wealthy, his name never appeared in any civic or charitable movement, but he was known to be very generous in a quiet way, and doing a great deal of good, much of which was not found out until after his death. He passed away at noon on a hot summer day, with the thermometer well over 100. Some city firemen came to me and told me that he was dying, and wanted to borrow an electric fan, as he was gasping for breath, and the housekeeper had been wielding palm leaf fans for hours. I told the boys there was no electric connections, not even a doorbell. They knew that, and had collected enough lamp cord and other wire to run an outlet in the engine house, across the lawn, and through a bedroom window.

I furnished a 16-inch fan, and in a very short time it literally blew the Elder right through the Pearly Gates. He was too weak to resist this modern thing that had come to him at the last moment of his long and eccentric existence.

My last adventure with the Minneapolis Fire Department came just a few years ago. I do not remember if I was coming to Rotary, but it was just at noon on a cold winter day, and I was just ready to cross Fourth Street, when I glanced up and saw smoke from an open window on the fourth floor of the Russell Hotel.

Everybody wants the chance to turn in a fire alarm, and here was my opportunity.

There was a keyless box on the northeast corner of Fourth and Nicollet, one of the old fashioned kind in that having a keyless door. I only hit the pavement once between curbs, before a big policeman yelled and started for me, and I knew that he wanted to pull the box himself. I beat him to it, by a split second, opened the door and pulled the hook down. By that time, the cop had me by the collar, and Rotary ethics prohibit me from repeating what he said. I pointed to the smoke and he said, "You damn fool, that is steam or hot air; I have been watching that for ten minutes." By that time things had begun to happen. A Nicollet Avenue box draws a lot of apparatus. The cop held me by the collar, and I longed for a hole to drop into. The boys from station "A" at Fourth and Hennepin were already set, the insurance patrol right behind them. No. 6 was roaring down Nicollet. Two chiefs were coming up Fourth

Street from the City Hall, followed by No. 1 from Sixth Avenue South. No. 3 had already turned the corner of Second Street and was coming up Nicollet. No. 11 from the east side was on the steel arch bridge ready for its run up from the G. N. Station. I could hear No. 4's sirens, as they came down Fourth Street from the Twelfth Avenue North station with all their equipment.

And there I stood, aghast at what I had done, and praying that no accident should happen that would sadden my life forever. The cops hand had dropped from my collar to my shoulder, but no one noticed me. There was too much going on. The big No. 1 ladder was raised, turned, and the upper end fell with a smash through the fourth floor window, two men, like monkeys, ran up the ladder.

Some day I hope to stand at the Pearly Gates, and have St. Peter say, "Come right on in Eddie." But his voice will be no sweeter than that fire chief as he cupped his hands and yelled, "Water on Number 10!" Well boys, it wasn't much of a fire as fires go (someone had dropped a match in a full wastebasket, curtains and woodwork were ablaze, and the room was a mess). But it was a fire.

A fire in downtown Minneapolis, c. 1900. *Minneapolis Public Library.* **Mpls. Collection.**

The West Hotel, located on the corner of Fifth and Hennepin in downtown Minneapolis, was opened to the public in 1884, and demolished, quite sadly and prematurely in 1940, in favor of a parking lot.* During its heyday—especially during the "Gay Nineties" and the first decade of the twentieth century—the West ranked as one of the truly "Grand Hotels" in the country, more often than not serving as the venue for the city's biggest and most important social events, as well as being the hotel in which most of the city's many celebrity visitors could be expected to stay.

Most of the large formal balls which took place in Minneapolis during this period were held either in the West Hotel ballroom, or else in the Masonic Temple, the only other place in town with a ballroom large enough to hold them. Among the biggest and most exclusive of these occasions was the Hostesses' Reception and Ball, which was held annually at the West from 1898 to 1906, and was the brainchild of Mrs. Thomas Lowry and seven other socially prominent Minneapolis ladies whose purpose it was to create an occasion upon which the city's socially prominent citizens could "present" their daughters to Minneapolis "society," as well, of course, as to give said sponsors a chance to make a conspicuous show of their wealth and status, and to then get to read about themselves (and the splendid impression they had made) in the society columns the next day.

In 1978 Loring M. Staples wrote a history of the West Hotel entitled The West Hotel Story: 1884—1940: Memories of Past Splendor. *Sandwiched amidst its various tales of murder, intrigue, terrible fire and tragic decline, was a chapter about "high society" Minneapolis at the turn of the century, a chapter in which Mr. Staples does a wonderful job of describing the manners and the mores of Minneapolis' most wealthy and influential citizens at the time of the West Hotel's (and perhaps high society's) greatest splendor. That chapter, which was entitled simply "The Hostess's Receptions and Balls," was the highlight of a most fascinating and useful book. It is reprinted here with the kind permission of the family of Mr. Staples.*

---

*Now the site of the Schubert Theatre, just moved from its old location in early 1999.

The West Hotel and the Hostesses' Receptions and Balls

by Loring M. Staples

This is a picture of the first stage coach to arrive in the city of Minneapolis. It was driven by Cyrus McComber and was parked in front of the West Hotel on the occasion of the Old Settler's Reunion, May 11, 1900. *Minneapolis Public Library.* Mpls. Collection.

American society in the late 19th century and, indeed, well into the 20th, was structured on a class basis: Upper Class or High Society; Upper and Lower Middle Class; and Labor or Working Class, to which should be added two separate and distinct outcasts, Indians and Negroes.

The Upper Class in America aped the upper classes of Europe, but, lacking an aristocracy or no-bility, was forced to use other methods of limiting its membership. Wealth was the principal test of admission, but wealth alone was not enough—many of the nouveau riche, who aspired to belong, found themselves rejected as "social climbers," which of course they were.

The yardsticks for admission were sometimes determined by ancestry, particularly in eastern cities, as in Boston, where the "Brahmins" of colonial ancestry ranked themselves above those of Irish descent without any consideration of comparative wealth. In New York, the "Four Hundred" as a synonym for rigid High Society received its name from Ward McAlister's calculation of the number of guests who could conveniently be accommodated in Mrs. Vanderbilt's ballroom.

To this hard core of wealth and ancestry were perforce added a sprinkling of professors, doctors, judges, lawyers, artists and men of letters; also included were emigrants from upper classes of other states or foreign countries, and, occasionally, the first generation of business men whose howling success at making money could not be overlooked, especially if they were liberal in contributing to charity or the arts. Their children always made it. There was a tendency to snub Jews, and a definite aversion towards actors and actresses.

A booklet, published yearly in the principal cities of the United States, entitled *The Social Register,* listed the names, addresses and progeny of the socially accepted group in each city of its publication. Divorced individuals and those who married "beneath them" were usually eliminated.

In Minneapolis, only a small percentage of the self-appointed upper class could boast of distinguished ancestry—they were mainly pioneers or descendants of pioneers who, unencumbered by income taxes or state and federal regulations on business, had taken advantage of cheap labor and the natural resources of Minnesota to make their fortunes in a hurry. Wealth was therefore a prime factor in delineating the ranks of the Upper Class.

Men of wealth in those days lavishly invested their incomes in palatial homes, staffed with cadres of servants, private art collections, ornate furniture, silverware, horses and carriages, and expensive gowns and jewels to adorn their wives and daughters. Mark Twain referred to the era as the "Gilded Age." Author Thorstein Veblen, not so amused, criticized the "Leisure Class," as he dubbed it, for advertising their affluence by means of "conspicuous waste." Veblen was only partially correct. Building expensive houses and buying expensive personal hardware is not necessarily wasteful, but the forms of entertainment indulged in by High Society were clearly wasteful. And because of the publicity they received, conspicuously so, since in the social columns of newspapers were regularly printed detailed accounts of teas, musicals, receptions, elaborate dinners and balls.

On the other hand these "Robber Barons," as the intellectual left of the time defined them, were in general quite generous in founding and supporting charitable and educational institutions, and more inclined than the wealthy of today to take an active part in politics, serving as governors, mayors and councilmen as well as devoting a great part of their time to promoting and donating money to support projects beneficial to the welfare and prosperity of the communities in which they made their living.

The ball was the height of social entertainment, and a large percentage of the mansions of the rich contained spacious ballrooms for receptions or dances, or both. Agnes Von Scholten, an observer and writer of the social life of that era, recalled that "For sheer elegance, costly material and lavish party accessories, today [1937] cannot hold a candle to the many balls (we never called them dances or formals) of the '80s. Dances, no, but 'Balls,' 'Germans,' and 'Cotillions,' yes."

Ballroom space in private homes was usually sufficient to accommodate only a limited number of guests, although there were exceptions. Senator and Mrs. Washburn introduced their debutante daughter, Mary, to 800 attendees at "Fair Oaks" and entertained 300 guests at a New Year's Eve ball in 1902. Over one thousand persons were invited to attend the marriage reception of James J. Hill's daughter, Mary. It was at the latter function that Hill presented a check for $5,200 to her as a marriage present.

Most of the large formal balls held in Minneapolis during the two decades from 1885 to 1905 were in the only two buildings, other than the Armory, that could supply the necessary space—the Masonic Temple and the West Hotel. The former had the larger ballroom, but the West Hotel offered far more attractive corridors and anterooms and as a consequence attracted most of the "'carriage trade." The social columns of the Minneapolis papers during the fall and winter, rarely lacked material for detailed reports of who attended and what was worn and done at elaborate balls—and balls to come—held mainly at the West.

The West Hotel. *Minneapolis Public Library.* Mpls. Collection.

The West Hotel

As my friend, "The Lounger," stated several weeks ago, there is little if any club life in Minneapolis in the approved sense of the word; but the men must spend their evenings in some place of public and fashionable resort, and as a natural consequence the easy chairs in the lobby of the West are filled each evening. Water finds its own level, and this homely physical axiom is broadened in its scope so as to include the men who meet evening after evening in the hotel lobby, the component parts of each little group being formed and cemented by the ties and mutual interests which each member thereof possesses in common with his fellow.

That large, fine-looking man seated in a chair at the left of the counter surrounded by a group of friends is the Col. John T. West, the proprietor and manager of the finest piece of hotel property in the Northwest. A mutual friend once said to me that Col. West was one of the very few men in the world who could stand prosperity, and this statement is borne out in the daily life of the good-natured proprietor. He is a true gentleman—as courteous and affable to one of his own bell-boys as he would be to the moneyed occupant of a room on the parlor-floor; yet his good breeding does not border on the familiarity which breeds contempt, and Col. West numbers his friends by the thousand. Now that he has taken upon himself the active management of his own property, Col. West's time is not his own, but he takes his customary horseback-ride every morning nevertheless. He has a penchant for professional people, and all theatrical men who stop at the West vote the Colonel the prince of good fellows.

The Eye, 1890.

To name a few: there was the Charity Ball, which started in 1886 and was attended by approximately 1,000 paying guests, with proceeds given to the Home for Children and Aged Women. The "Assembly" was somewhat more exclusive. It was attended by "invitation only" to 250 guests from the Twin City area and was held twice a year. Miscellaneous sub-species included the Golf Ball, the Jolly Club German, the Cotillion Club and New Year's Eve celebrations under various names.

But the most exclusive and elaborate of all was the Hostesses' Reception and Ball, held at the West Hotel from 1898 to 1906, and thereafter for a few years at the Radisson Hotel and the Minneapolis Auditorium.

On the afternoon of August 24, 1898 seven socially prominent Minneapolis ladies met at the home of Mrs. Thomas Lowry to consider the possibility of sponsoring one or more large, elaborate balls to be held annually, as the crowning event of the city's social season. Friday evening, November 18th, was chosen as the date for the first ball, and Mrs. Lowry agreed to talk to Colonel West and ascertain on what terms the West Hotel could be made available for the event.

The next week the same group met at the home of Mrs. Hugh Harrison, wife of the president of the First National Bank, to discuss and formulate a plan of organization. The first action taken by the seven ladies was to constitute themselves as a permanent committee with complete control of the enterprise. It was to be known as the Hostesses' Reception and Ball. There would be at least one ball every year during the Winter Season. The sponsors would be 50 women of social standing, all residents of Minneapolis, including the members of the Committee and 43 others to be chosen by the Committee. Each Hostess and her husband would be entitled to be present at the ball, and to invite ten guests of adult age residing in the Twin Cities, plus two guests from outside this area. In addition, each Hostess was given the privilege of "presenting" her daughters or nieces as debutantes at a reception preceding the ball. This was the plum in the Hostess' pie. Debutantes unrelated to Hostesses would have to be "presented" to society elsewhere. However, there was a way of circumventing the rule. A Hostess could transfer her right of presentation to a "substitute" Hostess.

Colonel West was enthusiastic about the project and promised complete cooperation. He also quoted a stiff price, because the hotel, as usual, was hard up, but the Committee decided it was worth while. After all, there wasn't any other really suitable place to go.

The first Reception and Ball took place at the West as planned, on Friday, November 18, 1898. It was a complete success. It was also a godsend to the dressmakers, since the Hostesses and their guests looked forward to the occasion as an opportunity to display their new gowns and jewels. The attendance was around 500, including many guests from St. Paul, who came over and rode back on a chartered streetcar.

The society editors of the Minneapolis press were ecstatic in their praise. The *Tribune* described it as: "An occasion to enter in the social annals of the city . . . The beauty and fitness of the West Hotel as a reception hall was never more apparent . . . In its realization, the Hostesses' Reception, stood for the cherished plan of a few society leaders, and called for the most brilliant assembly in many years."

Under the heading "A Long Felt Want," *The Minneapolis Journal* nominated the reception to the status of an "institution of the city," commenting that the women "to whom has been conceded the right to be society leaders have stepped aside during the past few years, and in consequence society has suffered, but they have come to their own again, and the result was the beautiful, dignified and delightful function last night . . . The decorations were carried out in exquisite taste."

Only three debutantes were presented, the Misses Nellie Winston, Eugenia Winston, and Marion Towne. But despite its restrictive features, it must be admitted, in all fairness, that the Hostesses' Reception and Ball had a high value. Everyone there enjoyed it, and those who were not there enjoyed, without envy, reading about it. As the society editors pointed out, it brought together the young and the old and enabled them to become acquainted with one another, and if the attendance was limited, what valid objection could be raised? Certainly not in 1898, when the social classes were defined, and were conscious of it. The *Journal's* conclusion illustrates this:

Elegant appointments and beautiful decorations were, however, wholly subordinate to the human interest of the affair and the throng made a fascinating study for the observing ones as well as a bewildering series of stunning pictures. It was at occasion for one's most stunning raiment and all the arts of costuming had been used most cunningly to supply telling effects, so that not the most captious critic could find fault with the ensemble, and the exquisite gowns were countless. In the beauty of her women and the gallantry of her men, the city need not fear to invite comparison. If the Hostesses' Reception is to be taken as the exhibition gallery.

When the Reception and Ball was held in 1900, the society editors found themselves groping for complimentary adjectives. It was "the most beautiful ever given," raved the *Minneapolis Tribune,* "the decorations were fairylike in their beauty. The entire first floor of the West was transformed into a Japanese garden, soft with the delicate lazy light of cherry blossoms."

It was a "scene of beauty . . . a brilliant affair," according to the *Journal.* "There was an illusive charm with a wealth of cherry blossoms that transformed the corridors of the West Hotel into a vast orchard."

The *Minneapolis Times* pulled out all the stops. The West Hotel was "a dreamland of Japanese grandeur . . . The women never seemed more beautiful in their costly gowns of silks and velvets with jewels glistening through laces and sparkling like dewdrops among costly flowers. For three seasons this body of charming women has been entertaining on a grand plan, but never before has a party been so delightfully arranged and the decorations so uniquely devised and so artistically carried out as last night at the Japanese Ball given at the West Hotel."

Eight debutantes were presented; 472 people attended; and the expenses amounted to $1,219.22, including charges of $577 by the West Hotel and $201.50 for the orchestra.

This is one of the first electric automobiles to show up in the streets of downtown Minneapolis. The owner is one Harold Sturgis (seated at left), and the car is parked in front of the West Hotel. April, 14, 1896. *Minneapolis Public Library.* Mpls. Collection.

By 1901 the society editors had nearly exhausted the supply of laudatory adjectives available in the English language and, beginning with the "Night in Italy" Reception and Ball of that year their descriptions became somewhat repetitive and also more restrained.

"Never before have the large reception halls looked more beautiful, never were the parlors appointed with more taste, and never was the ballroom decorated more artistically than last night," said the *Times.* But to the *Journal* the Ball was simply "a brilliant social event." Only the *Tribune* ranked it as superior to its predecessors. It was, "A grand affair . . . never before were the decorations quite so magnificent, so original and quaint in design, and it seems

that never before were there so many stunning toilettes and so many handsome women seen at a Hostesses' Ball in Minneapolis," adding that "the group of debutantes," (there were seven in all) "were fortunate in being launched into society under such charming auspices."

At the Charity Ball of 1902, Mrs. Sumner McKnight wore a gown of "heavy white satin with panne velvet, narrow panne velvet ribbons alternating to the flounce, which was heavily embroidered with pink roses. Point lace and embroidery beautified the bodice. Diamonds were worn. Mrs. John Vanderlip "was gowned in canary crepe-de-Chine with white chiffon. The full skirt was shirred at the waist and midway to the hem the shirring gave the appearance of a full flounce. The sleeves were full and shirred with an undersleeve of white chiffon. Velvet orchids were the corsage flowers."

And so it went—sometimes three or even four columns of fine print describing in detail the gowns worn by every female guest. Men's clothing was not mentioned. It was always the same—tailcoats, white tie, white gloves and starched boiler-like shirts with stiff starched collars and cuffs, beneath which the males of the species basted in their own alcoholic perspiration.

The society editors of the Minneapolis newspapers were much too interested in the decorations, dresses and debutantes to give much attention to the ceremonies. After all, they were not permitted to take part, but confined to peeking out from behind draperies. The ritual for those who did take part— the guests—was more active. Invitations to the Reception and Ball designated 9:30 p. m. as the time for arrival. Many arrived later, dallying over cigars, coffee and brandy at the many elaborate dinners that preceded the main event.

Nearly all came in horse-drawn carriages that formed a parade in front of the carriage porch on the Fifth Street side of the West Hotel. Since most of the guests were those of wealth, their carriages were driven by coachmen in full livery who lived above livery stables located in the rear of the mansions owned by their employers. Some came in rented carriages—the West did a profitable business at its hacking stand.

On arrival the guests were greeted by the West Hotel's doorman, resplendent in his tall hat and braid-trimmed uniform, who escorted them to the entrance and directed them to the first parlor on the second floor where stood the Receiving Line. Here were all the Hostesses and the debutantes they were to present, each dressed in a new gown for the occa-sion, heavily jeweled with all the household gems that could be shown with convenience and, at least in the case of the debutantes, bearing a sheaf of flow-ers—usually American-Beauty roses. As they passed down the line the names of the guests were an-nounced, and they shook hands with all those in line including, of course, the debutantes presented to them—most of whom they already knew. As far as the debutantes were concerned it was generally con-sidered to have been a great bore.

After the presentation, the fun began. There was a grand march, a cotillion with favors, waltzes, polkas, reels and lancers. There was a punch bowl and, later, refreshments and champagne. The ball usually ended around 1:30 a.m., when the coach-men, who had been left to fend for themselves dur-ing the festivities, were summoned by the whistling and bellowing of the West's doorman to drive their carriages back to the entrance and pick up the de-parting guests.

In 1907, the locale was shifted from the intimate splendor of the West Hotel to the newly built Auditorium and, for one year (1909), to the newly-built Radisson Hotel; then back to the Auditorium for the balance of its existence. Things were not quite the same—the Radisson was too small; the Auditorium too big and too plain.

Perhaps social emphasis had changed. The West Hotel and the Hostesses' Reception and Ball were vintage late-nineteenth century creations—products of the mauve decade, and they lost prestige together, although the hotel at least survived the first World War. The Hostesses' Ball did not. Somehow the steam had left the pipes. In October, 1914, at a meeting held at the home of Mrs. Lowry, where the idea of Hostesses' was first conceived, the Committee was dissolved; the Hostesses disbanded, and the cash on hand—some $2,500—was given to the Red Cross.

The Pence Opera House, about 1870. *Minneapolis Public Library.* Mpls. Collection

Even when it was nothing more than a raw and primitive frontier village, Minneapolis was a city that was always interested in the theater. Whether it was at Woodman's Hall (the city's first "true theater," built in 1867), the Academy of Music (built in 1871, and the city's principal theater until 1883), the Theater Comique (1874), the Standard (1878), the Grand Opera House (1883), the Bijou (1887), the Metropolitan Opera House (1894) or any of the rest, downtown was the only place to go to be entertained in the city's early days—a time when the theater could generate a level of interest and excitement that would be all but incomprehensible to the jaded and media-saturated patron of today.

In the following article, native Minneapolitan and Broadway leading lady Beatrice Morosco tells the story of the early theater in Minneapolis, that period of time "When Washington Avenue was the Great White Way." "When Washington Avenue Was the Great White Way" originally appeared in the Summer, 1972 issue of Hennepin History. *It appears in these pages in a slightly abridged form.*

When Washington Avenue was the Great White Way

BY BEATRICE MOROSCO

Even the earliest pioneer loved the theater. Washington Avenue was the first main artery of Minneapolis and it was only natural that places of amusement should gravitate there, close to the section then known as Bridge Square, where Nicollet and Hennepin Avenues converge. Contrary to the general plan of downtown Minneapolis, made by Colonel John Stevens, Washington was the only avenue to run east and west.

As far back as 1857, theatrical performances were given in the second floor auditorium of Woodman's Hall, located on Washington Avenue and Helen (now Second Avenue South) on the southeast corner. It was here the minstrel show made its debut and the first local performance of *Uncle Tom's Cabin* was given. When the citizens read that *The Octoroon*, the biggest success of the day, which was not only playing New York City but had four road companies, one of which was to play Minneapolis, there was great excitement.

The opening was scheduled for a matinee, a startling innovation established by Dion Boucicault, the very dramatist who wrote *The Octoroon*. The farmers were delighted. They were able to drive their wives to town to see the play and return in plenty of time for the evening chores. Tying down the teams and carriages was no difficulty since there were plenty of hitching posts. Little wonder there wasn't a vacant seat for that auspicious opening.

Although Minneapolis was inordinately proud of its new wooden sidewalks that had just been laid in the business district (elsewhere only dirt paths prevailed) nothing had been done about the dirt streets. When theater patrons gingerly stepped from the walk into the carriage that awaited them they were often mired ankle deep in thick Washington Avenue mud, a condition that was intolerable for the ladies since dresses were ground length while the more elegant gowns bore trains. But the muddy streets were to prevail for many years to come.

Not all the entertainment was for family consumption. At times there were "for men only" shows, which presented bawdy burlesque with obese, scantily clad chorus girls. Tights were not to be seen in any theater until the *Black Crook* would make its infamous debut in 1867. The clergy categorically condemned all theater performances whether they be Shakespeare or the shoddy *Sultan's Harem*.

Woodman's Hall soon met keen competition by Washington Avenue's pride and joy, the Palace Museum. Incredibly, it offered a complete minstrel show, a brass band in full uniform and a dozen circus acts for but ten cents. The two top floors were devoted to "freaks and oddities" and cost an extra dime. Quite frequently, for good measure, some celebrity, such as Calamity Jane, would be booked. By far the most talented of the celebrities was Annie Oakley with her shooting exhibition. By the 1880s, the Palace Museum was furnishing a full length melodrama along with a band and a dozen circus acts for a dime.

On June 21, 1867, Minneapolis dedicated its first real theater and cultural center, the Pence Opera House, located on the corner of Hennepin and North Second Street. The brilliant opening drew 1,300 patrons to the opening of *The Hunchback*. This offering was followed by *East Lynne* and a host of other popular plays for the next quarter of a century. These were the halcyon days of the theater when such thespians as David Warfield in *The Music Master* and Maurice Barrymore, father of the "Royal Family," Ethel, John and Lionel, trod the boards.

Maurice was a lovable character even though a bit

eccentric in his ways. He refused to go on tour unless he could travel in a private railroad car with his pet menagerie, which consisted of dogs, cats, rabbits, a monkey and a goat. The latter caused much concern to the other members of the cast who complained that their entourage did not smell like a bed of roses. Mr. Barrymore would then resolve to do better and start with fewer animals the following year, but as he picked up every stray that came his way his collection would soon be larger than ever.

A feminine favorite at the Pence was Lotta Crabtree, an outstanding musical star of the Gay Nineties and known as San Francisco's darling. After she donated her famous fountain for thirsty horses to the Bay City, she feared her gift might be misconstrued as a bid for publicity and refused to play San Francisco, her native city, for years to come. Her fountain, still a favorite trysting place, rivals only the cable cars as a tourist attraction. The story of her life was filmed as *The Golden Girl* with Mitzi Mayfair playing Lotta and she was the subject of two books. The Pence had scarcely opened its doors when two formidable rivals appeared only a mashie

shot away on lower Hennepin, close to Washington. The beautiful Academy of Music was rated the finest structure of its kind northwest of Chicago and it was here Ole Bull gave his second violin concert in the city. The Grand Opera House, less pretentious, was popular with the working man. For many years all three theaters were well supported until the Academy of Music met its unfortunate fate.

Winter arrived early that year of 1884, and on Christmas Day it was 24 degrees below zero. Invariably, it is on the coldest days the worst fires occur, and this day was no exception. The theater was already a mass of flames when the fire engines arrived. Little progress could be made because the subzero weather fast turned the streams of water into a solid sheet of ice.

There were few spectators. Most citizens were home eating their Christmas dinner, and at minus 24 even the hardiest Minnesotans do not stroll down the avenue. It took one hundred men all the next day to remove the cascades of ice so traffic could pass on Hennepin Avenue. No "Phoenix" arose from its ashes which meant less competition for the Pence.

The Academy of Music as it appeared after a fire on Christmas Day, 1884. *Minneapolis Public Library*. Mpls. Collection.

In show business, few things are more tragic than a star who outlives his fame. This is also true of a theater. After the fire destroyed the Academy, eighty years would pass before the Pence would give up the ghost. Its days of glory long passed, it had degenerated into a mission house for the city's indigent. When the building was finally razed in the 1960s, it rated a tear or two from those who love theater nostalgia and the newspaper writers paid it tender homage. There were even a few sentimental souls, including this writer, who thought it sinful to destroy such an historical landmark.

Washington Avenue gallantly made a last stand to maintain its reputation as the Great White Way even though its theaters would never be patronized by the city's elite. Two burlesque houses, the Dewey and Gaiety and a legitimate house, the Bijou, were erected on Washington, north of Hennepin, regarded as the "wrong side of the tracks". The Bijou booked second-rate productions generally referred to as "Ten, Twenty and Thirty" since these were the ticket prices. The season opened on Labor Day and seldom failed to produce the hardy perennial, *Dr. Jekyll and Mr. Hyde*.

Nevertheless, the Bijou made history. When the first motion picture, *The Great Train Robbery* was shown in Minneapolis in 1898 it nearly caused a riot. The picture was presented with a modicum of publicity in addition to the regular performance at the Bijou. Amazingly realistic sound effects with whistles and sheet iron were created by over-zealous stagehands until the audience grew so excited it panicked and tried to escape from the onrushing train on the screen by dashing out of the theater screaming like banshees.

But coming events cast their shadows before them. Even as frightened Bijou patrons fled Washington Avenue to scatter in all directions so did the theaters of the city. Perhaps the Bijou reached the peak of its career shortly before World War I, when "Buzz" Bainbridge took it over to run a highly successful stock theater. Although the Bijou was demolished at the same time as the old Pence, there was no obituary in the papers and no one to shed a tear for this truly elegant theater.

All Minneapolis watched the progress of the People's Theater, located on Marquette between 3rd and 4th Streets, which later became the Metropolitan. As it neared completion a ghastly mistake was discovered; there was no provision for a box office! Neither the architects nor the owner had given it even a passing thought. Hastily, a four foot space, under a stairway, was walled in to serve as a box office, forcing the unfortunate ticket sellers to scrunch themselves double getting in and out of their hutch.

At the grand opening in that year of 1894, gentlemen wearing Inverness capes and ladies with hair piled high and swathed in ermine, vied for attention with the show itself.

Not everyone who attended the theater came to be entertained. On the night of Dec. 3, 1894, Harry Hayward, the city's most handsome playboy, attended solely to establish an alibi. Having insured the life of his sweetheart, Catherine Ging, a pretty little dressmaker, to she tune of $10,000, he had hired Claus Alfred Blixt to murder her in a hired carriage on the northwest shore of Lake Calhoun while he was at the theater.

The alibi would prove too good. The friends he met in the lobby would remember how Harry kept pulling out his gold watch accompanied by such announcements as "The time is now nine o'clock" or "It is precisely half past ten," exactly like a trainmaster. The women of Minneapolis were oddly outraged with the jury's verdict of "guilty." While awaiting execution he was deluged with perfumed letters and officials were swamped with correspondence that Harry was "too handsome to be hanged." But hanged he was.

After the turn of the century came the salad days of theater, and the Metropolitan played the cream of Broadway productions for the next quarter of a century with such stars as Richard Mansfield, Sarah Bernhardt, Chauncey Olcott, Lillian Russell, Anna Held, Lenore Ulric and Charlotte Greenwood.

Before the Actors Equity Association was formed in 1919, stars indulged in the most outlandish of whims. Madame Bernhardt insisted she be paid $1000 *in gold* before each performance. Fritzi Scheff demanded that a red velvet carpet be placed from the street, where she alighted from her carriage, to the stage door. Anna Held badgered the harassed management into delivering ten gallons of milk to her hotel each day to encourage the press to

Looking west on Seventh Street from Nicollet, c. 1908. That's the Orpheum Theater at top, and the Radisson Hotel under construction. *Minnesota Historical Society.* Photo by Norton & Peel.

write about her famous milk baths, which were a colossal myth.

Strangely enough, although the Metropolitan was a "legitimate" house, playing top Broadway attractions, it also played a role in the advancement of motion pictures. In 1906, the news of the San Francisco earthquake, followed by fire, shocked the nation. Within a fortnight motion pictures of the disaster were shown at the Metropolitan, the first news reels ever shown locally and, despite the primitive, flickery photography, the public was fascinated. But this was only a public service, as the theater would continue for nearly half a century with its hosts of live and famous stars.

During this period, Oliver Morosco's two most successful plays, *Bird of Paradise* and *Peg O' My Heart* visited here. Lenore Ulric, who was born in

New Ulm, Minnesota, played the ill-fated Luana in the former. One of the most spectacular scenes ever witnessed closed the play—a smoking volcano which was so real that when Luana in her white feathery robe plunged into its gaping mouth, the awed exclamations of the audience were audible in the lobby.

Toward the end of the first decade of the century, the old Lyceum Theater on Hennepin Avenue between 7th and 8th Streets with the Dick Ferris Stock Company proved a great favorite. In the cast were Lew Stone who later played in the *Bird of Paradise* and still later became a top picture star (who could forget the Andy Hardy series with Mickey Rooney), and Leslie Morosco, brother of Oliver who played juvenile roles and later would become New York's top representative for actors.

The **New Garrick Theater**, between **Hennepin** and **Nicollet** on **Seventh Street**, 1917. The building at left occupied a spot in the middle of Seventh Street in 1917. It was a service center, housing the **YMCA, YWCA** and **War Camp Community Services. It was torn down after World War I.** *Minneapolis Public Library.* **Mpls. Collection.**

Florence Stone, then the wife of Dick Ferris, was the leading woman and the most adored woman in Minneapolis. This beautiful lemon-haired woman who later played stock at the Metropolitan, Bijou and Bainbridge's Shubert was one of the greatest actresses of the day. Her interpretation of Sardou's *Cleopatra* caused even the astute David Belasco to acclaim it as one of the greatest performances he had ever witnessed.

The Orpheum on Seventh Street, a block from Hennepin, brightened the horizon by offering the ultimate in Keith Circuit bookings. Irene and Vernon Castle, the world's most famous ballroom dancers who created *The Castle Walk* appeared here, as did Eddie Foy and the Seven Little Foys. Eddie Cantor, then an unknown, played here in a blackface act.

After playing The Orpheum in Minneapolis, Eddie Cantor continued on his merry way to Los Angeles, where his tour was to finish and he had grave misgivings about his career. He did a single act in blackface, wearing the white over-sized gloves and prancing back and forth in his own inimitable style. Oliver Morosco was casting a new show *Canary Cottage*, which he would "break in" at his Burbank Theater in Los Angeles before taking it to New York to open his new theater, the Morosco.

Accompanied by Earl Carroll, who wrote the music, as he had done for *Letty*, Morosco was so impressed with Eddie that he went backstage at once and signed a contract. Cantor ran away with the show and after the sixth week his name went up in lights. Unfortunately, Morosco did not sign a "run of the play" contract and a week before his New York opening in 1917, Flo Ziegfeld lured the comedian into the *Follies*.

Lucky are the people who lived in this era of thriving show business with its famous visitors in Minneapolis. It can never be repeated.

In the spring of 1970, Hennepin County History editor Joseph W. Zalusky wrote an article for that publication in which he reminisced about June 18, 1954, the day he and a lucky handful of other guests had the privilege of taking part in Minneapolis' last streetcar ride. Inspired by the restoration and revival of "Old 1300," one of the city's last and most venerable streetcars (in 1970 this old warhorse was to be up and running again, on 3000 feet of track between Lake Harriet and Lake Calhoun), Mr. Zalusky's recollections served not only to evoke fond memories of those "galloping, sweet-smelling, turn-of-the-century trolleys," but also of the heyday of the downtown Minneapolis that they had so long and faithfully served.

Mr. Zalusky's article, which was originally entitled "Old 1300," and which originally appeared in the Spring 1970 issue of Hennepin County History, *is reprinted here along with two other articles, one written by Mr. Zalusky for the Winter, 1961 issue of* Hennepin County History *("Fares, Transfers and Other Pertinent Facts About Streetcars, 1873–1960"), and one which was an account of the first electric streetcar ride, which originally appeared on December 24, 1889 in the* Minneapolis Tribune. *Both of Mr. Zalusky's pieces appear with the kind permission of the Hennepin County Historical Society, the other by that of the* Star Tribune.

The Trolleys

BY JOSEPH W. ZALUSKY

An early horse-drawn trolley. *Minneapolis Public Library.* Mpls. Collection.

The Minneapolis Street Railway Company was organized on July 1, 1873, with the following incorporators: D. Morisson, W. D. Washburn, Wm. G. King, R. J. Mendenhall, W. P. Westfall, J. C. Oswald, Paris Gibson, R. B. Langdon, W. W. McNair. All of these men were prominent in the building of the city of Minneapolis.

It was not until July 9, 1875, nearly two years later, at the annual meeting of the board of directors that the following officers were elected: President, Philo Osgood; Vice President, Thomas Lowry; Secretary, Wm. B. King; Treasurer and General Manager, James Tuckerman.

On the same day the City Council of Minneapolis passed an ordinance granting to the company a franchise during the life of its charter, for construction and operation of a street railway system and providing regulations for its operation.

The ordinance provided for the building of two lines of street railways. The first street car line in Minneapolis opened September 2, 1875. This line started at Fourth Avenue North and Washington Avenue; thence to Hennepin Avenue, thence along Hennepin Avenue across the river along Central Avenue to Fourth Street S. E. and along Fourth Street to 14th Avenue S. E., a distance all told of 2.1 miles.

This line was completed within four months. The second line was to extend from Plymouth Ave. along Washington and to 12th Ave. So.; thence along the most practical route to Franklin Avenue, and was to be built within one year.

The City Council reserved the right to designate other lines as were demanded by public necessities and also for the extension of existing lines.

The rate of fare for carrying a person, including hand luggage, from one point to another within the city limits was not to exceed five cents on any line, the city reserving the right to alter and regulate the rates to be charged at the expiration of five years from the approval of the ordinance. The ordinance was accepted by the company on August 18, 1875, and cars began to run September 2, 1875. Two cars were operated and their total receipts for the first day were $21.50. At this time the area of the city was 11 square miles and the total population was 26,765.

Streets were not graded, in fact, no grade was established. The tracks were bent plates, 23 pounds per one yard, and spiked to wooden stringers five inches square, which in turn were spiked or drift bolted to the ties. The cost of construction was $6,000 per mile. The cars were primitive, 10 feet long and drawn by one horse or mule. The car mounted on four light wheels and weighed about 1,000 pounds, two long seats in each car accommodated 12 to 14 passengers. The fare box was placed in the front end of each car and in it the passenger was expected to deposit his fare on entering the car; some had to be reminded by the ring of the bell. After dark the car was illuminated with an oil lamp which often leaked, gave a feeble light and always had a bad odor. In winter, heat was supplied by a small sheet iron stove in the middle of the car. Hay was used on the floor to assist the "heater" in keeping the passengers' feet warm. Under the ordinance no car was permitted to run at a greater rate of speed than six miles per hour. The driver stood on the platform protected only by a sheet iron dash which extended a short distance above his knees. Under these conditions he drove his horse, kept a sharp lookout for passengers, looked after the disposition of the passenger's fare, and made change. He was on the car from 12 to 16 hours each day with 20 minutes relief for dinner. During the first six or seven years he had to wash his car either at the beginning or at the end of the day. For all these services the driver was paid the sum of $35 per month.

The horses cost the company from $135 to $150 each, and six horses were required for each car operated. On the horse's collar a bell was suspended which told of the car's approach. The company's car-house, barn, blacksmith shop and office was located at 3rd Ave. N. and 2nd St. Two men operated the entire plant, including the blacksmith.

During the horse car days the writer well remembers the streetcar on Franklin Avenue. On entering the car, adults (children under seven rode free) would put their fares in a slot that ran across the car windows to the driver who was also the conductor. If change was to be made the passenger would go to the front of the car and get his change from a little cup in the door, deposited there by the driver.

A brass token was sometimes used. These tokens were slightly larger than a nickel with a street car drawn by two horses and the words, "Good for one fare" on one side, and on the other side, "Minneapolis Street Ry. Co." If the passenger forgot to deposit his fare a gentle ringing of a bell reminded him of his obligation. No transfer "checks" were given at this time. There was no date on the token.

And now for the transfers. Probably the first transfer was issued in 1890, a small one (3-1/2" x 1-1/2"). A copy of one is in our collection and is called a transfer check and dated December 25. Wording, "Good only on this date. Must be used before hour and only on connecting line punched." The transfer was an idea that contributed considerably to the growth of the street car system. Although they had tough sledding at first they finally won out and kept the passenger totals climbing. It was argued that if you made street car riding more useful to people, more people would ride.

Prior to this time (1894) the street car company was having trouble coping with the public. At a transfer point where nearly all streetcars met (Washington and Hennepin avenues), riders would be given transfers. The unused ones were either thrown away or given to alert kids who in turn would sell them for two cents apiece to those that didn't care to pay a nickel for a ride home or to work. Many people displayed a strong impulse to try to use transfers for stop-over purposes. A woman would ride downtown, get off the car, get a transfer, do her errands and use the transfer to go elsewhere.

In order to stop the trolley riders of that day from passing transfers at the end of a trip to other persons waiting to board cars, the company put into use a new type of transfer. At one end of the transfer were printed seven faces, five were of a masculine type,

Passengers board for the last streetcar ride, June 19, 1954. *Minneapolis Public Library*. Mpls. Collection.

each decorated according to the tonsorial fashion of the day. There were the full bloom beards, a chin whisker type, the heavy handle barred mustache species, a sideburn look reserved for the city slicker and a smooth shaven gent who probably couldn't whistle if he wanted to. Two types of women were represented, one was what was known as the flapper type of today, the other a middle aged matronly type. When you boarded a street car and requested a transfer at a transfer point, it became the job of a transfer agent to give you the once over and punch the face on the ticket that most nearly resembled yours. Unless you stopped for a shave or paid a visit to a beauty parlor, the next conductor would accept your transfer at face value for the rest of the journey. This was fine as it went, but apparently it went too far. Many people became peeved at the puncher's estimate of the riders and protested to the company. The result was that in a few months the faces were eliminated from the transfer and the "race track" idea remained for the balance of the year.

The Last Trolley Ride

Friday afternoon, on June 18, 1954 at 12:25 p.m., eight old, rather tired streetcars loaded to capacity with streetcar and city officials and friends, left the East Side Station (301 1st Avenue Northeast), bound for their last resting place, there to be dismantled and destroyed. The car on which the editor rode was number 1678. A long table, running lengthwise, and all set for a luncheon of shrimp or chicken salad, greeted the 36 guests who were to occupy this car.

The cavalcade of cars, each individually operated, left the station and started slowly down East Hennepin Avenue and crossed the east and main channels of the Mississippi River, thence to First Street, westerly to First Avenue North, southerly to 11th Street, thence over to Hennepin Avenue and to Washington Avenue South. We were escorted through the Loop by police cars which stopped traffic at each intersection. All this time the guests were visiting, eating their luncheon, and enjoying themselves.

The streets were lined with people wondering what it is all about. Some waved at us and we responded. We proceeded slowly and easterly on Washington Avenue, which gave us time to finish eating and to get a good view of that part of the city.

In our car were the City Engineer, the Traffic Engineer, and several others from the city departments. All were in for a little "ribbing" when we came to the Washington Avenue Bridge, thought to be unsafe for many years for heavy loads. The city engineer told us that there was no danger, but I did notice that only one car crossed the bridge at a time.

It didn't take us long to get to the "Snelling Yards" in St. Paul, which was by this time converted into a cemetery for the old, tired, worn-out cars. When the car came to a stop, it was a sort of signal for some of the guests to get souvenirs as reminders of the last official streetcar ride. Then the guests watched the president of the company put a torch to one of the cars to give the occasion a dramatic ending. After securing our souvenirs, it took but little time for other souvenir-inclined people to take possession of flags, bells, hangers, poles, signs and anything that could be easily taken. This "legal vandalism" was being done as the old condemned car, which must have been saturated with oils and grease, sent tongues of flames and heavy black smoke high into the sky.

The cars on which we started our trip were by this time too tired and worn out, I think, to take us back home. We were told to board a special new bus which brought us safely back to our starting place.

The Street Railway Service

The street railway service of the Twin Cities is, in many respects, satisfactory. But there are so many little defects which could, it would appear, be easily remedied, that it will not savor of "kicking" to call attention to them. For instance, it seems asinine on the part of the management to run double cars on lines where there are not half enough passengers to fill one car at most hours of the day, while one car trains do duty on the line between St. Paul and Minneapolis, where the travel is heavy at all hours of the day, and where on each car the people are wedged in like sardines in a box. There may be some good excuse for this arrangement, but it is not apparent to the public.

There must be a different management of this interurban service if the street railway company expects to compete with the steam roads. In the first place, cars must leave Minneapolis earlier than 7:20 in the morning. The conductors must have a club used on their craniums in the hope of pounding into them a little sense—say enough to teach them that the people don't want to freeze because it is easier for a conductor to leave a door open than to shut it. There must be more cars for each train. The time must be shortened. And some arrangement must be made to obviate blockades at the Market House. At present it requires about ten minutes for a train to make the distance between Seventh Street and Smith Park.

The Eye, 1890

Hennepin Avenue, c. 1940s. *Minneapolis Public Library.* Mpls. Collection.

Minneapolis' First Electric Streetcar Run
Minneapolis Tribune, December 24, 1889.

At exactly four o'clock yesterday afternoon eight new electric street cars on the Fourth Avenue line began to move from Second Avenue and Third Street on the first trips for the transportation of the public. The drivers and conductors, with long ulster coats buttoned about them with brass buttons, swelled out their breasts, looked straight ahead and felt even more dignified than the passengers aboard who looked out upon their friends standing upon the pavement. Ding, ding, ding, around the corner and straight out Fourth Avenue they swept majestically, while the hundreds of lookers-on pronounced them "just the thing," as they ran smoothly as it is possible to be conceived. As the last one turned the corner and entered upon its long run, an astonished son of the Emerald Isle thrust his hands deep into his pockets and proclaimed:

"Well yees can hang the loikes of me. I've heard of people talkin' through the tellmephone and writin' letters on the tellmegraph, but ridin' on electricity is too much. They'll foind McGinty yet."

During the remainder of the afternoon and evening and up to a late hour last night the cars ran with but few interruptions. Each car carried fully as many people during the time they ran as a Fourth Avenue horse car did during an entire day. Everybody pronounced it a grand improvement, especially the matter of time. The electric cars made the round trip in 48 minutes, while the horse cars made it in 64 minutes. The run to Sixteenth Street is made in 14 minutes, and the horse cars made it in 16.

A. J. Russell on the steps of the old Minneapolis Public Library. *Minneapolis Public Library.*
Mpls. Collection.

A. J. Russell *entered newspaper work in Minneapolis in 1885 and for 45 years wrote a column for the* Minneapolis Journal. *In this column (known by many names over the years, but lastly and most famously as "With the Long Bow") Mr. Russell practiced a variety of column writing that we no longer see today, a variety of writing which was as much philosophy and poetry as anything, one which his colleague John K. Sherman once described as "the graceful, humorous essay in the genteel tradition." This style also served Mr. Russell well in his career as a writer of books (he was the author of nine), especially in a privately published little volume entitled* Fourth Street, *his nostalgic, sentimental and altogether romantic retrospective of that once great street and of its legendary "Newspaper Row." Published in 1917,* Fourth Street *was a book that could only have been written by Arthur J. Russell, a man whose attachment to Fourth Street can only be called mystical, and a writer the likes of which we just don't see anymore.*

Fourth Street

BY A. J. RUSSELL

In the geography of streets, Fourth Street is a paradox. It runs west to go north, and it runs east to go south. A study of the map of Minneapolis, showing the bends of the Mississippi River, explains something of this paradox. Fourth Street also runs downward towards the center of the earth till it opens to the imagination the old caverns hollowed out in the sandstone by the curious, underground, wandering river, reaching with creeping indefinite fingers for the distant Gulf. Into these caverns the engineers of the city's Sewer Department penetrated. While they did not consider them a menace to the city's stability, they did, nevertheless, shore them up with massive pillars of cement and rock to make certain that there would be no future "faults" or slips in the strata. Fourth Street's foundations are firm, despite sensational stories to the contrary sent to eastern newspapers.

Winding upward again, the street touches heaven. Charing Cross is but one of the terminals of Jacob's Ladder. Another is found on Fourth Street And at all times of the day and of the night, I have seen the patient people going up and down, each carrying his burden. The dull rain fell or a deadly cold enveloped, and everything seemed like a tale often retold. But on special days, as the evenings came in, I have seen the clouds break, and down the wide street the poet's "pure splendor poured." Then appeared the celestial highway and the celestial host.

Like the people who traverse them, streets have their genders. Some are feminine and constant. Others are masculine and venturesome. And I have wandered, late at night or on dreary Sunday afternoons, down long reaches of neuter streets—and found nothing. Moods of their own, optimistic, melancholic, witty, gay, and lively, streets also have; and characteristic voices as well—either inarticulate cries or spoken words. Other streets maintain an impassive silence. Whatever noise of men or of traffic would break in upon it by day or by night, the real note of Fourth Street is too deep to register in the human ear. But an inner sense obtains it nevertheless. I love these deep soundless streets.

"Uncle John" Daubney, of Taylor's Falls, who, at the age of 96, returned to Minneapolis for a brief visit, heard, seventy years ago, the leafy murmur of Fourth Street or of the place where it was to be. In the year 1846, a cow would have found no path here. Instead of a city and a highway, Mr. Daubney saw a plateau covered with brush and scrub oak trees. Where the Globe building now stands, and so on to Hennepin Avenue, a little green hill covered with brush and trees sloped gently up and away. Another hill in the general vicinity of Fourth Street and Second Avenue South was cut through during the Civil War to let Second Avenue downtown. The indignant inhabitants, whose homes were left high in air, called the avenue Dutch Gap, from the name of a fierce battle of that bloody year. A thousand times I have constructed for myself the Fourth Street location as it was before Colonel John H. Stevens laid it out on his farm and gave it a name to endure as long as men run up and down upon it.

The curtain of the nearer past lifts an edge and we begin to catch more familiar accents. Plymouth Church stands on the corner of Nicollet Avenue and Fourth Street, facing downtown, where the Thompson store today dispenses soda and medicines. On the site where the Vendome Hotel now offers more material hospitality, Westminster Presbyterian Church looms up. On the lot north is the old Pettit home. Across the street Beal's pioneer photographic gallery, just moved up from Washington, offers to take your likeness for posterity to admire. Dr. Sample resides next door. Miss Grabill's millinery establishment graces the corner of Fourth and Nicollet where the Milwaukee railroad now sells tickets. Two of the private houses that attract the eye by their magnificence are the Deshon place, First Avenue and Fourth Street, and, directly across the avenue, the old S. C. Gale homestead.

These are the years called "the '70s." Mollie Deshon dances gaily out of the house and across the lawn, springing to the Fourth Street sidewalk to greet her nearest friend, Luella Brigham, from the Brigham house, where the Loeb Arcade now assists us to turn the Fifth Street corner at Hennepin Avenue. Together they go cheerfully up the street. The beautiful Kate Deshon looks after them from the doorway. Across the avenue Eddie Gale is playing on the lawn. Around the corner like a deer, dashes little Carl Wallace on his way up First Avenue to escape capture by Billy or Bud Deshon. Miss I. M. Grabill walks sedately down the street to her millinery store. Ed Bromley meets Ed Clement on the street and they stop to wonder what Fourth Street will see in the way of new buildings and improvements by the beginning of another century. They pronounce the wonderfully suggestive figures "1900" and look at each other smilingly, doubting if they live to greet that far time.

In the winter of 1880, William Webster, foreman of the composing room, saw from the bay window of his Fourth Street boarding-house, where the Palace Building now stands, a woman, "a beautiful woman," come out of the Deshon house, then a boarding-house itself. It was a bitterly cold day and the streets were icy. As she turned from the private walk to the street, she slipped and fell. A passing stranger helped her to arise and ascertained that she was unhurt. Who was she? Where is she today? Do her grandchildren walk these streets? Foolish questions! All trace of her is lost. The curtain has lifted just an edge, has shown the picture, and has dropped back again.

Fourth Street is now to the Gale family tomcat what Fleet Street was to Dr. Johnson. When the Northwestern Bank Building was constructed on the velvety lawn of this cat's former residence, the Gale descendants saw to it that a stone inscribed "To the memory of Tom (as) Cat" was firmly imbedded in the walls to serve as a puzzle for future antiquarians. The Northwestern Bank, "the bank with the props," is the monument over the last resting place of this animal.

I own the street. No matter who may hold title to its real estate and to the splendid buildings that line it, the street itself is mine, by right of actual possession (pedis possessio) over this long term of years.

Its moods having been my moods and its trodden ways my ways for so long, it lacks nothing that Fleet Street, New Oxford Street, Broadway, Tremont Street, Michigan Avenue or Canal Street might offer. In this year of 1885 the street was entirely unpaved and it was deep with the snows of winter and thick with the mud of fall and spring.

Someone has elaborated a theory of the interpenetration of worlds. These worlds are in the same place, but one sees his own world only, never the other persons. Death does not result in a change of place, but gives another point or view of the same place. We apprehend the place by means of another sense apparatus and find it not the same, although it is the same.

In similar fashion, there is necessarily an interpenetration of Fourth Street. To the foreman of the composing room, my street is a fantastic and surprisingly unreal thoroughfare, a subject for laughter and for sonic contempt, as the vision of a partially deranged man, or of a humorist, one willfully humorous, something that to the warped imagination appears to be, but is not. The tired businessman from his Fourth Street shop also looks upon my street with wrinkled and disrespectful eye. For my street cares little for the value of the land by the front foot, it is totally oblivious of the rental values of the buildings that line it, or of the number of persons and vehicles that pass a given corner in a given time, astonishing the mind that there are so many who seem to wish to be elsewhere and who try to get there by way of Fourth Street.

To the animal that pulled the hack that once rattled the pavements and awoke the midnight echoes, Fourth Street was merely a percept. To the animal man who walks it, the street begins to be something of a concept. He brings to it whatever of mind he has acquired in his climb, and his Fourth Street becomes as complex as the closet where Frank Nimmocks' vests hang. This concept of the street comprises the gambolings of the Flubdub Club, the profundities of the Eternity Club, R F. Jones' tall hat and the heated discussions of the Bonehead Club. In it Tiger Dan, Dr. Ames., Doc Levi, Joe Murch and the cafes flourish and the bright lights shine.

The artist's conception of the street becomes still more complex. He begins to feel something of the soul of it, to listen to its music, to catch intermittently the deep sounding of its three great bass notes, and to detect the traffic of its ladder to heaven. The street is not merely asphalt and stone and people. William Blake, the poet-artist, vehemently denied that the sunrise was to him the apparent appearance in the cast of a material ball of fire arid light. "No, no," he said, "I see a multitude of the heavenly host shouting, 'Holy, holy, holy, Lord God Almighty!'"

Something spiritual and profound exudes from the pavement of a well trodden street and escapes into the air. One breathes in the spirit of the street and knows it not. What millions of complex influences are poured every twenty-four hours into its vital air!

I was standing on a corner of Fourth Street and First Avenue South rather late in a summer evening of 1886, leaning against the area-way railing on the *Journal* corner of the old Tribune building—and lonesome. I was thinking so intently about something of no importance that I barely noticed a rather trim little girl who walked past the corner once or twice and glanced in its direction. In a few moments she passed it again and this time she turned around and spoke:

"It's a mean world!"

"Well," I replied, rather taken aback, "it has its outs."

She hesitated a moment and then continued:

"If you haven't anything else to do, what's the matter with coming up to my room?" It was the first time that I had been accosted in this manner on Fourth Street and I hastened to reply in the spirit if not with the exact words of Dr. Samuel Johnson on a similar occasion: "No, no, my girl; it won't do."

On a late-in-November night in 1889, memorable forever, I saw the first slender, swaying column of flame rising perpendicularly like a great red streamer from the western end of the old Tribune Building, now the Phoenix, and waving itself out into nothing high in the darkness above the great structure old friends and fellow workers are crowding out of the windows, picking their perilous ways cautiously around the narrow cornice still in place on the seventh floor of the present Phoenix Building. I see them falling from the fire escape ladder on the alley side of the building, Milton Pickett coming down as if swimming on his back, landing heavily on the pavement of the alley between the building and the present bank. I hear the cries of terror and of hurry and sounds of men swearing and crying!

Yes, a photograph of the street misses much that is clearly there. The annals and the life histories of the pioneers and transients who walked it and helped to make it what it is do not contain it. All the trivial happenings one can gather from the waste paper basket of his memories, disappointing the judicious who are looking for wisdom or for information and discovering their husks, do not carry the whole spirit of the history of the street, though I sometimes think that they come nearer to it than do the more pretentious histories.

With Tennyson's "mystic," angels had talked and "showed him thrones." The spirits of Fourth Street past, present, and to come have spoken to me things not to be lightly uttered nor quickly forgotten. Yet not these things, but rather the "trivial fond records" are what I wish to place upon paper before walking gladly up the street for the last time and turning the familiar corner of Hennepin Avenue to— Heaven.

In searching through the mental records of a long past Fourth Street, running not quite back to the time when E. R. Barber lived on the street at its intersection with Second Avenue South, it has occurred to me that I remember the date when the bluff of being abnormally busy and driven beyond the powers of endurance was first put up. It was known as "hustle." Everybody in the business world assumed the breathless air of tremendous activity. Did you call on a business man, he received you brusquely:

"Well, what can I do for you?"

"This is my busy day," "Hustle, get it off your chest," "I'll give you just five minutes," and "Get a

The Tribune Building, at Fourth Street and First Avenue S., destroyed by fire in 1889. *Minnesota Historical Society.* Photo by Wheeler & Haas Landscape Photographers.

move on you," were some of the watchwords. Men with no particular errand were seen rushing wildly up Fourth Street and having arrived nowhere were seen a few minutes later rushing as wildly back. They were "hustling."

This old hustle and assumed brusqueness was broken up by a joke. The hustler, when approached by someone who wished to do business, would greet him:

"Well, I'm in a hurry. What do you want?"

And the standard reply became:

"I would like a few kind words." Some of the more genial and universal natures of the street were undisturbed by all this undue and artificial activity and continued the even tenor of their ways up and down the street. Mr. E. A. Bromley might have been hurried a little at times, but he never hustled. Yet he was always "on the spot." Mr. Bromley, in the days of his most fruitful activity, was staff photographer of the *Times,* a lamented organ that housed itself on Newspaper Row. He was only slightly flurried one morning when, on alighting from his street-car at the corner of First Avenue and Third Street, he ran

Newspaper Row

Newspaper Row formerly extended along Fourth Street in Minneapolis from the Spectator Building between First Avenue North and Hennepin to the Globe Building between Nicollet and Hennepin; then across Nicollet to the *Minneapolis Journal*, Regan's Restaurant, the *Pioneer Press*, Stern & Van Winkle, the old Tribune Building now the Phoenix, the *Penny Press*, the later Tribune Building, containing the *Morning Tribune*, to the Press Café; thence across First Avenue South to take in the former *Minneapolis Times*, the Augsburg Publishing House, Lund's Topics in 10-Point and, still further east, the sunrise. Now from Newspaper Row "all are gone, the old familiar faces," except that of the new *Minneapolis Times* which is valiantly holding a bridgehead on Fourth Street, the Augsburg, Lund's Topics and the sunrise. A detour took in Schiek's Café and Powers' Book Department on adjacent streets.

The general sentiment of any surviving member of the Old Newspaper Guard today is well expressed by the comment of a former janitor of the *Journal* (though not in his exact words) when he passed the vacant lot formerly occupied by the *Journal* Building but now utilized as a parking space:

"And all my mother came into my eyes and gave me up to tears."

A. J. Russell

head on into a gentleman engaged in murdering his wife. Forgetting those things which were behind, Mr. Bromley remembered only that he was staff photographer. Unlimbering his camera and wheeling into position, he secured a negative of the "tragedy," "shot" the policeman in the very act of making the arrest, secured a negative of the excited crowd and a photograph of the murderer as he was

held pending the arrival of the "wagon." Then, in full consciousness of duty done, the staff photographer went on his way to the office to take whatever assignment was on the book. As the finest case of what was then known as "Johnny-on-the-Spot," this event has been celebrated in Fourth Street song and story.

"Some day," said John the Janitor, when I asked him about his Fourth Street, "we'll all be gone and other darned fools will be walking here."

I looked for a long time today at a photograph of the street as it was in the sixties and the early seventies. Old country road flavors hung about it. The usual dusty grass and thistles were in its borders and it had ragweed and goldenrod decorations. Morning-glory vines and the eternal woodbine adorned the porches of the white houses. The front yards showed hollyhocks and asparagus. These white houses had the clean, old-fashioned, country smells of woodshed and kitchen and the mustier but no less pleasant odors of spare room or parlor.

The street has become harder and surer. The once quiet corners roar with the traffic and voices of the city. The simple mud-road has become iron, asphalt, and cement. The white houses and wooden churches have given place to stone, steel, and brick in towering structures. How must this new street look to the children who were born in these lovable old homes? Sometimes I feel the sadness of it all coming up through the pavements.

The keys in which this olden time music are set are the keys of chance and change.

I have felt sometimes that it might be pleasant to live on a street that never changes, where the old home places wait through the ages, where there are no chances and changes, unless there are a few happy ones for variety's sake, and where, when we are once at home, we are at home forever. I have had waking dreams of turning a corner of life and of establishing a residence on the Fourth Street of Security in the City of Permanence. It may not have golden pavements nor "everlasting spring" abiding as a climate, though I find no fault with either.

Newspaper Row. Fourth Street South, just off Nicollet, c. 1927. *Minnesota Historical Society.* **Photo by A. D. Roth.**

Regan's Lunch Room, between Nicollet and Marquette on Fourth Street, "Newspaper Row." *Minneapolis Public Library.*

Regan's

"Regan's!" The name is deeply cut into the annals of the street. Fourth Street and youth walked hand in hand and dined at Regan's. The restaurant was at one time on Nicollet Avenue, but it was near the essential street and it finally moved over. It lacked something, perhaps, of being Sherry's, but we knew that the proprietors served no article of food which they themselves were not willing to eat. They gave their customers a square deal and every man his money's worth. In this humble place, Fourth Street history was made. Hundreds of graduates of the University of Minnesota, or of some neighboring business college, return to Fourth Street today and look in vain and possibly with dimming eyes for Regan's. There, while working their way, they obtained their "three squares" a day for months at a time, "waiting on table," or otherwise making themselves useful.

"Regan's!" How many breakfasts of "brickbats and coffee" with a doughnut on the side I ate at Regan's, only the books of the recording angel will show. What mighty questions and weighty problems we settled here daily, found then unsettled again on the next day and again took them up for discussion! The closing of the doors of the old place occurred on February the 28th, 1914:

My pen trails listless at its theme,
I cannot do my stunt,
The life of the noon hour has fled
with Regan's Restaurant.

I know that it is vain to grieve,
Mortalia omnia sunt,
Yet that itself adds to the grief
For this lost restaurant.

A. J. Russell, 1893. *Minneapolis Public Library.* Mpls. Collection.

The Bookmen of Old Fourth Street

Good hunting was found along Fourth Street even after it became half civilized and the rabbits had ceased to run. This hunting was not by dog and gun accompanied. Some small technical knowledge of the values of rare books, a bit of nerve to back investment, and a reasonably small salary made up the necessary equipment While still nothing of a woodsman along the street, I watched with interest and some awe a muscular and well dressed young bank clerk cautiously prowling—or perhaps I should change the whole hunting metaphor and say that he was flitting from flower to flower; that is, from old bookstore to old bookstore.

And the old bookmen that "the trade" has known on Fourth Street or near it! It would take an artist to put them properly upon paper. Thompson's! Do you remember Thompson's on Fourth Street next to the *Journal* office? Later, when rents went up by leaps and bounds, he moved down the street somewhere below the Oneida block. Glorious moments I have spent in Thompson's! I still see, when I close my eyes at night, shelves full of early editions of Emerson, Thoreau, Whittier, Longfellow, and Bayard Taylor in the old green, black, and brown cloth. What might have been among them, or what unknown literary treasures were there, I dare not even hazard a guess. Thompson had the books and he prospered financially until he felt the coming on of the strange mental aberration that he was cheating his customers. It was the result of abnormal conscientious, I guess, for no man was honester. He talked with me about it one day, and explained that the fear was always with him that he was short-changing his friendly customers. Having just bought a book I thought to try him out. I suggested that perhaps I had not received all the change coming to me on the late deal. Mr. Thompson smiled. The abnormal fear was absent in this case.

And there was Raymer, whose sidewhiskers are so imperishably connected in my mind with first editions; and an Old Roman named Alexander who was taciturn and studious and knew books, but who sometimes looked upon the ruin that entangleth; and Goodyear on Hennepin, and Nevius on lower Nicollet, the latter of whom the subtle alchemy of "the trade" had transformed into "Devious"; and Jim Adair who has survived them all and is here today, but not in the old place. Ah, that old corner of Washington and Nicollet. Many happy moments have I spent there.

Chapter Three

Downtown Minneapolis: The Twentieth Century

Armistice Day celebration in downtown Minneapolis, between Sixth and Seventh streets, 1919. *Minneapolis Public Library*. Mpls. Collection.

When the Great War ended on November 11, 1918, the celebration in downtown Minneapolis was unprecedented. The Minneapolis Tribune *ran the following account of that momentous day on page one of its November 12, 1918 issue. It appeared under the headline, "Victory Joy Continues to Sweep City."*

Armistice Day: November 11, 1918

From the Minneapolis Tribune, *November 12, 1918*

At 2 o'clock yesterday morning it began.

At 2 o'clock yesterday afternoon it was increasing.

At 2 o'clock this morning it was diminishing—slightly.

For more than 24 hours Minneapolis forgot everything but that supreme moment in the history of the world when the official news arrived that the war had ended.

Blackening with the shadow far more of the earth's surface than any other war in history; costing in lives, suffering, energy and wealth so dearly that the price of all other wars fades into insignificance; marking the end of right upon the scaffold and wrong upon the throne, remaking the human science of things, the lifting of the noisome cloud sent the sunlight of happiness over nearly the entire face of the globe and the sorrowing sons of men lifted their faces to the radiant sky in a world-wide song of praise and of thanksgiving.

"The world is free."

This was the cry heard in the lifted voice of the victorious Allied countries, and this is the knowledge shared by all humanity which will make Peace Day an international holiday forever, taking a place above all single national holidays and standing with New Year's Day and Easter Day and with Christmas Day.

The news reached Minneapolis shortly before 2 o'clock yesterday morning. Minneapolis instantly awoke to full realization of its meaning: Lights flashed, windows and doors opened, people began pouring into the streets and in less than half an hour a multitude of men and women were down town reviewing their celebration of world peace: singing, shouting, laughing, weeping, ringing bells, blowing horns, pounding impromptu cymbals and bestowing affectionate felicitations upon those who were strangers the day before, who were all brothers and sisters of freedom in the bright hour that had come at last.

It is estimated that the downtown crowds increased at the rate of 200 per cent every hour, and by the hour usually designated as "breakfast time" (though few stopped for breakfast yesterday) Nicollet and Hennepin avenues and all the cross streets below Tenth presented the rare spectacle of an American carnival in full swing.

America does not go in very much for carnivals, just as she does not go in very much for wars; but when she celebrates she does it as hard and as tirelessly as she fights, and yesterday was her high tide of celebration, not only in Minneapolis but in every community of every state in the Union.

The deafening din of joyousness lasted all day and far into the night. Early in the day parades began to appear, made up of the ranks of employees of factories and shops that had closed for the great day; of civic and fraternal organizations led by blaring bands; of orderly ranks of young soldiers and sailors who had hoped to march against the Huns, but were generously celebrating the achievements of their more fortunate comrades whose better luck had taken them overseas. Other parades had no particular excuse for being; they simply sprang into noisy existence because everyone felt like being in a parade.

Automobiles and auto trucks, covered with flags and bunting, sounding continuous horns, dragging clanging metal tails of tin and iron along the protesting pavements and overflowing with shouting boys and girls, filled the streets until all traffic was blocked, and nobody cared. Paper streamers, scraps of town paper and rainbows of falling confetti made the dizzy air as noisy to the eye as it was to the ear.

Small boys dragged stuffed effigies of William Hollenzollern, former Kaiser of Germany, along the asphalt and shrieked with glee as an automobile ran over their dummy enemy. Impromptu community sings and dances went on all over the place, wherever a band played a singable or danceable tune during that memorable day.

By evening the din was indescribable and the streets were nigh impassable. Someone said it was like a thousand New Year Eves and Halloweens rolled into one; but America doesn't think in thousands any more, but in billions.

It was appropriate that Minneapolis should have joined hands with the world in the greatest celebration in history, for the greatest day the world has ever known called for such a festival.

Armistice Day at Donaldson's, November 11, 1918. *Minnesota Historical Society.*

In 1967 Bradley L. Morison wrote a history of the Minneapolis Tribune *on the occasion of its hundredth birthday. It was entitled* Sunlight on Your Doorstep: The Minneapolis Tribune's First Hundred Years, 1867–1967, *and among its many fine chapters was one entitled "Fourth Street: Was it Heaven?" an account of his life and career on "Newspaper Row," that portion of old Fourth Street (between Nicollet and Marquette) that was for many decades home to both the* Minneapolis Journal *and the* Minneapolis Tribune *(as well as the* Morning Times, *the* Penny Press, *the* Svenska American Posten, *the* Irish Standard, *and a number of other publications) and which was, of course, memorialized earlier in this volume by A. J. Russell, that greatest and most romantic of all of the lovers of Newspaper Row.*

No one was more qualified to update the saga of Fourth Street than was Bradley Morison, who was a lover of Newspaper Row in his own right and a man who for over 40 years was a reporter, editor, editorial writer and executive for the Minneapolis Tribune. Sunlight on Your Doorstep *was published in 1967 by Ross & Haines. The following excerpt is reprinted with their kind permission, and also by that of the* Star Tribune.

Fourth Street:
Was it Heaven?

BY BRADLEY L. MORISON

A. J. Russell, "With the Long Bow" columnist for the *Minneapolis Journal* for many years, once likened Fourth Street to heaven. But there were many who held a contrary view.

William J. McNally, looking back on Fourth Street from the *Tribune*'s new home on Portland Avenue in 1943, called it a "street filled with glamour and romance." In his "More or Less Personal" column he added: In all Minneapolis I doubt if you could find a better locale for a novel than Fourth Street of long ago."

Many old timers will agree with McNally's estimate. It is difficult to pin down and dissect the "glamour and romance" he found along the street where the *Minneapolis Tribune* and the *Minneapolis Journal* sat in close but competitive intimacy for several decades, and where the *Times* and other less

enduring newspapers waxed and waned. Perhaps these qualities seem more impressive in retrospect. But they were indisputably there.

The *Tribune* and the *Journal* stood on the south side of Fourth Street, barely 100 yards apart, between Nicollet and Marquette Avenues, across from a site occupied today by the Sheraton-Ritz Hotel. This was Newspaper Row, and for many of us it was the center of the universe in those now misty days when Babe Ruth and Bill Tilden and Floyd Olson and Col. Charles A. Lindbergh and the Great Depression and the New Deal and the trial of Leopold and Loeb and the bloody truck drivers' strike were all part of an exciting and often tragic news panorama.

I was fond of Fourth Street, but I never thought of it as the heavenly place of Russell's sentimental fan-

The office of the *Minneapolis Times* on a rainy night, sometime around 1910. *Minneapolis Public Library*. Mpls. Collection.

cies. Until the Newspaper Guild was born, salaries were low (as a sports writer I got $65 a month in 1918), raises infrequent, vacations brief and fringe benefits hardly worth mentioning, unless one considered a company-financed office picnic at Lake Minnetonka an important beneficence.

In the *Tribune* newsroom we sweltered through summer without air conditioning at battered desks, and those unfortunate enough to work in the composing room on the fifth floor knew what it was like to be slowly roasted on a spit.

Company-financed travel was a luxury I never knew in more than 20 years on Fourth Street. Although I wrote countless editorials on affairs centering in Washington, D.C., it was not thought important to send me there to absorb background material. Only once was I dispatched outside the Twin Cities on assignment, but my horizons were not much broadened by the experience, since my destination was Duluth.

But Fourth Street had its compensations, including the great number of newspaper "pros" who populated it. Some were hard drinkers, some had no college background. There were "floaters" and deadbeats among them. Yet most responded to the challenge of a big news story, like a fire horse to an alarm; and in the heat of competitive strife, many a news triumph was forged and many sparkling piece of copy written under deadline pressure.

Competition inevitably imparted zest to the pursuit of news. Perhaps it even helped us to forgive the thin pay envelopes, which reached the nadir of their inadequacy in the depressed thirties, when two 10 per cent salary cuts in quick succession caused a great gloom to encompass the *Tribune* building. In such dark moments, it was scant consolation that we received' occasional movie passes or that some of us carried police press cards, which made us feel important if hardly affluent.

A crowd gathered around the offices of the *Minneapolis Journal*, c. 1900. They appear to be watching a scoreboard, and are probably following the progress of a baseball game. *Minneapolis Public Library.* Mpls. Collection

There was the Metropolitan Opera House (a road-show theater) only half a block away and beyond that, on Third Street, the dark mahogany cavern of Schiek's Cafe, which had been founded in 1862, five years before the *Tribune's* birth.

On the way to Schiek's, through a dim and dingy alley, one might encounter greatness at the Metropolitan's stage door, perhaps in the person of Sarah Bernhardt, Julia Marlowe, John Drew, Katharine Cornell or David Warfield. How brightly Broadway sometimes shed its glamour in that narrow alley! And in the friendly, convivial atmosphere of Schiek's, where the newspaper rivalries of Fourth Street often mellowed, one might be rewarded by a glimpse of Sinclair Lewis, John Barrymore, Otis Skinner or other celebrities.

When the *Tribune* moved to Portland Avenue in 1941, it was to find no more glamorous neighbors than General Hospital, the Armory and Bemis Bro. Bag, all worthy institutions but somehow failing to cast the magic spell under which we labored on Fourth Street.

From the old Tribune building we might escape to the white-tiled restaurant glitter of Child's around the corner on Nicollet Avenue, where chorus girls from the Metropolitan used to snack at midnight; to Hill's Cafe down the street on Marquette, a *Tribune* nightside hangout better known for its steaks than its decor; or to Perley McBride's saloon, even handier to *Tribune* bons vivants, where many a deadline worry was dissolved in lager beer and good fellowship. Later on the Covered Wagon was a center of Newspaper Row conviviality.

It is hard for me to stroll down Fourth Street today without recalling the great and lowly of Newspaper Row who once gave it a vitality and color never recaptured. Many of them are now dead. Many have dropped from sight. Many others were to become *Minneapolis Tribune* and *Minneapolis Star* staffers on Portland Avenue, bringing their competence—and sometimes their luster—to the Cowles newspapers. But all of them, in some way, helped to create those Fourth Street memories still pleasantly held by a steadily diminishing company of survivors.

There was Lorena Hickok, the *Tribune's* amply proportioned, pipe-smoking girl reporter of the twenties, later friend and confidante of Mrs. Franklin D. Roosevelt. "Hick's" front page coverage of the Minnesota Gopher football games was the envy of many a male sports writer. She could report a murder trial with a grand flourish of exciting detail. Many pecksniffs judged her by her pipe. Her associates judged her by her competence.

There was the *Tribune* bowling writer, "Dad" Hull, first name unknown, who couldn't write a line of his crudely pencilled copy without his precious list of "ajatives" (synonyms) which told him that "pins" could be called "maples," that bowling balls could be termed "spheroids" and that "superlative" and "terrific" were interchangeable. One day a great personal tragedy occurred: "Dad" lost his synonym list and was completely immobilized, in a literary sense, until he found it a week later. Meanwhile, so far as the *Tribune* was concerned, the bowling world had spun to a complete stop.

There was Tom Moodie, a shaggy, disheveled newsman who had served on many papers before he drifted onto the editorial page staff in the early thirties. Tom's roving feet later carried him back to North Dakota where he was elected governor on the Democratic ticket in 1934 and served for just 30 days in that capacity. Someone had discovered Tom's name on a Minneapolis polling list and he was shortly removed from office because he could not fulfill North Dakota's five year residential requirement. While Moodie occupied the office next to mine, his editorial meditations were frequently interrupted by visiting Indians whose pleas for a half-a-buck or two-bit "loans" this kindly, rough-hewn man rarely refused.

McNally was probably Fourth Street's brightest literary light, but Delos and Maud Lovelace would have to be given husband-and-wife team honors. Delos was night editor of the *Tribune*, Maud Hart a slim brunette who wrote feature stories soon after the end of World War I. Lovelace gained distinction as a syndicated columnist, short story writer and author of several books. His wife was best known for her historical novel of Minnesota, *Early Candlelight*, and for her Betsy Tacy books.

When I walk down Fourth Street today I think of Bob Harron, with whom I worked on a three-man-*Tribune* sports staff back in 1918, a preacher's son destined to become assistant to the president of

Newspaper Row. Looking down Fourth Street from Nicollet, c. 1929. *Minnesota Historical Society.* **Photo by A. D. Roth.**

Columbia University. There comes to mind sports editor Fred Coburn, who gave me my first *Tribune* job, the fastest man at turning out good newspaper copy I ever knew. And I recall Demaree Bess, son of a Macalester College president and later associate editor of the *Saturday Evening Post*, who shared the triumphs and frustrations of a cub reporter with me.

I am reminded, too, of Dr. James Davies, the genial and scholarly professor of German at the University of Minnesota who succeeded Caryl Storrs as *Tribune* music critic; of wise-cracking, witty Jim Shay, whose bland copy as a reporter never caught the Damon Runyon sparkle of his conversation; of City Editor Neil Kelly, thinner than a rail and as competent as he was thin; of big, handsome George

Akerson, *Tribune* Washington correspondent and political writer who became President Hoover's press secretary; of Charlie Johnson, a high school junior writing sports for the *Tribune* in his off-hours, tagging after sports editor Frank Force, determined to be what he eventually became—a big wheel in the sports world. And in later years there was reporter Arthur Naftalin, destined to serve several terms as mayor of Minneapolis.

These were just a few players on old Fourth Street east.

With the sale of the Journal to the Cowles interests in 1939, the *Tribune* became the sole survivor on Newspaper Row, which soon, in any literal sense, ceased to exist.

Cedric Adams. *Pavek Museum of Broadcasting.*

At the time of his death in 1961, Cedric Adams may well have been the most well-known person in the state of Minnesota, perhaps in the entire Upper Midwest. (WCCO surveys regularly showed that his name was recognized by as many as 98 per cent of the people in their listening area.) His evening newscasts were so popular, in fact, that when airline pilots would fly over "'CCO-Land" they could invariably be counted upon to comment in amazement at the nightly phenomenon whereby the lights in small towns and in farm houses would all seemingly go off almost in unison at the conclusion of Adams' extraordinary popular, "Cedric's Nighttime News."

In addition to his radio work, Cedric Adams was a popular columnist for the Minneapolis Star, where for many years his column, "In This Corner," was consistently one of the Star's most widely read. On April 7, 1957, and again on August 10, 1958, Adams devoted his column to reminiscing about downtown Minneapolis, remembering with special fondness his family's visits to his grandmother's house, located at Seventh Street and Second Avenue South. Each of these pieces has been abridged slightly for the purposes of this book. They appear together here under the title, "Grandma's House."

Grandma's House

by Cedric Adams

Characters somehow seem to be missing from our scene these days. We aren't completely without them, but today's persons of distinguishing attributes fall short of the collection we had in Minneapolis three or four decides ago. My exposure to the characters whom I'm about to chronicle started during my early boyhood visits to "The Cities," when my father and mother took turns visiting my grandmother taking me with them most of the time. One of my first fascinations was a train caller in the old Union Station. His career began long before the public address system or even the use of a megaphone. Tones tumbled out of his gravel throat completely unaided to fill the high-ceilinged waiting room of the depot. It was always a joy to stand bug-eyed in front of him to watch his mobile mouth as he so magnificently announced the towns through which the next departing train would go.

Grandmother's house was located on 7th St. and 2nd Ave., on the present site of a parking ramp. One of the frequent journeys Grandma and I made together was to Donaldson's Glass Block. I enjoyed watching the huge steam engines in the basement with fly wheels which extended to the ceiling as they drove generators for the store's electricity. But the store had a character I'll never forget. His name was Sadler and his title was superintendent, a post most department stores have abandoned. Mr. Sadler officed on the balcony, had a waxed mustache, dressed meticulously, was never without a red carnation in the button hole of his lapel. He toured the store twice daily to check on operation and personnel. But his route and timing varied daily. As he strolled through each department his presence sent out a kind of shock wave. Saleswomen would tidy up their hair, their counters, their stock.

When Father and I visited "the Cities," there was always one occasion when we dined out together and it was usually at Schiek's. When mother and I ate out, it was usually in some tearoom. Mother was an avowed "dry." Father liked a flip now and then. That's why we so often went to Schiek's and that's how I met another character, the charming and delightful Louis Schiek. It was Louis who taught me first how to drink a toast properly. He had a stein of dark beer; I had water. He said, "When you drink a toast, you must look each other in the eyes, raise your glasses, touch them gently, never, taking your eyes off one another, and then drink."

When Grandma moved from 7th St. up to 10th St. on 2nd Av., I was exposed to another character. Across the street from her rooming house was a mansion that hadn't yet been converted into a rooming house. It was owned and occupied by the man who built it, a grain merchant named Petit. He and his wife lived in the huge house alone. As I recall, he resembled the late John D. Rockefeller. He was a wizened man who carried a cane, an instrument I always felt he'd be willing to put to other purposes if necessary. Mr. Petit had a car that had irresistible charm for me. It was really an electric limousine. Mr. and Mrs. Petit sat in the back and the chauffeur sat completely unprotected out in front.

When my mother and I moved to Minneapolis, after my father's death, we took a flat (nobody called them apartments in those days) in McKinley Court, on 14th and Stevens. Hard by the rear of the building was an old frame house with a single occupant, a widow deep in her 80s named Mrs. Kitts. Wrinkled, but sprightly, you could call her. No one ever knew the source or the amount of her income. She never had company, she never worked. She kept the outside of her premises and her front porch immaculate. The thing that made her a character was her

The Great Northern Depot, c. the 1920s. It was built in 1914 and demolished in 1978. *Minneapolis Public Library.* **Mpls. Collection.**

means of transportation. She rode a bicycle everywhere. She had a sort of string protector over the back wheel that kept her skirts from catching in the spokes, a basket on the handle bars for her shopping and a hand bell to warn vehicles and pedestrians of her approach. Her hosiery never varied—long black woolen stockings.

The traffic cop on 7th and Nicollet was another character known to thousands. He had a Santa Claus shape, red veins that showed in his cheeks, a waxed mustache, and wore his uniform exceedingly well. The traffic semaphores in those days were mobile affairs that were moved to the middle of the intersection and were operated by hand. A quarter turn set the flow in one direction, charged it to the other. In the summertime the semaphores had spreading umbrellas to protect the officer. It was always a production when this rotund policeman rolled out his semaphore for the rush hour traffic. The loop knew another main distinction—Fish Jones, owner-operator of the famed Longfellow Gardens. Fish appeared periodically in the loop in stovepipe hat, cutaway coat white gloves striped trousers. Now and then he had a seal trailing him. At other times he led a couple of swans on a leash. Yes, characters all. You may argue that we have a brand of them today. Into the category you might put Nell Palmer or Russell Plimpton or Myndall Cain or Augie Ratner or the Shinder boys or Virginia Safford or Billy Graham. Notable traits they may have, but will they be inscribed as indelibly as the symbols of our earlier era?

———

May I give you the saga of Second Avenue today? Have you had one street that has played a very important part in your life? Maybe it was the main street in your home town, a lane where you wooed and won your mate, a tree-arched boulevard where you cycled, an alley that provided a shortcut from your home to downtown, a particular street that offered a sliding hill when winter traffic was shut off. I have developed a curious fondness for Second Avenue South in Minneapolis. My love for this street goes back to the days when I, as a 5-year-old, first

visited Minneapolis. My grandparents, on my father's side, lived in Minneapolis, and for several years I was the only kid in Magnolia who had ever been to "The Cities," as we called them. These visits I made periodically, sometimes as often as twice a year, with either my mother or my father.

My grandmother lived on Second Avenue South and Seventh Street in what was called "the old Pillsbury mansion," which had been converted into a rooming house that my grandmother ran. When I traveled with my father, we always took a hack from the Great Northern Depot to grandma's house. My mother was a conservative, so the two of us would take a streetcar at quite a saving. This Pillsbury mansion was located on the corner where the parking ramp is now just across the street from the WCCO building and the Minneapolis Athletic Club. Grandpa Adams maintained a beautifully-kept lawn. I remember sitting out on the grass and listening to the Newsboys' band concert in a park where WCCO is now located. I remember, too, the laying of the cornerstone of the Minneapolis Athletic Club.

On the site of the present Baker Building there was a Greek candy store and ice cream parlor with its huge electric fans hanging from the ceiling, its windows filled with the sounds of fresh chocolates and bon-bons, its white-aproned Greek proprietor behind the soda fountain, its fly-specked menus on the white marble tables. Grandpa Adams and I made it over there two or three times during my visit for a chocolate soda. I haven't tasted chocolate like that since.

Second Avenue South in those days was a kind of hub for my metropolitan visits. Little did I dream, as I sat on the lawn of grandma's house on Seventh and Second to watch the new Elks Club Building going up, that some day I'd have an office there and do 25 broadcasts a week from that very building. Now and then as I walk out the front door of WCCO and look across the street at the new parking ramp. I can still visualize my grandfather's green lawn, my grandmother's well-kept rooming house and the little squirt in bangs and a Buster Brown suit teasing his grandfather for a chocolate soda. Even 50 years haven't blurred the memory. That's why I love Second Avenue!

Aerial view of downtown Minneapolis, c. 1950s. The Foshay Tower is at right-center. *Minneapolis Public Library.* Mpls. Collection.

When William B. Foshay was but a boy of fifteen, he made a pilgrimage to Washington D.C., where, it is said, he was greatly impressed by the simple, yet powerful, design of the Washington Monument. So impressed was Foshay, in fact, that when it came time to pay tribute to himself as the grown-up founder of a great banking, newspaper and public utilities empire, he decided to do so by erecting a monument in the form of a giant 447-foot office building which took the shape of the Washington Monument and was called—of course—the Foshay Tower.

Completed in August of 1929, the Foshay Tower's opening ceremonies lasted three days, attracted 25,000 revelers, and made Foshay and his 32-story landmark famous all over the Midwest. Almost overnight, however, Foshay's fame was to turn into "Foshay's Folly," as the great magnate was soon to find himself in legal trouble, and would, along with almost everyone else, fall victim to that year's ruinous stock market crash. His story is told here in an article that originally appeared in the March, 1966 issue of the old Twin Citian magazine. It was written by the noted Star-Tribune reporter James Parsons, and is reprinted with his kind permission.

Foshay's Folly

BY JAMES PARSONS

Slithering lines of delirious students, feverish from a Rose Bowl invitation, have inundated Minneapolis' streets.

Thousands have mobbed the downtown area in bellowing, honking, screaming, wonderful pandemonium to celebrate the end of the world wars.

Thousands more, especially the young, have gaped as lumbering elephants hauled the Greatest Show on Earth into town . . . squealed at the Aquatennial Jesters or watched a presidential motorcade with enthusiastic awe.

But none of the mass hysterias of the past or that of the future is likely to match the prolonged ballyhoo that marked the arrival of the Foshay Tower to its dominant place in the city's skyline.

No building in the state ever had such a lavish "coming out" party, but then, the Foshay Tower was not just any new building.

Back in 1929, it was the tallest building (32 stories) in the Northwest. And it still is. It was patterned after the Washington Monument in the nation's capital and it had the Italian marble, African mahogany and the gold-plated knobs that you would expect of the extravagant gaudy Twenties.

But more than anything else, the tower had Wilbur H. Foshay.

Or rather, Foshay had the tower.

And the short, pudgy baron of a utilities empire decided that everyone should know he had the tower. So he invited 25,000 dignitaries from all over the nation, Alaska, Canada and several Central American countries to the dedication.

A member of the president's Cabinet, many senators, representatives, governors, and diplomats took Foshay up on his all-expenses paid invitation.

So many came, in fact, that they had to have committees of local dignitaries to entertain the visiting dignitaries.

The whole thing must have set some sort of endurance record, running for three days.

They came by the tens of thousands to take in the view from the observation deck and tour the building hopefully getting a glance at the 27th and 28th floors that Foshay had staked out as his own office and living quarters.

Even for an era that had champagne baths, Foshay's private suite was supposed to be the ultimate. Rumor had it that the great man had a bathtub of gold.

That wasn't quite true, but let a reporter who was allowed to walk across those African mahogany floors describe it:

"The tub, to be sure, is not finished with gold leaf. But it is a leviathan of bathtubs, of black enamel, and the spigots are of delicate design and gold-plated. Italian Siena marble are the walls, and through glass panels in the ceiling drifts a pale, mysterious light, as if the chamber were under the sea.

"Nine gold-plated faucets gleam within the glass shower bath cabinet. Its sides are etched with the coat of arms of the Fouches of France and the Foshay of Minneapolis."

There was a magnificent library with a fireplace, three bedrooms, three baths (including the $10,000 one off the master bedroom), a dining room, kitchen, breakfast room and butler's pantry.

Besides the mahogany, there was teakwood, rosewood, oak, walnut and mahajua wood in the apartment.

The price tag for all this—a mere $125,000.

The street floor arcade of the tower almost matched Foshay's private suite. The marble—Violette de Brignolles from France, Botticini from Italy and Belgian and American—was worth $15,000; another $22,500 was put in hand-wrought iron grill work; the massive ceiling was gold and silver-plated, and the terrazzo floor was put in by experts from Italy.

But back to the dedication of this office building, which Foshay intended to be the headquarters for his $23 million empire—an empire that stretched from Alaska to Nicaragua and California to Pennsylvania.

Foshay really began beating the drums when construction began in 1927. A publicity release announced that workmen had dug 50 feet to solid rock before sinking concrete caissons into the bed rock. A cofferdam was built around the entire excavation to protect the surrounding property from cave-ins.

The steel structure was anchored to the concrete, giving the building such a sturdy base that it could take on a 100 mile-an-hour gale without even blinking an eye.

A year later, Foshay escorted the Minneapolis mayor and a delegation of business and professional men to the top of the tower to pound in the last rivet—a solid silver one—in the steel framework.

At the time, the tower wasn't finished. It was just a skeleton.

The first 18 floors were not so bad. The well-dressed gentlemen went up the elevators used to hoist material to the workmen.

For the next 10 floors, a stairway had been put in and the well-fed gentlemen found the going just a bit puffy.

The last four floors were the real test. Over 400 feet in the air and with nothing but ladders for support, some of the well-meaning gentlemen allowed as how enough was enough and forgot all about that silver rivet. But the pluckier ones carried on and had ringside seats as the mayor whacked in that final bolt.

That Christmas Eve, lights in some or the offices were left on to outline the "world's largest Christmas tree." The Minneapolis City Council was so pleased with the huge "tree" that the aldermen passed a resolution commending the W. B. Foshay Company for its civic and Christmas spirit. The council also said of the tower: "As a work of architectural grandeur it is unsurpassed."

By mid-1929, people were already getting tours of the unfinished tower. The Foshay Company bused 200 state legislators over from St. Paul and gave them the deluxe treatment, including dinner in the basement.

The newspapers sadly reported that the law makers felt compelled to sing for their supper, trying "Sweet Adeline" and "Let Me Call You Sweetheart" and others less painful. Mercifully, the sounds were lost in the elevator shafts.

Another first that year was the radio broadcast from the 27th floor to celebrate the Fourth of July. There had to he something novel, of course, so they had 16 cornet players blaring at the listeners.

These little forays were just the preliminaries.

Foshay was busy putting the final touches on a "boyhood ambition"—to build a monument to George Washington.

To whoop up local interest in the dedication, there were contests.

A St. Paul woman won $100 for coming the closest to guessing the height of the tower from the ground line to the top of the airplane beacon. (It was 5,443 inches or 452 feet, 9 inches. The beacon has now given way to a radio and television antenna and the height of the building itself is 447 feet.)

A man in Taylor's Falls, Minnesota, received $250 for reportedly seeing the beacon's beam from the farthest distance, 74 miles. In all, the company shelled out $640 in prize money. Then came August 30th.

At 11 o'clock that morning, the bombs began bursting in the air. Hundreds of bombs—the fireworks variety—and thousands of small American flags sprouted out of the observation galleries at the top of the tower and showered the watching throng in the downtown area.

Then a brass band took over. It was not just any 75-piece brass band. It was John Philip Sousa's band.

Foshay—as he did with all the details of the dedication—personally made the arrangements to get the maestro of the march to come to Minneapolis.

"I am especially anxious that the children of our community hear this band," Foshay said. "One of the impressions that will remain with me always was when, as a boy, I first heard John Philip Sousa playing at Manhatttan Beach some 35 years ago."

Miss Marjorie Moody sings at the dedication ceremonies for the Foshay Tower. The band director is John Phillip Sousa. *Minneapolis Public Library.* Mpls. Collection.

Sousa, the man who had played for presidents and traveled throughout the world with his "Stars and Stripes Forever," "Semper Fidelis" and other marches, was more than equal to the occasion.

Besides giving seven concerts, Sousa unveiled his latest composition, the "Foshay Tower—Washington Memorial March."

The rotund impresario of the tower was obviously pleased. And when the maestro autographed and presented to Foshay the original piano score, Foshay responded by handing Sousa a $20,000 check.

That afternoon, the man in whose memory the concrete spire was built, was honored. Three busts of the father of the country were unveiled with the aid of a color guard of Fort Snelling soldiers. Said Foshay, "We believe that the tower, which occupies such a prominent place in the northwest, may well be accepted as the west's memorial to George Washington."

Next came the lovely "Scherzo."

Foshay Tower dedication ceremonies, August 30, 1929. The bronze statue at center has just been unveiled. The sculptress was Harriet Frismuth. *Minneapolis Public Library.* Mpls. Collection.

Every great building, like every park, needs a statue and fountain. For his, Foshay commissioned Harriet W. Frismuth, a sculptress of considerable acclaim, to mold a statue that would commemorate the beauty of woman.

While a group of young girls dressed wispily as water nymphs tripped about the fountain, the gracefull bronze nude was uncovered. "Scherzo," who received her name from the musical term applied to light, graceful symphonic movements, was too much for mere adjectives for one chronicler of the day's events.

"Scherzo," he wrote, "is as adorable as Phyrne (a Greek courtesan of compelling beauty), as vivacious as Lais of Corinth (who entranced the eminent and wealthy with her beauty), as divinely slim is Sappho (a Greek poetess who actually is better known for her poems than her trim waistline), as mysteriously ravishing as Aspasia (another Greek lady known for her wit, beauty and political brilliance)."

That evening, the governors, foreign ministers and the like were entertained at the Minikahda Club and, along with practically everyone else in Minneapolis, watched the tower again explode with a crescendo of colorful fireworks.

The next day—Saturday—was devoted to speeches.

Secretary of War James W. Good represented President Herbert Hoover. The president's secretary, George E. Akerson, was also there to join Foshay in a triumphant parade down Nicollet Avenue.

Nineteen guns, hauled into the city to salute Good, erupted as the band and men of the Third Infantry from Fort Snelling escorted the dignitaries to the tower.

Good was awed by the building. It could have been that his speech writers in far off Washington were "awed," but, anyway, he said:

"We are met today in the shadow of a mighty edifice, a shining monument situated in a fair and fertile country. What more appropriate place for so majestic a tower, so fit a memorial to Washington? Happy the man who daily could ascend its towering pinnacle, to be inspired by the compelling beauty around about him. What could be more inspiring than the view of this new Canaan, a promised land in which the promise has been realized? Here the creator, using the majestic glaciers as puny men would use a plow, molded a region which would be a jewel in the diadem of an empire. Here fields extend a generous welcome to the sower and the reaper. Here gem-like lakes, sparkling in the green settings of the forests, are linked together by the strands of the sky-tinted streams."

He went on like that a bit longer. Then he talked briefly about General Washington, a bit about politics and a great war about the hoped for development of an inland water route through the St. Lawrence River and the Great Lakes.

Sousa's crew, perched on top of the two-story building that surrounded the tower, took over for an hour. Following that, Foshay feted all the stockholders—whose money was making the whole thing possible—at a banquet in the tower's block long arcade.

Newsreel cameras recorded the proceedings and the flamboyant parts were later shown in theaters throughout out the country. It was the first time an event in the northwest had been so honored and it even rated a sound recording with the film.

Sunday was "Tower Consecration Day" with a 2-hour religious program of music and addresses by representatives of the Jewish, Roman Catholic and Protestant faiths.

Sousa's band completed the program and the three-day dedication with a concert of sacred music.

All of the guests went home with solid gold watches as souvenirs.

And Foshay, who was still waiting to move into his tower quarters, went home with two bills. One was a gargantuan $3,750,000 for the construction of the tower and the other $116,449.38 to dedicate it.

But the cost scarcely seemed important. Foshay had seen the realization of a boyhood dream, and in process of honoring George Washington his own name had been immortalized in concrete.

Foshay and his company also got great chunks of free publicity as a side benefit for building the tower. His attorney, Josiah E. Brill, commented years later that "Foshay was first and foremost a promoter. He conceived the building as a huge promotion for his utilities interests.

"Foshay kept clippings of all the newspaper stories written about the project. 'Look at all this free publicity,' he once said to me. 'If I had bought this much advertising space, it would have cost me far more than the tower.'

The building carried Foshay's name, all right. But it was his for only two months after the now-fabled dedication.

The stock market crash knocked the props from under the nation's businesses. Foshay's empire, except for the concrete and steel structure, came crashing down with a fatal thud.

The skyscraper and its majestic apartment were soon in the hands of a court-appointed receiver. By mid-December, 1929, the building was losing $8,500 a month. The building corporation was nearly $3.2 million in debt, the heat bill was unpaid and a cut-off-the-lights campaign introduced.

Foshay wasn't just broke. In another six months the federal government had him under investigation and mail fraud indictments were returned against him and six other Foshay Company officials.

They were accused of enticing thousands of people into investing in the company by advertising that the firm was earning and paying large dividends on its stock.

Actually, their enterprises were losing money and they were using the funds pouring in from investors to create the illusion of profits. There was also some book juggling by company officials to convert the red ink to black.

The trial in Minneapolis Federal Court almost created as much of a circus as the dedication.

Hundreds of investors came to hear how they had been bilked. They listened for six weeks as accountants and inspectors testified about the company's finances and the misleading financial statements to encourage investments.

Then the jury of 11 men and one housewife began deliberating. The men voted almost immediately for conviction but the housewife, Mrs. Genevieve Clark, stubbornly held out.

The men pounded away for seven days, but there was no changing the mind of Mrs. Clark, the mother of two younger boys. She frequently refused to listen to the men's arguments. She reportedly told them at she had little sympathy for the government as prosecutors in the case because "of the way they (the government) treated the soldier boys when they came back from France" at the end of World War I.

A mistrial was declared and an aura of intrigue crept into the case.

It was discovered that Mrs. Clark wasn't even a member of the original group picked for jury duty. A slip with her name was added to the box containing all the prospective jurors names at the eleventh hour by a clerk who could not remember why he did it. The jury had been isolated during the entire trial, but officials found out that a U. S. Marshal had allowed Mrs. Clark to call her husband and see him on several occasions during the trial. It also came to light that Clark, who was formerly a St. Paul bank president, knew Foshay personally and had had business transactions with the Foshay Company.

When Mrs. Clark was being questioned as a prospective juror, she thought it unimportant to mention that at one time she had worked briefly for the Foshay Company. Mrs. Clark was charged with contempt of court for withholding this information. She was convicted in Federal Court and sentenced to six months in prison. A Supreme Court appeal failed,

At this point, the case turned macabre.

On the day she was to surrender to authorities, the Clark family disappeared. Later, Clark, his wife and the boys, Rowland, 11, and Deane, 7, were found in their car in a secluded area several miles from Minneapolis. All four were dead from intentional carbon monoxide poisoning.

Since Mrs. Clark's now-tragic hold out had resulted in a hung jury, a second trial began for Foshay and H. H. Henley, a company officer. The five other company officials that were defendants in the first trial had pleaded guilty in the meantime.

The second jury found the two men guilty and they were sentenced to 15 years in prison.

Both men were now broke and did not have enough money to pay lawyers to appeal the verdict.

Josiah Brill, who defended the men, said later that Foshay "went down with his ship. He was sure his company was sound, and he invested every cent he had in its common stock. After the crash, he didn't have enough money left to pay for his court expenses."

Henley acted as the attorney for the two men, preparing long legal briefs for their appeals. Two years after the trial, in May, 1934, their final appeal

The Foshay Tower c. 1930. *Hennepin County Historical Society.*

was turned down and both men were taken to Leavenworth Penitentiary.

Foshay and Henley, along with thousands of others acting in the men's behalf, began bombarding President Franklin D. Roosevelt with requests for pardons. After three years in prison, the president finally granted their pleas.

Foshay came home to Minneapolis. It was a bit like 1915 when the former art student at Columbia University in New York came to Minneapolis to make his fortune.

He was broke at the time (had to mortgage his furniture to guarantee payment for his family's train fare). With an office force of one—a stenographer—he started a small utilities company and soon began buying other electric properties. He sold stock to meet his monthly expenses and kept buying more utilities and selling more stock.

In a few years, he had an empire. He sold that one; built another, sold it and number three was in full bloom when the stock market fell.

Now, eight long years after the collapse, he stood looking at the tower—the symbol of the wealth and applause that had been his.

"All this was mine, once," he said, arching a wrinkled hand in the direction of the stately tower.

"Rebuild my empire? How can I?" he asked newspaper reporters. "I even have to find a job in order to live. I don't have a red cent."

Then he had to ask for permission to walk across the mahogany floors of the suite that was once his—the suite that he never got to occupy.

Foshay was resilient, however, and was soon working in Colorado where he had several friends. There, he continued doing what he did best—promoting. Only it was not utilities this time, but the small town of Salida where he headed the Chamber of Commerce.

He moved on to similar jobs in two Arizona towns. In 1951, a reporter asked him if he would swap his unhurried and modest life in Winslow, Arizona, for the "hectic but elegant existence of a Minneapolis millionaire."

"Not on your life," Foshay replied. "Mind you, I wouldn't kick at having to pay the kind of income taxes I used to, but just piling up money is not enough to make me enjoy life."

In his last years, he returned to Minneapolis and lived in a convalescent home. He was much thinner but still quick with a smile. In 1957, at the age of 76, he died. Ironically and perhaps fittingly, he died on the 28th anniversary of the dedication of the tower.

In 1962 James Gray wrote the official, authorized history of Minneapolis' greatest department store, a book that was entitled simply, You Can Buy it at Dayton's. *In this volume Mr. Gray tells us the story of February 7, 1946, the day that Dayton's made 90,000 pair of nylon stockings available to the war-deprived, stocking-starved women of the city, thus causing one of the most extraordinary scenes in the history of downtown. "Everyone was well aware that when the stockings were put on sale that there would be a dramatic scramble to get them," writes Mr. Gray. No one, as he goes on to tell us, could have ever predicted "The Battle of the Nylons" that was to follow.*

The Battle of the Nylons

BY JAMES GRAY

Women had behaved extremely well about the privations of the war, But now that it was over, normal desires began promptly to reassert themselves. Probably no limitation of choice in the buying world had disturbed the well-groomed American woman more than the inability to keep herself supplied with stockings. On her private program of postwar planning, item number one was to fill this lack in her wardrobe.

Dayton's had prepared for this moment. Its own plan had been to accumulate enough nylons to make fair distribution among its customers possible. By February, 1946, there were enough on hand to justify a sale. Some 90,000 pairs were available. The point was to offer these in such a way that women would be conscious of the effort made on their behalf. Dayton's wanted once more to earn the friendship, as well as the patronage, of its customers.

Everyone was aware that when stockings were put on sale once more there would be a dramatic scramble to get them. The suggestion was even put forward that Dayton's should hire a large public building—the Minneapolis Auditorium, perhaps, in which to stage the event. But Nelson Dayton was opposed to the idea. He did not want it to become some sort of extraordinary athletic event that would go down in the social history of the community as a great impersonal happening divorced from any association with the store. As always, he was determined that women should think of Dayton's and of their re-

lationship to it as the provider of necessities and comforts. No matter how difficult the great sale might prove to be, it must take place inside the store.

All kinds of special preparations were made for what was obviously going to be an unprecedented event. Before the stockings were put on sale packages containing two pairs each—the limit to a customer—were made up and put in the sub-basement fur vaults for safekeeping. It was planned that customers would be admitted by the Eighth Street door, carried by elevator to the third floor and then into a queue that made its way by escalator down to the second floor. There the line would wind through the toy department, the boys' and mens' wear departments and the yard goods, coming at last to the cashiers' windows where their money was received in advance. With a receipt in hand, the customer would continue her journey to the counters where she would find what she was looking for—the stockings, stacked by sizes and by price. Having received her merchandise, it was hoped that she would go home to gloat quietly over her achievement.

Every kind of precaution had been taken to prevent misadventure. The police department had agreed to send twenty-one officers in a special detail under a sergeant. There were to be eight firemen as well under the supervision of the chief himself.

Still no one had quite anticipated what was to happen on that morning of February 7, 1946. It wrote a dramatic page into the record of the social

Thousands of shoppers line up at Dayton's Eighth Street entrance for a chance to buy the first nylon stockings made available to the public after World War II. *Minneapolis Public Library.* Mpls. Collection.

history of a community as seen from behind the department store counter.

The day was cold and all night long snow had fallen, building up to a typical midwestern blizzard. Yet at 6:30 in the morning the streets were already full of women wearing masks of resolution such, one observer said, as would make the cartoonist's traditional image of the bargain-hunter seem bland and placid by comparison. The moment was a tense one in local history. A killer had just escaped from the Hennepin County Jail and the police were in pursuit of him at that moment. But even this absorbing subject was temporarily forgotten by some 15,000 people whose fixed idea was simply to get inside Dayton's.

In the preponderantly feminine crowd there were actually many men, one in six, according to the estimate of a newspaper account. Among them were many GIs, a scattering of officers, and one intrepid soul on crutches. But the tone of the session was treble and the male additions to its chorus were lost except as occasional outbursts of jocularity.

Staff members coming to work at the normal hour had to battle their way through ranks so tightly drawn as to be virtually unable to give passage. Rubbers were torn from shoes—even feet out of shoes—as the crowd milled and surged about in the street.

The very pressure of this human mass had resulted in a certain amount of minor damage even before the store opened. The glass in several doors was broken, the police were forced to hold back the customers for their own protection. Nelson Dayton, en route to his office, stopped on the balcony to look anxiously at the throng. He called a hasty conference after making further arrangements for the safety of the crowd. Women who fainted were to be escorted to the children's barber shop to recover.

It was a relief to everyone when the iron gates were swung back at last and the crowd could discharge its tensions by motion, slow as that was certain to be. A mass of human beings filled the entire area of the first floor and one more could have been added only by starting a second layer on the shoulders of the others.

Inevitably the atmosphere was one of mild hysteria. The volume of voices, heightened by excitement and made piercing by tension, escaped in a succession of sighs, groans and shrieks of delight whenever the line was able to inch forward. There was even an occasional quite authentic, scream. Above this torrent of sound roared the orders of the police. "Don't push! Don't get out of line! Slowly!" and the blaring of the public address system, describing the progress of the battle in portentous tones. Except for the absence of gunfire the experience was, according to a young woman reporter with a lively imagination, "a little like being in the rush that followed the opening of Oklahoma territory."

Other participants were reminded of more recent historical scenes. As fainting women were carried out of the line, and even a few men collapsed. A burly Colonel, mopped his brow and murmured: "I'll take the Battle of the Bulge any time."

The police sergeant was similarly rueful. "I'd have had a quieter day," he said, "if I'd been assigned to recapture George Sitts (the escaped killer)."

But, actually, there were no crises worse than the fainting spells. Among the articles reported lost were many rubbers, many head scarves and one girdle. A mystery which was never cleared up and which leaves in the curious mind a haunting image of the scene had to do with the loss, reported by a customer, of "a large turquoise blue feather hat."

Memories of the sale kept the community well supplied with jokes and gossip for many days. One woman appeared at a party wearing the heel of a stocking pinned to her shoulder. "I've been decorated," she announced. "Battle of the Nylons." Cedric Adams, contributing "Notes from the Nylon Front" to his column in *The Minneapolis Star,* dismissed the rumor that a baby had been born in the midst of the line but verified the story that a small war had been averted by the narrowest of margins when one woman confided to another that she did not know why she had taken the trouble to join the queue because she already had fifteen pairs of nylons at home.

For three days the sale continued, paralyzing every other activity of the store. Then on Saturday morning Dayton's advertised with an emphasis that seems fairly to be shot from the newsprint: "There will be no sale of stockings today," and the crisis was over.

In 1934 the city of Minneapolis, like cities all over the country, found itself in the throes of the Great Depression. Its flour and lumber milling industries were in decline; workers were desperate; and Minneapolis' business community, fearful of financial ruin, was fighting those workers and their attempts to bargain collectively, with a ferocity and intransigence that is scarcely comprehensible, even in this anti-union age.

On May 21 and May 22, 1934, this long-simmering conflict came to a head, erupting into what could only be called class warfare on Minneapolis' downtown streets, when for two consecutive days, strikers from Truck Drivers Local 574 and the forces of the police and the pro-business Citizens Alliance engaged in a club swinging, rock throwing (and occasionally gun-firing) brawl which left two people dead, dozens of others badly injured, and chaos and anarchy to reign on the city's Market District streets.

In 1936, noted writer Charles Rumford Walker moved to the city of Minneapolis, where a year later he wrote American City: A Rank and File History, *a classic study of its great summer of labor strife. Although* American City's *perspective was plainly and avowedly leftist, and although Walker's sympathies were entirely on the side of the strikers, he does, whether one shares his sympathies or not, provide us with an invaluable account of the tumultuous events of Monday May 21, and Tuesday May 22, 1934, those events which came to be known to history as "The Battle of Deputies Run." The story of that "battle," which originally appeared as Chapter Thirteen of* American City *and was entitled "Battle in the Streets," is reprinted here in a slightly abridged form.*

Battle in the Streets:
The Great Truck Driver's Strike of 1934

BY CHARLES RUMFORD WALKER

To the historian in retrospect, the "Battle of Deputies Run" as an episode in class warfare, appears clearly as a two-day battle and not a one-day engagement, in spite of the fact the second battle was the more sensational and has received the widest fanfare of publicity. Monday's battle was the more interesting and well ordered as a strictly military engagement between two forces of armed men. Tuesday's battle, though it completed Monday's work and in effect ended the war except for minor engagements, was tactically speaking, both a rout and a riot. A story of the Monday battle as seen from the viewpoint of a union leader follows:

"We built up our reserves in this way. At short time intervals during an entire day we sent fifteen or twenty pickets pulled in from all over the city into the Central Labor Union headquarters on Eighth Street. So that although nobody knew it, we had a detachment of six hundred men there, each armed with clubs by Monday morning. Another nine hundred or so we held in reserve at strike headquarters. In the market itself, pickets without union buttons were placed in key positions. There remained scattered through the city, at their regular posts, only a skeleton picket line. The men in the market were in constant communication through motorcycles and telephone with headquarters. The special deputies (Citizens' Army) were gradually pushed by our pickets to one side and isolated from the cops. When that was accomplished the signal was given and the six hundred men poured out of Central Labor Union headquarters. They marched in military formation, four abreast, each with their club, to the market. They kept on coming. When the socialites, the Alfred Lindleys and the rest who had expected a little picnic saw this bunch, they began to get some idea what the score was. Then we called on the pick-

An elderly woman striker engages in hand-to-hand combat with a female deputy, May 21, 1934. *Minnesota Historical Society.*

ets from strike headquarters who marched into the center of the market and encircled the police. They (the police) were put right in the center with no way out. At intervals we made sallies on them to separate a few. This kept up for a couple of hours till finally they drew their guns. We had anticipated this would happen, and that then the pickets would be unable to fight them. You can't lick a gun with a club. The correlation of forces becomes a little unbalanced. So we picked out a striker, a big man and utterly fearless, and sent him in a truck with twenty-five pickets.

He was instructed to drive right into the formation of cops and stop for nothing. We knew he'd do it. Down the street he came like a bat out of hell, with his horn honking and into the market arena. The cops held up their hands for him to stop, but he kept on; they gave way and he was in the middle of them. The pickets jumped out on the cops. We figured by intermingling with the cops in hand-to-hand fighting, they would not use their guns because they would have to shoot cops as well as strikers. Cops don't like to do that.

"Casualties for the day included for the strikers a broken collar bone, the cut-open skull of a picket who swung on a cop and hit a striker by mistake as the cop dodged, and a couple of broken ribs. On the other side, roughly thirty cops were taken to the hospital."

The Minneapolis *Star* gives the following account of the same episodes in Monday's battle:

"Two brief but heated clashes between police and a yelling throng.. . resulted in dispatch of nearly one thousand special officers (the citizens' army) and regular police to the area.

"Although the truck operators had announced they would move perishables, *no attempts were made* (italics mine) after the first outbreak near the Gamble Robinson Company, 301 Fifth Street, N."

This was the strikers' first offensive described above.

"Clubs, pipe, rock, and in one instance a knife were used by the crowd after police watched two truck loads of strikers enter the district and unload. A third truck drove up, bearing the sign, "All organized labor help spring the trap. Rid the city of rats!"

"The men jumped from the truck at Third Avenue, N. Some hundred police armed with sawed-off shotguns . . . attempted to halt the advancing group."

This is the honking truck of shock troops mentioned above.

"Advancing while approximately 1500 others turned up, the pickets dared the police to halt them. An arm rose, wielding a club. One policeman went down.

Strikers and police engage in hand-to-hand combat, May 21, 1934. *Minnesota Historical Society.*

"Other police leaped into the battle, using their night sticks in retaliation. Rocks hurtled through the air. Half a dozen police dropped. One policeman was stabbed on the back of the neck with a knife. Strikers and others in the crowd fell to the ground. The crowd then retreated, taking with it its injured.

"Several of the injured police were taken into packing houses for emergency treatment, and later to various hospitals.

Nearly an hour later, a second battle broke out at the corner of Sixth St. and Third Ave., N. One of the crowd tossed a club at Patrolman Wm. Mealey. Three policemen were lying on the ground when reserves pushed back the crowd. Several strikers were injured in this battle.

"The crowd cheered as the injured officers were loaded into an ambulance, and taken to General Hospital."

At no time did the bystanders—the bulk of whom were not strikers—show sympathy with the police or the deputies.

"The crowd grew. At the same time, additional special police and special deputy sheriffs, one wearing a football helmet, arrived. One of the special deputies was Alfred Lindley, Minneapolis sportsman and mountain climber. He was dressed in polo jodhpurs, and wore a polo hat. The crowd jeered Lindley constantly. One picket reached out a club and flicked Lindley's hat to the street.

"When reports of the disturbance reached Johannes, he ordered the night shift of regular officers back to duty. . . Ass't Inspector Georgan ordered the deputies to form a line and marched them back to headquarters . . . This move brought cheers from the crowd."

John Wall, the sheriff of Hennepin County, commented to me on these episodes. "It was a mistake" he said, "to use men without uniforms. You see," he explained, "the strikers regarded them the same as strikebreakers. But the chief of police was hollering for more men so we tried it."

The events of the next day were to amply justify the sheriff's analysis that the strikers regarded the deputized business men as the same as strikebreakers, and to them somewhat more detestable than the police who at least were paid for it. In fairness it should be said that a considerable number of the

"deputies" neither anticipated or relished the role they were called upon to play.

Despite the ferocity of Monday's battle, and the fact that the union had succeeded again in halting the movement of trucks, and that many police and special deputies, as well as strikers and bystanders, were seriously wounded, the employers saw no reason for either halting or modifying the character of their offensive. Negotiations for a settlement of the costly and bloody warfare continued after the battle for fourteen hours up to three o'clock the next morning. The Minneapolis-St. Paul Regional Labor Board summarizes laconically the results:

"The employees demand that a written contract directly with the union be entered into. This the employers positively refuse to do."

Employers' strike headquarters in the West Hotel, in collaboration with the army which was still gaining recruits at 1327 Hennepin Avenue, still had its heart set on settlement "without the intervention of the union." They prepared to throw even greater forces into the market place. Chief of Police Johannes, despite Monday's slaughter, encouraged them. "It was a religion to Mike Johannes," remembered an officer of the Citizens' Alliance later, "to keep the streets of Minneapolis open."

On the day of the Battle of Deputies Run, the newspapers reported, "By late today there will be nearly 1700 police including special officers—an additional 500 are being sworn in for active duty." The strikers too were gaining recruits. Nearly every worker who could afford to be away from his job that day, and some who couldn't, planned to be on hand in the market. No one had announced a second battle, but twenty to thirty thousand people showed up in the market place on the morning of May 22.

As Dobbs, who is strategically minded, put it to me a little regretfully, "A planned battle was almost impossible on that day." The two sides were simply there in force, and fought it out. Men and women, boys and girls, crowded windows and stood on roofs above the armies waiting for it to begin. The news photographers were all ready, the movie men present, and a radio announcer for KSTP right in the middle of things to report the battle like a football game to listeners in all parts of Minnesota. The newspapers had reported that morning, "several large produce houses are . . . to move perishables into their warehouse; other trucking operations are resuming on a small scale." This was the issue of the battle: Will they move the trucks or won't they? And the crowd knew it. Will the strikers lick the cops and the business men or the business men and the cops lick the strikers? They were all waiting for the kick-off.

Finally it came—a trivial incident. Some petty merchant moving some crates of tomatoes—and a striker throws one of the crates through a window. The shattering of that glass was enough. The two sides joined battle, hand to hand, sap, black-jack, lead pipe, and night stick. It was actually over in less than an hour, with the Police and the citizens' army back in their headquarters, or hiding out, or in hospitals, and the strikers in control not only of the streets of Minneapolis but for the moment "of the situation."

No succinct account of the battle was written or could be, least of all by the reporters with deadlines to meet who found it impossible to be in fifty places at once rather a hundred and fifty, for the battle with the deputies and police in retreat spread to all corners of the city. As late as ten o'clock that night the pickets continued to mop up, or to settle individual accounts in alleys and bars. Nevertheless the individual episodes were so lively and significant, and the individual emotions engendered so various and heated, that it is worthwhile recording a few from eye witnesses on both sides.

One of the leaders and organizers of the citizens army records his side of it as follows: "There came news that there was going to be trouble in the market district, and Colonel Watson (the military leader of the special deputies) agreed to help with these men. We had long conferences beforehand with the sheriff and with the chief of police; everything was mapped out and organized. I didn't go to bed for three days at the time of the trouble. Well, on this day, we were ordered to be in the market place at four a.m. Everyone was divided into sections and it was agreed there would be a uniformed policeman with each section.

"Once in the market we were in touch with our headquarters constantly, with the sheriff and the chief of police. Our men, you understand, were not armed except with a small stick. Colonel Watson had refused to arm them, a good many having no military experience whatever. He was undoubtedly wise. Well, the police did not hold the crowd back. They simply held up their hands to their shoulders and allowed themselves to be pushed till the crowd entered the market. Then unexpectedly the police on duty were relieved and a new detail appeared, which as far as we can discover had no instructions whatever regarding our outfit. There were two or three trucks to be moved that day, to be convoyed. Well, after the trucks had been moved and had gone out, suddenly these strikers and bystanders rushed in, thousands of them, the police hung back, and you know the rest. The strikers were armed with lead pipes, baseball bats—with barbed wire around them, and every other goddamn thing. Arthur Lyman was killed and there were a great many serious injuries. Colonel Watson, Major Harrison, and a few others were in headquarters afterwards. And this crowd came around. They were ready to murder us. We armed ourselves with shotguns and side arms, and went out and stood there facing 'em. Well when they saw the guns they stopped, and jeered at us. Finally we managed to push our way out. Another incident—a truck load of our men, citizens, were chased all the way from the market to our headquarters. We opened the door, drove the truck in, and shut the door. Our fellows were beaten up and bleeding and in a terrible condition.

"After the trouble in the markets I carried side-arms and arranged for special protection for my wife and children. I carried a gun in the office or anywhere I went for three months.

When the battle was over we tried to keep the men together for a while, but they fell away. They refused to be exposed to the slaughter when the police offered them absolutely no protection. And besides there was no more need for them; the strike was settled shortly after."

Here, on the other hand, is the battle as Dobbs saw it: "Some twenty thousand people jammed the market area. The actual spark which started the battle after several hours of waiting was a crate of tomatoes thrown through a plate-glass window. Instantly it became a free for all. Arthur Lyman was killed while running to cover in a grocery store—between the curb and the door. But it made no difference who it was provided he had a deputy's badge or a

Striker kills Arthur Lyman of the Citizens Alliance, May 21, 1934. *Minnesota Historical Society.*

club. Just to show you how dangerous it was to be a deputy, several of our fellows picked up the clubs from fallen deputies, and were immediately knocked cold by pickets. Our boys didn't look in a man's face—all they saw was the club. Hours after the battle deputies were getting theirs as far from the market as Nicollet and Twelfth Street."

Bill Brown, president of the truck drivers' union, gives his experience as follows:

"I went down there with a couple of truck drivers who were supposed to be my bodyguards, but they kept seeing fights they wanted to get mixed up in, so that bodyguard stuff didn't work very long. You know the market—well, imagine sixty thousand peo-

ple in there. (Dobbs reports twenty thousand, but Bill's Imagination is at least three times Dobb's in a fight.) People upon the roofs, a radio announcer, guys with cameras. Everybody waiting for the kick-off. I happened to be quite near where it started. Somebody brought a crate of eggs or tomatoes or something out of a little store. And a little blond feller, I don't know who he was, yelled, 'Hey, there's a fink here, starting to move goods!' That was enough. They busted everything in the place. Somebody took the crate and crowned him with it. I can see him now, standing there with the crate around his neck like a collar, then the blond feller yelled: 'Come on, let's get em,' and the crowd swept forward against the deputies. A picket captain yelled, 'Some of you guys get over on this side.' So they completely surrounded 'em. The harness bulls [police] fell back but the crowd went after them. In an hour there wasn't a cop to be seen on the streets of Minneapolis. About six o'clock I rode down Hennepin Avenue—about fifteen blocks from the market—there were no cops; our fellers were directing traffic."

Another striker: "I seen one cop under a car, and a picket poking underneath with a stick to get him to come out."

Another striker: "We brought a bushel basket of deputies' and cops' badges back to headquarters; and two polo helmets. One feller had a captain's badge he was pretty proud of."

Another striker: "Fourteen cops hid in the Armour cooler; they didn't come out for almost twelve hours."

The last tale may be apocryphal; I couldn't say, but my informant is usually reliable.

At all events, it is known when the pickets returned to headquarters they decided that the officers regularly stationed on adjoining streets to watch over the union should be dispersed. The officers were "chased away" by strikers, and police headquarters did not replace them for the duration of the strike.

The list of wounded for the Battle of Deputies Run was a long one, on both sides, and two deputies from the citizens' army were killed. One of them was Arthur Lyman, prominent Minneapolis citizen, attorney for sixteen years for the Citizens' Alliance and vice president of the American Ball Company.

Those personally involved on the side of the employers remember the battle with some bitterness. The average middle-class citizen, however, took it somewhat as a sporting event, and admits when questioned that he thinks "the damn fools who went out as deputies got what was coming to 'em."

Police open fire on strikers who had just rammed a truck guarded by police, July 20, 1934. *Minnesota Historical Society. Minneapolis Tribune.*

Editors note:

Although an agreement between the striking truck drivers and their employers was reached on the following Saturday, the employers failed to live up to their end of the bargain, and on July 16, a new strike was called. It began peacefully, but on July 20, a truck filled with policemen ambushed a group of strikers, killing two of them and wounding sixty-seven. Fearing a resumption of open warfare, Governor Floyd B. Olson called out the National Guard, and on July 26, he declared the city to be operating under the rule of martial law.

Finally, President Franklin Roosevelt (a visitor to the city that summer) came to the aid of the truck drivers when he let it be known that unless the Minnesota Employer's Association recognized the union he would deny to Minneapolis firms all monies then being made available to them through the Reconstruction Finance Corporation. The Employer's Association soon gave way under this considerable federal pressure, and two weeks after Roosevelt's ultimatum it agreed to recognize the union and to enter into collective bargaining agreements with its workers.

Back in 1938 a man named Paul Ferrell published his autobiography. It was entitled Michigan Mossback, and was the incredible story of a life which had brought him from a backwoods cabin in the Michigan forest to the twin cities of Minneapolis and St. Paul, where, if we are to take his story at face value, he was to experience one of the great "frame ups" of all time. Betrayed by a cynical and calculating wife, falsely imprisoned on eight occasions by a corrupt municipal government, Paul Ferrell's story is an eye-opener—a shocking tale not only of his own ruination (it is, unfortunately, beyond the scope of this book to relate his personal odyssey in any great detail; suffice it to say, however, that he tells the story of a wife who divorces him, takes his money and his child, and in the process transforms him from a respected and prosperous Washington Avenue businessman into a workhouse inmate and a skid row bum), but of the "big city rackets" of the prohibition years in Minneapolis and of the cesspool of corruption that the city had become. In the following excerpt from Michigan Mossback we find Paul, who has just been discharged from the St. Paul Workhouse and who has just rented a cheap hotel room in the notorious Gateway District, providing us with a habitué's eye-view of life in the nether regions of downtown.

Michigan Mossback:
A Michigan Backwoodsman in Downtown Minneapolis

BY PAUL FERRELL

Habitués of Gateway Park, February 22, 1946. *Minneapolis Public Library.* Mpls. Collection.

After my discharge from the St. Paul Workhouse on October 19, 1926, I went to live at a cheap hotel in the Minneapolis Gateway District, as the little money I had left was rapidly diminishing.

This Gateway District—or "The Gateway," as it is sometimes called—is also known as "Bridge Square," and some call it "The Balkan States." It extends below Washington Avenue to the Mississippi river, from Second Avenue South to Hennepin Avenue, which is an area of about three or four blocks square. This district is composed, principally, of cheap hotels, barbershops, pawnshops, second-hand clothing stores, cheap restaurants, employment agencies, and so-called "soft-drink" saloons. The human scum of the world can be found there.

In this district all types of transients congregate by the thousands. Lumberjacks from the lumber woods of Northern Minnesota and Wisconsin; dirt movers from state road construction; gandydancers from railroad construction; harvest hands from the farms of Minnesota, Wisconsin, North and South Dakota, and Iowa. Sometimes there are also well-dressed out of town businessmen, looking for adventure—and they usually get it.

Many of the so-called soft-drink saloons in this district were operated by barmaids. Each girl usually owned her own place, and generally had another girl for an assistant. These barmaids, all dolled up and painted like burlesque showgirls, stood behind their bars and beckoned to the lumberjacks, gandy-dancers, etc. It was an unwritten law from the police department that they could not stand outside on the street or in their doorways to solicit business, but they were allowed to stand behind their bars and beckon potential customers.

Most or the barmaids had men, and their men as a rule did not work, although a few of them tended bar in bootlegging places not operated by barmaids. These girls and their men usually lived in swell apartments uptown.

When a barmaid enticed a man into her place, if he was not already drunk, she would try to get him in that condition, then she would get him in the back room of the joint, entertain him and rob him. Sometimes they would take him to a room in one of the many flop-houses in the neighborhood and when they were through with the victim, his money would be gone. Before the barmaid was through with him, at some time she would slip her hand into his pocket and relieve him of his bankroll. As I heard a landlady say once in that district, "It was a dumb girl who couldn't pick up for herself from $500 to $700 a month around one of those joints. But they spent it as fast as they got it. They were high livers and each had a man to support, who dressed nicely and spent lots of money."

The victim was usually too drunk on poisonous moonshine that was sold in those joints to know that he had been robbed; or if he did know, there wasn't anything he could do about it. If he went staggering up the street and told his troubles to a police officer, he was told to move on—or he was arrested for drunkenness or vagrancy and thrown into jail. The next morning, when he appeared in court, he was either discharged or sent to the workhouse. In either event, his money was gone. It was not often that the victims reported things to the police.

Soft-drink saloons not operated by barmaids were owned by a group of bootleggers. Among themselves and their confidants these bootleggers called themselves "The Syndicate." In the syndicate saloons, men were employed as bartenders.

These bartenders who were employed by the syndicate saloons were known as "fall guys," or "Big-hearted Jims." The city soft-drink licenses were usually in fictitious names. It was mighty seldom that these places were raided by city officials; but occasionally they were raided by federal officials, and, in such cases, if liquor was found on the premises, the "fall guy," or the "Big-hearted Jim" would assume this fictitious name on the license and claim ownership of the place. Then he was arrested and put into jail, and the syndicate saw that he was bailed out. Later on, when his case was called for trial, he usually pleaded guilty, as by pleading guilty he calculated to receive a lighter sentence than he would if he stood trial and was found guilty. Bootleggers called this pleading guilty "copping a plea." The syndicate paid the "Big-hearted Jim" his regular salary, usually about five dollars a day, during his confinement.

I remember meeting a young man, whom I had had in my employ several years before, and who at that time was a nice, industrious young fellow. This man stopped to talk to me, and I said to him, "Eddie, what are you doing now?" (Of course, Eddie was not his real name.)

He said, "Mr. Ferrell, I don't work anymore. I am a Big-hearted Jim. I've been running a beer and moonshine flat for _____. He mentioned the name of a prominent bootlegger. He also said, "You know my boss stands big with the city officials. We have no fear of them, as my boss has everything 'fixed'. But the Federals raided the place and arrested me, and I have just come back from doing time." Three or four months, I think he said, he had been in some county jail. "I got five dollars a day for all the time I put in, and my boss says he will start me in another home brew beer and moonshine flat."

After one of these locations had been raided and liquor found several times by Federal officials, the United States government usually put an abatement on the premises—that is, they padlocked or closed it up for one year. Then the bootlegger syndicate moved to a new location close by, sometimes next door. When the year's abatement expired, the bootlegger usually moved back to the old location.

It was apparent that the bootlegging syndicate and the police department were in close league. The so-called Purity Squad—to my knowledge—never raided a syndicate place. They went around town and raided a few people who were selling a little beer or moonshine, and dragged them into court; but the syndicate places seemed to be immune.

In the fall of 1927, the syndicate had a moonshine saloon at 127 Marquette Avenue. The place had been raided several times by the federals. In fact, in the fall of 1927, the place was raided and some liquor found. A Big-hearted Jim took the fall and did 30 days for this place. So the syndicate moved out.

In the fall and winter of 1926 and spring of 1927, I saw many men short-changed, strong-armed and robbed around those syndicate saloons. Men were even robbed of traveler's checks, as there were "artists" around those places who could imitate almost any signature.

I remember one time a fellow came in from some place, I think Montana. He had a book with traveler's checks and some cash on him. They gave him a knock-out drop and he went to sleep in a chair. They robbed him of his cash and his traveler's checks.

The corner of Nicollet and Second, 1948. *Minnesota Historical Society.*

There were six of these checks for 20 dollars apiece—120 dollars—a writing artist signed his name to them the same as he had signed it above. They went to the bank along with the daily deposit of one of the bootlegging joints and there was never any complaint made about it. I remember this case in particular.

Sometimes these robberies amounted to several hundred dollars. I remember one day when I was in one of the syndicate saloons. In one of the chairs was a man who was very drunk. He had just struck town that morning, off from a big construction job, and he had a big bank roll. In walked two Big-hearted Jims from one of the other syndicate saloons. They went over to this fellow and said, "Come with us. We are your friends, and if you stay around here you will be robbed."

Entrance to a Gateway Hotel. *Hennepin County Historical Society.*

Well, the fellow did not want to go with the Big-hearted Jims, so they grabbed him—one by each arm—and led him out of the place. It was all the same gang. The same syndicate owned the saloon he was sitting in and the one they were taking him to. Both of these Big-hearted Jims were employed by the syndicate. I knew them well later. The man was remonstrating with them all of the time, saying that he did not want to go, but they kept saying to him, "Oh, you are all right with us. We are your friends."

This was in cold, below-zero weather. The next day I met this man on the street, and he did not have an overcoat. He told me that he had been robbed of over $300, his watch, and his overcoat. He said he had been drunk and he didn't know who robbed him. It would not have done him any good if he had known!

I know of another instance where a man was strong-armed in one of those places. He afterward went to the police department in city hall about it. The police simply made no move whatever in regard to the matter.

On another occasion, I was walking down Hennepin Avenue in the year 1928. At the corner of Third Street I met a man who spoke to me and said, "I don't think you're acquainted with me, Ferrell." I told him that it seemed as though I knew him from sight, but could not place him. He said, "I come to Minneapolis a couple of times each year, and I know you by sight, as I have eaten in your restaurant several times when you were in business on Washington Avenue."

He then proceeded to tell me that he worked in a packing plant in Sioux City, Iowa, and had just arrived in Minneapolis the day before. He said he was in one of the saloons down in the Gateway, the night before, where he took several drinks, went to sleep in a chair, and when he woke up he didn't have a cent on his person. He said they "took" him for something over $400. He had just been to a telegraph office and wired home for money to return on.

He asked me what I thought he could do in regard to regaining his money. I told him I thought there was nothing he could do, and for him to stay out of the Gateway, for if he went down there and began to talk about his loss, he probably would be beaten up, thrown out on the streets, and arrested, and he might take a trip to the workhouse on a drunk or vagrancy charge, before he got a chance to return to his home in Sioux City. I said to him, "You wait around *uptown* for your money, and when you get it, buy a ticket and get for home as soon as you can, as I have seen scores of men robbed, beaten up, and railroaded from that district to the workhouse."

One day I stood on the sidewalk in front of one of those syndicate saloons talking to a member of the syndicate, whom I knew well. He was a big shot in the booze racket in the district—a close personal friend of the big "fixer" of the city. Along came a man who was connected with the Minneapolis Police Department and who had formerly been head of the Purity Squad in Minneapolis. The bootlegger said to me, as this man passed by, "That fellow certainly has got his nerve, and he is surely sitting on a lot of money. When he was head of the Purity Squad, there were not many bootlegging or gambling places or houses of ill fame that he missed shaking down. He had the nerve to shake me down, when he should have known that I control this district below Washington Avenue, and I pay my money to the official fixer, and I can say who can go and who can't go in this district."

I knew that to be true. Then he said, "This big stiff came in to my place here (and he pointed to the door of the place before which we were standing) and he said to me, 'What are you doing here?' And I said to him, 'What do you s'pose I'm doing here? I'm selling moonshine. How much money are you looking for? He said, 'I should have $25 a month.' Well I thought just to get along with him, I would pay him the $25 a month, which I did. But if I had wanted to, I could have had him removed from his position as head of the Purity Squad and put back on a beat again where he belonged."

I knew of one instance in particular where this same official, when head of the Purity Squad, shook down a gambling joint for several hundred dollars each month.

I remember a sergeant in this district who evidently thought that the city laws meant something, so one day he raided one of the syndicate saloons, or so-called soft-drink parlors, and arrested one of the real members of the syndicate. This fellow stood trial and was eventually acquitted, but the sergeant didn't last long down there. He was soon transferred out of the district.

In 1957, David Rosheim, "as a small-town adolescent, and very naïve about cities," visited his cousins in Minneapolis where, as he tells us in the prologue to his wonderful book, The Other Minneapolis: Or the Rise and Fall of the Gateway, The Old Minneapolis Skid Row, *he for the first time became acquainted with Washington Avenue, "that derelict-lined thoroughfare, the main street of the old Gateway, the Skid Row." Many years later David Rosheim wrote a history of Minneapolis' Skid Row, doing so, he tells us, because he felt the need to discover "why men dwell sometimes in the 'down and out' parts of town." In the following excerpt from* The Other Minneapolis *he tells the story of the Gateway during its last, declining years. This excerpt originally appeared as the greater part of a chapter entitled "Last Call."*

Gateway Park as it appeared in the early 1950's. *Minneapolis Public Library.* Mpls. Collection.

Last Call

by David Rosheim

Twilight was now hanging over the skid row. It came for many reasons and through various avenues. Social change was a major factor. The post-war era was not like that which followed the First World War. It was not 1919. The skid row continued to lose its population because of new legislation and a series of social welfare benefits running the gamut from education to psychiatric treatment enabling most World War II veterans to return to civilian society with more ease than any of their predecessors. Very few found their way to the skid rows.

Instead, they found their way to the rapidly growing suburbs. The new shopping centers meant that there would be less revenue for the central city. This, in turn, led to a strong desire to make the inner city more commercially competitive by modernizing it and rebuilding it to suit the new group of consumers

The Gateway, pathetically, tried to adapt to the post-war world. The merchants there hoped to attract a more lucrative trade by painting and putting up new store fronts. Leading the way was one of the fine old restaurants, Schiek's, at 45 Third Street South. The quaint old Ladies Entrance was removed. Diners of both sexes then were able to enter through a single stately granite portal. New lighting was installed which banished some of the accumulated gloom and revealed long-hidden artwork on the ceiling.

Despite the face-lifting, Gateway behavior continued to be on the obtuse side. For instance, in May of 1946, Edward Prouix, a cripple, who lived at the Victor Hotel at 36 Washington Avenue South, was jailed for hitting another Skid Row man with his crutch. His victim, Axel Berg of 211 Nicollet Avenue, was minding his own business when Prouix approached and asked him for some money. When he saw that no money was forthcoming, Prouix swung his crutch and hit the other man on the nose. Mr. Berg went off to the General Hospital and Mr. Prouix went off to the cooler. Both reportedly had been drinking.

A sixty-one year old policeman by the name of George Aby retired in September of 1947. Old-timers in the Gateway remembered Aby well. He had spent most of his career there keeping order in a period when brawls were commonplace and when whores and card sharks inhabited old Block 20.

Cedric Adams heard an item from the information people at the Great Northern Station, the station on Bridge Square. A Gateway dehorn (canned heat drinker) would go to the Great Northern Station after becoming intoxicated. "Once inside he takes his place between the waiting room and the train arrival corridor, pulls himself up to as full a height as his condition will permit, and then in tones that echo through the entire station, goes into a traincalling routine. He's always a little mixed up on his stations. For instance, he'll announce, 'The Empire Builder now leaving for Miles City, Memphis, Winnipeg, Oshkosh, Denver, Atlanta, International Falls and points west. Leaving on track ny-un.' About one call, and he's bounced out. Undoubtedly, he's a thwarted individual and has discovered that curious means of self-expression."

In the 1930s 121 Nicollet Avenue was a bar named Angelo's which had the usual cheap hotel above it. But by 1947, it was the location of the Minneapolis Revival Mission. Its supervisor and co-founder was Marie Sandvik, a Norwegian immigrant. In 1940, she felt she had received a call to spread the Gospel in the Gateway district after she had learned from a repentant prostitute about the conditions there. She received enough contributions to buy the former bar and set up the Mission.

She was proud of the many conversions, some undoubtedly sincere, although, she said, "There is much greater work to be done here now than ever before. The drinking problem in the Gateway is greater than it has ever been. During the war there wasn't so much drunkenness. Now it is worse than before the war. When we took over the hotel upstairs, we cleaned out all the whiskey bottles. They filled our basement when we stored them there before they were hauled away."

On September 25, 1947 Federal Indian Service Agents closed down the Silver Dollar Bar at 207 Nicollet Avenue. In that period there was a federal law on the books which forbade the selling of intoxicants to Native Americans. There was even a sign to that effect in the Silver Dollar. Despite it, half of the patrons were Indians so the bartender was arrested and held without charge.

There wasn't, in short, much that was new in the Lower Loop in the immediate postwar era. In the greater city, the progressive spirit prevailed. Hubert H. Humphrey was elected mayor for his second term. In October of 1947, he appointed five men to serve as the members of the city's first Housing and Redevelopment Authority. He had visions of a renewed Minneapolis, but he soon left the city for national politics.

On May 6, 1950, Mayor Eric W. Hoyer, who had succeeded Humphrey in 1949, announced that money had been raised to conduct a survey of conditions in the Gateway District. The survey was to determine the human factors creating the skid row conditions and also to determine what to do about them. This unpretentious announcement was the actual beginning of the huge urban renewal effort which was to annihilate Skid Row, although it was not obvious at the time

How did people live on Skid Row during its last flowering (or floundering)? In the *Minneapolis Star* for June 27, 1950, a Gateway tough told how he made beer money: "Every night there are guys with dough who come down here. I go along with them. Then kick the devil out of them and take their dough. They can't complain, It's a cinch,"

It was a cinch in many cases because the victim was a homosexual who would not report the attack because he feared exposure, the same reason why people don't take pictures in gay bars. The preying thieves didn't use guns, but beer or whiskey bottles, or they had friends along to provide more muscle. They also robbed sleeping drunks or those who were so badly intoxicated that they couldn't resist or fight back.

The owner of the former Sourdough Bar, John Bacich, said a small group of homosexuals would sometimes frequent his bar. He did not allow people to harass them. Mostly, however, the gays patronized the Trocadero Bar at 253 Second Avenue South. Perhaps their most noted nightspot was the Dug Out at Third Street and Third Avenue South. Reportedly people were attracted there from all over the United States.

Even the old age pensioners were robbed by unscrupulous transients. Because of this the old-timers would avoid carrying cash around as much as possible. They would instead buy meal tickets which were good for a month at the skid row restaurant of their choice. They also paid their rent in advance so, even if they were jackrolled, they could still get by until the next pension check.

A former streetcar motorman told of one incident on the Washington Avenue of that period. A man charged out of one of the grittier bars and jumped on board. As soon as he bad taken a seat, he fell sound asleep. The streetcar went out to Fort Snelling and back several times before he woke up again. The revived man said that someone had slipped a Mickey Finn, some knock-out drops, into his drink and that he had to get away from there before he passed out and lost all his money. His tactic worked. One of the bartenders may have been the culprit. Many of them were as bad as the jack-rolling toughs in relieving them of their funds.

On February 7, 1952, in the last year of the Truman administration, the Gateway survey was presented to the City Planning Commission by Herman E. Olson, City Planning Engineer. It was a very comprehensive study and contained all the data on building use, age, physical characteristics, and probable fire-resistance but not too much data on the human causes of Skid Row. The survey also contained a Loop businessmen's thoughts on how the area should be improved, some of which were

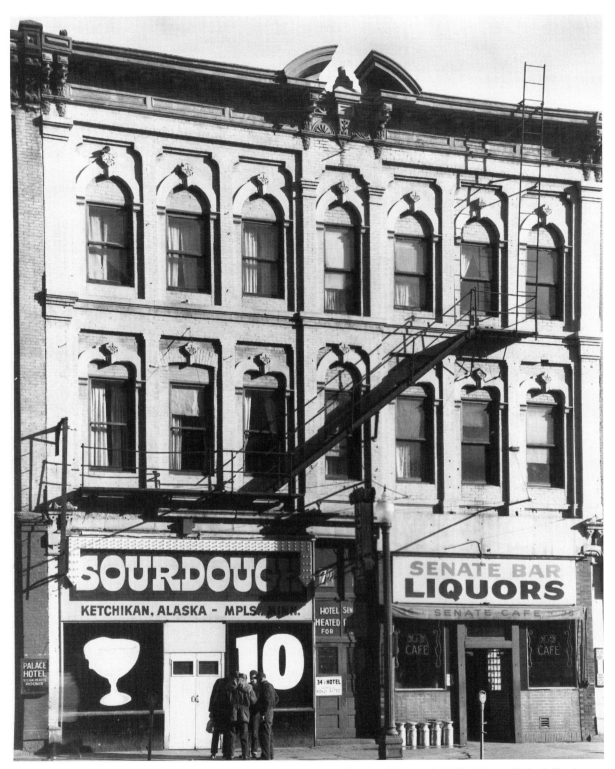

The notorious Sourdough Bar in downtown Minneapolis' old Gateway District. *Minneapolis Public Library*. Mpls. Collection.

Washington Avenue, c. 1950s. *Hennepin County Historical Society.*

rather drastic (though not as drastic as what the HRA had in store for the area).

Some loop businessmen and industrialists had ideas for the improvement of the Skid Row. Among these ideas were: move single permanent residents to Nicollet Island; clean up the district; have uniform law enforcement; eliminate undesirable businesses; obtain better parking; replace the streetcars with busses and remove Gateway Park. The suggestion about removing the streetcars seems somewhat extraneous to the discussion. The bus lobby must have already been at work.

The last-mentioned proposal meant the demolition of the Gateway Building which had been so ceremoniously dedicated in 1915. In 1952, Charles E. Doell, Parks Superintendent, inspected it and found it in bad condition. He also counted about 200 whiskey and wine bottles in its vicinity. By 1954, the park had a new look. The objectionable streetcar

passenger shelter and public comfort station was razed and workmen had put in trees, flower beds and an ornamental iron fence 48 inches high which stretched all around the park. There would be no more loafing there!

Many had thought that the view of all the poor men sitting around the old Gateway Building had not given train visitors a favorable first impression of Minneapolis. These people finally saw their cause vindicated, at least in part. The few arrivals to the city would see pretty flowers and a lot of idle men leaning on the wrought iron fence, not sitting and loafing as they had done formerly, but standing and leaning instead.

On July 7, 1953, a once-proud theater, the Palace at 414 Hennepin was torn down. But the Grand Theater at 242 Hennepin was still active. So much so that Jake Sullivan, the head of the police morals squad, ordered Sam Berger, its proprietor, to stop showing a film about a newspaper reporter's adventures in a nudist colony. Previously in the summer of 1953, Berger had shown a film called "French Peep Show" for which he had been fined one hundred dollars.

Talk of impending doom circulated in the Gateway in 1953. It originated with the civic leaders and the architects and engineers and filtered down to the 62 liquor outlets and 77 lodging houses in the 18-block Skid Row.

In 1953, a visitor to the scene would see a group of three- and four-story buildings of brick and limestone built in the 1890s or earlier a block up from the Great Northern station. On the Nicollet side, there was a bar, an old hotel, a revival mission then a quick-lunch place, a second-hand book store, yet another mission, another bar and another quick-lunch.

Continuing up Nicollet, across Second Street, was a rooming house and three bars right in a row. Beyond it, another hotel, a good cafe, a barber college, another hotel and finally, a liquor store. On these streets were men in overalls, and men in slacks and T-shirts, men young and old. Behind these streets, in the alleys, little groups of men formed "bottle gangs" to split a jug of wine. The alley in back of the Sourdough Bar was commonly known as Party Alley and was an object of police scrutiny.

One of the frequenters of this alley explained to a *Minneapolis Star* staff writer why he lived in the

Skid Row: "I like to drink. Drinking is my only recreation and source of pleasure. I like living on Skid Row because of easy drinks for one thing."

"And there's the cheap restaurants and places to sleep, a person doesn't have to be too careful about his appearance. Mainly it's the drinks."

The speaker was in a probation office, about to leave for the Willmar State Hospital for rehabilitation, if possible. He told of his life on "the avenue."

"In the morning I usually hang around the mission or take in a sermon at the Salvation Army so I can get a bowl of soup, some bread and weak coffee.

"If I run into drinks first, I forget breakfast. You can always find a drink if someone has the necessary buck. You develop a sixth sense about spotting a bootlegger. You ask him if he has a drink, give him a dollar and he slips you a bottle of wine.

"All day long you keep looking for a drink. That's the important thing. After the first drink, the others come easier. You may run into somebody who has a railroad compensation check, or a rocking chair, social security.

"Or you find a spot at an employment office (commonly called the 'slave market'). It's rough work that nobody else wants, like unloading boxcars. You can make five or ten dollars. "This is gone by next morning. You always have help drinking it up. There are many friends when a bottle is to be had. Men hang around the liquor stores to see who's going to buy a bottle. "I like whiskey best but can't afford it. Sometimes we buy canned heat at a hardware store. We don't like the taste, but it's highly alcoholic, and its the effect that counts.

"At night, if I have money, I can get a place in a flophouse for fifty cents. It's a cage, a partition of boards and chicken wire with a cot inside. Flophouses are dreary. They are lit by 20-watt bulbs and are dirty. There's always the chance of getting lousy.

"If one has any possessions, he seldom hangs on to them because there's always somebody who wants them more. One night somebody let a string down through a cage and hooked my shoes.

"The workhouse is a real lifesaver which has prolonged the lives of many men. It's a home and lots don't like to leave. There are men who have done twenty-five to thirty years out there on the installment plan.

"Outside of feeling that I'm looked down on when I'm drunk and carelessly dressed, I have no resentment.

"You can find a certain kind of comradeship on the Row. As long as men drink together they are friends. When the wine gives out, the friendship is over."

Who were the people of the 1950s Gateway? The 3,000 residents, who stared out from the windows of second-story lobbies or who lined the evening pavements, leaning on the parking meters, and chatting with friends, who were they?

They were pensioners, migratory workers (in much smaller numbers than forty years before), men without a family who included a minority of real alcoholics in their midst. The oldsters lived there on relief allotments of up to sixty dollars a month and survived because of the cheapness of

Entrance to the Twin City Hotel. *Hennepin County Historical Society.*

rooms and food in the Gateway. Many of them lived on railroad pensions. Others were physically handicapped or even emotionally disturbed.

Then there was the transient or floater population, exact numbers unknown. About 80 per cent of the 11,000 drunks and vagrants brought into municipal court in the course of a year came from the Gateway District. Another group to be found in the area added to the complexity. These were the Saturday night drinkers. They came from other sections of the city when they grew bored with their neighborhood taverns. They came to see the bright lights and floor shows of The Lower Loop nightclubs. It was estimated that at least sixty-five per cent of the patrons of saloons on Washington Avenue came from the outside.

A recovered alcoholic of the period indicated some of the conditions prevailing in the Skid Row of those days. The police, he said, did pretty much as they liked. It all depended on how many people were needed at the workhouse or the workhouse farm. But in many cases, enforcement was lax. In the Nicollet Inn which was on the other side of Washington Avenue from the Nicollet Hotel and kitty-corner to it, there was a Blue Room where the drinkers of cheap red wine could relax with their beverage of choice, although the Nicollet Inn was supposed to be a 3.2 beer joint. Wealthy people who stayed at the Nicollet Hotel would sometimes go over to the Inn, thinking that it was a regular sort of place. They were not deceived long.

There was one man who used to make money by picking potatoes in the Red River Valley. He would get his pay and come back to the Gateway where he would quickly drink it all away. Men who had just been paid often lost their money to Chicago jack-rollers who would come to Minneapolis during the harvest season when the men were collecting large amounts of pay. Washington Avenue was still the central area but there was a lot that went on along the two avenues that converged on The Great Northern Station. The heaviest crowds were to be found along Washington in the block between Marquette and Second. In that block the Persian Palms, with its glittering lights and double entrance, dominated the night scene, and men and women flowed into and out of it constantly. Other bars near it were also crowded.

The Palms was noted for its aggressive b-girls. It was known as a "clip-joint". Some who visited it thought of it as a rather elegant place patronized by many well-dressed couples. The owner of the Sourdough Bar across the street was more explicit. He said the b-girls would hustle men to buy them bottles of champagne, sometimes at twenty-five dollars a bottle. When the Veterans of Foreign Wars had a convention in Minneapolis, one of their number ended up spending several hundred dollars for champagne in the Persian Palms in just one night. If the tipsy customer wished to write a check, the bartender would let him write one and make sure that his signature was on the check. Then the management of the Palms would refuse the check, claiming the signature was illegible. They would insist on a second check after crumpling up and tossing away the first one. But when the customer had gone, they would uncrumble the first check and cash it too. The poor customer would have paid twice for his entertainment and drinks.

In the majority of the bars the patrons would be roughly dressed, and would be mostly male. They also drank more beer as a rule than was drunk in spots uptown. The men wore wool shirts, dark pants and gray suspenders if they were railroad men. Casual laborers preferred gaudy sports shirts and khaki pants.

A typical night would always have incidents. Three policemen would walk a beat along Washington Avenue watching for them. One incident took place in a bar near Marquette and Washington. A reporter described it:

"There was a sudden commotion at the entrance. Then the limp body of a man was sprawled across traffic on the sidewalk.

"His khaki pants looked clean, but his new sports shirt, gaily checked in red, blue and gray, hung in ribbons. A tan cap lay by his side, exposing his bald head.

"Police and an ambulance reached the scene almost simultaneously and as the ambulance men pushed their way through the crowd to see what was wrong, an excited figure in the white shirt and white apron of a bartender rushed outside.

"This guy," he said, "take him away and lock him up."

Habitués of the Persian Palms, August 1945. *Minnesota Historical Society.*

"How about the ambulance?" one of the policemen ventured.

"Not for him. Not for him," came the retort, "that's for the girl inside. This guy smashed a glass of beer in her face, I threw him out."

These nights went on brightly, gaily, cruelly. But they could not last forever. Change was approaching the Gateway with increasing speed.

The postwar improvements had been only skin deep, as the Gateway survey indicated. Trash littered the alleys. New utilities, water pipes, electric conduits, and gas mains had been installed through the years, cutting through the solid limestone walls of the nineteenth century. The openings in the walls had been sealed with soft mortar and thin lathes. Man's ancient scourge, rats, ate their way in through this flimsy material. Old, old fears, unconscious perhaps, of the bubonic plague and typhus, both rat-borne on rat-fleas, revived. The slap-dash temporary constructions also raised fire hazards appreciably.

177

Study of the area continued. An issue of *Greater Minneapolis* in the middle 1950s listed the number and the kinds of businesses in the Lower Loop:

Liquor taverns	62
Manufacturing	59
Wholesale	48
Lodging and rooming houses, Hotels	71
Loan and pawn shops	24
Cafes and restaurants	35
Warehouses	11
Hamburger shops	10
Clothing stores	9
Furniture stores	10
Hardware stores	2
Drug stores	6
Barber shops	15
Miscellaneous (cigar, laundry)	63
Offices	5

The rooming houses, also known as flophouses, varied widely in quality. The worst of them would have as many as 150 men on a floor, trying to sleep in five by seven cribs with the well-remembered chicken wire over the top. These 150 men also had to share a single bathroom which law required each floor to have. John Bacich, who owned some hotels as well as the Sourdough Bar, paid for the burial of those who died while residing in his rooming houses. Otherwise, they would become cadavers for the University of Minnesota Medical School.

Death was no stranger in the Gateway. A typical occurrence was the death of an old-timer on the Row. One old railroad worker died there in a April of 1956. He had been drinking double brandies with beer chasers most of the afternoon when he suddenly collapsed in his booth. While the police removed the body, the juke box played the "Rock and Roll Waltz" and the drinking went on without a pause. His friends at the flophouse, however, were saddened at his death. He had lived on Skid Row with fellow old railroadmen since his wife had died twenty years before.

Two sisters owned what they called a mission house next to a rooming house run by Mr. Bacich. They appeared only once a month to collect rent front the residents, A few days after one man paid his rent, he died in his room. He lay dead in bed for

twenty-one days until men in the adjoining flop house noticed the smell and had the police investigate. None of the dead man's fellow residents had seemed to notice.

The roomers of Mr. Bacich, only twenty on a floor, would mop up the place and clean it each day, like in a military barracks. He would give them a gallon of wine as compensation for their work. As a result, the four hotels he owned were much cleaner than many, or most, of the others.

The dead poor were less of a problem than the dead property owners. Much of the Lower Loop was owned by dead people. This dead property was also bound by long-term leases. Such leases made it difficult to acquire property in large blocks and thus seriously hindered renewal.

This legal problem was difficult but not insurmountable. Looking beyond it, Curtiss C. Coleman, then president of the Minneapolis Chamber of Commerce, wrote: "We must have a plan for something more than the status quo, a plan for new development—a plan for something inspirational, a plan that will encompass elements of beauty as well as overcome physical and psychological objections."

What may have been objectionable to the Chamber of Commerce was not at all objectionable to the drifter. In 1955, Mayor Eric Hoyer complained of the coast-to-coast reputation Minneapolis enjoyed as being a soft spot for panhandlers. It was easy for them to panhandle a dollar a day and they could easily get by on that amount.

The Sourdough Bar had a bell in it. Whenever someone bought the house a round of drinks the bell would be rung. One panhandler liked to to keep the bell ringing and he made enough money from sympathetic passers-by to do so. He worked alone and told people that he was a disabled World War II veteran, which was very likely true. He said he only needed a little to get by. They helped him out. He also sold little packets of pins and needles to shopgirls on their way home to their apartments and would get back considerably more than what he paid for the pins. Sometimes he made fifty dollars in three hours. It's fair to assume that he knew the territory.

The other major group of Gateway solicitors, the hookers, continued as a problem. Oddly enough, the use of penicillin added to the Lower Loop's difficulties. It kept the old prostitutes healthy and active, much to the despair of city officials who wanted them to retire. Even so, in the Nicollet and Washington Avenue area the gonorrhea rate was fourteen times the city rate and syphilis about six times. Skid Row led the city in homicides.

In May of 1956, the federal government granted Minneapolis $50,000 for the planning and survey necessary to qualify the project for broad federal assistance. Renewal was on the way. It was estimated then that the total Gateway redevelopment would cost twelve million dollars.

Following that news, the city planners next considered how and where to relocate all the Skid Row dwellers. As the seriousness of this problem became apparent, there was talk about using the facilities of the Union City Mission and the St. James Hotel or of building single unit public housing for them.

While they conjectured, the Gateway saw a forerunner of more modern tastes. A Skid Row resident was discovered cultivating marijuana plants around the Memorial flagpole in the summer of 1956. He was plucking the blue flowers to encourage more blooms when some killjoy tipped off the authorities.

In 1956 a number of businesses on the block bordered by Third and Fourth Streets and Marquette and Second Avenues South received their walking papers as the federal government finished the plans for a new Federal Courts Building. This was the first major dent in the old city. The businesses were: Oudal Bookstore, 315 Marquette; Minneapolis Bar, 317 Marquette Avenue; Hip Sing Association, 319 Marquette Avenue; Ted's Cafe, 323 Marquette Avenue; Wendell's Inc., 325 Marquette Avenue; the Oneida Building, 104 South Fourth Street; Kvalsten

Washington Avenue, 1948. *Minnesota Historical Society.*

Electric Co., 110 South Fourth Street; Minneapolis Liquor Store, 108 South Fourth Street; the Strand Hotel, 110 South Fourth Street; the Typewriter Clearing House, 112 South Fourth Street; and The Covered Wagon, Inc. (a bar popular with the newspapermen) on 114 South Fourth Street. All had to vacate by May, 1957.

The Persian Palms, however, would not go out without some final lurid happenings. Edward L. Berdie, the night manager of the Palms was robbed of $400 and a diamond ring worth $2,500 in August of 1955 as he got out of his car in front of his home one night. The bandit who robbed him was familiar with his habits and addressed him by name.

An even grimmer event, a murder took place on the premises of the Palms.

A brooding Lower Loop saxophone player sat in the establishment on a Thursday night, July 17,1958. His estranged wife, Barbara Jean LaCount, 24, was an exotic dancer employed by the Palms. She did a number called the "Black Cat," whatever that may have been. When she finished her number, she took a seat at the bar. The brooding man, Stanley LaCount, produced a pistol and shot her. She fell backwards from the bar stool screaming, "Somebody help me! He's killing me."

Her husband then knelt beside her and fired several more shots into her body, according to Ted Berg, bartender at the night club at 111 Washington Avenue South. Berg said he dropped to the floor behind the bar and crawled to the front office to call police, then he ran out the front door to summon a beat officer. LaCount surrendered readily to police. He had been on parole from Stillwater where he had been sentenced for armed robbery.

In 1958, the Gateway must have been alive with researchers and students of the Skid Row life, judging from all the studies and reports of that time. One study dealt with the income of residents there. The researchers found that of 3,000 residents, mostly male, 572 had an income of less than $600 a year, 1,056 had between $600 and $999, 362 had between $1,000 and $1,499, 562 between $1,500 and $2,499, 198 earned between $2,500 and $3,499 and 41 had from $5,000 to $9,999. None made over $10,000. One old Finnlander who owned a number of houses in south Minneapolis but who lived with his old friends on the Row must have been one of the top earners.

A student of skid rows, Samuel S. Wallace, did some on-the-spot research in Minneapolis. He wrote of one incident in the final year of the Gateway:

"The Star Bar had been recommended to me by several different people as a nice place, a comfortable place, a place where the toilet is good (a crucial point) and the drinking water is adequate, and as a friendly place.

"One of the b-girl dancers came and sat down and asked if I would buy her a drink, I said I was busted and she moved away. Then another girl came up to me and asked if she might join me.

"'Sure, sit down.'

"The bartender poured her a drink and said, 'That'll be one buck, sir'

"What's that?"

"'That'll be one buck for buying the lady a drink.'

"'I didn't buy anybody a drink. Hell, I'm broke.'

"The girl looked depressed, 'Gee, how come you're so cheap?'

"'Wait a minute. I'm sitting here drinking, minding my own business, and you come up to me and ask if you can join me, What's the scoop?'

"The bartender poured the drink back into the bottle and the girl sidled off."

Some of the methods used to coerce drinks were cruder than that. The owner of a South St Paul liquor store, who once tended bar in the Gateway, said that certain obnoxious older women would spread their legs and threaten to urinate on the floor unless they were given free drinks.

There were continuous jackrollings right up to the end. Once a drunken pig farmer appeared in the Sourdough Bar and announced that he had $400 from a sale of his livestock in South Saint Paul. The bar owner urged him not to advertise the fact but the farmer foolishly did so. He was mugged later on in the evening a few blocks from the Sourdough. He came back into the bar understandably irritated. The police soon appeared to investigate but it was no use, only another case of "we told you so."

Some of the bartenders and owners, like the owner of the Sourdough, tried to take care of their customers. Some of them gave drunks a free morning drink to help them face the new day. Liquor store owners did many things for their customers. They cashed checks, extended credit to sober clients (intoxicated ones couldn't remember what they'd bought), and refused really inebriated people service often telling them to go back to their rooms and sleep.

Other businesses were also helpful. The Skid Row restaurants offered regular menus of plain but good food. Hans' Lunch was one of those. A barber college (Moler Barber School) now moved up to Nicollet to Grant Street, cut the men's hair at a price they could afford. And there were the all-night movie theaters which provided shelter and entertainment, and some exhibitionism if you sat near the wrong person.

Policemen too were well-treated on Skid Row. Bartenders would often give officers change so they could afford an extra pack of cigarettes. Sometimes they received complimentary bottles of whiskey. In response the police would offer a little more aid when necessary.

The police were helpful in removing passed-out drunks from bars. They would generally know their names and how long they'd been drinking. The experienced drunks would go along quietly. The police were also good about putting the men they found passed out in doorways, or wherever else during the vicious Minneapolis winters into warm jail. Many lives were saved by such action. When the drunk tank was abolished in 1971, a Minneapolis policeman was worried about having no place to put the drunks he found on cold nights. The solution was the present detoxification center which dries the men out with more concern for the dangerous alcohol withdrawal symptoms than the old drunk tank evidenced. The men are also no longer made to feel that they are habitual lawbreakers, since public drunkenness is no longer a crime in Minnesota.

Gateway "renewal." *Hennepin County Historical Society.*

Back in 1977 Dick Chapman of Minneapolis *magazine wrote an article in which he took a nostalgic look back at the "old" Hennepin Avenue, the pre-70s Avenue, "the street," he tells us, "where it all happened in Minneapolis":*

Hennepin Avenue (not Nicollet, not Lyndale, not Washington) was where it all happened in Minneapolis. There was action almost 24 hours a day from East Hennepin down to the parade grounds. From Augie Ratner's Theatre Lounge to Walkers' Art Gallery to the bustling business and financial offices on second and third floors—the Avenue was always humming. There was: the Alvin, Curly's, Andy's, Brady's Bar, the Lyceum, Rogers Hotel Bar, the Music Box, the Olympia Fruit Store, the Majestic, Andrews and West Hotels, the Casablanca, the Frolics, Schieks—all (over the years) either on or just off the Avenue.

Restaurants such as Dutro's, the Cafe DiNapoli, and the 620 Club featured full tables during that era, with the 620 Club (located just off of Seventh and Hennepin) and its famous 620 Roundtable serving as the hub of all the action, "as the melting pot," said Chapman, "as the center of the universe for every bindlestiff, Working-Joe or Bon Vivant of the times."

In 1967 Gretchen Tselos of the old Twin Citian magazine paid a lunchtime visit to the 620 Club at a time when it was one of the last great institutions from the "old Hennepin," from what she called the "real Avenue," the "class Avenue" of the decades that had gone before. We join her now for lunch at the 620 Club, as Max Winter, Ernie Fliegel, George Mikan and the rest of the 620 Roundtable regulars grab their beers and turkey sandwiches and settle in for an hour or two of talk. Politics, entertainment and sports will be the topics of conversation. Pull up your chair and stay awhile.

The 620 Club

BY GRETCHEN TSELOS

Seventh and Hennepin, 1939. The 620 Club is at left center. *Minneapolis Public Library.* Mpls. Collection.

In the half-hour before noon there are a hundred handshakes. They come in, the sporting crowd, punching each other, smiling, stopping for "howayahs" as they draw back into the restaurant to a round, black table. Some move briskly to seats at the table, others are more tentative, and some approach with nervous eyes, looking for a friendly nod, and veer off to eat a turkey sandwich elsewhere, or stand in the dim light of the long oval bar to drink a beer under the photographs of old fighters like Dempsey and Barney Ross. By noon the atmosphere is set. The fourteen seats at the round, black table are filled with the barons of old Hennepin, all members of the 620 Roundtable, and the day's guests.

Then comes the talk. Politics, entertainment, sports, past, present and the future. Around the table on a given day might be George Mikan, Max Winter, a Chicago sports announcer with a White Sox rookie in tow, Morris Chalfen and a bantam weight wearing the light suit and dark tan, and, Ernie Fliegel, co-owner of the 620 Club with Henry Winter, Max's brother.

Outside, Hennepin Avenue is aging and a little down at the heels. Too much joyless bumping and grinding away of a couple generations of conventioneers. There are only a few pieces left of the real Avenue, the class Avenue. One of them is the 620 at noon. To understand why, you have to go back 57 years when a Rumanian kid named Ernie Fliegeltaub started hawking newspapers along Hennepin the day after he came to town. He was six years old and, from the beginning, a fighting newsboy.

According to Dick Cullum, long time *Minneapolis Tribune* sports writer, Fliegel would fight another news-boy from the hardship paper, the *Minneapolis Daily News*, for the 15 free newspapers it gave the winner. To a kid trying to help his immigrant parents make a go of it in their new country, such a take was a big deal. News alley, where the *Journal*, the *Tribune*, and the *Daily News* dropped papers for their newsies, was the scene of countless amateur fights. Making one cent on every two cent newspaper was usual, and 15 free made a substantial difference to any newsboy. So Ernie often came out of news alley crying or with a bloody nose, but almost always with that bundle of 15 free papers clutched at his side.

After a short stay in a northside community of Russian Jews, Ernie Fliegeltaub's family, mother, father, sister and Ernie, settled on the southside of Minneapolis in the Cedar-Franklin area where a large colony of Rumanian Jews flourished. It was there Ernie met a neighborhood kid with whom he was to form a life-long friendship—Charlie

Saunders, whose restaurant, using his first name, would later enjoy a wide reputation.

In 1910 Ernie was only a newsboy, one among many—Benny Haskell, Augie Ratner, and Morris Chalfen—who were part and heart of Minneapolis life. Not delivery boys, these, but real agents of the press, hollering the news from corner to corner.

The locus for most of this activity was Hennepin and Washington Avenues down to Seventh Street and east as far as Second Avenue. The kids, for whom these pennies were so dear, ran from their grade schools to Hebrew School, and then to News Alley and the streets. Every minute lost was a penny lost to some other kid. When they had sold all but one, these six and seven year olds, then Benny Haskell Zucknian, Ernie Fliegeltaub, and the like, walked to the main streetcar interchange, and cried, "Paper for your transfer, paper for your transfer!" So each day ended, and the boys went home exhausted.

Newsboy hawking papers at the corner of Hennepin and Washington avenues, 1904. *Minneapolis Public Library.* Mpls. Collection.

Ernie grew up fast as did most of that generation. Fighting made men of the youngest, and ethnic groups, Jewish, Irish, Swedish or German, fought from the time they left their homes till they returned. "You fought on your way to school and from school, as well as for your right to be a 'newsie,' says Ernie. "This was true here as well as in New York City, Boston, and Chicago." Augie Ratner recalls his first meeting with Ernie Fliegel:

"Two new kids come down selling papers on my corner. Boy, I chased them and made those two kids, none other than Ernie and his brother, Joe, buy those papers back from me." These corners passed on as private property from one newsie to another, and the prized corners sold from $150 to $200. And the rivalries showed themselves; northside newsies and shoeshine boys were tougher or so they thought, than southside boys.

Boxing was a natural for kids who learned early to defend themselves. From 1910 through the early '40s baseball and boxing were virtually the two major American sports, and although college football also flourished, the big time professional audience wasn't there. Bernie Slater, a roundtable regular until the day before his recent death, cited boxing history from Nat Fleischer's *The Ring*, pointing out that boxing was "The Way Up" for a youngster who fought from age six or seven for survival. "Today," explained Slater, "a kid who needs money and is interested in sports, doesn't need boxing. Being a golf caddy will open the same doors that boxing did in the early days."

Surprisingly, to a '60s generation, Jewish boxers dominated boxing circles in the late-teens and early '20s. The list included Max Baer, Barney Ross and "Battling Levinsky." The Irish had come before and Italians and Negroes were to come after, for as Slater explained, "Economics! Boxing is the sports of economics. A hungry fighter is the best fighter, and those immigrant boys needed a meal. Now the Negro and Puerto Rican largely capture our boxing titles. They're the hungry ones today. And these Jewish boys, however slight or small, were able to find a niche in the different categories of boxers."

Ernie Fliegel first fought as a bantam-weight, 118-pound limit, and later as a feather-weight, 126-pound limit. George Barton, present secretary of Minnesota's Boxing Commission, refereed many of Fliegel's pro fights. He describes Fliegel as "very clever in the ring—a boxer, not a puncher."

Bernie Slater concurred, terming Ernie a "scientific pugilist." "He always knew what was happening—that's why he never ended up on queer street."

Early in his boxing career Ernie's path crossed that of another Jewish Rumanian immigrant, Bennie Haskell. Ernie trained at Pott's Gymnasium which Haskell then operated after previous stints as both fighter and manager. The two became close friends, and Haskell, sitting at his small desk in his liquor and wine emporium near the Radisson, reminisces that "even then, there was an unusual quality of loyalty about Ernie. He was a cut above the average guy. You could respect him."

Haskell, too, literally had to "fight" his way while growing up. Like Ernie, who changed his name from Fliegeltaub to Fliegel, Benny Haskell Zuckman took his father's first name as his last when he began to fight. It was a practical and personal decision. High schools didn't allow their boys to play football and play professional sports. What else could a South High football player named Benny Haskell Zuckman do? He shortened his name, and neither school nor Jewish parents knew for sure about the boxing.

One morning, following work as a messenger in the copy room of a paper, Benny had gone directly to school. He tells how his principal followed him into the latrine and said, "Zuckman, you don't want to be in school, do you?" "No sir. My mother wants me here." That night Benny high-tailed it, age 13, to Duluth, on to Chicago, St. Louis, and parts unknown. He boxed all over the country, picking up a manager in each town, as so many boxers did.

Eventually Benny returned to Minneapolis, where he fought in the first legal bout in the state of Minnesota.

This 1915 bout of Haskell's marked the end of a strange era in Minnesota sports history when boxing was a felony, punishable by one year in prison, a $1,000 fine or both. George Barton described how it became a crime. "In 1891, two Australian boxers were to meet in St. Paul in a highly promoted middle-weight championship bout. The impending fight attracted so much publicity that church and reform groups of the day demanded that Governor Merriam stop the match. Despite his request for cancellation, the promoters went ahead pointing out that there was no state law prohibiting boxing. On the day of the match, the governor called out the militia and surrounded the arena, preventing the fight on the grounds that no law existed allowing boxing. The next legislative session passed the bill making boxing a felony. But many policemen and officials sympathized with the sport and so the fights went on."

By 1915, sentiment had changed enough for boxing to regain legal status. Fliegel took advantage of the repeal, worked out and was on his way up. One of his friends and competitors Augie Ratner (then known as "Little Bull"), now owner of Augie's Theatre Lounge, recalls one fight. "Though I thought I was tougher, Ernie was in better shape and so in the armory that night, the ticket winner was Ernie Fliegel." Ernie boxed hard and a handsome winner he was-his trunks were fancy black silk made from the remnants of his mother's old synagogue dress. She had finally accepted her son's fighting career.

These boxers ushered in the Jazz Age. "The Roaring Twenties were upon us," says Eddie Schwartz who used to run copy in the loop for his publisher father. "Hennepin Avenue was the Great White Way. It was the Rialto of Minneapolis and it was busy almost 24 hours a day." From East Hennepin down to the auditorium, day and night activity abounded. Ernie Fliegel fought in the all-star bouts which climaxed the 1927 dedication of the new Minneapolis Auditorium and to earn extra money he boxed in the theaters after the amateur nights were over. Further up on East Hennepin, Augie Ratner ran a place called the White Swan whose clientele represented still another characteristic of the times. Dillinger and his friends frequented it, and according to Ratner, "they checked their guns before coming in my place. Even so there was a vacant lot in back covered by a huge spotlight, so if any disagreements took place, they took place out there." Hennepin Avenue, east through downtown, was the highlight for all visitors, the epitome of night-life and had much significant daytime activity—Walker opened his art gallery at 8th and Hennepin, the Public Library was downtown, and Eddie Schwartz tells of the bustling business and financial activities in the second and third floor downtown office buildings.

Ernie gave up fighting in 1927 as a result of an eye injury, but he gave up nothing else. From 1928 until '33 and then some time later, Fliegel managed boxers; he took on only quality, never quantity. As many boxers and sports figures were idolized and often led a night-time life, they often went into evening busi-

nesses. Bars, restaurants and liquor businesses provided natural openings for a generation that had had little time for education and had boxed nights for a good part of their lives. So Ernie Fliegel opened up The 620 Club in 1933 and felt comfortable on the street of his youth. His restaurant fit into the downtown milieu of such fancy candy stores as Saint Terese's, the Imperial and the Arcadia where everyone took his best girl to be served sundaes on marble counters. There were exotic restaurants too, the Golden Pheasant and the Peking featuring Chinese food. And finally the vaudeville theaters, The Unique and the Grand, and dance halls like the Bucket of Blood. Everyone congregated on Hennepin Avenue where the lights flickered and where the fun was plentiful.

From the first year on, the 620 Club became known as the restaurant "Where Turkey is King." The differences between it then and now were the soda fountain which prevailed until Prohibition lifted and really served only sodas; and pool tables and dance space where the back rooms and the kitchen are today. Jack Dempsey, close friend of Ernie's, came in for the opening of the Club and so tradition began marking it as the gathering place for sports and entertainment figures. It was in those days, that the forerunner of the Round Table began. Known as the "Carcass Club", it had membership cards and met after showtime at the vaudeville houses. The succulent turkey remains were gnawed at by burlesque queens and sports greats.

Prohibition knocked a dent in Hennepin social life but mostly it was just an inconvenience. "For most there wasn't much change," says Ernie. People drank all the way through Prohibition." Bootlegging fronts, or "Grand Pigs" took care of sources of supply. But it was still a cause for celebration when Prohibition was lifted in 1934. Augie Ratner recalls, "The piling of beer cases dead center in the White Swan took place in minutes. It fizzed away and that was the end of Prohibition, though there were still some who preferred bathtub gin."

Eddie Schwartz, owner of Ad Art Advertising Company, admits that, in those days, "between Ernie and Jack Dempsey, I never ran out of humorous material."

This sense of humor also bound Ernie and Charlie

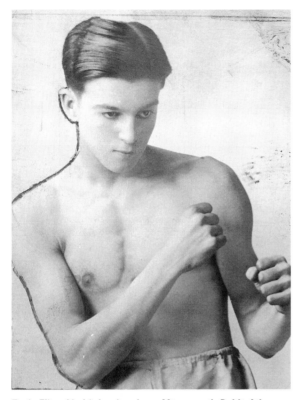

Ernie Fliegel in his boxing days. *Minneapoils Public Library. Mpls. Collection.*

Saunders. Louise Saunders, Charlie's widow, testifies to her husband's and Ernie's love of practical jokes, particularly, but she feels that as important to Ernie and Charlie's friendship was the warmth and love which Ernie and his lovely wife, who died last year, felt for one another and which they shared with others.

"She had been introduced to him in New York by Jack Dempsey. Aileene Albee (her stage name) had been Aileene Aalbu from Minneapolis. She and her three sisters formed a rhythmic foursome which toured from New York City to the West Coast. She encouraged Ernie in his love of music and she taught him to play the organ. Many an evening was spent with Aileene at the violin, Ernie at the organ, a neighbor, Judge Leslie Anderson, on the flute, and Aileene's sister at the piano.

Last year when Ernie was honored for 50 years of service to Pillsbury Settlement House, be expressed his opinion that "more settlement houses and fewer home social work calls might work better in the poorer neighborhoods." Ernie has poured back into "Pill House" what he had received as a kid; he taught boxing at their summer camp and in their gym and donated money and time even when there seemed to be none available. Ernie states, "Kids need somewhere to go, something to do, and if there's a place to work off frustration, then there might not be so much vandalism. Sure, talk is fine, but kids are geared for action."

Ernie Fliegel knows because he remembers. And so do the others who still gather at noon for the Roundtable after years of wear have changed the Avenue around them.

Benny Haskell says, "The change started coming just before World War I. Vaudeville was on its way out and the downtown way of life suddenly shifted." Eddie Schwartz sees the beginnings of change coming at the same time. "World War I stepped on vaudeville, World War II almost killed it and TV knocked off whatever was left." There were other problems. Schwartz says: "Between the coming of parking troubles and the tearing out of major downtown institutions like the West Hotel you were bound to have changes."

And the Avenue's composition continues to change. It's still the theater center, but they're movies, not vaudeville. There are still the girlie shows and the markets, but the flavor is gone. And, as for boxing, Ernie says: "Boxing no longer gets enough superior athletes. Youngsters are exposed to higher education and who wants to box when you have the knowledge to do something else? It's better this way."

But the bright colorful years of Hennepin still survive in anecdote and at places like the 620 Roundtable where the men who gave the Avenue class still meet and probably will until they, themselves, are no more.

Says Hy Shinder: "Why you could never wean any of us from the Avenue, let alone Ernie Fliegel."

The following two pieces were written by guys who didn't have a seat at the 620 Roundtable, guys whose experience of Hennepin Avenue was a little bit different from that of the Roundtable regulars, the "Barons of Old Hennepin" who had long run the show. In the first, Dave Hill (described by his editors as a "career eccentric" and an "ex-con turned Jimmy Breslin school of writer par excellence") writes from the perspective of a guy who still yearns for the "grimy pleasures of the Hennepin Avenue of his youth, that time, as he tells us, "when Hennepin Avenue used to be a street to conjure with—a bad-ass street given over to the business of sin." In the second, Willie Bingstad writes from the perspective of a self-described con-man, "a lazy, lushing bum" who used to live (and work) on the street. Willie Bingstad's story, entitled "Salad Days on the Avenue," originally appeared in the July, 1967 issue of the old Twin Citian magazine. Dave Hill's, entitled "Street Story," originally appeared in Zibeta magazine in February, 1972.

Shinders, 1920. *Minnesota Historical Society.* Photo by C. P. Gibson.

Street Story

BY DAVE HILL

Hennepin Avenue used to be a street to conjure with—a bad-ass street joyfully given over to the business of sin, falling apart in places, yet held together with a sinister dedication to the grimy pleasures of life.

And now it's something different, something less. Time was when the pimps dressed the part and stood arrogantly on the corner while the all-day theaters flaunted their leering marquees and made no pretense about offering art films.

Today the street is cleaner, the hustlers are efficient and check their watches, and the dingy old dives have been replaced by fast food franchises, boutiques, and anonymous parking lots. A government office building now stands in faceless splendor, looking like the box for an electric razor, where once the State Café offered a hamburger for a quarter and a booth to sleep in on a cold, dark night.

Worst of all, the pinball machines are gone: no more magic balls to buy for a nickel . . . shooting for the elusive four-hole in the win section on the Bally's machine . . . hoping to rack up 600 games to cash in for thirty bucks.

In some ways I suppose the street is better now; it's cleaner, safer, more All-American.

But when I was a young man, just starting to make my way in the world some 20 years ago, Hennepin Avenue was a far different street: a dazzling classroom in the school of hard knocks.

At the far north end there was the great old Victorian Library, complete with marble angel. Around the side on 11th Street, were the steps leading down to the public restrooms. There, it was said, you could always find a fairy in the urine-smelling tiled darkness. We often talked of rolling a queer, but never did.

Near Eighth Street was the famous Kin Chu Café, headquarters for the almost-legendary Kin Chu gang, young hoodlums with long, greasy hair, ducktails, one-button rolls and Mr. B shirts with knit ties. They were bad and they stood on the street, looking evil, hustling the young girls as they walked past.

A few doors away was the infamous Lincoln Recreation, rumored to be the nerve center of big-time gambling in the city. But we were too young then to put five bucks on the Dodgers at a run-and-a-half. We played pool, eight ball and nine ball and rotation. We were good.

We also stole a lot of beer. Downstairs at the Rec where the bowling alleys were, was a phone booth by the storeroom door. Four or five of us would go down there in our trench coats, and stand around in a mob while someone pretended to make a call.

That was the cover. One at a time we'd sneak into the storeroom filling our pockets and waistbands with bottles of warm Grain Belt. They never caught on, never locked the storeroom. We would always empty out a full case or maybe two cases, and put the empty with the rest.

Then we'd saunter up the alley, and climb up on the roof of Bridgeman's to drink. Sometimes we really got smashed and began lobbing bottles at the street cars, trying to break windows.

That ended in the summer of 1953, when the last of the great old trolley cars rumbled down the avenue.

Our hangout in those days was Shinder's News Stand and Coffee Shop, on the corner of Sixth and Hennepin. They had three pinball machines—the horse racing kinds—where you could win as many as 600 or 800 free games.

We weren't interested in the free games: we played for money. Eight hundred free games were worth 800 free nickels—40 dollars. Sometimes, when we were flush, we'd get two rolls of nickels for four dollars and play our asses off. Then we'd hit it—the big one—and the ball would plunk into the four-hole in the Win section, with all four lights, and we'd stand back, smirking with pride, as the machine dutifully racked up 630 games.

"Check this—I want to cash in," we'd tell Danny or Art Shinder. And they'd come over, verify our score, step behind the cash register, and flip a switch. Click-click-click—the games would be tallied off, and one of the Shinders would count our winnings—$31.50.

"Don't put it back in the machines, now—get the hell home!" Art would say.

"Well, give us the $1.50 in nickels anyway."

By 4 a.m. we'd be totally broke, and Art would loan us a dollar for coffee and streetcar fare.

Down at the other end of the street were such places as the Bijou Theatre—"Continuous Shows"—where the most desperate of the perverts lurked in the dark, boxes of popcorn in hand.

At the very end of the street were the bars, blending around the corner into the jungle of Washington Avenue. The 24 Club and the Sourdough, the Pacific and the Oak, the Stockholm with its famous nickel beer, and the Persian Palms, where everything was for sale.

On that end of the street our business was in the old Gateway Park, where the winos slept off their nightmares in the summer afternoons.

We'd wander around, fending off the moochers, until we'd find one who would buy us some booze. Usually we'd give him the money for two six packs of Stite (whatever happened to that marvelous, bitter brew?) and half a buck to buy himself a pint of muscatel or white port.

We had to follow him all the way to the liquor store, and wait outside. We always had one guy stationed in the glass-littered alley to make sure the wino didn't sneak out the side door.

Once we saw a liquor store owner catch an old wino stealing a quart of sherry. We helped him hold the old man while the storeman poured the whole quart down his throat. He was a sick, but happy, man.

All that is gone now. No one sleeps on the lawn at the Towers apartment, no bootleggers lurk in the lobby of the Sheraton-Ritz, no peroxided hustlers stand on the plaza of Hansford Pontiac, shaking their asses at the Johns as they pass.

The Avenue is cleaner today. Almost sterile. A place to transact your business and leave.

Looking east on Seventh Street toward Hennepin, c. 1947. *Hennepin County Historical Society.*

Salad Days On The Avenue

BY WILLIE BINGSTAD

Did you ever sleep inside a twenty-five cent locker? The kind they have in bus depots? I mean, just crawl inside one, and curl yourself snugly around a pint of Arriba wine and sleep. It can be done, though it's kind of a drag. I did it once, even though I had a perfectly good bed waiting for me in the Radisson Ramp.

This dates back to my salad days (1959–1960) when I inaugurated my own war on penury.

I could say I was rebelling against conformity, or trying to "find myself" in a mad, mad world. But the truth is simpler: I was a lazy, lushing bum.

Here's how it worked: the first essential was a place to sleep at night, winter and summer, that was warm, dry, and quiet. I hit on the Radisson Arcade, which was open all night at that time, just having been opened. I haven't checked out the protocol or architecture there recently, but when I moved in, it was ideal.

The place to sleep was in a small area just back of a waist-high wall slanting off from a bank of phone booths. On this wall were plants, which provided shade and refuge. It was completely hidden from the main arcade. On the other side was the corridor to the Radisson, almost never used in the wee hours. All I had to do was come in at night, slide a shoppers bench behind the wall, make my bed, and sleep.

The bed making was easy. I had a friend running a penny arcade who allowed me to keep a suitcase containing two quilts and a pillow under the counter. When bedtime came I just picked up the suitcase, went to my quarters, and made up my bed.

It would have been awkward, of course, to have been discovered there in the morning. But I had a friend who baked at a nearby hotel who thoughtfully awoke me each morning at 6:00 as he walked by to work. After stowing my bedding in a large locker (without paying, as no one would be in to steal anything for hours) I'd join him in the bakery for coffee and everyone thought I was on the early busboy shift, and I had rolls for breakfasts for months.

By the time I was nourished enough to hit the avenue, it was perhaps seven a.m., which presented a problem: what do you do for kicks downtown at 7 a.m.? I usually compromised on the sad scene by making it to a little cafe where I kept some clothes (in the walk-in cooler) and got dressed for the day. A suitcase with some essentials and a spare shaving kit I kept in a Hennepin Ave. tavern. The rest of my clothes I stowed in lockers in the ramp, at a cost of ten dollars a week in quarters, since it cost a quarter every time I had to get out a fresh shirt or change suits.

By the time the big stores opened I was hungry again, and I usually ate at one of the big dime stores. For the big breakfast, ham, eggs, and such, I paid a dime. It worked like this: I made a point of going into the place, and picking out the most homely young waitress in the place. Her I would cozy up to, and put some story on. The best shot was simply to be mysterious and sort of in need of a big sister. Within a few days I could have her trained so she'd give me a 10-cent tab for any meal on the menu. So, for a dime a trip, I could get meals to burn. It cut corners plenty, since my clothes cost so much, sitting in pay lockers.

Thus nourished, I usually embarked on pastimes. The old standby was a movie, most of which opened by 11:00. And getting to know a ticket taker was a simple matter, with a minimum of con work involved. At one time I was in thickly enough to get into seven downtown theaters with no more than a smile and a wink.

As far as cold cash income is concerned, let me

tell you a classic tale, and end this chronicle with an account of the great record swindle.

Remember the payola stink? Stations suddenly found their little piles of disc jockey records an odious mess, and didn't know quite what to do with them. To have a huge library of sample records was to leave yourself open to cries of Payola!" Yet they were worth too much to simply discard them.

Hearing of a leading station's intent to divest itself of a thousand or more such records, one fine Saturday morning, I rounded up another friend as clean-cut and wholesome looking as myself, and a third party, who had such a deep and solemn voice that everyone called him "The Rabbi."

After making my friend with the deep and sonorous voice memorize a speech, I had him call the station, with the message (as best I recall the wording), "This is Father St. Hilaire and I'm a direc-

tor of the Ascension Youth Club of the holy church. I understand you have records . . . oh. . . . you would donate and I would be most pleased to have them."

Ten minutes later my friend and I hit the station with shopping bags, and announced ourselves as the boys from Ascension.

We swung out with a little over 1,100 records, all 45s.

I peddled them at teen hangouts downtown for weeks. Three, four, or even five for a buck, and stayed in wine till summertime.

Just last week, in fact, I found a few of the very worst of the lot in an old suitcase of mine.

I have long since given up the bottle, and no longer do I court poverty.

But when I swung, I swung . . .

Hennepin Avenue as it appeared from the fourth floor of the library, March 1945.
Minneapolis Public Library. **Mpls. Collection.**

Back in September of 1979 the distinguished British travel writer Jonathan Raban paid a visit to the city of Minneapolis where, after a brief stay in a downtown motel, he rented a 16-foot boat and headed on a journey down the Mississippi. The story of the journey (inspired by Mr. Raban's boyhood reading of Huckleberry Finn*) was told in his book* Old Glory, *portions of which have been excerpted below. It's fair to say that Mr. Raban was not favorably impressed by the "completely synthetic urban space" he found in downtown Minneapolis (he was especially unimpressed by its much vaunted skyway system), calling it "the city that had gone indoors."*

The City that had Gone Indoors

BY JONATHAN RABAN

In Minneapolis a boat was waiting for me. I was going to ride the river for as long and as far as I could go and see whether it was possible to stitch together the imaginary place where I had spent too much of my time daydreaming and that other, real, muddy American waterway.

I was being interviewed by the radio pastor of WWID, Ladysmith.

"Have you said yes to Jesus yet?"

No.

"It's by His grace you're saved through faith. Exercise your faith and fly. 'Lord, I'm receiving You as my Lord and Savior.'"

My headlights picked out the twin marmalade eyes of a raccoon in the road. I swerved just in time.

"Henry Slotter tells the news at nine, straight up, and then *Sunday Hymnsing* to follow, on this second of September, Labor Day Weekend. Now hear this. The Oklahoma Baptist Festival Choir. 'It Is Well with My Soul.' That says just about all that needs to be said, folks. "It Is well with My Soul . . ." The opening chords on the electric organ quivered with pious tremolo: then came the voices, the sopranos sounding as if they were crying for joy, the baritones and basses adding a counterpoint of moderation and common sense, as if getting on the right side of the Lord were just good business practice. I turned up the volume and joined the Interstate, singing my way into Minnesota along with the Oklahoma Baptist Festival Choir. After all I was in no position to jeer at other people's dreams of personal salvation. I had my own hopes of becoming a born again something, even if it wasn't a Christian. *It is well with my soul, pom, pom . . well with my soul.*

I was jolted back into an America I recognized without affection. The bald glare of the sodium lights over the highway had flattened the landscape and robbed it of shadow and color. The exurban fringe of the twin cities of Minneapolis and St. Paul was the usual mess of neon doodles. Curlicues of mustard. Trails of ketchup. The motels, taco houses, Radio Shacks and Pizza Huts stretched away in a bilious blaze of American mock-Alpine. I remembered poring over the Victorian atlas, playing with the exotic syllables of Minneapolis as if they spelled Samarkand. Even now I wasn't quite prepared for the thoroughgoing charmlessness of this five-mile strip of junk food, porno movies and the kind of motels where you expect to find blood running down your shower curtain. There was a brief, merciful break of darkness. Then the illuminated crap began again.

It was only after I had gone on another mile or so that I realized I'd crossed the Mississippi. I had crossed the Mississippi. It had dropped through a crack in the lights of Minneapolis, and I hadn't even seen it go.

I pushed on deeper into Minneapolis until I found myself driving up a street that felt like the heart of something. Hennepin Avenue. Louis Hennepin had been a seventeenth-century Franciscan friar who had been chaplain to the La Salle expedition which had charted the upper Mississippi in 1680. I'd just been reading about him in Francis Parkman's *La Salle and the Discovery of the Great West,* and was interested to see how his name had been commemorated here. Hennepin Avenue was blocked solid with gay bars, massage parlors, bright little boutiques with vibrators and dildos displayed in their windows, and the offices of pawnbrokers and bail bondsmen, now shuttered and pad-locked for the night. Perhaps Father Hennepin had been an altogether merrier priest than Parkman had made him sound. Or perhaps the ruderies of Hennepin Avenue were intended to convey what Protestant Minnesota thought of foreign papists.

I stopped at a bar that looked and sounded rather more straight than its neighbors: MOBY DICK'S— FOR A WHALE-SIZED DRINK. Having just missed out on one American epic by oversight, I had better catch up with whatever classics I could find. A few doors down the street, no doubt, there'd be a sex shop called "The Scarlet Letter."

In the three-quarters dark, the walls of Moby Dick's were bright with sweat. It was the kind of place where all the loose ends of a city tend to shake down together. A glazed-looking Indian in a booth had a pitcher of beer for company. Two blacks, wearing enviably sharp hats and suits with lapels as narrow as switchblades, were feeding the jukebox with quarters. At the bar, a drunk was getting nowhere with the barmaid as he tried to sweet-talk her into betting on the outcome of the New England-Pittsburgh football game.

"Come on, honey. Just a little bet . . . a *gennelman's* bet . . . whaddaya say?"

On the TV screen above his head, someone dressed up in medieval armor was running for a touchdown.

"A *dollar.*"

The barmaid squirted whiskey from a tube into my glass.

"I said a *gennelman's* bet. One dollar. What's a dollar between friends?" He sprawled across the bar toward the girl in a sudden access of inspiration. "Hey . . . you can take Pittsburgh."

"Straight up or soda?" said the girl to me.

"Go on, what's a dollar?"

"Food, clothing and a place to sleep," I said. Bob Hope had said that in a movie once.

The girl faced the drunk for the first time in minutes. "It's too early in the season. I ain't into the teams yet."

Defeated, he settled on me, grabbing at my sleeve as I started to leave the bar. "Where you from, fella? Where you from? I can tell you ain't from around here," he said with the triumphant cunning of a man who has got the better of half a bottle and can still pull off feats of amazing detection.

I headed for the empty booth next to the pickled Indian's.

"Hey, where you going? Where you going, fella?"

Far away, I hoped. South with the Monarch butterflies. Downstream.

I needed to lay in some provisions. Thoreau had taken a supply of melons and potatoes on his trip. Huck and Jim had loaded up with traps, setlines for catfish, a lantern, a gun and a Barlow knife. I went shopping in the city, hoping that if I acquired a few symbols of pioneer self-sufficiency it would bring about a transformation of my character and turn me into a proper outdoor adventurer.

Minneapolis itself, though, had gone indoors. When it had done all it could to tinker with the Mississippi; when the bridges, mills, power plants, locks and dams had been finished; then the city had turned its back on the river and focused inward on itself. Now it was engaged in yet another exercise in utopian gadgetry; building a city within a city, a perfumed maze of artificial streets and plazas set in midair, four stories above the ground.

No wonder the streets had seemed so empty. The city had gone somewhere else and cunningly hidden itself inside its own facade. To go shopping, one had to take the elevator up to this other Minneapolis. It was a completely synthetic urban space. Glassed-in "skyways" vaulted from block to block, and the shopping plazas had been quarried out of the mid-

Nicollet Mall, c. 1975. *Minneapolis Historical Society.*

dles of existing buildings like so many chambers, grottoes and tunnels in a mountain of rock.

Here, fountains trickled in carpeted parks. The conditioned air smelled of cologne and was thickened with a faint, colorless spray of Muzak. The stores were open-fronted, like the stalls of a covered Arab souk. Like all the best utopias, this one was only half-built. It was the nucleus of a dream city designed to stretch out and farther out until Minneapolis-in-the-air would be suspended like an aureole over the deserted ruins of Minneapolis on-the-ground. If one put one's ear to the walls, one might hear the distant reverberation of workmen with pneumatic drills tunneling out more corridors and plazas in the wider reaches of the city.

The skyway system was as vividly expressive of the peculiar genius of Minneapolis as the roller-coasting freeways are of Los Angeles or the glass-and-cement cliffs of New York: Only a city with really horrible weather could have arrived at such a thing. Here people had left their local nature behind altogether. It was something nasty down below, and the skyways floated serenely over the top of it.

"Nature" here was of the chic and expensive kind that comes only from the most superior of florists: ornamental palms and ferns, rooted not in soil but in coppery chips of synthetic petroleum extract.

Voices melted into the musical syrup of Andre' Kostelanetz that trickled from hidden speakers in the palm fronds. Footsteps expired on the carpeted halls. At a mock-Parisian street cafe, the shoppers sat out at gingham tables, drinking Sanka with non-saccharin sugar substitute. Skyway-city turned one into an escapee. It was a place where everyone was on the run—from the brutish climate, from carcinogens, from muggers, rapists, automobile horns. Even one's own body was being discreetly disinfected and homogenized by the deodorant air. Up here, everything was *real* nice: we were nice people who smelled nice, looked nice and did nice things in nice places.

Four floors below, we could see the nasty world we'd left behind. Hennepin Avenue was stretched out in front of us, famous for the Original Sin in which it wallowed. Beneath the skyway, a crummy little store sold rubber wear and shackles. Posters for the blue-movie houses showed nipples and pudenda so imaginatively colored and airbrushed that they'd ceased to look human in origin. A wino pissed in a doorway, watched by his dog. It was a pregnant bitch, and looked vaguely ashamed of its owner.

Looking down on that fallen world from the standpoint of this temporary synthetic Eden, I thought that perhaps Minneapolis and I were really on much the same track, traveling hopefully, never arriving. I loved the audacity of that American principle which says, When life gets tainted or goes stale, junk it! Leave it behind! Go West. Go up. Move on. Minneapolis had lit out from its river. Now it was trying to wave goodbye to its own streets. The skyways were just the latest stage in its long voyage out and away. "Where ya goin'?" said the truckdriver to the hitchhiker at the end of *Manhattan Transfer*. "I dunno. Purdy far." It was the same answer that I'd given to the drunk in Moby Dick's, and on the skyways the whole city seemed to be echoing that classic traveler's statement of intent.

Our voyages, though, led in separate directions, and I seemed to have made yet another knight's move away from the river; so I was cheered to see a rack of corncob pipes in a cigar store, They weren't called corn-cob pipe that would have been too straightforward for this realm of artifice and invention. They were advertised as "Missouri Meerschaum," and I bought two of them, along with a tin of Captain Black Smoking Tobacco, which sounded suitably swarthy, and a Zippo windproof lighter. Drifting idly through more chambers of glass and ferns and tea-garden rumbas, I picked up a corkscrew, a thermos flask and a khaki rain hat. I reached my hotel room half a mile away without ever touching ground.

I first happened upon Brian Hammond's wonderful little book Keep Harmon Open: An Urban Homesteader's Journal, *in my friend Steve Anderson's old Snelling Avenue bookstore, just before it closed a couple of years ago. I had never seen it before that time, and have never seen (or heard) of it anywhere since, though it's a book which certainly does not deserve such obscurity, and one whose partial resurrection in these pages (we've unfortunately been able to include only those portions of it which deal most directly with life in downtown Minneapolis) constitutes an invaluable addition to our understanding of that downtown neighborhood called Harmon Place.*

There's no easy way to describe Keep Harmon Open. *In fact, I feel so inadequate to the task that I'm not even going to try. Instead, I've decided to quote from the blurb which appears on the back cover (I assume it was written by Mr. Hammond) and allow him to describe for himself as quirky—and as uncatagorizeable—a book as any of us is likely to find.*

Keep Harmon Open *is a story about the clash between urban renovators and the culture of the streets. Caught between purveyors of the skin trade amid the bible pushing enterprises the author bears witness to the battle of the spirit and the flesh. Tried by his own conscience and tempted by his visions, he sketches the theatre of the streets from his bathroom window. His neighbors are hookers, pimps, winos, and con artists. The Massage Parlors, day labor pools, alleys, public restrooms, and soup kitchens are his neighborhood. The streets are a parade of pimpmobiles and sandwichmen, nomadic wine tasters and nature lovers who wrap themselves in cardboard and sleep in the interstices between buildings . . .* Keep Harmon Open *is a search for transcendence: A quest for the pivotal chord, the existential cul de sac, a retracing of one's steps in search of passage through the dead end streets.*

Hennepin Avenue at Harmon Place, looking west on Harmon Place toward Hennepin, c. 1963. *Minnesota Historical Society.* Photo by Norton & Peel

Harmon Place

by Brian Hammond

It seems like only yesterday that Harmon Place was igneous rock, monocotyledons, and dinosaur dung. But as the millennia came and went, and the various conflagrations smoldered, the earth became rich in rubber, chrome and used car lots. The early Indians of the area held these nomadic herds of used cars sacred, and gave them ancient, ancestral names like Pontiac, Cherokee, and Comanche.

Then the white man came, and monumental names like Bill Boyer Ford and Don Peterson's Downtown Chevytown towered over Harmon Place. Goodyear, Uniroyal, Firestone, and Anderson-Crane dealers lined both sides of the street like a four-block long patch of laid rubber. Harmon Place had become the automotive capitol of the Upper Midwest.

But as America moved to the suburbs, so did the car dealerships. Today, all that remains of the once mighty automotive empire are vacant display rooms, empty buildings with parking on the roof, and Walker Auto Supply.

Transubstantiation

The Kenosha Apartments, a four-story brick building constructed in 1894, is located on the corner of Twelfth and Harmon Place. I live on the second floor. My older brother lives in Kenosha, Wisconsin, although I don't think there's any connection, unless synchronistically, in the Jungian sense. Across Twelfth Street is the Walker Auto Warehouse, and some six blocks away, across from Loring Park, is the Walker Art Center. Now, here is a connection—perhaps not strictly speaking in the Kantian sense of a necessary or even a contingent one but a connection, none the less—suggested by the billboard for Gabriel Shock Absorbers which is affixed to the side of the Walker Auto Warehouse. The billboard is the

primary view from my living room window, and renders in red, white, and blue the Strider, the Red Rider, and the Hijacker—Gabriel's three top-the-line shock absorbers.

"GABRIEL—THE SHOCKING DIFFERENCE."

As I peer through the dusty film on the windowpane. I hope to catch a glimpse of the billboard becoming pop art right before my very eyes.

Urban Homesteading, or How the Kitchen Was Won

"Like to build a sleeping loft, have an interior brick wall, sanded hardwood floors, view of the downtown skyline?" was the advertisement in the Sunday Want Ad section that aroused my curiosity about the possibility of renting an apartment on Harmon Place. The thought of living downtown was enticing in a sort off Heideggerian sense of "transcending *into* life." Since I had never been able to save enough money to move to British Columbia, it also appealed to my fantasies about being a modern pioneer—even though this would be more in the line of urban homesteading. And, speaking of Heidegger, like the contradictoriness of an existential truth, urban apartment remodeling was, I found, both a lot of fun and a royal pain in the ass.

The apartment. in which I was particularly interested was a one bedroom for one hundred thirty-five dollars. It had a large living room painted light blue, a dining room painted light green, a yellow vestibule, orange kitchen, pink bathroom, and a bedroom with sheets of burlap pasted on the wall. Viewed from the doorway, the apartment had a prismatic effect potent enough to induce vertigo. I wondered why the molding hadn't been painted flat black to set off the colors a bit.

According to rumor, a family of eight had been the former tenants and had lived for two years out of unpacked boxes. These boxes had been stacked along the walls in warehouse fashion, with aisles leading from one room to another. Chairs were placed at strategic locations, to reach second or third story boxes.

I suppose that's as good a rationale as any: Why unpack when you'll just be moving again in a year or two anyway?

I was struck by the peculiarity of another architectural feature, too, namely the window on the wall that separated (or perhaps I should say joined) the kitchen and the bathroom. That's exactly what I said, "What a weird place for a window!" We're probably all a little voyeuristic by nature, but this was really indecent. And I refuse to believe it was placed there for ventilation purposes. About the only sense I could make of it at all was by way of a sort of Freudian psycho-alimentary metaphor. I had once seen a play, written by a local dramatic group, in which bathroom fixtures did have definite cosmological overtones. Hot and cold running Yin and Yang, and I believe the toilet bowl was the great Tao—"that which receives everything and rejects nothing." I tried to find a large, reasonably priced sheet of semipermeable membrane to cover the strange aperture, but had to settle for three-eighths-inch sheetrock.

The kitchen was like a hopelessly incurable psychosis. I caught myself sneaking up to the entry and peering around the corner, fearing that a ninety-pound silverfish might be hiding in the deep shadows. Prowling around your own kitchen with a flashlight may seem slightly absurd, but as there were no windows and the light (wherever it was) was burned out, it seemed an intelligent solution—especially for anyone who has the slightest doubt about being protected by a guardian angel. Besides, I had seen those programs on *Twilight Zone* where somebody accidentally leans against the wrong wall and gets sucked up into the void.

Having replaced the light bulb and figuring all is safe when the lights are on, I took hold of a loose corner of contact paper just above the oven. Praying that it wasn't infectious, I tore it from the wall in one panicky motion. You wouldn't have believed it. I mean the greasy filth was like someone had fried up two whole pounds of bacon and put the grease in a bowl, then cleaned out the toaster, stirring in six year's worth of crumbs, stood about a foot away and slowly poured the mixture down the side of the wall. Dead cockroaches, ants, slugs, and an occasional fly still shuddering in death's agony, seasoned it and gave it the appearance of something from the Book of Revelations.

I was seriously considering boarding up the entry to the kitchen—like those rooms in old mansions that have remained locked for more than a hundred years—but I decided instead to enter herein wearing rubber gloves, a face mask and a crucifix, thus exorcising the chamber of horrors once and for all.

Meanwhile, I would eat my meals out.

Stalking The Wild Cheeseburger

Harmon Place has no dark forests or grassy hillsides on which one may spread a tablecloth to picnic on fruits, cheese, French bread, and white wine. Some blocks away, however, one will find a Burger King and a shortcut to it through the back alleys.

The street transients often have their picnics in these back alleys, toasting life with a pint of Thunderbird wrapped in a brown paper bag. I have seen more than one of these nomadic winetasters talk affectionately to the parking meters, just as one might talk to the pines of the deep forest or to the willows alongside sandy streams. In the spring, they sleep in the tarred parking lot behind the H. A. Holden building, under Harmon's starless skies. In the winter, some find a dark corner in the stairwell of my apartment building. The real nature-lovers wrap themselves in cardboard and wedge their bodies between the two-foot space of neighboring buildings. Some die from exposure or pneumonia, most from the Thunderbird.

"Blacky," the local sociopath, crosses Harmon Place daily while making his rounds. He's usually peddling hot merchandise or lids of oregano (maybe it's Minnesota Green). At one time or another, he's tried to sell me a tape deck that he ripped off from somebody's car, a suede coat that he was convinced was just my size, and an expensive Japanese camera. If other locals hit me up for drinking money, I usually give it to them, not to support their addiction, but rather to reinforce their honesty. I'm sure they don't understand that, but I really hate those guys who come on with the "Hey, Brother, I need some busfare to get across town to pick up my paycheck to send to my sick mother" Bullshit. If a bum says, "Buddy, can you help me out?—I need a drink real bad," I give him the money.

One evening, while tracking down a double-meat cheese whopper hold-the-tomato, light onion, I was stopped by a tall man in a heavy storm coat. He startled me, standing there in the alley looking like a big green pine tree in the oversized coat. (The coat was his home). But no, he wasn't a pine tree in the alley. He wanted me to "borrow" him fifteen cents for a "cupacoffee." I stopped and said I was going to Burger King, and that I would lend him the change if he wanted to borrow it, making a futile attempt to uphold the rules of grammar, even if it were only an alley off Harmon Place. He told me that I was a gentleman and a scholar.

At the Burger King, I ordered my pine tree friend his "cupacoffee," and the cheeseburger "my way." Our waitress looked about fourteen, slightly anemic, and so skinny I had my doubts that she could even carry a whopper. I paid for the order, received my change, and watched the meat patties bounce down the conveyor belt toward the five-inch diameter buns. I waited. Five minutes went by—a long time when it's supposed to be fast food. The kids on the hamburger line were laughing and clowning around, and even our waitress seemed to be getting a little perturbed. I assumed the manager was out. Seven minutes, and still no goods. Finally the waitress came over again and asked me in her frail, dreamy voice, "What did you order again, sir?"

"A double-meat cheese Whopper no-tomatoes light-onion, a milk, and a coffee."

"Sorry you've had to wait, I don't know what those guys are doing back there. I'll be right back." The waitress disappeared through the Keep Out doors that led to the hamburgers.

My friend in the green storm coat seemed quite calm as he picked dried pieces of snuff from his lapel. He was used to waiting.

Then a voice that I never in a million years would have credited to our frail little waitress, yet it was hers, all right, boomed out of the back room: "Will you guys get your SHIT TOGETHER and get those orders out here?! These people have been waiting for ten minutes now!"

My Whopper tasted even better because of the delay, and my pine tree friend thanked me again and again, assuring me once more that I was a gentleman and a scholar. He headed back out into the streets to drink his coffee.

Spring on Harmon Place

Today I took a walk on Harmon Place to behold the beauty of the first few days of spring. Daffodils and narcissi, nasturtiums and rhododendrons, sweet peas and petunias all pushed themselves from the damp ground and into the sunlight somewhere, but not on Harmon Place. Here, spring and winter are actually quite indistinguishable—except, of course, to the trained eye. The first real signs of warm weather are the winos passed out in Loring Park and the used condoms in the Community College parking lot. Trees in the park sport dazzling orange stripes; not a sign of spring, however, but of Dutch elm disease. Young children laugh with glee as they drop large rocks into the goldfish pond, while the others on bicycles aim for the tame squirrels by the park benches.

The hookers also have shed their winter coats and parade their sassy young bodies in flashing purples and canary yellow dresses. Their hair is orange or lap-dog brown. From my window I can hear the soft jingling of coins in their underwear.

Things like soybeans, corn, and turnips don't seem to grow very well on Harmon Place. It's not for lack of rain, for it does rain and often rains hard, but rather because the soil is so inaccessible. Anyone intending to do any serious farming on Harmon Place needs to supplement his hoe and spade with a jackhammer. There's also a lot of social pressure against those who would sledgehammer through the sidewalks or tear up the asphalt to sow their spring seeds.

Russian immigrants to Harmon Place have a difficult time adjusting to life on a land where either buildings or pavement cover all of the soil. More than once have I seen them congregating on the street below the Gabriel Shock Absorber sign shouting protests and espousing the wisdom of Dostoevski:

"One has to grow on the soil where the corn and trees are growing and from which the whole order, freedom, life, honor, the family, the children, the church—in one word, everything of *value* comes."

The Dance of Anger

A shiny, black Lincoln Continental with a tan Naugahyde top, tinted windows, white walls, a pink pussy cat with electric eyes in the back window well, and enough antennae to be a small television transmitter station, was parked on the other side of Harmon, just barely visible from my bathroom window. A young dude in maroon velvet hat and blue sunglasses slouched in the driver's seat, sneering out of the corner of his mouth. Outside the car, in six-inch green platforms, and a leopard-spotted porkpie, another man paced back and forth, alternately shaking his head and throwing his hands up in the air.

I stepped into the bathtub and poked my head into the opened window. My nose pressed against the screen. I could hear only bits of the conversation, due in part to the distance, and in part to the tape deck which was blasting Earth, Wind and Fire out of the car window. I should have been minding my own business in the first place, but things do get slow, even on Harmon Place.

"You mean to tell me that you gonna let some motherfucker come up to you and. . . sheeyit . . . I mean, man, I don't gotta take that kind of shit from no honky! . . ."

The guy in the leopard-spotted porkpie now raised his cap above his head, as if to throw it on the ground, but didn't. Then turning his back on the car, he began to march away, still spouting, "Christ Almighty, Man!" Not yet finished, however, he about-faced, walked up to the glistening hood of the car, spat on the Olympic trophy-sized grill ornament and swatted the hot, black metal. SMACK! Slowly reapproaching the driver, he began to poke little holes in the turbulent air with an accusing finger.

"I mean nobody comes up to me man, and do you read me, man is that perfectly clear to you what I'm talking about?! GOD DAMN IT!"

Still slumped against the steering wheel, the cat

in the blue sunglasses straightens up and slowly gets out of the car. He fixes his shirt at the waist, and shakes his leg to get the crease of his slacks straight.

Oh shit, I said to myself excitedly. The fur is going to fly now, I chuckled, thinking how much better this was than television.

But instead of blows and blood, what ensued was more like a cockfight, with ceremonious strutting, puffed plumage, and territorial bluffs.

As if preparing him for fight or flight, a silver sweat broke out on the face of the man in the blue sunglasses. Blowing himself up to twice his normal size, skin glowing in fluorescent green highlights, teeth bared in a venomous snarl, he began pacing around the aggressor in tighter and tighter circles. Slowly the cadence began to build, with feet stomping the asphalt, elbows cutting V's in the air, hands thrashing, heads shaking with low threatening growls.

The dance of anger continued until the rhythms gradually subsided, and the words began to cool. Then a woman's head appeared on the driver's side of the car, and said coolly, as if she'd slept through the whole affair:

"You turkeys gonna stand there jiving each other all night, or you gonna take me uptown?"

As both men got back into the car and drove off down Harmon Place, cat eyes blinking in the oval back window, I couldn't help but again marvel at the complex ethology of the inhabitants of Harmon Place.

Memoirs of a Parking Lot Attendant

By ten o'clock in the morning, three blasting space heaters had warmed up my shack only to about thirty-five degrees above zero. Outside it was twenty-eight below, with a wind-chill of sixty below.

That's about as much as I care to go into winter at the parking lot.

When I started this job almost four years ago, I had no idea that I was going to stretch it out into a life's work. I suppose there are those of us who are called to such professions, although I don't exactly equate my occupation with the essence of my inner being. But it does seem strange that I should earn my living in connection with some of the things I

Aerial view of downtown Minneapolis, c. 1972. Note that the IDS tower is under constuction and that Harmon Place is at center. *Minneapolis Public Library.* **Mpls. Collection.**

hate the most—namely, cars, driving, mechanical problems of any sort. Talk about what you've got under the hood, and the foul smell of a catalytic converter.

After 1957, all cars began to look alike to me, and it has taken considerable research and study on my part to attain the skill I now possess in identifying the various species and phyla of automobilia. Aside from the task of identification, the parking lot attendant must also correctly match up car and car keys. Because I am able to do this, I have often been called a genius. I don't mind being hailed in this way, but I'd rather get bigger tips.

I have a little trick that I do with change, too, that often impresses people. After four years of having ninety cents dropped into your hand, the palm begins to develop a special sensitivity to even subtle variations of coinage. If someone tries to trick me by substituting a penny for the dime in the basic "three quarters, a dime and a nickel" combination, one flip of the five coins in my hands tells me right off that something's amiss.

Integrity is especially important to me as a parking lot attendant, and I didn't work myself up to $4.75 an hour by screwing around on the job. When asked what I find most satisfying about this line of work, I answer without hesitation: breaking into a locked car with a clothes hanger. Nothing can match the breathless suspense of slipping the specially looped end of the wire through the window seal and lowering it ever so carefully down upon the little lock button. I get an almost criminally orgiastic delight in accomplishing this feat. I think back to all the time I spent trying to make the high school varsity football team when I could have been out there stealing cars!

There are plenty of frustrations to being a parking lot attendant, however, and other than its probably being the lowest status job in the county (this parking lot is for employees at the Hennepin County Medical Center), it is a thankless job. For example, how many nurses screech into the lot, nearly smashing over the "Sorry, Full" sign, and demand that I park them because they're late for work. They expect me not only to be responsible for the care of their cars, but for getting them to work on time as well. I've noticed that some of these nurses, whom I imagine must have an extremely hard time getting to work on time, take orderlies or young interns home with them overnight to help overcome this difficulty.

Another predictable and extremely annoying scene is the car that pulls in looking for public parking. I spot right away that this isn't an employee, because I know all the employees—that is, I know their cars. So I press the play button and a prerecorded voice comes out of my mouth, saying (click): "I'm sorry, but this is a private lot for employees of the Hennepin County Medical Center." (Pause).

The response is inevitable: "Well that's where I'm *going,* the Hennepin County Medical Center!"

(Click) "I'm sorry, but this is a private lot *just for employees* at the Hennepin County Medical Center."

Some of the harder cases then start in on: "Well this is a county parking lot, isn't it? Well, then, I live in this county and I pay my taxes and I've got a right to park here same as anybody else!"

You know what else really bugs me are all those people who are so concerned about me not getting enough sun. I choose to sit inside my shack and read or write rather than sacrifice my body to the blazing sun of the shadeless, asphalt-covered, inner-city, ninety-degree August morning. People think I'm weird because of this, but I've never been fond of having my epidermal covering blistered and scorched like that of a broasted chicken. It is, at times, a tossup, however. The shack has a metal exterior, with approximately nine square feet of floor space, and is stuffy, hot and gloomy. Outside there's no shade, no grass, and blowing gravel. So, it's either stay inside out of the direct sunlight and suffocate, or sit outside with an occasional gravelly breeze and fry.

The shack itself doesn't permit many shenanigans, either. There are few options. You can sit cross-legged, stand up straight, turn a full circle and talk on the phone. There's certainly not enough room for somersaults, handsprings, or jogging. Some days I wish there were at least enough room to pace. There's something about spending six and a half hours a day in a space equivalent to that of a phone booth that creates a certain intensity to life.

Other customers are very perplexed over the cap that I wear. Since it's a permanent part of my portraiture from September to May, when I do take it off for the summer, everyone thinks I've just grown a beard or gotten new glasses.

I get comments like: "Oh, I like your new haircut. No, that's not it. You took your hat off! Gee, good for you. I hardly recognized you. I bet it's a lot cooler, isn't it?"

The thing that really throws them, though, is when they can't find a good excuse or legitimate rationalization for me to be a parking lot attendant.

"Going to school?" I'm asked.

"No."

"Looking for another job?"

"No."

"Waiting for something better in the hospital?"

"No."

"Well, what do you do all day long? Seems a shame to waste all that education parking cars."

So I start telling them this is the first and only job I've ever had that actually allows me time to use my education, but they're not really interested.

There is a poetic side to the parking lot that not everyone can understand. From my peaceful bodhi-tree shack, I watch the sparrows pick dead insects out of the car grills, hear the piercing screams of the patients on the psych ward, and witness the billboard changers do their paste-and-brush ballet. Or, there is the slow, daily trek of the indigents on their way to Brother DePaul's House of Charity or the methadone clinic.

There are the parking lot classics, too. Like the nurse who pulls into the lot, leaves the car running, and locks the door with the keys still in the ignition. Or the guy who stops his car in the main aisle, gets out, pees against the side of the car, gets back in, and drives off. Once, a fellow was taking a shortcut through the lot, mumbling and smiling to himself when suddenly he stopped dead in his tracks, threw his arms up over his head and shouted to the heavens: "Thank you, Jesus! Thank you, Jesus!"

A young doctor who has a rotation at the hospital every Thursday is very amusing. He's obviously a fitness fanatic, with golf clubs, jogging shoes, racquetball outfit, and other sports paraphernalia crammed into the back of his car. He squeals into the lot, leaps out of the car, throws me the keys from halfway across the block and sprints toward the hospital,

hurdling the divider cables along the alley in Olympic style.

I've pulled a few boners myself. For example, making a flippant remark to a customer—who turned out to be one of the county commissioners—that I was going to work my way up from county medical center parking lot attendant to head of brain surgery. Or the time this alluring young woman in a short skirt drove in and so flustered me that I replied: "I'm sorry, but this is a private lot just for exposed thighs."

Much of the time I must appear to be a walking zombie, for people actually have the audacity to disturb me—when I'm deeply engrossed in a good novel or working on some writing or having a delicious fantasy—and want to park their car in my lot. Can't they see that I'm busy?

I try to make up for times like that by relaying a good story I've heard on the radio. One winter's morning after a blizzard, a radio commentator told this one: "Do you know why they call Minnesota the winter wonderland?"

"Because people wonder why we live here in the winter."

I used that line on just about everyone who came in for the next month.

Excuse me. I'll have to go now. Somebody just pulled into the lot and parked a Winnebago in the main aisle.

Frank and Joe's Coney Island

During Minnesota winters on Harmon Place, it's not uncommon, particularly in January and February, to have wind-chill factors of fifty-five below zero. It's like cold fire on your cheeks, the wind. Your eyelashes freeze, and your cuticles crack and bleed.

If, by chance, the temperature happens to rise to a big fifteen above, the contrast is so sharp that people assume it's spring and start acting crazy. Well, this was just such a day, and as I walked toward the bus stop to make a transfer, I found myself thinking of flying kites and going barefoot. When a busload of school children drove by, I knew that it was indeed spring, for a strange compulsion came over me to make faces at them.

It must have also been this midwinter delusion,

this fifteen-above heat wave, that made me stop by Frank and Joe's Coney Island. Frank and Joe's is a greasy spoon seating about ten patrons. Entering the place, I felt as if I should have a tape recorder and some prepared questions for a sort of on-the-road-correspondent report. There's no denying Frank and Joe's Coney Island is, indeed, a special feature.

I figured the coffee was probably safe enough to drink, so I ordered a cup and even decided to take a chance on some apple pie. Anything alive in the pie would be taken care of by the coffee (the coffee being strong enough to stand on its own two feet) and with the grace of God, the empty cup would reveal only the spirit of Zen. (Note the ecumenical metaphor.)

The waitress at Frank and Joe's was overweight and rather badly complexioned, but obviously quite a hit with the regulars. Her suitor, the short-order cook from the grill down the street, smoked Winston Longs with a shaky hand. Their conversation centered on the possibility of juggling shifts for Friday night, so as to get to Mousey's before closing time for a few drinks and whatever. They looked to be a nice couple, really, and I wondered if they went right over to Mousey's in their cooking "whites," or changed clothes first.

Mousey's is an infamous bar replete with hookers, hustlers, fights, and knifings. Next door is the Romp and Stomp (a massage parlor), neighbored by a pawn shop and a temporary labor pool for the unemployed. What I imagine takes place nine times out of ten, although I've never actually counted, is this: Some guy works an eight-hour shift on a temporary assembly job through the labor pool, heads for Mousey's with twenty-two bucks in his pocket, drinks up half his money, goes next door for a little "romping and stomping," spends the rest of his money on a fifteen-dollar coconut oil bath and massage deluxe, but finds out that the "deluxe" is another twenty dollars, leaves drunk and pissed off, coathangers a car window, rips off a camera or a tape deck, pawns it and heads back to Mousey's to drink away the rest of his frustration. A day and a half later, the hangover nearly squelched, it's back to the labor pool to earn some more bucks.

A neat little lesson in ecology.

The pie wasn't really all that bad, and I felt no im-mediate ill effects. I think the fact that it was served on a real plate (the kind that breaks if dropped), rather than packaged within a sealed cellophane pouch encased in a styrofoam box and automated, IBM encoded cardboard—somehow enhanced the flavor.

Still able to walk, I left Frank and Joe's. Outside, Mike Freedom was passing out pamphlets entitled, "I too, used to be a Robot." He has on his beanie cap with a propeller and a sandwich placard vest with warnings of apocalypse amid senescence. His Schwinn is parked in the street at a meter, for with the extra baskets filled with handouts and empty pop bottles, and the rear training wheels, the bike is nearly the size of an automobile. I imagine myself to be like him when I'm fifty-five.

At the bus stop, a young man in some kind of brownish gray service uniform kisses an enormously fat woman dressed only in a slip, bathrobe, and overshoes. She pinches him in the ass and says, "Now don't try to start anything you can't finish."

"That's my trouble," laughed the man, "I always finish everything I start." He twitched his leg, raised his shoulder, and did a little Elvis Presley thing with the left corner of his mouth that seemed to say: "You don't think I'm telling you the truth?"

A plot went through my mind, that this guy was a military man on leave, and had picked up this woman (probably at Mousey's) partly because she reminded him of his own mother (and was quite likely the same age), and partly because he liked to go about things in a "big way."

"You know what I need?" he whispered to the fat woman.

"I can guess!" she laughed. No, I need some new shoes. I went to this one place, but all they got is kid-sized shoes. I need some man-sized shoes. I mean I'm man-sized all over. I got man-sized hands, and man-sized fingers, too. And I've even got a man-sized tongue."

The fat woman let out a screech, as he bent down and licked the inside of her ear.

"And I got one hell of a man-sized . . . "

"Mouth!" the woman interrupted, laughing uproariously.

Just then my bus pulled up.

The downtown Minneapolis skyline as seen from the direction of Harmon Place. St. Mary's Basilica is in the foreground. *Minneapolis Public Library.* Mpls. Collection.

Revelation on Harmon Place

When my mother first learned of my intention to rent an apartment on Harmon Place, in the midst of downtown Minneapolis in an area with a reputation for prostitution, homosexuality, pornography, dereliction and homicide, she was nearly beside herself. I wrote her a letter explaining that my apartment was less than a block away from Billy Graham's Minneapolis headquarters. She was immediately consoled, knowing that her son was under the protective wing of God's secretary-treasurer. For her, it was as if God Himself had a branch office on Harmon Place.

I read recently that Billy's been prodded into revealing more than just the word of God. Not only is his multimillion dollar Billy Graham Evangelistic Association being scrutinized by the Minnesota Commerce Department and the Better Business Bureau, concerning a "gift-annuity plan" and shielded assets totaling $22.9 million, but local tennis players in Loring Park think it is downright unfair of him to use divine intervention to get a court. Shouldn't he have to hang up his racket, just like everyone else?

One might say the streets of Harmon are quite literally paved with gold, with the millions of dollars flowing into Graham's Minneapolis office from Crusade contributions. Then with the boarding up of Don Peterson's Downtown Chevytown's main display room and the locking of the doors to the Pink Poodle Massage Parlor I wouldn't be surprised to see Loring Park transfigured into the Lake of Fire. Harmon's already been closed at Hennepin to begin construction on the twelve gates with the twelve jewels of the apostles. Downtowners are being warned daily of the seven torches of fire, the scroll of the seven seals, the seven angels of the seven seals, the seven trumpets of the seven angels of the seven seals, and of course the seven plagues.

Is Harmon Place about to be resurrected? It is indeed having a conversion experience.

The Closing of Harmon Place

Things had just gotten too weird on Harmon Place. The wide open spaces of urban tenements were being staked out and the rich top soil was blowing right into the bulging pockets of the private developers. As the steam-gilled, fork-toothed, stegosauric trail blazers gouged and stampeded across the land, they trampled whatever lay in their path.

The settlers had circled the wagons, but were defenseless against the snorting, rubber-treaded beasts. This pre-fab formula, specialty shopping mall-mold mentality had blighted the land, jumping claims right and left. Local homesteaders had been ferreted out of their encampments again and again, bowing to Red Barn and Burger King chains, Dinkydales, highrise developments, condos, and greenways. The corner neighborhood joint had been transmogrified into an eating and drinking emporium. Mortuaries were resurrected as restaurants—with grave prices indeed, while the Walker Auto Supply is now a designer court. Dives that had formerly smelled of flat beer and stale tobacco, now reeked of ambience.

I had been sent ahead to scout new territory, as I understood it, and report back my findings. Actually I felt more like a pocket gopher who had poked his head out of his burrow and come face to face with the apocalypse.

With the Scientologists and Pentecostalists at one end of the street and the pornographers and skin-traders at the other, a real battle between the spirit and the flesh had ensued.

Harmon Place was closed down. You got as far as Fifteenth and ran right into the community college. I pondered if this symbolized education as a dead end street, then tried to retrace my steps, searching for a passage or an outlet. I seemed to be trapped in an existential cul-de-sac. Perhaps when you're at the end of the road and up against the wall, the only exit is into life.

Garrison Keillor needs no introduction. We're just glad that he wrote the following piece (which originally appeared in Time *magazine), and that he has so graciously allowed us to reprint it in the pages of* Downtown.

Murray's—The Age of Elegance

BY GARRISON KEILLOR

These perfect fall days make me sad, and there have been so many of them lately in Minnesota. My cure for sadness is, first, to clean off my glasses and, second, to take a fast ride on a bicycle. If that doesn't work, I go to Murray's. The next step is to join the Men in Their 50s Coping with Melancholy group, and I've never had to do that.

Murray's is a restaurant in downtown Minneapolis that's been around longer than I have. In my childhood, there were the Big Three, Charlie's, Harry's and Murray's, and only Murray's survives. It is the sort of grand old joint you find in any big city, restaurants with pink drapes and a 70-year-old coat-check girl and a pianist who plays *Deep Purple* and the waitresses have names like Agnes and Gladys and the menu harks back to the Age of Steak; a place where a fiftyish couple can enjoy a Manhattan and tuck into a chunk of cow and au gratin potato. Murray's serves the Silver Butter Knife Steak for Two. That's the special and it's been around since I was learning to read—I saw it advertised on billboards around town. I'd form the words MURRAY'S and SILVER BUTTER KNIFE STEAK phonetically, and say them aloud as we passed, and the mystery and elegance of them stuck with me.

My parents never went to restaurants. We ate at the homes of relatives—we were sensible people, not spendthrifts or dreamers. Once a year we went to the state fair and had Pronto Pups. That was it. Every Sunday morning, however, my father drove us to church, and the route took us past Murray's, and I would glance up from my Bible and the verse I was

memorizing for Sunday school, and there was Murray's big marquee and the name written out in orange block letters and, above, a sign that said COCKTAILS / DANCING, and over the years, memorizing one verse after another, you build up an intense interest in a place like that. You imagine walking in and finding yourself in a movie—the maitre d' takes your coat and hat and nods toward a corner banquette, and there sits Fred MacMurray, your boss at Acme, stubbing out a Lucky, grinning, and you realize it's all true—you're assistant manager now, you got the big raise, you and Sue and Becky and Little Buddy can move out to Sunny Acres.

I saved up for Murray's for years, and then, when I turned 21, I couldn't go there because I was under the terrible burden of being hip—it took years for that to wear off, during which I ate what hip people were eating in Minneapolis then, ethnic food, most of it awful. I thought of Murray's as a den of Republicans: steaks became (in my mind) politicized. And then, on the very last day of my misspent years in graduate school, my role model and hero Arnie Goldman said, "School's out—what do you say, let's go to Murray's," and so it was cool. We put on our corduroy sportscoats with the leather elbow patches and had dinner, and he ordered us martinis, and the gin made me as witty as Robert Benchley. We swapped timeless repartee for a couple hours and ate liberal Democratic steaks and felt the glow of scholarly brotherhood.

I have gone back about once every three or four years, and the magic seems never to wear off, the

Photographs courtesy Murray's.

sight of the pink drapes, the mirrors, the cadelabrum sconces, the red plush chairs, the candles flickering on the white linen—it still elates me, the Silver Butter Knife feels like a bright sword in my hand. And last year I returned with four old friends and my wife Jenny. It was one of the happiest nights I can remember, everyone yakking and laughing, eating steak, drinking a big booming red wine, feeling flush and lovable. And then I went back one night last week with Jenny and my son and his girlfriend. We strolled in, and I saw the pink drapes, and I felt the old euphoria rise in my heart, and it dawned on me that I had invented Murray's: as a child, reading the words SILVER BUTTER KNIFE STEAK FOR TWO off billboards, meditating on them, I had created a kingdom of elegance more durable than any restaurant where an immaculate young waiter introduces himself and tells you about the broiled marlin served in fennel mustard sauce on a bed of basmati rice and topped with shredded asiago cheese and lightly toasted pine nuts. I would never take out-of-towners to Murray's. Nobody whom I wanted to impress. Only my dearest friends. Only old Minnesota pals who grew up with Murrayism and know it is a symbol of all we hold dear.

On a beautiful fall day, when I recall what was grand and exalted and now is gone forever—the Burlington *Zephyr* and the *North Coast Limited*, the *New Yorker* of my youth, Memorial Stadium where we spent Saturday afternoons cheering for the Golden Gophers, the Earle Browne farm that was turned into a mall and a subdivision—I think of the SILVER BUTTER KNIFE STEAK FOR TWO, looming above me on a billboard, our car stopped at a red light on Lyndale Avenue in 1952, the Bible on my lap open to *Ecclesiastes,* my head anointed with Wildroot hair oil, and I feel restored. Some glories remain. You for sure, and me, perhaps, and, absolutely, Murray's.

Part Two
Downtown Saint Paul

There is no doubt that at some future period, mighty kingdoms will emerge from these wildernesses, and stately and solemn temples, with gilded spires reaching the skies, supplant the Indian huts, whose only decorations are the barbarous trophies of their vanished enemies.

Jonathan Carver,
upon his visit to the
future site of St. Paul
in 1767.

Early St. Paul, looking west from Third Street, 1857. *Minnesota Historical Society.*

Chapter Four

A Brief History
of Downtown Saint Paul

by David Anderson

Father Lucien Galtier's church. *Ramsey County Historical Society.*

The first white resident of that plot of ground we now call the city of St. Paul was Pierre "Pigs Eye" Parrant, that hideously one-eyed French Canadian Voyageur (his blind eye was described by J. Fletcher Williams, St. Paul's first historian, as "marble hued and crooked, with a sinister white ring glaring around the pupil, giving a kind of piggish expression to his sodden low features") who was also responsible for setting up the city's first business establishment, when in June of 1838 he opened up a tavern in the hovel he had built at the foot of Fountain Cave.

Parrant's establishment, strategically located in this high-traffic area (there was a stream flowing out of Fountain Cave which allowed his customers to paddle right up to his door) specifically for the pur-

Fountain Cave, c. 1875. *Minnesota Historical Society.* **Photo by Illingworth.**

pose of selling bootleg whiskey to the soldiers and Indians in and around Fort Snelling, was strictly illegal (Indian agent Taliaferro had expressly prohibited the notorious Parrant from entering Indian territory for any purpose), and like most drug-selling schemes which possess the benefit of being prohib-

ited by law, extraordinarily profitable (one poor addict is said to have paid $80 one cold winter night for a bottle of whiskey that probably cost its pig-eyed purveyor all of a buck!).

By the spring of 1839 business was booming for Parrant and his fellow whiskey-sellers, booming to such an extent, however, that Major Plympton of Fort Snelling had become alarmed by the vast quantities of illicit hooch that his charges had consumed during the previous winter and by what the surgeon of the post had called "the most beastly scenes of intoxication among soldiers of the garrison and Indians in its vicinity."

Soon thereafter Major Plympton and the Army resolved "to immediately adopt measures to drive off the public lands all white intruders within 20 miles of Fort Snelling," and in May of the following year the whiskey-sellers and the Swiss refugees from the Selkirk Colony who had for the last two years settled in their midst, were forcibly evicted from what by that time had legally become reservation lands. Having no option but to move (the soldiers had burned down their houses and destroyed much of their property) the unfortunate squatters reluctantly gathered up what was left of their belongings and moved en mass to that piece of land at the heart of what would one day be known as the city of St. Paul, but would for its first few years be known by a somewhat less euphonious name. Edmund Brissett, a young French Canadian habitué of Parrant's new tavern (after being forced out of his old location, Parrant had opened a new establishment at the foot of what would one day be Robert Street), explained to J. Fletcher Williams how the fledgling settlement came to receive its first name:

> I looked inquiringly at Parrant, and seeing his old crooked eye scowling at me, it suddenly popped into my head to date it [a letter he needed to mail] at Pig's Eye, feeling sure the place would be recognized, as Parrant was well known along the river. In a little while an answer was safely received, directed to me at Pig's Eye. I told the joke to some of the boys and they made lots of fun of Parrant. He was mad and threatened to lick me, but never tried to execute it.

In 1844 Parrant sold his claim at the Lower Landing for ten dollars, and shortly after losing another (in a rancorous dispute with his neighbor, Michel LeClaire), he left town and headed for Lake Superior, though he never got there, "dying en-route," reported Williams, "of a disease resulting from his own vices."

The name "Pig's Eye" lives on, of course, as we now find it attached not only to Pigs Eye Lake and Pigs Eye Island, but also to St. Paul's newest lager, Pigs Eye Pilsner beer. Pigs Eye Pilsner is said to be selling well in England and will soon be introduced in Japan and Russia as well. Perhaps one day the name of St. Paul's founder will be known to the beer-drinking public all over the world. Few people at all familiar with the early history of the city of St. Paul would argue that its original namesake could be remembered in any more appropriate way.

And so if Minneapolis was a city conceived in water power (as the famous old adage used to go), St. Paul was a city born in whiskey, making, according to Williams, "brutes of the white men and demons of the red men . . . there being no knowing what depths of abasement might have awaited it, had not a mighty and powerful moral influence been thrown into the scale against rum—and that was the Christian church."

The Catholic branch of the Christian church arrived to "throw itself into the scale" in the spring of 1840, and was represented in the settlement's early days by the single person of Father Lucien Galtier, a 29-year-old French priest who had been recruited to come to America and minister to the handful of Catholics at Mendota and the new settlement of Pigs Eye. Not long after his arrival, Father Galtier saw to the construction of a rude little log basilica on a spot near Fountain Cave, and in November 1841 he blessed his new church and dedicated it to "Saint Paul, the apostle of nations." Years later, in 1864, he wrote a complete account of the building of St. Paul's first church, and of how he came to rescue his new village from what the historian W. B. Hennessy called "the swinish appellation it was given at the hands of Edmund Brisset."

I expressed a wish at that time that the little settlement would be known by the same name [St. Paul] and my desire was obtained. . . . When Mr. Vital Guerin was married, I published the bans as being those of a resident of 'St. Paul.' A Mr. Jackson put up a store and a grocery was opened at the foot of Gervais' claim. This soon brought the steamboats to land there. Thenceforth, the place was known as 'St. Paul Landing,' and later on as 'Saint. Paul.'

In its early days the newly named little village was largely a French-speaking community whose log houses, tiny hovels and Indian tepees were mostly owned by French-Canadians, Swiss refugees from the Selkirk Colony, Yankees and Indians. Of St. Paul in the year 1843 one chronicler wrote, "It had but three or four log houses with a population not to exceed twelve white people, and was a mixture of forests, hills, running brooks, ravines, bog mires, lakes, whiskey, mosquitoes, snakes and Indians."

With the steady arrival of new immigrants, however, (most of whom arrived via the great Mississippi steamboats), the little village's population gradually increased, reaching 910 souls (including 14 lawyers!) by 1849, the year in which the city was to experience the last of its "arcadian days," that period, said Williams, "when the easy going simplicity of the people, isolated as they were from the fashions, vices, and artificial life of the bustling world," was to give way to the crush of newcomers brought into town by the announcement in April of that year that congress had granted Minnesota territorial status and that St. Paul had been named as its capital.

This flood of immigration brought thousands of new people into the city and is said to have actually *doubled* its inventory of buildings from 70 to 142 in its first three weeks. For a time, people were pouring into the new capital at such a rapid rate that the great paddleboats were disgorging them at the Lower Landing to the tune of five-hundred or more per day!

Inevitably, however, this great crush of newcomers caused prices in the city to rise and the crime rate to go up. The massive influx of immigrants, "many of them greedy for speculation, selfish and unscrupulous," said Williams, "had changed the people of St Paul, transforming their steady going habits and plain manners into a maddening avarisciousness for gold."

By the mid-1850s, speculation in real estate was rampant. Nobody wanted to work. Food actually had to be imported into the city, as it seemed as if every man fancied himself a real estate tycoon and nobody wanted to farm. "This mad, crazy, reckless spirit of speculation" could not, of course, last, and when the Ohio Life Insurance Company failed on August 24, 1857, it set off a disastrous chain of events which led to the inevitable crash. Williams described its devastating effect upon the fortunes of the city of St. Paul as follows:

To St. Paul, this prickling of the bubble of speculation was more ruinous and dire in its consequences than perhaps to any other city in the West. Everything had been inflated and unreal—values purely fictitious, all classes in debt, with but little real wealth, honest industry neglected, and everything speculative and feverish—that the blow fell with ruinous force. Business was paralyzed, real estate actually valueless and unsaleable at any price, and but little good money in circulation. Ruin stared all classes in the face. . . . Everybody was struggling to save himself. The banking houses closed their doors. . . . All works of improvement ceased, and general gloom and despondency settled down on the community. In a few days, from the top of the wave of prosperity, it was plunged into the slough of despond.

Things got worse before they got better (fewer than 20 percent of the city's businesses survived the panic, and its population was to shrink almost in half), though over time, and especially beginning with the advent of the St. Paul and Pacific Railroad in 1862, the city began to rebuild itself upon a more sound financial foundation. The next two decades saw railroad lines being built through the state in all directions, enabling St. Paul, which had developed into their regional hub, to establish itself as a major transportation, wholesaling and manufacturing center. By 1893, when James J. Hill had extended the railroad lines all of the way to the Pacific, St. Paul had secured for itself the status of being "Gateway to the Northwest."

The Railroads, The Trolleys and Early Downtown St. Paul

Beginning around 1850, St. Paul had begun to establish itself as the head of navigation of the Mississippi, the principle point of debarkation for the people and supplies headed for St. Anthony and points beyond. During these years the Upper and Lower levies were the principle engines of St. Paul's economic growth (the fur trade and its famed Red River Oxcarts were, of course, also of great importance until they were put out of business by the railroads), though the inherent unreliability of the river as a mode of transportation (it was often dangerous and always closed for six months out of the year), made it inevitable that the railroads, once sufficiently established, would quickly take their place. Between about 1875 and 1920 St. Paul was a town dominated by the railroad, one which, says Paul Hesterman in his *Ramsey County History* article "The Mississippi and St. Paul," would do whatever it took to establish the city as the commercial capitol of the region.

To establish the city as the commercial capitol of the region its citizens and entrepreneurs vigorously pursued a policy of building a rail system focused on St. Paul. City government subsidized most of the early rail lines with the sale of city bonds, and St. Paul businessmen were prominent investors and officers of the companies The St. Paul Chamber of Commerce worked to facilitate this development and to guide the city's commercial growth. As the rail system grew, businessmen built warehouses to make the transfer of goods among rail, river and wagons more efficient. James J. Hill's transfer warehouse built along the river at the Lower Levee was the most prominent.

Although the railroad was the principle instrument of St. Paul's growth into a major regional trade center, it was also a principle culprit in the destruction of much of the city's considerable natural beauty, especially along the Mississippi river, whose bluffs were chopped off and whose channel was filled in whenever the railroads found it necessary to build more tracks. By 1880 the city had filled, leveled, diverted, chopped up and chopped off so much of the

Downtown St. Paul and adjacent railroad yards as seen from Dayton's Bluff, c. 1925. *Minnesota Historical Society.*

downtown area's once spectacular natural setting that not only were the city's original forests gone, but many of its waterfalls, streams, hills, lakes and wetlands as well. There's little evidence that the city troubled itself much over this wholesale destruction of its natural environs. It's attitude was probably more or less summed up by William W. Howard of *Harpers Weekly* when, in 1890, he said of the city that "St Paul cares about as much for the picturesque and poetic side of the river traffic as she does for the riparian laws of the Hottentots . . . Her interest is one of business."

The photographs from St. Paul's early days demonstrate conclusively that the early settlement was not a thing of beauty. They reveal, in fact, little more than a bleak, muddy and debris-strewn landscape, one in which it seems to have occurred to no one to plant so much as a flower or a tree. The buildings downtown were all made of wood (these early wooden structures demonstrated an alarming propensity to burn down; St. Paul lost fifteen hotels alone during the fifties and sixties, and 34 buildings in a single fire in 1860) and stood in a jumble, arranged in no discernable order on streets which were narrow and crooked and named and numbered according to no discernable

plan. "Never was a city laid out as badly as St. Paul," said the editor of the *Minnesota Democrat* in 1853. "What a maze of confusion—what a labyrinth some portions of our goodly city exhibit," groused the *St. Paul and Minneapolis Pioneer Press* some years later, "streets beginning anywhere and ending anywhere—running into and out of each other at every conceivable angle, but often not connecting with other streets at all."

The simple fact of the matter was that early St. Paul seems to have been platted to no end other than to serve the city's commercial interests. While there may have been other reasons for the city's narrow streets and sidewalks, or even for its complete failure to provide space for alleyways or parks (i.e. its rugged and hilly setting), one cannot help but suspect that such "amenities" were felt by many to be a waste of land that was much better used when it was subdivided and sold for a profit. Early St. Paul was not a city to be bothered with parks, or even with arranging its streets to take advantage of its spectacular river views. The business of early St. Paul was business, and "progress" was the order of the day.

The heart of downtown St. Paul during the 1860s and 1870s was to be found in the Wholesale District

View of early downtown St. Paul featuring the first State Capitol (at center), 1857. *Minnesota Historical Society*. Photo by B. F. Upton.

A storm over downtown St. Paul, July 13, 1890. *Minnesota Historical Society.*

of Lowertown. Stretched along East Third and Fourth streets, the Wholesale District featured narrow streets, three and four-story brick buildings on both sides of the road, and a bustling commercial atmosphere that had become distinctly urban, and that had definitely acquired the feeling of "downtown." It was during this period that St. Paul, its population soaring from roughly 13,000 in 1865 to more than 41,000 by 1880, became a full-fledged modern city, installing its first gas street lights in 1867 (electric didn't come until 1882), water system (1869), sewer (1873), paved streets (1873), telephone service (1877), and horse-drawn trolley system (1872). These horse-drawn trolleys, known widely at the time as "cracker boxes on wheels," seated fourteen and a ride cost a nickel. They traveled at a pace of roughly six miles-per-hour and were running on about twenty miles of track in 1880, when they began to be replaced by cable cars. When living space downtown began to run out in the 1870s, the trolleys made it possible for the city's new immigrants to build its first inner-ring of neighborhoods (West Seventh, the North End, Frogtown,

the East Side and the West Side) and still be able to work downtown. The trolleys also of course made possible the more distant suburban real estate developments that would become such city neighborhoods as Merriam Park (1882), Macalester Park (1883), St. Anthony Park (1885), and Groveland (1890).

By 1893, all of the city's streetcar lines had been converted to electricity, and by 1920, the system's heyday, the car lines served some eighty square-miles of neighborhoods, and were readily accessible to most any resident of the greater metropolitan area. By this time the lines had also long since been extended well beyond both city's limits, running as far as White Bear Lake to the north, Minnetonka to the west, Stillwater to the east and South St. Paul to the south.

The establishment of the trolley lines as a cheap and efficient mode of transportation (once fully electrified, they became, arguably, more efficient than any system before or since) was of tremendous significance to the growth and development of the city. The trolleys funneled thousands of people downtown every day, and made possible the critical mass of department stores, specialty shops, theaters, restaurants, offices and *people* necessary to create the lively and bustling atmosphere that we have come to define as "downtown." The downtown St. Paul of this era—or the downtown of any American city during this era—would have been no more possible without the trolley lines than the Mall of America would be without freeways and the automobile today. It was the trolleys that made possible the huge, acutely concentrated centers we came to call "downtown," just as it has been the automobile that has shaped the suburbs and the "Edge Cities"* in which we live, work and shop today.

The 1880s and 1890s: Downtown Comes of Age

Despite the great depression of 1893, the decades of the 1880s and 1890s were a period of tremendous growth and development for the city of St. Paul. Entering the eighties with a population of only 41,473, by the turn of the century the city's population had grown to 163,000 and its total area had been expanded to its present size of approximately 55 square miles. This population explosion was accompanied by soaring land values and by a building boom which, fueled by speculation and by massive amounts of eastern capital, was little short of incredible. In 1883 alone, $9.5 million was spent on construction projects within the city, fourth most of any city of any size in the nation. By 1889, four years before the crash was to ruin many of them, the city was said to be home to some forty millionaires!

Despite this period of tremendous growth, St. Paul was still in many ways quite raw and undeveloped in the 1880s and 1890s. The air smelled badly (slaughtering houses, rendering plants, and the city dump were among the most egregious offenders); sidewalks were made of wood; streets were muddy and mostly unpaved. Because there were no zoning laws of any kind (they would not come until well into the next century) the downtown environment of this era can only be described as being one of

great extremes, one in which says St. Paul architectural critic Larry Millett, in his wonderful book, *Lost Twin Cities*

Splendor and squalor cohabited on downtown streets in a landscape of startling juxtapositions. Skyscrapers rose next to shanties, elegant retail emporiums overlooked rolling wooden sidewalks and streets choked with mud and manure. Backyard privies stood in the shadow of grand hotels. Although both downtowns by 1890 were densely built up along most streets, blocks tended to remain open in the middle, where a disorderly collection of sheds, shacks, and other outbuildings formed a now-vanished back-alley that might be called the interstitial city. Created overnight as though exploded out of a cannon, downtown St Paul and Minneapolis were also paradigms of a society addicted to change. In this helter-skelter urban world, the shock of the new was so pervasive that no one could escape its electrifying touch. Everything seemed to be moving and changing all at once: great office towers rising out of mud holes, houses wheeling on the streets on their way to new destinations, old monuments falling to the relentless roar of progress.

The 1880s also saw the advent of the "skyscraper" in downtown St. Paul. These early "skyscrapers," though they were in no sense tall buildings by modern standards, were nevertheless impressive for their time, and served as the same monumental symbols of downtown's commercial prosperity that fifty, sixty or one hundred-story structures do today. The first skyscraper to be built in downtown St. Paul (that is, the first commercial structure to exceed the previous limit of five stories) was the seven-story Ryan Hotel, built at the corner of Sixth and Robert in 1885. A number of six-story buildings (including the Chamber of Commerce at Sixth and Robert, the Union Block at Fourth and Cedar and the Bank of Minnesota at Sixth and Jackson) would follow in 1886. For a brief period the ten-story Globe Building at Fourth and Cedar, (1887) was the tallest commercial structure in the Twin Cities. It was soon

---

* See *Edge City: Life on the New Frontier*, by Joel Garreau. Readers of this volume will find this wonderful book of special interest.

topped, however, by the thirteen-story Pioneer Building (1889), which remained the tallest building in the city until 1915. The Pioneer Building and the Germania Bank (1889) are the only representatives of this early group of skyscrapers still standing.

The Pioneer Building, at Fourth and Robert, built in 1889. *Ramsey County Historical Society*

Old Third Street

Prior to the 1880s St. Paul's downtown commercial core was centered on Third Street and bounded more or less by Wabasha and Wacouta. During its prime it featured five banks between Wabasha and Jackson, as well as the majority of the city's older and more established stores (Zabel's Shoe Store, the D. D. Merrill bookshop, Farwell's Hardware Store and Ingersoll's Dry Goods were a few of the more prominent). In addition, the theaters and halls near Third and Wabasha helped establish Third Street as the main center for St. Paul's entertainment and social activities (as did, of course, its virtually numberless saloons), and it was also the street on which virtually all city parades, circuses and Winter Carnival events took place. After gas lights replaced kerosene as the state-of-the-art method of street illumination, the city began the annual custom of celebrating State Fair Week by erecting at intervals, from Wabasha to Sibley, arches of gas pipe which spanned the width of the street, each filled with about fifty gas jets and a pyramid of nine lights at each end. At dusk the gas jets would be ignited, enabling thousands of celebrants to promenade under a spectacular array of flickering lights.

In the early 1890s old Third Street began to change. The retail shopping district moved north to Sixth and Seventh Streets (Schuneman's moved in 1890, and Mannheimer Brothers in 1892), and the commission merchants, second-hand stores and employment agencies began to dominate the blocks west of Jackson. By 1915, however, the commission men had for the most part moved their operations to the market district on Jackson Street, leaving Third Street to settle into a long period of decay and decline.

By 1928 the city had finally decided to stem the tide of Third Street's sad decline, as voters approved the creation of Kellogg Boulevard, a mall which would extend from Jackson Street to Seven Corners and would finally create the wide avenues along the river bluff that many city residents had long desired. Such an avenue had long been needed, as the buildings which had lined both sides of Third Street from the 1870s on had blocked off most of the city from what should have been a spectacular river view. The offending buildings (forty-three in all, including many of the city's most historic commercial structures) were torn down in 1929, finally providing a public viewing ground from which the great sweep of the Mississippi could be beheld.

Looking west down Kellogg Boulevard (old Third Street) shortly after its completion in 1932. The Robert Street crossing is in the foreground. The new City Hall (under construction) is in the distance. *Minnesota Historical Society.*

Interior view of Field, Mahler & Co. Dry Goods, c. 1890s. *Ramsey County Historical Society*

Doorman in front of the Fifth Street entrance to Field, Mahler & Co. Dry Goods (predecessor of Field Schlick). Although the date of this photo is unknown, the Field, Mahler building was constructed in 1890 and designed by E. Townsend Mix. *Ramsey County Historical Society*

Mannheimer Brothers Department Store as pictured in *Northwest Magazine*, February, 1888. *Minnesota Historical Society.* From *Northwest Magazine*, Feb. 1888.

The Department Store

With the exception of the skyscraper, no other phenomenon is more associated with the rise of downtown than is the institution of the department store. The department store as we know it emerged in most American cities during the last two decades of the nineteenth century (St Paul's first true department store was Dickinson's, built on St. Peter between Fourth and Fifth Streets in 1885), evolving from dry-goods stores which sold fabrics and pre-sewn clothing, into massive, multi-faceted shopping emporiums designed to sell all manner of products to the newly liberated woman of the burgeoning urban middle class. The department store's wisely chosen strategy was to treat this "new woman" as their most important customer (most offered special services for their female clientele such as nurseries and restaurants), making their stores safe, orderly, hospitable and, above all, according to urban experts Bernard J. Frieden and Lynn B. Sagalyn in their book *Downtown, Inc.,* . . . magnificent!

Department stores . . . succeeded by making shopping magnificent. Their buildings were often palatial in design, with interior grand courts, rotundas, columned galleries, chandeliers, thick carpets, and polished mahogany counters. Large windows and skylights brightened the shopping areas, window and floor displays were lavish and the huge number of products in one place was like a world exposition where everything was for sale. In Zola's phrase of the time, the department store 'democratized luxury.'

By making downtown more accessible to women, department stores changed shopping forever, transforming, as Frieden and Sagalyn go on to point out, an activity that had once been considered a chore into a form of recreation and entertainment:

> Newly liberated from home and neighborhood, middle class women began to spend hours in town on shopping trips. As the nearby sidewalks turned into promenades, other merchants opened businesses between the streetcar lines and the department stores. Soon long rows of specialty shops, restaurants, and a variety of stores created shopping thoroughfares around big stores. By the turn of the century the heart of most big cities was a popular retail district in which department stores, specialty shops, restaurants and entertainment places all complemented each other.

Schuneman's Department Store, Sixth and Wabasha, c. 1923–1925. *Minnesota Historical Society.* Photo by C. P. Gibson.

Schuneman & Evans

Among the notable accessions to the retail interests of St. Paul during the past year, the most important to all Northwestern people is the opening of Schuneman & Evans' magnificent department store. Messrs. Chas. Schuneman and B. H. Evans, the members of the firm, came to St. Paul a little more than three years ago and engaged in the retail dry goods business, occupying the three story building at Nos. 53, 37 and 59 East Third Street. Their business though comparatively small at first, was remarkably successful and within less than a year it was necessary to build a large addition to the building. It was soon evident however, that the building would not long be adequate to the increasing trade, and preparations were accordingly made for removing to more commodious quarters, and it was then that the project of the present great store was conceived. The location, corner of Sixth and Wabasha streets, is one of the best in the city, for retail purposes; it is equally accessible from all parts of the city, every electric car passing the main entrance. The building, which was erected especially for Schuneman & Evans at a cost of more' than a quarter of a million dollars, is an imposing five story and basement structure of iron terracotta and glass; the total area of the six floors is more than five acres. The store is modeled somewhat after the Fair of Chicago, Macy's of New York, or Wanamaker's of Philadelphia, and is fitted with every modern convenience to facilitate business and add to the comfort of patrons. An idea of the comprehensiveness of the stock may be gained from the fact that there are at present fifty-five distinct departments in the store; this wide range of merchandise includes most everything required to clothe man, woman or child and every article of furniture and house furnishings ordinarily in use. The first or main floor is devoted to the sale of dry goods, shoes, books and stationery, music, jewelry, gentleman's furnishings, notions, underwear, hosiery, etc. etc. On the second floor are kept men's and boy's clothing, millinery goods, ladies' muslin underwear, corsets, cloaks, furs, etc. etc. The third floor is occupied by the carpet, rug and upholstery departments; the fourth floor after March 1st will be devoted to the sale of furniture; the fifth story is used for reserve stock; here also are located the advertising office and mail order department; in the large, light basement saleroom, are generous stocks of crockery, silverware, fine bric-a-brac and cut glassware, pictures and easels, toys, dolls, baskets, trunks and valises, house furnishing goods, kitchen utensils, etc., etc.; a portion of the basement is also used for receiving and shipping goods, in which a large force is employed; in the basement annex are located the steam heating plant; electric lighting plant and engines. The private offices of the firm, are located on the entresol midway between the first and second floor. The ladies' waiting room surrounds the light well on the second floor, from which point a view of the entire main floor and portions of all the other floors are obtained. The counters, shelving and woodwork are of antique oak. It is needless to state that this great store has been a success from the opening day.

St. Paul Dispatch
Souvenir Edition, 1891

The corner of Wabasha and Fourth Street, 1917. The second City Hall and Ramsey County Courthouse is at right. *Minnesota Historical Society*. Photo by C. P. Gibson.

The Twentieth Century

While the downtown St. Paul of the nineteenth century had to quite literally be carved out of the wilderness, the movers and the shakers who set out to create it anew in the twentieth were compelled to tear down the old (or what passed for old in a city founded scarcely three generations before) in order to put up the new. The restless push for "progress" so characteristic of this era ensured that no building, whatever its historic or architectural significance, was safe from the wrecker's ball. Most people during this period could only interpret the destruc-

tion of many of the city's landmark structures as being a sign of "progress," and with no institutions in place to protect them (this was, of course, long before such protections as the National Register of Historic Places), such notable buildings as the Old Cathedral Church, Dickinson's Department Store, the National German-American Bank, the Minnesota Club, Capitol City Panorama, the Metropolitan Opera House, the State Savings Bank, and the St. Paul City Hall—Ramsey County Courthouse were all torn down.

The Paramount and the Orpheum theaters, on Seventh Street looking east from St. Peter toward Wabasha, 1945. *Minnesota Historical Society.*

The first three decades of the twentieth century saw not only the destruction of many buildings, but also the construction of many new and important civic and commercial structures. Among them were the new Ramsey County Jail (1903), the second St. Paul Armory (1904), the St. Paul Auditorium (1906), the Minnesota Historical Society (1917), the St. Paul Public Library (1916), the Hotel St. Paul (1910), The Emporium (1911,1915) and Golden Rule (1915) department stores, the Minnesota Club (1915), the St. Paul Cathedral (1915), the Merchants Bank Building (1915), and the First National Bank (1930-31) which at 33 stories was for many years St. Paul's tallest building. During this period downtown also sprouted many new theaters in its entertainment district (centered mostly along Wabasha and Seventh Street), including the Star (1901), a burlesque house on Seventh and Jackson, the original Orpheum (1906), a vaudeville house at Fifth and St. Peter, the Princess (1910), the Schubert, later known as the World (1910), the Alhambra (1911), the Empress (1911), and the New Palace (later the Orpheum), completed in 1917. Only the World and the Orpheum remain.

By the 1930s and 40s, however, the great depression and World War II had taken their toll (in 1936 *Fortune* magazine had characterized St. Paul as being little more than a decaying, crime infested wasteland, finding it "cramped, hilly and stagnant. Its streets narrow and its buildings small . . . Its slums . . . among the worst in the land"), with this era being far more notable for the buildings it tore down than for anything significant that it put up. Among the many victims of this era were the old City Hall and Courthouse, the second State Capitol, and the Customs House on Wabasha. Each might have been judged worthy of preservation in a later age. But given the exigencies of the depression (many buildings were tax delinquent and became the property of a government which could not afford to maintain them) and the mood of the times, there was probably not a realistic chance that these, or any of the many others lost during this period, could have been preserved.

Demolition of buildings on the southwest corner of Fifth and Minnesota to make way for the new Minnesota Federal Savings and Loan Building. The Ryan Hotel can be seen in the distance at upper right, March 31, 1957. *Minnesota Historical Society.* Photo by *St. Paul Dispatch-Pioneer Press.*

The Decline, Urban Renewal

The end of World War II brought with it, of course, the by now all too familiar phenomenon of suburban flight and the concomitant rise of the regional shopping mall. As millions of middle class city dwellers bought cars, took out VA loans (after the war, the Veterans Administration and the Federal Housing Administration subsidized homes for nearly fourteen million families) and headed for the suburbs, they brought their money and their jobs with them, leaving many of the nation's downtowns—including, of course, downtown St. Paul— more or less for dead.

A sterile and uninviting scene at the intersection of Fifth and Minnesota, July 16, 1975. The building at center is the American National Bank and Trust Co. *Minnesota Historical Society*. Photo by Steve Plattner.

Looking down Sixth Street toward Twin City Federal and the American National Bank, September 11, 1978. *Minnesota Historical Society*. Photo by E. M. Hall.

By 1954 retail sales in downtown St. Paul had fallen some $15 million from what they had been in 1948. Downtown property values had plummeted more than 50 percent since 1930. By 1975, when the federal highway and urban renewal programs had gotten through with them, fewer than 160 of the over 400 stores that had been doing business downtown in 1963 remained.

In St. Paul, the first great wave of urban renewal took place in the State Capitol area. By the time Interstate Highway 94 had finished cutting its swath through the city in 1967, virtually every historic building in the 103-acre renewal-area was demolished (the only exceptions were the buildings in the Capitol complex itself) and virtually all of the old streets destroyed. Not only were the "slums" of the Capitol approach area cleared, but many historically and architecturally significant structures as well. Among the more significant casualties were: The John Merriam House (razed 1964), Trinity Lutheran Church (razed 1952), Central Park Methodist Church (razed 1960), and numerous residential structures such as the Newport (razed 1952), the Virginia (razed 1956) and the Elsinore (razed 1960). Such irreplaceable public spaces as Central Park and Park Place were also lost.

For Sale sign on the Riviera Theater, between Seventh and Ninth Streets on Wabasha, serves as a grim reminder of the decline of downtown St. Paul in the 1970s, as do the empty store fronts on the buildings adjacent to it, 1980. *Minnesota Historical Society.* Photo by Dale Ailport.

By the early sixties, it had become obvious to most people that downtown St Paul, like downtowns all over the country, was dying. In response to this crisis, St. Paul's business leaders put together an improvement committee and hired an array of architects and planners to propose a new "downtown plan." The committee's proposal, known as Capitol Centre, soon became the basis for a comprehensive downtown renewal project which between 1965 and 1970 demolished virtually every structure in the twelve-square-block area at the heart of downtown (notable exceptions were the Endicott and Pioneer buildings). Put up in their place, however, was a drab, dreary and uninspired group of office towers, commercial buildings and parking ramps, all of which were connected to each other by St. Paul's much vaunted skyway system, which, despite its obvious attractions, had the highly unfortunate effect of giving an even more depressing and deserted atmosphere to downtown's already dingy and half-deserted streets. Larry Millett described the overall effect of the skyway system on the ambiance of downtown as follows:

> The skyway system provided welcome comfort and convenience, especially in winter, but was not an unmitigated blessing. The skyways pulled life up and away from the street, damaged historic facades (such as that of the St. Paul City-Hall Ramsey County Courthouse), obscured important vistas (again, a particular problem in St. Paul), encouraged new building designs that were bleak and uninviting at street level. In 1988 that peerless student of cities William H. Whyte, dubbed St. Paul 'the blank-wall capitol of the United States,' after touring the skyway system.

Revival

By the time George Latimer became mayor of St. Paul in 1976, it was obvious to him, as it was to most everyone, that downtown was in desperate shape and that dramatic steps had to be taken if its fortunes were to be reversed. Of particular concern was what to do about its so-called "superhole," that two-block field of rubble at the heart of what used to be the Seventh Street retail district, which had been a source of civic embarrassment to the downtown community ever since it had been created during the heyday of urban renewal. After much debate, Latimer and the city ultimately decided to replace "superhole" with Town Square, a mixed-use development, which, when finished in 1980, covered two city blocks, and allowed shoppers to walk through three levels of stores to its spectacular enclosed rooftop city park (the park features some 250 species of plants and is said to be the largest of its kind in the country). Town Square's retail center is flanked by a hotel on one side, and by two office towers on the other. The entire complex is connected to Dayton's department store and to the surrounding office buildings by tour skyways which are in turn connected by other skyways to 26 additional downtown blocks. Developed through an unprecedented public-private agreement between the city of St. Paul and the Oxford Development Group and the Carlson Companies, Town Square was the city's first major attempt to revitalize downtown by bringing it back under "middle class control," its strategy being to recreate with Town Square the atmosphere of a shopping mall, one in which suburbanites, many of whom hadn't been downtown in years, would feel safe and comfortable, where they could bring their families, and where their teenagers could safely hang out.

While Town Square undoubtedly went a long way towards serving this function (despite its mixed record of success, it certainly has brought more people downtown than "superhole" ever did), it was also responsible for turning downtown even more inward, being, as Frieden and Sagalyn point out, one of the main reasons that William Whyte declared downtown St. Paul to be "the blank-wall capitol of the United States."

> Although Town Square is well connected to downtown at the second-story skyway level, it is not at all inviting at street level. From the sidewalk it has the appearance of a gray-walled fortress. No store-fronts enliven the street, and the most prominent openings are driveways to the hotel entrance and the underground garage. Only a few small doors lead from the sidewalk to the skyway area. . . .The barrier walls at street level are especially disappointing.

After getting off to a slow start in 1980, the Town Square Project gradually picked up steam and by 1984 had achieved 100 percent occupancy. During the next few years city officials and Oxford Executives were encouraged enough by Town Square's performance that they began searching for ways to build upon its modest success, hoping to finally be able to create a critical mass of stores that would give downtown a chance against its many suburban competitors. Unfortunately, neither of its main efforts in this regard, The World Trade Center or Galtier Plaza, another "upscale" mall, located across from Mears Park in Lowertown, was able to accomplish this task. Galtier Plaza was a particular disappointment, opening in a largely vacant and unfinished condition in 1985, and declining steadily into bankruptcy from there. Things had gotten so bad by 1989 that Mayor Latimer was quoted as saying, "It's just delightful," when informed that the city would finally be able to extricate itself from the Galtier fiasco and would lose only $9 million of the almost $26 million it had put up for the deal.

Galtier Plaza, in downtown St. Paul's Lowertown neighborhood. *Randy Jeans.*

The World Trade Center tower. *Randy Jeans.*

The St. Paul Public Library and Hill Reference Library, designed by New York architect Electus Litchfield and built in 1917. *Ramsey County Historical Society*

In 1986 Oxford sold Town Square and most of its other U. S. holdings to Bell Canada Enterprises, who eventually merged it with the World Trade Center and renamed the new entity St. Paul Center. As of this writing, however, both centers are plagued with low retail occupancy rates, casting a pall over the prospects for a true revitalization of retail business in downtown St. Paul. Of particular concern is the recent cancellation of plans for a $43 million makeover of the World Trade Center (its current owners, Principal Financial Group, are looking for a buyer who will be better suited to revive its retail fortunes), and the fact that Town Square, though fully occupied and remodelled, is now no longer so much a retail center as it is a nondescript office tower. Downtown St. Paul's one remaining "selling-point" would appear to be its so-called "Cultural Corridor" which though it has been highly touted by city officials and though it is certainly composed of many distinguished and estimable attractions, could

be seen by a skeptical observer as being "nothing new," and as little more than a new label attached to a group of organizations and institutions, most of which have been with us for a considerable period of time (the wonderful new Minnesota History Center and the Children's Museum being the most significant exceptions).

The concept of the "Cultural Corridor," defined officially by the St. Paul Convention and Visitor's Bureau as being "a new name for the western side of the downtown area," does however seem to be as good a way as any to promote downtown's more than 25 arts organizations, cultural facilities and visual and performing arts groups. Among the most significant of these are: The Landmark Center (an impressive renovation of the turn-of-the-century Federal Courts Building, now used by a number of arts organizations and as an adjunct to the Minnesota Museum of Art), the magnificent Ordway Music Theater, and the St. Paul Public Library, which are all, along with the

The Landmark Center (the old Federal Courts Building) which was one of the 1970s' first preservation and restoration projects, and which reopened with great fanfare in 1979. *Ramsey County Historical Society*

beautifully restored Hotel St. Paul, grouped in a striking setting around Rice Park. Other prime attractions considered by the Convention and Visitors Bureau to be part of the "Cultural Corridor" are: The Science Museum of Minnesota and its Omni Theater, a very popular and truly world-class attraction; the Great American History Theater, located in the Science Museum's original space and across the street from The Science Museum building on Wabasha; the Seventh Place Theater, on the deserted and lifeless "plaza" that used to be the heart of the Seventh Street theater district; the Fitzgerald, (formerly the World) Theater, at Cedar and Tenth Streets (beautifully renovated for Garrison Keillor's "Prairie Home Companion," and a variety of other attractions); the newly-renovated St. Paul Civic Center; the St. Paul Chamber Orchestra; the Minnesota Museum of American Art, and the new Minnesota History Center. A new Science Museum, on the riverfront, is under construction at the time of this writing. It is scheduled to be finished in late 1999.

The Future

In June of 1993 a study commissioned by the city of St. Paul and its Chamber of Commerce found that although the retail world of downtown St. Paul is in considerable trouble, it is not entirely dead. The

The new Science Museum, October 10, 1999. *Cartwheel* © 1999.

$60,000 study, based in part upon a survey of downtown residents and shoppers, concluded that downtown was "not a ghost town," that the loss of Carson's had not significantly reduced St. Paul's overall "drawing power" (the study was occasioned by the loss of Carson's and West Publishing in 1992), and that the Woodbury Outlet Mall and the Mall of America had not had a noticeable impact on downtown St. Paul. One major key to the future of downtown, it said, was to find a way to motivate downtown workers, who currently shop almost exclusively on their lunch hours, to return downtown for shopping and recreation during the evenings and on weekends. It pointed out also, of course, that more St. Paul area residents must be enticed into shopping downtown.

The other major findings and recommendation of the Chamber survey were as follows: 1) Dayton's is the anchor of downtown retailing. "A potential loss . . . of Dayton's is the greatest tangible and direct threat to St. Paul," says the study. It recommends promoting and sprucing up the department store possibly with money generated by the sale of its parking ramp to the city. 2) Downtown parking is perceived by most shoppers—or potential shoppers—as being inconvenient, expensive, unsafe, dirty and out of repair. Clean it up, says the report. Build new facilities and offer free or validated parking. 3) Downtown is perceived to be dirty, dark, uninviting and unsafe. Spruce it up says the report. Improve signs and lighting, dress up vacant storefronts, address safety issues and create a common theme for street signs, trash cans and banners. 4) A large store, such as Target, Wal-Mart or Montgomery Wards should be convinced to open a store downtown. Efforts should also be made to retain and attract other occupants. 5) Strong leadership, especially from the private sector, is needed if these recommendations are to be put into place. The recommendations will be executed in phases and will be paid for by public and private money.

As self-evident as these findings and recommendations might seem, they do serve, if nothing else, to underline the nature of downtown St. Paul's problems. Unfortunately, just like the 1989 plan to revitalize downtown, and a 1990 "Immediate Action Plan," (and probably most of the other plans to come after it, including "St. Paul on the Mississippi," and the most recent, a study by the Gibbs Planning Group of Birmingham, Michigan*), this plan, for all its good intentions, is probably doomed to have a very limited impact, at best. "For the most part it's a very difficult uphill battle," said Kurt Barnard, of Barnard's Retail Study Group. "In most cases plans such as St. Paul's will just slow the deterioration." "All through the years you have all these so-called experts talking about things that were going to make a difference," Richard Witham, owner of Skyway Opticians, told the *Pioneer Press* shortly after the study was released. "Town Square was going to make a difference. The Trade Center was going to make a difference. St. Paul is basically a 9-5, Monday through Friday town. I don't think there's anything anybody can do to change that."

Those of us who would like to see downtown St. Paul returned to at least some semblance of its former glory would love to be able to disagree with Mr. Witham. Unfortunately, given the social and economic realities which underlie the decline, and given what we know about the efficacy of most such plans, it is all but impossible for anyone but the most partisan observer to be genuinely optimistic about the immediate chances for a true revival of the retail fortunes of downtown St. Paul.

The loss in recent years of such corporate tenants as Amhoist, West Publishing and Carson Pirie Scott, and the headquarters of Burlington Northern, combined with the demise of the Athletic Club, Peck and Peck, Nina B. Boutique, Woolworths, Bachman's and Liemandt's (just to name a few) have dealt the downtown retail scene some terrible (if thankfully not quite fatal) blows. These losses, when combined with the failed promises of such glitzy construction projects as Galtier Plaza (its movie theater has just closed, leaving downtown St. Paul without a single movie house) and the World Trade Center (its proposed $43 million makeover has just been cancelled) have done much to diminish the great

---

*This study concluded that downtown St. Paul's shopping district has a $35 million "leak" that could be plugged with the right mix of stores and restaurants, street and skyway improvements and a newer, smaller version of Daytons. It also concluded that downtown St. Paul's main retail market consists of 40,000 workers, 200,000 people who go there on business, more than 3000 residents and 1.25 million visitors.

achievements of the late seventies and the eighties (i.e. Town Square, the Science Museum, the Ordway and the restoration of the St. Paul Hotel and the World Theater), though such recent additions as the Radisson Inn, Lawson Software, the Ecolab expansion, the new hockey arena (for St. Pauls new NHL franchise) and the newly renovated Convention Center are a credit to the administration of Mayor Norm Coleman and do, along with the city's proposed riverfront development (the new Science Museum, the restoration of Harriet Island, possibly a new baseball park), provide hope for the future.

"Riverfront development and downtown development must be one," said Richard Broeker, in a recent editorial for the *St. Paul Pioneer Press*. "A working 'riverfront- downtown' chock full of small, homegrown businesses would evoke the spirited characteristics of the downtown of the 1940s. An integrated waterfront-downtown, of pleasing scale and proportions, would offer a dramatic alternative to the Mall of America, or downtown Minneapolis—an alternative in increasingly short supply."

Given St. Paul's inability to effectively compete with the regional malls, and given that it has little else upon which to pin its hopes, the city of St. Paul and its Riverfront Corporation (an agency launched by Mayor Norm Coleman to promote riverfront development and to help integrate that development with downtown and its surrounding communities) would be well advised to listen to Mr. Broeker when he says that "the key to building a genuine 'waterfront downtown' is restoring the downtown, the waterfront and the Capitol grounds as the single place it was meant to be." The city might seriously consider his proposal for a fixed rail shuttle (a shuttle that could be slung under the Wabasha Street Bridge, connecting the south river bank to the History Center and the Capitol, and looping around Rice Park and Lowertown) that would serve the vital purpose of tying together the ten-by-ten block area from the Capitol to the Mississippi River, thus partially restoring at last a portion of the community fabric so terribly rent asunder by the great gash of I-94, and possibly setting the city upon a course of action that could eventually lead to the rejuvenation of downtown St. Paul sometime early in the 21st century.

Downtown St. Paul as seen from Harriet Island, 1998. *Elcio Rodriguez Filho.*

Chapter Five

Downtown Saint Paul:
The Nineteenth Century

In 1850 the city of St. Paul was still a crude little frontier settlement, scarcely ten years old. It was not at all a thing of beauty (at least it wasn't if one is to judge from the few photographs available), but was, instead, a city that made an "altogether unfavorable impression on the first-time visitor" (at least if we are to believe Mr. J. W. Bond, the chronicler to whom we are indebted for the following account). "A Stranger Sketches St Paul" originally appeared in the Minnesota Pioneer *on February 6, 1851, and subsequently in a book entitled* Minnesota and its Resources, *published in New York in 1853. * It is an invaluable account of life in St. Paul's early downtown, and of that "promiscuous multitude" that daily crowded its "tumultuous streets."*

Red River Ox Carts in front of Cheritree and Farwell Hardware on Third Street, 1859. *Minnesota Historical Society.*

---

*This article also appeared in a book entitled *With Various Voices,* Itaska Press, 1948. The editors of that volume were not aware of the identity of its author, however, and credited it, as did the *Minnesota Pioneer,* to "an anonymous stranger."

A Stranger Sketches
Early Downtown St. Paul

BY J. W. BOND

St. Paul, Minnesota Nov. 5, 1850. A stranger is generally somewhat astonished and not infrequently very much amused at the scene presented for contemplation on his first arrival at the St. Paul Landing. In short, his first impressions with regard to the state of society here are altogether unfavorable. He is welcomed by an unusual and motley group of human beings, gathered from all parts of the Union, the Canadas, the Indian lands, and Pembina, besides the curiously mixed up race of natives. This is indeed a most peculiar feature of the capital of Minnesota, which in respect to its inhabitants differs materially from anyplace I have visited in the west. Being an old settlement of French and half-breeds and the present seat of government for the Territory, situated near the head of navigation and contiguous to the Dakota land, a strange spectacle is often presented to the uninitiated. All the different classes, however, mingle together, forming a singular mass, variously habited, speaking different languages, and distinguished by a variety of complexions, features and manners. Yet all this appears quite common, and excites no curiosity among those who have resided here but a few months.

But how different the spectacle appears to the stranger and visitor. Chained, as it were, by a spell of astonishment, he pauses a moment to view the scene, before setting foot on shore, to mingle in the promiscuous multitude. A variety of persons attract his attention. Merchants in search of newly arrived goods; editors, anxious for the latest news; citizens, receiving their long expected friends from the East or South; carmen and coachmen with their teams,

all, indeed, join in the tumultuous strife and enjoy the excitement. A little removed from the crowd may be seen another class, which by the way is too numerous for so small a community as that of St. Paul. This is composed of a host of lawyers, politicians, office-holders and office-seekers, whom we may perhaps call refugees from other States, though actuated by the hope of gaining some honorable position and a share of the public spoils. They are discussing very boldly, perhaps, a subject pertaining to the Territorial Government, or the late doings of the long Congress.

Amid the busy crowd may be seen the courteous and sociable Governor Ramsey, conversing freely with his fellow citizens, or politely receiving General A., Colonel B., or some other distinguished personage just arrived. Close by the side of his Excellency a Dakota, Winnebago or Chippewa warrior strides along as boldly and quite as independent as the greatest monarch on earth. He is attired in a red or white blanket, with his leggins and mocasins fantastically ornamented with ribbons, feathers, beads, etc., while his long braided hair is adorned with a number of ribbons and quills, his face is painted with a variety of colors, giving him a most frightful appearance. In his hands he carries a gun, hatchet and pipe. As the noble fellow moves along, so erect, so tall and athletic in his form, a feeling of admiration involuntarily fills the stranger's mind. He pronounces the Indian warrior the lion of the multitude, and is forced to respect his savage nature. The eye follows him along till he joins, perhaps, a company of his own tribe, some of whom are quietly regaling themselves at the end of a long Tchandahoopah,* others gazing at the white man's big canoe. Now the astonished gazer beholds a group of dark-eyed squaws, some carrying their heavy burdens, others with papooses on their backs, with their bare heads sticking above a dirty blanket. The little things may be sleeping and as the mother walks carelessly along, their heads dangle about as though their necks would break at every step. They sleep on, however, and do not heed the scorching rays of the sun shining in their faces. The stranger, having become satisfied with the contemplation of such and similar scenes, at length concludes to debark, and soon he too becomes one of the promiscuous multitude. He soon forgets the oddities that so much excited his curiosity among us. He finds a great multitude of French half breeds and Dakotas; yet the character is decidedly Eastern. The Redmen, who are now so numerous, will ere long flee away before the influence of civilization, while the native French, half-breed, will be absorbed by an Eastern society. In short, every thing is fast partaking of a Yankee spirit, and yielding before the influence of Yankee enterprize.

Improvements are going on in Saint Paul with an astonishing rapidity. A great change is noticeable every month: but the greatest change that has taken place of late is with regard to churches. Three months ago all the houses of public worship to be seen here were the Methodist house, a very commodious brick building, besides an old Catholic church built of logs. Now we have, in addition to these, a Presbyterian house which would not compare unfavorably with those of Chicago, and the Baptist and Episcopalian, all of which are ready for public services. They occupy the most prominent points in the embryo city and can be seen from a great distance in approaching the town from the Southeast. We consider the building of so many churches, in so short a time, a good enterprise, indeed, for a place two years old, and containing only twelve or fifteen hundred inhabitants.

The restraining influence of the churches here is already felt to a great extent, notwithstanding the number of each denomination is small. The Methodists, who organized a church in December, 1848, and built the first Protestant Meeting House in Minnesota, have now about fifty members, being the largest of any denomination in Saint Paul.

The Presbyterians and Baptists organized churches nearly all the same time last season. They have, for the most part, held their meeting in school houses and other inconvenient places. Their new houses being nearly completed, they hope soon to exchange their places of worship. for these that are large and more convenient.

As yet we have no very good schools in Saint Paul, owing to the mixed state of society, and newness of the place. The prospects, however, are very encouraging, as we have a free school law, and a community anxious to carry it into effect. The district schools are now being organized under the provisions of the late act. The pioneer teachers were ladies sent out from the East by the Board of National Popular Education. Two of these teachers have taught here a long time and had charge of our schools almost entirely. We have now a good many teachers, and those who are, we trust, competent to conduct either the common schools, now being organized, or higher institutions, as soon as they are needed. Our hope for the future prosperity and greatness of Minnesota is founded upon her school system, which if properly carried out, will doubtless make her truly the New England of the West, as far at least as education is concerned.

*Tchandahoopah, is the Dakota name for their pipe, which is from two to three feet in length. The lower part, or howl, is made of the red pipe stone found on the Sioux River; the stem is made of wood.

The First Sidewalks

Our Side-Walks—Under the efficient guardianship of the City Fathers, our town is now becoming liberally supplied with good wooden sidewalks—a great convenience to the pedestrian. The best one in the city is that in front of the Catholic Chapel. This is broad and of *stone,* which is more substantial and better than those of other material. Bishop Cretin, in all of the improvements he has made, and they are not a few, has sought to combine beauty with durability. With none has he succeeded better than with that referred to above.

St. Paul Pioneer Press, 1854

Dance at the Capitol

Our city had the honor yesterday of a visit from several hundred Winnebagoes, with their squaws; and during the day they paraded the streets in all the gaudy finery, which is the sure token that they have recently been in the receipt of government annuities. Most of the chiefs and braves, with Little Hill at their head, were in a party, and during the afternoon a grand dance took place in front of the capitol.

Quite a number of ladies graced the official realms of the Governor and Secretary with their presence. In order to obtain a view of the proceedings, the Capitol steps were crowded, and the lawn in front was thickly covered with Indians, some of whom were in their gayest dress, and others, and not a few of them, as nearly naked as they could be. The dancers, about fifty in number, occupied the centre space of the lawn; around them a ring of braves were seated, and behind them a circle of squaws, papooses, etc. Two Indian and one American flags, were stuck in line, at proper distances, in front of the Capitol, and before them sat the band, which thumped drums and blew whistles with unceasing energy. The dance was protracted for nearly or quite two hours, and formed a wild and exciting scene which can hardly be described.

St. Paul Pioneer Press, 1855

Offal Debate

At the meeting of the City Council, on Tuesday evening last, a proposition was made by an individual to clean the streets, cart off all dead animals, and remove all offal from public houses and private dwellings. A compensation was demanded, and this gave rise to a debate which resulted in suspending the final consideration of the matter until the next meeting.

We think that this is a matter which our citizens should at once take hold of. It is an absolute necessity as a sanitary measure, and all the influence which can be brought to bear, should go towards it adoption and authorization. The city needs the regular cleaning proposed, and especially at this season of the year, it can hardly be a question of a small amount of money, which should be permitted to stop that which tends directly and practically to be the maintenance of the city's health. Quite enough has been paid by the corporation for expenses growing out of disease contracted in impure localities, and it is well worth considering whether it would not be a matter of economy to put in practice the measure proposed. Nothing, certainly, can be lost by it, and if it is true that an ounce of prevention is worth a pound of cure, we think it but the proper duty of our City Fathers to set up this as one safe-guard of the city's health.

If this proposition is accepted, as we hope it will be, it will induce the necessity for the passage of an ordinance requiring housekeepers to provide receptacles for offal, and to place them where the City Scavenger may have ready access. It is the practice in the eastern cities, and does admirably. We have no doubt that our citizens will give their hearty approbation to the measure itself, and further its enforcement in every way.

St. Paul Pioneer Press, 1855

Those Onions on Bench near Roberts street, should be thrown into the river. They are not adding to the health of the city in their present location. Will the Marshall take a peep around that corner?

St. Paul Pioneer Press, 1854

Mark Twain visited Minnesota on three occasions, twice as a traveler, and once as a platform speaker. Though he had planned a trip to the upper Mississippi as early as 1875, it was not until April, 1882, that his first such trip was finally undertaken. The great writer arrived in St. Paul for the first time on a cold and windy Sunday morning on May 21, 1882, and though his first impression of the city was a decidedly unfavorable one (he had left a tropical New Orleans only ten days before and was appalled by the cold, snowy weather he had found in the northern river valley), he soon decided that St. Paul, despite this rather considerable drawback, was "a wonderful town."

The result of Mark Twain's 1882 journey to the upper river (his other two trips were in 1886 and 1895) was his famous book, Life on the Mississippi, *in which, among his many other observations, he recorded his opinions of Minnesota and its two principle cities. Although the chapter on Minnesota is hardly vintage Mark Twain, and although in it he touches only briefly on the subject of the two downtowns, it is well worth reading, if only to find out what one of America's greatest writers thought about us at a time when the two cities were growing so rapidly (they were growing so fast, said Twain, "that pretty soon a stranger will not be able to tell where the one Siamese twin leaves off and the other begins"), and also for his famous philosophical dissertation on whiskey, that "great van-leader" of culture, and the "earliest pioneer of civilization."*

Speculations and Conclusions on Early St. Paul

BY MARK TWAIN

View of downtown St. Paul, featuring the second State Capitol (at center), c. 1890. The second State Capitol served as a storage facility after it was abandoned in favor of the current Capitol. It was torn down in 1937-1938. *Minnesota Historical Society.*

We reached St. Paul, at the head of navigation of the Mississippi, and there our voyage of two thousand miles from New Orleans ended. It is about a ten-day trip by steamer. It can probably be done quicker by rail. I judge so because I know that one may go by rail from St. Louis to Hannibal—a distance of at least a hundred and twenty miles—in seven hours. This is better than walking; unless one is in a hurry.

The season being far advanced when we were in New Orleans, the roses and magnolia blossoms were falling; but here in St. Paul it was the snow. In New Orleans we had caught an occasional withering breath from over a crater, apparently; here in St. Paul we caught a frequent benumbing one from over a glacier, apparently.

St. Paul is a wonderful town. It is put together in solid blocks of honest brick and stone, and has the air of intending to stay. Its post office was established thirty-six years ago; and by and by, when the postmaster received a letter, carried it to Washington by horseback, to inquire what was to be done with it. Such is the legend. Two frame houses were built that year, and several persons were added to the population. A recent number of the leading St. Paul paper, the *Pioneer Press,* gives some statistics which furnish a vivid contrast to that old state of things, to wit: Population, autumn of the present year (1882), 71,000; number of letters handled, first half of the year, 1,209,387; number of houses built during three-quarters of the year, 989; their cost, $3,186,009.

The increase of letters over the corresponding six months of last year was fifty per cent. Last year the new buildings added to the city cost above $4,500,000. St. Paul's strength lies in her commerce—I mean his commerce. He is a manufacturing city, of course—all cities of that region are—but he is peculiarly strong in the matter of commerce. Last year his jobbing trade amounted to upward of $52,000,000.

He has a custom-house, and is building a costly capitol to replace the one recently burned—for he is the capital of the state. He has churches without end; and not the cheap poor kind, but the kind that the rich Protestant puts up, the kind that the poor Irish "hired girl" delights to erect. What a passion for building majestic churches the Irish hired girl has! It is a fine thing for our architecture; but too often we enjoy her stately lanes without giving her a grateful thought. In fact, instead of reflecting that "every brick and every stone in this beautiful edifice represents an ache, and a pain, and a handful of sweat, and hours of heavy fatigue, contributed by the back and forehead and bones of poverty it is our habit to forget these things entirely, and merely glorify the mighty temple itself, without vouchsafing one praiseful thought to its humble builder, whose rich heart and withered purse it symbolizes.

This is a land of libraries and schools. St. Paul has three public libraries, and they contain, in the aggregate, some forty thousand books. He has one hundred and sixteen schoolhouses, and pays out more than seventy thousand dollars a year in teachers' salaries.

There is an unusually fine railway station; so large is it, in fact, that it seemed somewhat overdone, in the matter of size, at first; but at the end of a few months it was perceived that the mistake was

Assumption Catholic Church (built in **1874**) whose twin spires dominated the **St. Paul** skyline for many years, 1886. *Ramsey County Historical Society*

distinctly the other way. The error is to be corrected. The town stands on high ground; it is about seven hundred feet above the sea-level. It is so high that a wide view of river and low land is offered from its streets.

It is a very wonderful town, indeed, and is not finished yet. All the streets are obstructed with building-material, and this is being compacted into

St. Paul's second Market House, located on the north side of Seventh Street between Wabasha and St. Peter, replaced the city's first Market House (built in 1853) in 1881. On Saturday morning—market day—it was descended upon by thousands of buyers and sellers—so many, in fact, that soon many other markets were needed in other downtown locations for supplemental use. The Market House burned down in 1915, taking with it over 100,000 library books (the Public Library was located on its upper floor). The St. Francis Hotel and the Palace Theater (later the Orpheum) was built on its site in 1917. *Ramsey County Historical Society*

houses as fast as possible, to make room for more—for other people are anxious to build, as soon as they can get the use of the streets to pile up their bricks and stuff in.

How solemn and beautiful is the thought that the earliest pioneer of civilization, the van-leader of civilization, is never the steam-boat, never the railroad, never the newspaper, never the Sabbath school, never the missionary—but always whisky! Such is the case. Look history over; you will see. The missionary comes after the Whisky. I mean he arrives after the whisky has arrived; next comes the poor immigrant, with ax and hoe and rifle; next, the trader; next, the miscellaneous rush; next, the gambler, the desperado, the highwayman, and all their kindred in sin of both sexes; and next, the smart chap who has bought up an old grant that covers all the land; this brings the lawyer tribe; the vigilance committee brings the undertaker. An these interests bring the newspaper; the newspaper starts up politics and a railroad; all hands turn to and build a church and a jail—and behold! Civilization is established forever on the land. But whisky, you see, was the van-leader in this beneficent work. It always is. It was like a foreigner—and excusable in a foreigner—to be ignorant of this great truth, and wander off into astronomy to borrow a symbol. But if he had been conversant with the facts, he would have said: Westward the Jug of Empire takes its way.

This great van-leader arrived upon the ground which St. Paul now occupies, in June, 1837. Yes, at that date, Pierre Parrant, a Canadian, built the first cabin, uncorked his jug, and began to sell whisky to the Indians. The result is before us.

All that I have said of the newness, briskness, swift progress, wealth, intelligence, fine and substantial architecture, and general slash and go and energy of St. Paul, will apply to his near neighbor, Minneapolis—with the addition that the latter is the bigger of the two cities.

These extraordinary towns were ten miles apart a few months ago, but were growing so fast that they may possibly be joined now and getting along under a single mayor. At any rate, within five years from now there will be at least such a substantial ligament of buildings stretching between them and uniting them that a stranger will not be able to tell where the one Siamese twin leaves off and the other begins. Combined, they will then number a population of two hundred and fifty thousand, if they continue to grow as they are now growing. Thus, this center of population, at the head of Mississippi navigation, will then begin a rivalry as to numbers with that center of population at the foot of it—New Orleans.

Minneapolis is situated at the falls of St. Anthony, which stretch across the river fifteen hundred feet, and have a fall of eighty-two feet—a water-power which, by art, has been made of inestimable value, businesswise, though somewhat to the damage of

---

The Temperance Tide

A Public Procession Last Evening, Followed by Another Large Meeting at the Opera House.

The temperance procession last evening was certainly the largest and most imposing demonstration of the kind ever seen upon the streets of St. Paul, and the large number of persons who thus gave public evidence of their faith in the temperance cause was certainly highly complimentary to Mr. Doutney, under whose auspices the affair was conducted. The procession was formed in Rice Park, and headed by brass band paraded the streets indicated on the programme published yesterday morning. A considerable number of clergymen took the lead, and they were followed by several hundred men in all conditions of life, including quite a sprinkling of men who have sacrificed all but their lives to the intoxicating bowl. The rear of the column was tapered off with young men and youths in their teens. The whole line extended over a distance of five or six blocks, and fully a thousand persons of all classes took part in the cold water demonstration. A string of carriages containing ladies and children brought up the rear, while the sidewalks all along the route of march were lined with the interested spectators of a scene the likes of which was never before seen in this section of the country.

St. Paul Pioneer Press, 1877

the Falls as a spectacle, or as a background against which to get your photograph taken.

Thirty flouring-mills turn out two million barrels of the very choicest of flour every year; twenty sawmills produce two hundred million feet of lumber annually; then there are woolen-mills, cotton-mills, paper and oil mills; and sash, nail, furniture, barrel, and other factories, without number, so to speak. The great flouring-mills here and at St. Paul use the "new process" and mash die wheat by rolling, instead of grinding it.

Sixteen railroads meet in Minneapolis, and sixty-five passenger-trains arrive and depart daily.

In this place, as in St. Paul, journalism thrives. Here there are three great dailies, ten weeklies, and three monthlies.

There is a university, with four hundred students—and, better still, its good efforts are not confined to enlightening the one sex. There are sixteen public schools, with buildings which cost five hundred thousand dollars; there are six thousand pupils and one hundred and twenty-eight teachers. There are also seventy churches existing, and a lot more projected. The banks aggregate a capital of three million dollars, and the wholesale jobbing trade of the town amounts to fifty million dollars a year.

A steamboat as pictured in *Harper's Weekly*, December 7, 1878. *Ramsey County Historical Society.*

A native of St. Paul, Alice Montfort Dunn's roots in the city stretched all of the way back to the 1880s where as a young girl she lived in the old Windsor Hotel, located at Fifth and St. Peter in downtown St. Paul. The hotel was owned by her father (her grandfather was James Wickes Taylor, American Consul at Winnipeg from 1870 to 1893) and as one of the city's most prominent such establishments, put the young Miss Montfort at the very heart of the fledgling city's social, economic and political life.

Young Alice was a most perceptive observer, and, as you will soon discover, took full advantage of her strategic position (both downtown and as a member of one of the city's most prominent families) to observe the manners and the mores of the inhabitants of early St. Paul. Her vivid and colorful recollections (originally arranged for publication in the Spring, 1952 issue of Minnesota History *by her son, James Taylor Dunn, and reprinted here with his permission) constitute an invaluable contribution to our understanding of social life in the early days of the city.*

The Windsor Hotel, located at the corner of Fifth and St. Peter, c. 1890. *Minnesota Historical Society.*

People And Places In Old St. Paul

BY ALICE MONTFORT DUNN

Alice Montfort Dunn. *James Taylor Dunn.*

As a child and a young girl, I lived much of the time with my aunt, Mrs. Frank Summers, in my father's hotel, the Windsor, located at Fifth and St. Peter streets where the St. Paul Hotel now stands. In the 1880s, when I lived there, it was a spot of historic interest—in a sense the political center of Minnesota. Convention after convention was held there, with one wing given over to the Republicans and the other to the Democrats. Strange to say, harmony reigned over all. Once I heard a man trying to bribe a senator. In an apparent burst of indignation, Mr. Senator said in a Stentorian voice, "Sir, how dare you insult me! I am an honest man," and then almost in a whisper, unaware of the little girl standing behind a pillar, he remarked, "My coat is hanging in the lobby, you can put the money in the pocket."

In the dining room a table in the corner was reserved for the bachelors—Stone Gorman, Dr. George Coon, Dr. Cornelius Williams, Judge Westcott Wilkin, Orland Cullen, my handsome Uncle George Montfort, and others. Celebrated authors frequently dined at the Windsor—Ignatius Donnelly, Hamlin Garland, Sir Gilbert Parker, who came to St. Paul to visit his brothers, and hosts of others. When he played in St. Paul, the actor Richard Mansfield always engaged the entire first floor wing on the St. Peter Street side of the Windsor. He was not very tall, quite English in appearance, and arrogant and dictatorial. But he could be very nice when he was pleased.

The hotel's main dining room was long and had plate-glass windows on one side. Each window had a border of stained glass, fruits, flowers, birds, etc, set in lead designs. A wide strip of crimson carpet ran the entire length of the room. A separate dining room had curtained booths lining the walls. All in all, the atmosphere was cheerful, cozy, and happy, conducive to good digestion. And such an enormous amount of food to choose from! The menu listed oysters and little neck clams in season, appetizers, three varieties of soup, fish, four or five entrees, and a similar variety of meats, salads, and desserts. In addition, a small decanter of wine was served to each individual. The price—seventy-five cents! I once heard woman say to her son, "Peter, stop drinking water. I didn't pay all that money to have you fill up on liquids."

Each evening the city's hotels featured itinerant musicians, usually playing the harp, violin, cello, and flute. Italian songs and excerpts from operas were given, as well as such favorites as "Old Black Joe" and "Old Folks at Home." In addition, typical songs of the day, such as "Daisy Bell," "My Sweetheart's the Man in the Moon," "Where Did You Get That Hat?" and similar selections made up the repertoire of these traveling musicians.

Chairs on the sidewalk in front of the Windsor were always occupied by men who did not sit up straight, but tipped back in them. I do not know how they managed to keep their equilibrium. Young girls who passed by found the experience very disagreeable; it was almost like running the gauntlet.

Two blocks south of the Windsor Hotel was Third Street, now Kellogg Boulevard. This was the city's fashionable promenade and main thoroughfare. About four in the afternoon the local boys and girls would gather to walk up and down crossing from one side of the street to the other as they window shopped. Two jewelry stores were especially interesting—Theodore B. Myer's and Edward H. Brown's—just below Bridge Square at Third and Wabasha—for they displayed superb rings, necklaces, and brooches. Obed P. Lampher's hats, caps, shirts, and men's furnishings were to be seen on Third Street, and located there also were Daniel D. Merrill, of the St. Paul Book and Stationary Company, the Misses Julia and Martha Jones' millinery shop, Russ Munger's music store, and James V. Steen's art shop, one of the best we ever had. Our old friend, Charles A. Dibble, had a small clothing shop farther down the street on the corner of Cedar. I thought it lots of fun to sit on one of the round revolving stools they had all through Mannheimer Brothers' store on Third and Minnesota streets, and dizzily whirl myself. I can still see Junoesque, handsome Mrs. Cushman K. Davis there, with diamond rings up to the knuckles of every finger except the thumb, and on her ample bosom a watch pinned with a gold fleur-de-lis. Chisleft's shoes were great to behold. At one time I bought a pair of bronzed leather boots that made me the envy of the girls. They came nearly to my knees and had large round pearl buttons all the way up.

Herman Grote's Tivoli restaurant at Bridge Square was an attractive resort built out over the bluff on the south side of Third Street and affording a lovely view up and down the Mississippi. The building itself was quite historic because it was one of St. Paul's first brick structures and had been used at various times as a post office and newspaper printing plant. The vine-covered platform surrounding the Tivoli was very German in appearance. At the small tables, with red and white, and blue and white checked cloths, lager beer and real German food were served. It was pleasant to saunter down Third Street on a warm Friday evening, listening to the music featured at Grote's—Seibert's Orchestra, the Great Western Band, and others. Readers at the Public Library in the Ingersoll Block across the street had a box seat to these performances. I am sure that the Tivoli was perfectly respectable, but for some reason I was never invited to go there, except a few times with Papa.

Farther east on Third Street was Louis B. Smith's candy and fruit store—an after-school meeting place for the young. Another favorite spot was the Ryan fruit and confectionery shop on Robert Street across from the Rand Hotel. This spectacular fruit and candy store during the 1890s was moved by its proprietor J. George Smith up the block on Sixth Street into the Chamber of Commerce Building, adjoining the then new Metropolitan Opera House. Huge baskets of luscious fruits—pineapples, pomegranates, bananas, oranges, Malaga grapes, and other exotic edibles—were displayed on a sloping stand set in a large window. All the baskets were different. Some had high twisted handles tied with enormous wired bows and bright red, purple, or yellow tulle; some were fisherman's baskets with open lids; others were shaped like trunks and were covered with steamship labels or European hotel stickers. Above the entrance to Smith's shop, extending from the second story, Cupid sat in a pink shell, driving six pure white doves. He sported a blue girdle, and the reins he held were all the colors of the rainbow. Inside the shop, the counters were piled high with candies, mixtures of a thousand colors, and with candied fruits in round boxes edged with frilled paper. The fruit came from the French Riviera, for California was not yet in the business. To the rear, there were small marble-topped tables, each in a glass candlestick, in which one day all the candles would be red, another yellow or lavender. To top it all, S. George Smith served delicious homemade ice cream. My favorite was peach, with great chunks of the fresh fruit all through it. Here, too, was once exhibited the new Edison Kinetoscope, called "The living picture in motion." Culturally speaking, this was a step ahead of the dime museums near Seven Corners.

Some distance up from Seven Corners was the descent from Summit Avenue which led streetcars

Downtown St. Paul as it appeared looking south from Merriam's Hill. *Ramsey County Historical Society*

down a very steep hill from where the cathedral was later built. That was where the cable car ran. Early in the afternoon of January 27, 1888, during the St. Paul Cable Car Company's first week of operation and in the midst of Winter Carnival festivities, the grip car's brakes failed and from the top of Selby Avenue it and the passenger car plunged at an unmanageable and terrifying speed down the precipitous hill, jumping the tracks at the Third Street curve. Several people were seriously injured and badly burned. Young Louis Robert had his arm torn off and 48-year-old Merville L. Saunders was killed. I asked my friend Mrs. Warren S. Briggs, who at that time lived along the curve of the hill, if she remembered the frightful accident. "Remember it?" she

answered, "I certainly do. The injured were brought into our home because my husband was a doctor, and Mr. Saunders died on the sofa in my parlor."

On Seventh Street, which was called Fort Street above Seven Corners, were located the city's dime museums—amusement places which provided great thrills for boys and girls. There were to be seen the freaks of the day—Jo-Jo the dog-faced boy, sword swallowers, ossified and tattooed men, and numerous malformed creatures who held a great fascination for the youngsters. There, too, one could see a series of fast-moving photographs by looking through a small aperture and turning a crank after inserting a nickel in a slot. These pictures were

View of Third Street during the Winter Carnival in 1886. Picture from *Northwest Magazine*, April, 1886. *Minnesota Historical Society*.

mostly amusing. They depicted young women jumping up on chairs to escape tiny mice, ladies lifting their skirts above their ankles as they crossed muddy streets, little girls playing with dogs, and similar simple situations. I suppose these pictures were the forerunners of the movies.

There was also roller skating, a popular pastime, in a large structure called the Exposition Block, on Fourth Street between Wabasha and St. Peter where the Medical Arts Building and Field-Schick are now located. During January, 1885, the entertainment

given at the Exposition Skating Rink was a fair with booths representing different countries, somewhat similar to our present day Festival of Nations. In fact, it was called a "Carnival of Nations."

A side room was fixed up as a Turkish corner with a deep, three-cornered, rug-covered seat and ornamental Orientals draped over spears at the front and side. I was sitting a distance away in another corner. The lights were very dim so I was not seen when one of St. Paul's famous beauties and a man with a perfectly enormous nose drifted in. I was then and there initiated into the mysteries of ardent love making and a proposal of marriage such as no author has penned. I was almost afraid to breathe for fear of being discovered; and I certainly did not want to miss a word. The climax was reached when he dramatically fell to his knees and kissed her hands over and over again, begging her, "Darling, say yes. She promised to give her answer soon. Months passed, and finally their engagement was announced, much to my relief.

The midwinter festival of February, 1886 saw the first Ice Palace adjacent to Central Park, a tastefully laid out enclosure of some twenty acres near the present-day state capital. Uncle Delos Montfort was the villain of this celebration—the first of the Fire Kings. The Carnival of January 1887, however, was undoubtedly the most exciting and beautiful ever held. That was really a palace worth having, with its massive walls and towing 140-foot turrets; it was bigger, more elaborate and impressive than the palace of 1886.

During the lengthy festivities there were all kinds of sports and wonderful parades which the many toboggan and snowshoe clubs participated. Some of the floats were truly works of art, and the prize winning Windsor float, in which I rode, was lovely. Lengthwise seats were filled with pretty girls dressed white and blue striped blanket suits and wearing blue Tam O'Shanters. At the back of the sleigh were three half-opened sea shells lined with pink. A canopy over the top was light blue with a white fringe and the sleigh was drawn by eight white horses sporting enormous blue feather plumes on their heads. The men also wore blanket suits the same color as the women's, only they had on stock caps instead of Tam O'Shanters and walked in a double file on each side of the float. At night they paraded with confident, elastic step through the illuminated streets of St. Paul swinging kerosene torches over their shoulders. Mrs. Earl Goodrich Lee (she who was Jane Wood) has recently shown me a diary kept by Charles J. Ingles when he was a twenty-four-year-old clerk at the St. Paul Public Library. He thought that the Windsor float was the finest of them all. "It represented a ship of blue and white," went his description, "with a canopy of the same colors. Two swans, restrained by blue ribbons, and driven by a little child, were at the prow.

The float was filled with handsome young ladies in uniforms of blue and white, all reclining on beautiful white fur robes."

A newspaper reporter in the special Carnival edition of the *St. Paul Dispatch* made official the public's enthusiastic reaction: "There are the Windsors," he writes, "in the loveliest float that St. Paul ever saw, one that easily grasps the prize from all competitors. More than three queens are in this barge, for every Windsor girl seems a queen in blue and white."

When the Fire King rode through the streets of St. Paul in his chariot drawn by three elks, the people who thronged the streets were delighted. The Indian encampment near the Palace where gaudily dressed and painted aborigines performed their war dances, was a unique, fascinating, yet terrifying sight. The 1886 celebration was the first Winter Carnival ever given in the United States, but the 1887 Carnival was the best of them all. As I have said, the Palace that year was the most imposing with its high, crenellated, hundred-foot Norman tower and handsome doorway. The storming of the castle and the mock battle between the Fire and Ice Kings, the beginning signaled by the loud explosion of a bomb, was a grand spectacle. It was especially magnificent when Vulcan set his torch to the great walls of ice, and streams of fire poured out from the tower and red lights shone through the clear blocks, while smoking, colored fireworks skyrocketed overhead to turn night into day!

Within easy reach of the Windsor Hotel was Rice Park, the square which the St. Paul Public Library now faces. It was very pretty in the 1880s. Centering from a large fountain of cast iron representing a boy clutching a goose by the neck, gravel paths and beds of colorful flowers spread out through the park. Band concerts were given there each Friday night in the summer, and people in every imaginable kind of equipage would draw up alongside the square or drive slowly past as they listened to the music. There were phaetons with fringed canopy tops, buggies with horses wearing elaborate fly nets and cute little caps on their ears, elegant landaus with uniformed coachman on high seats in front and sometimes footmen at the back, dogcarts, tandems drawn by two and sometimes three horses hitched one in front of the other, commercial hired hacks in which the driver operated from a high seat in front and the riders occupied two seats facing each other below. One hack driver was Jock, who drove for S. B. Cook and Son from the Union Depot, near its present site, to the Windsor Hotel. Since he knew my father well, he would sometimes call out to me, "Little girl, don't you want a ride?" And proud as Punch, I would ride in state two or three times around Rice Park.

Lower Town, just beyond Smith Park, now in the heart of the St. Paul wholesale district, was a fashionable residential section in the 1880s. My dear friend Mice Pope and her sisters, Gussie and Elsie, lived in that neighborhood with their mother and grandfather. They were granddaughters of the famous Henry H. Sibley, who had been a general in the Civil War, commanded the military forces sent to quell the Indians in the Sioux Outbreak of 1862, and served. as the first governor of Minnesota after it became a state in 1858. Loads of boys used to call on Alice at the Sibley mansion on Woodward Avenue. At nine o'clock Grandpa Sibley would shake the coal stove furiously. At ten, he noisily wound the tall grandfather clock. After that hour, poor Alice was on pins and needles for fear Grandpa would appear at the top of the stairs in his long white nightshirt and stocking cap to demand in a loud voice, "Young woman, do you and your guests realize how late the hour is?"

Many of my friends and relatives lived in the neighborhood of Irvine Park just west of Seven Corners and two blocks south of Fort Street. Though it was so close to the St. Paul business district, the park was as secluded as a suburb. No road passed through it, and the families who lived there made their own laws socially speaking, and established their own social customs. It was well understood that within the park precincts, no lady need put on her bonnet to make a friendly call. She might, if she chose, even wear her sewing apron. Without fear of censure or disapproving glances, she could tie up her head in a kerchief when she sat in the park or visited across the nearest back fence. The park and many of its stately houses remain, though most of the families who lived there in the 1880s have removed to other parts of the city.

Many brilliant and distinguished people lived on Irvine Park and the adjacent streets. Captain Henry Carver and his daughter Helen, a Vassar graduate, always most punctilious in speech and manner, lived on Walnut Street. Across the street from them was the home of Joseph L. Forepaugh, set in a beautiful garden, the pride and joy of the entire neighborhood. When I was a wee mite I often pressed my face against the high iron fence around Governor Alexander Ramsey's Exchange Street house, where a grand queen lived, his daughter Mrs. Charles E. Furness. I always expected to see her appear with a crown on her head. Her daughters still reside in the great gray stone mansion on the edge of Irvine Park. Many other interesting people whom I did not know lived on or near Irvine Park, and others with whom I had a slight acquaintance; the Bigelows, D. R. Breed, Miss Annie Semple, and Mrs. Samuel Robbins.

Directly opposite Lawyer Horn's house on Irvine Park, my beloved great-aunt, Mrs. William A. Spencer, lived. In her pantry there was always an enormous pitcher of lemonade to pass around to the neighborhood children along with sandwiches, cookies, and cake. On a hot summer's day a long hill back of the house was a thrilling place to roll down. Aunt Nettie, with her hair always in a smooth water wave, not a strand out of place, was so placid, calm and serene; I wonder if she could have kept that serenity in this day of rush and hurry. During any illness, neighbors took turns tending the sick. Aunt Nettie was invariably the first to appear. When people entertained, all the neighbors pitched in and helped prepare the refreshments.

Aunt Nettie Spencer was noted for her light, flaky, delicious cakes, and her chicken salad in which only white meat was mixed with hearts of celery, a few bard-boiled eggs, and mayonnaise made with oil beaten drop by drop with a silver fork. Critics of taste and discrimination declared that her apple pies had a special charm of their own. She was also celebrated for her brandy peaches. A temperance worker once dined with her before giving a lecture. When she asked him if he would have some more peaches, he said, "No thank you, madam, but I will take a little more of the juice, if you please." Governor Ramsey introduced this speaker at the lecture by saying, "Mr. So-and-So is an old friend of mine. Many is the drink we've had together." The speaker, quite perturbed stirred uneasily, until the governor added, "I drink the whisky and my friend drinks the water."

Aunt Nettie was the heroine of another story. At times the peaceful Irvine Park neighborhood would have its intruders. Far below, under the bluff, lived the O'Rourkes and O'Hoolahans. Occasionally the small members of these families climbed by round-about paths from their dusty, hot shacks to the cool shade of the park. But they knew they were tolerated only as long as they were on their good behavior, and that no bird-nesting or stone-throwing would be permitted.

One day a new tribe of small Berserkers appeared, and in open defiance of the unwritten laws, sent one of their number up a tree after a robin's nest. Promptly Aunt Nettie appeared in front of her house. The boy was bidden to come down and cease operations forthwith. It was evident they were newcomers for they mocked at my aunt, laughing at her as the boy climbed higher and higher. A moment's pause and she turned and disappeared with the house. An instant later down her front walk Aunt Nettle marched with stately tread, her shoulders squared, her head high as one who goes forth to war. In her hands was a large, long-handled ax, the edge of which she was tying in a bloodcurdling fashion, glancing from time to time toward the boys.

As the awesome figure appeared, a hush stole over the group. The boy above stopped climbing, and those below looked at one another in dismay. She didn't speak a word, but marched steadily forward until, as she reached the park, wild panic fell upon the culprits. The climber slid down in hot haste regardless of trousers, and with yells of fear they rushed headlong from the park. The next morning Aunt Nettie was seen passing lemonade and gingerbread over her back gate to those same boys, binding them by vows (which were well kept) to let the birds nest in peace.

Great-grandmother Langford divided her time between two of her daughters, Mrs. Spencer and Mrs. Governor William Marshall. Even as a child of three I can recall the awe and admiration that filled me when I was in her presence. She was the sweetest, most attractive old lady I have ever known; her snow white hair was dressed with three curls on each side of her face, and she wore an enormous cap of thin material, stiffly starched, and with two streamers that hung down to her shoulders. Her complexion, even when she was well over ninety, was free from wrinkles, fresh pink and white—not from a box either. Her maiden name was Chloe Sweeting, and the Sweeting apples were named for her. The apples are pink and white too. She raised thirteen children and never lost her keen sense of humor and her gift for making friends.

On her birthday it was customary for all the old settlers to pay their respects, bringing gifts. On that day her rooms were filled with flowers. Papa always gave her a bottle of whisky and when no one was looking she would call him over to her. As he leaned down she would whisper, "Charles, your present was the very best one I had. Of course I only take a little drink once in a while for my stomach's sake." The way she said it, with a sly wink, was charming.

Yes, my mind often reverts to Irvine Park. I can never catch a glimpse of butterflies fluttering over red butterfly-weed without remembering a bunch of it which grew on the north side of the old park. The common old columbine, too, I always associate with the wooded slope.

As the years have brought an increasing knowledge of life in a large city I have a feeling of thankfulness that my early days were spent in a real neighborhood, a kindly little community where large yards, vacant lots, and parks gave breathing space—where there were friendliness and kindliness and the good life.

Bridge Square, looking down Third Street from Wabasha, 1871. *Minnesota Historical Society.* Photo by Illingworth.

In its early days virtually all of downtown St. Paul's buildings were made of (and heated with) wood. Because of this, the threat of fire was constant, and large and devastating fires were common. (St. Paul's worst fire occurred in March of 1860 when 34 buildings on old Third Street—now Kellogg Boulevard—went up in flames.) On May 17, 1870 there was another terrible fire on Third Street, this time at the tailor shop of the brothers August and Charles Mueller. The story of that fire, of the brothers harrowing escape, and of the great impact the conflagration was to have on their lives and the lives of their families, is told in the following article by the daughter of August Mueller, Mrs. George R. Becker. The story that she tells is of interest not only because of the lively and exciting account that it provides of the fire, but also because of the fascinating details that it provides about life in early downtown St. Paul, and about the manners and the mores of the people of that day. Mrs. Becker's article, entitled "Memories of Early St. Paul: Perilous Escape From Fire Down Eighty-foot Bluff," originally appeared in the Fall 1973 issue of Ramsey History.

Memories of Early St. Paul:
Perilous Escape Down Eighty-foot Bluff

BY MRS. GEORGE R. BECKER WITH GEORGE A. REA

In 1870 my father, August Mueller, with his brother Charles, owned and operated a tailor shop located on Third Street (present-day Kellogg Boulevard), which at that time was the heart of St. Paul's business district. It was near the site now occupied by West Publishing Company, and their establishment was located on the top floor of a three-story building. The weather was cool and windy on the afternoon of May 17, 1870. The windows in the shop were closed, the coal burning stove was going strong and the Mueller brothers, just back from lunch, were busy with their work. A shipment of some bolts of cloth, probably men's woolen suitings, had just arrived. The two tailors may have been drowsy, just after lunch, or maybe their thoughts were elsewhere. They were soon to be married to two sisters, Augusta and Louise Albrecht.

One of the brothers may have stopped stitching to put more coal on the fire, and may have passed close to the window. At any rate, he said to his brother, "Listen, don't you hear somebody shouting in the street below?" "It's just those boys from the business college yelling and fooling around now that school is over for the day," his brother may have replied. Byant and Stratton Business College was located across the street on the north side of Third Street.

One of the brothers opened the window to hear what the boys were shouting, and he heard them shouting, "Fire! Fire! Fire!" They were pointing to a blazing fire coming from the livery stable next door. Then he noticed that their own building was on fire. The brothers ran for the small hall which was the anteroom to their shop. From it the stairway led to the first floor. They saw at once that a thick, black cloud of fumes and smoke was pouring up the stairway. Their only means of escape was on fire. So they ran to the windows facing the steep bluff overlooking the river.

First one, then the other climbed out on the sill. They realized that if they jumped they might be killed. Spectators on the bluff below shouted, "Don't jump. Wait until we put up some ladders!" The fire department had raced their horse-drawn engines and hook and ladder rig to the site and were placing ladders against the side of the bluff, but the ladders were many feet too short.

By this time, flames were bursting out of the stairwell, and the heat, the fumes, the smoke made breathing almost impossible. The front of the building was ablaze. There was only one chance—the two men would have to jump out of the back windows facing south onto the river. It was a drop of eighty feet down the almost vertical sandstone bluff. If they stayed in the building, they knew they would be suffocated or burned to death. They hung by their fingertips to the window sills as long as they could. Then, one after the other, they dropped to the slopes below.

Miraculously they were not killed. However, they both were so severely injured that it was thought they would not survive. In the meantime, the wind had tossed huge, fiery streamers of burning straw and hay from the livery stable fire onto the houses of squatters who lived nearby along the edge of the Mississippi river, forcing them to evacuate their possessions. The injured men were placed on some mattresses which had been hastily discarded during the panic. Later they were taken by wagons to the home of their sister and brother-in-law at 45 Mississippi Street, about a mile away.

The heat from the fire had been so intense that windows were broken and paint blistered on buildings across the street. The building where the Mueller

Third Street, the heart of early downtown St. Paul, between St. Peter and Wabasha, 1866-67. *Minnesota Historical Society.* **Photo by Illingworth.**

tailor shop was located was damaged so severely it had to be razed. After the fire was over, the body of Mrs. Ella Topley, a dressmaker who had her shop on the second floor of the building, was found. As she had no immediate relatives, she was buried in Oakland Cemetery in the family plot of George Siebert. My father pointed out her grave to me some years afterwards.

My father and my Uncle Charles were in such critical condition due to internal injuries, that they stayed at the home of their sister and brother-in-law all that summer. The lives of both men were greatly affected by the injuries they sustained. Charles married Augusta and was able to return to tailoring, but he was always handicapped by poor health and he died in 1885.

August, my father, had suffered a broken arm during his fall, his right hand was crippled, and one elbow was stiff. He could not continue to work as a tailor. Late in 1870, he went to Chicago to see a bone specialist. His arm was re-set, but the operation did not relieve his disabilities.

For a while, he ran a fruit and confectionery store on Jackson Street, near Seventh, in the hope of being able to recoup some of the heavy financial losses from the fire. Soon after his marriage to Louise Albrecht, they established a fancy goods store, aided by the advice and encouragement of Louise's brother, Ernst, who was the founder of Albrecht Furs. Louise was an accomplished needle woman and she took orders for knitting, crocheting, and embroidery work while August waited on trade and did the stamping.

The stamping of material—all done by hand—was used in the process of transferring patterns for embroidering on cloth. It left a light blue pattern on the fabric, similar to the machine-made stampings on cloth today. After the patterns were made, the stampings were reproduced from them onto the cloth.

The Mueller Fancy Goods Store was first located on Jackson between Sixth and Seventh Streets. About 1880 it was moved to 191 East Seventh Street. There were living quarters above this store and this was one reason my parents decided to move. I was born above the second store in December of 1885. My uncle, Ernst Albrecht, continued to give my parents invaluable assistance. Not only did he give them advice, but on his yearly trips to the world fur market in Leipzig, Germany, he bought goods which could be sold in the fancy work store—A music box in the form of a lady seated at a piano playing the "Blue Danube Waltz" was part of the first consignment of these imported toys ever to reach the Northwest.

It is now at the Minnesota Historical Society and it still plays. German toys were much sought after and my parents' shop must have been a busy place, especially around Christmas. Without Uncle Ernst Albrecht's help, it is certain that my parents' store would not have succeeded as well as it did.

I remember our neighborhood vividly. On the corner of Sibley and Seventh Streets stood Collier's Drug Store, with tall red and green lamps in the window. Next door to the west, there was a tobacco shop run by a Mr. Tengler. Out in front of his store, instead of the usual cigar store wooden Indian, there stood a huge wooden, painted figure of Atlas carrying the world on his shoulders. Next to that was Schugard's wallpaper and picture framing store. Then came my parents' store, and above it, our home.

Behind us, on the corner of Eighth and Sibley, was Dr. Pomeroy's veterinarian barn and livery stable. On Seventh Street at the west end of the block, at Jackson, was Allen's Drug Store.

There was a great demand for "fancy work" materials at that time. Almost all the ladies of a household in those days were accustomed to working with colored silk, woolen knitting materials, or cotton thread. They embroidered designs or monograms on tablecloths, luncheon tray cloths, napkins, pillow cases, and sheets.

They knit all sorts of useful garments, especially woolen socks and stockings, caps and scarves. They tatted or crocheted anti-macassars, tablecloths, bedspreads. They had a great deal of time on their hands, as most of the housework was done by maids. It was a poor household which did not have a "hired girl" who was paid about $30 a month, plus room and board. They were on duty from morning to night, did the washing and cooking for the family, and had a holiday on Thursday afternoons and Sunday mornings. Thus, the ladies of the house, in order to keep busy, did a great deal of fancy work, the raw materials for which were supplied by my parents' shop, among others.

Another reason young women kept busy with fancy work was that in those days there were few occupations deemed appropriate for women. They generally had three choices—marriage, teaching, or nursing. Working as maids, waitresses, cooks, or as clerks in department stores was done only out of economic necessity. Very few girls worked in business offices; those who did usually were stenographers.

Most of the entertaining for young people was done at home. The young man was invited to dinner several nights a week, if there was a prospect that an engagement might be forthcoming. The social customs of those days were strictly observed. For instance, it was considered undesirable for a young man to give a young lady, even if they were engaged, anything that might be considered "support," such as articles of clothing, fur coats or muffs, or gifts of food. Flowers, books, jewelry, and candy were the acceptable presents, giving rise to the saying, "First the watch and then the ring." The watch was usually given at Christmas and the engagement ring around Valentine's Day, with the wedding planned for June. Boxes of candy, dried fruit, bananas, and oranges, such as my father sold in his fruit and confectionery store, were popular presents for young ladies. A girl would be considered "fast" if she ate dinner at a public restaurant, such as Carling's Uptown. It was, however, thought proper for her to have an occasional meal at a hotel dining room, such as at the Merchants or the Ryan Hotel, especially if she were travelling.

As department stores came into being, my parent's business diminished, and about 1900 they sold out and built a home on Dayton's Bluff.

I remember that it took a half hour to walk from our new home to the old Central High School at Minnesota and Tenth. I don't recall ever taking the cable. The standard school girl costume consisted of a winter-weight suit of woolen underwear, long black wool stockings, high-button shoes encased in sturdy four-buckle overshoes, and a black or dark blue woolen suit, the skirt having a "mud flounce" to protect the ankle-length skirt around the edges. Over this suit jacket, I wore a heavy woolen winter coat that reached to my calves, or an astrakan lamb finger-length jacket on more dressy occasions. My winter outfit was completed with the addition of a heavy knitted wool hat or beret-fashioned cap called a "Tam-O'-Shanter," and a woolen scarf which was long enough to wrap around my neck and then cross over for double protection under my coat. Thus warmly dressed, I walked back and forth to school every day. My good health in subsequent years undoubtedly was helped by these hourly walks during my early years. My school books and homework papers were carried in a leather strap fastened with a brass buckle. I always had a nickel in one pocket for "rain money," so I could take the horse-car tram if necessary.

As our high school classes were over by 1:00 p.m., I didn't eat lunch at noon but waited until I returned home. Often, I carried a small sandwich and a piece of cake or fudge, wrapped in wax paper, to eat at the 10:30 recess.

As I look back over the years I can only surmise how our lives might have been different if there hadn't been that fire in 1870 with its near-tragic consequences. Yet, we still managed to make the most of life, despite circumstances.

Back in the winter of 1887, E. V. Smalley, the well-known editor of Northwest Magazine, *took up his pen to write an article for that magazine's special Winter Carnival issue (this was on the occasion of the city's second Winter Carnival; the first had taken place the previous year), an article entitled, simply, "A Cold Day in St. Paul." In this piece Mr. Smalley takes us on a winter tour of his beloved city, providing us with an invaluable trip down the streets of its early downtown. Mr. Smalley was a fine and perceptive writer who was possessed of excellent descriptive powers. We are much in his debt for the following account.*

A Cold Day In St. Paul

BY E. V. SMALLEY

A flash of rosy light comes from the East. In the deep valley of the Mississippi all objects are wrapped in the pearl-gray veil, which flushes as the light falls on it from above. As the day dawns, a tile column of blue smoke can be seen rising as straight as though they were of solid substance, so still in the cold air. There is a steel blue color on the snow-covered roofs, indication of an unusually low temperature. All sounds are heard with surprising distinctness—the bells on the milkmen's horses, the rumble of distant trains, the tramp of early pedestrians on the crusty snow. Doors are opened with a creak and a snap. The curious citizens come out to look at their thermometers, hung under tile shelter of the porches. Thirty degrees below zero! In the warm houses, with their double windows, storm doors and furnaces there is no hint of the severe cold, save on the thickly frosted panes.

How curiously still the air is! When you first go out, you feel no chill. You doubt the record of your thermometer, the atmosphere is so mild and pleasant. In a few minutes, however, you feel a little biting sensation in your ears and you pull down your fur cap. Then there comes a peculiar aching sensation. In the middle of your forehead, and down comes the cap still lower, until your eyes look out from just below its warm border. The end of your nose stings a little, and you thrust it into the beaver collar of your overcoat, first on one side and then on the other. Now you are quite comfortable, and you can laugh at the utmost efforts of Jack Frost, who can do no more than cover your beard with ice and make stalactites in your mustache. How invigorating is the still, crisp air! Everybody walks with a springing step. In their muffling, with little of their faces visible save their eyes, you would hardly recognize your best friends if you were not familiar with their fur coats. You distinguish them as you distinguish animals, by the color of their hides. Here is A. in his new mink coat, very proud of it, too; tells you it cost him a hundred and twenty-five dollars. There goes B. in his buffalo—a "silker," he would have you know, always very rare, these soft fine-haired buffalo skins, and not to be had at all now. "Wouldn't trade it for a mink," he assures you. This is C., the bank-cashier in a beaver, and with him is D., the successful real estate speculator in a seal skin that must have cost him a good three hundred at least. Next comes F., the editor, whose musk-rat coat he thinks is about as good as mink, although it cost only one-third as much. The hack-driver, his vehicle hung by the wheel-less axles upon four runners, wears a bear skin that comes down to his feet; that cardriver's coat is of Japanese dog skin. Your neighbor, the railroad man, is arrayed in Russian lambskin, the wool curled to resemble Astrakhan. Thus, in time, you come to know people by their external garments. How much of casual, cold-weather conversation is about these fur coats! Men who would never think of mentioning their ordinary clothes will chat with

Downtown St. Paul on a winter's day, c. 1925. *Minnesota Historical Society.* **Photo by C. P. Gibson.**

great interest about this, that, or the other kind of fur, where it comes from, how much it cost, how to keep the moths out in summer and so on.

The streetcars are rarely obstructed, for the snow is dry and is easily pushed from the tracks by the scrapes hung in front of the wheels. Formerly, every car had a little stove on the front platform and connecting with it was a register that admitted the hot air to the interior. This winter a new plan of heating has been adopted and a small stove in a sort of zinc-lined box stands in the car on one side occupying about the room of one passenger. Many people think the old plan was best, for the car when crowded is usually uncomfortably warm, especially to passengers wearing furs.

In the car the passengers compare the records of their thermometers and no two of them ever exactly agree. They ask each other how their furnaces are working and talk of the price of coal. The car-wheels make a ringing, musical sound on the rails. You cannot see out of the window because of the accumulation of frozen moisture from the breath of the passengers. The sun is well up now and the streets are flooded with brilliant light, but there seems to be no warmth to it. At noon the mercury has risen a little, but it does not go above twenty, and towards evening it falls again. Trade goes on briskly in spite of the cold. The streets are musical with sleigh-bells and with the metallic sound of the sleigh runners on the hard snow. In the afternoon the ladies are out shopping, wearing sealskin cloaks or cloth cloaks lined with fir, their heads muffled up with soft, knit fabrics, their cheeks red enough now without the aid of art.

You walk home to avoid the crowded streetcar and to enjoy the brisk life of the streets. Your breath is like puffs of steam from a locomotive; your blood seems to rush through veins and arteries at an unusual speed; you feel an exultant sense of vital force. Once off the stone pavements of the business streets, the board sidewalks snap and creak under your feet and from the sides of the houses come sharp reports like pistol shots, produced by the contraction of the wooden walls. The walk seems much shorter than it used to seem in the summer and fall, and what an appetite it gives you for your six o'clock dinner! How pleasant seem the warm rooms, after you have hung up your fur coat in the hall, pulled off your arctics and settled yourself in your big easy chair by the fireside. Every sensible man has at least one fire in his house that he can see, no matter how efficient may be the furnace in his cellar.

Only the languages of cold countries possess the beautiful, the incomparable word home. In warm countries life is too much outdoors for sentiment and deep attachment to gather around the domicile. The Italians say la casa mia, which means only "my house." The French recognize fire as the center of domestic life reverence le foyer—the hearthstone. We of English speech have a word that means at once house and hearthstone and family and all tender domestic ties of home.

There are many compensations for the rigors of our northern winters in the pleasures of the household and of social life. Nowhere else are such pains taken to make the home cozy and attractive. Southern houses, even those of wealthy people are finished and bare in comparison with northern interiors, with their fur rugs, their many pictures, their warm carpets and cushions. In our northern winter homelife there is much reading of magazines and books, the piano is rarely silent a whole evening, neighborly calls are frequent, and whist parties and progressive euchre parties are favorite forms of social diversion. A prudent man always looks to his furnace the last thing before going to bed. When you have done this you may, perhaps step out on your piazza to take a glance at your thermometer. "Down to thirty-two below—going to be the coldest night of the season," you say. You glance at the white street, where the moonlight sparkles on the myriad crystals of the snow and up to the heavens, where the stars seem to shine with a supernatural brilliancy. A sound of sleigh-bells and of laughter comes round the bell striking the hour in the distant steeple seems close at hand; the whistle of a locomotive far off in the valley is as loud as though it were but a block or two away. How the snow creaks under the tread of a passer-by. But the keen night air nips your face and makes light of your heavy clothing; so you shut the outer hall door and the inner door, and return in a moment from the arctic regions of the outer world to the tropics of your warm parlor.

In August of 1889 an anonymous correspondent for the newly established magazine of St. Paul "high society" called The Eye *(*The Eye *billed itself as "a journal of society, literature, drama, fiction, politics etc.," though a perusal of its few extant issues shows it to have been at least equally interested in the purveying of gossip, scandal and racist cartoons), took a stroll down old Third Street for the purpose of reporting back to its readers on "the person-alities of the town as seen every day." Though the modern reader might find himself offended by the snooty and elitist attitudes so shamelessly purveyed by* The Eye *(its primary audience was, after all, "the Four Hundred," an exclusive list of St. Paul's wealthiest and most promi-nent citizens), he will, if he is at all like me, be eternally grateful that it saw fit to send "The Stroller" down old Third Street on that hot summer's day of over a hundred years ago. Reading "Down Third Street" is the closest any of us will ever come to walking the streets of early downtown St. Paul. We would be well advised to accompany its author on his "stroll."*

The northwest corner of Third and Wabasha, showing the Warner Block, 1887. *Ramsey County Historical Society*

Down Third Street:
Personalities Of The Town As Seen Every Day

by "The Stroller"

It is a hot August afternoon, the new court house bells have just chimed out four o'clock in unmelodious peals, and the city lies baking in the rays of the hot summer sun. On Third Street all the town is abroad—that is, all the town which is not lying negligently in hammocks by the lakeside, or riding in whirling tires upon a summer jaunt. Pedestrians are hugging the shady side of the street, and the roadway is filled with handsome carriages with gaily-attired occupants. A peripatetic springing-cart is wending its way slowly down the hill, deluging the hot paving of cedar blocks with rivulets of water; at the crossings ladies are pausing irresolutely before launching themselves upon their heels into the thin coating of mud; the narrow pavements are crowded with a well-dressed throng, strolling or bustling along on business, as the case may be. The sight is indicative of the day, of the hour, of the place. Third Street is a curious street—curious, firstly, because in no two places between Sibley Street and Seven Corners is it of the same width; secondly, because it is composed of two distinct parts, the one alive, the other dead—the former the great retail district between Sibley Street and Wabasha Street, the later, west of Wabasha Street. It is a cosmopolitan street, and it is, par excellence, the fashionable promenade of the city. It is to St. Paul what Broadway is to New York, Chester street to Philadelphia, Pennsylvania Avenue to Washington, Piccadilly to London, and *Boulevard des Italians* to Paris. It is not a pleasant promenade; but it is all St. Paul has, and it is the only place where one may go upon a search for someone and be tolerably sure of meeting him; it is not more of an artery than Seventh Street, but it is infinitely more convenient of location to the places of importance, and sooner or later, every man, woman and child who has occasion to come downtown will find himself, herself or itself on Third Street.

Starting down the street from Bridge Square, one meets people whose faces and names are familiar friends, even without an introduction. Here, coming out of the Second National Bank, is D. A. Montfort, white-mustached and erect, the very personification of the banker. As we walk behind him, admiring his trim figure and assured carriage, we can better imagine him as a dashing cavalry-officer, perhaps but his whole air is that of the successful man of affairs—his success indicated, moreover, by the fact that he has aged but little in the last decade.

A little further on we step aside to allow stalwart Judge McCafferty to pass by. Here is a man who is every inch a man—and he has a good many inches, too, both circumferentially and vertically. His frank eyes and pleasant smile must inspire confidence in the most suspicious, and I am sure that one cannot look upon him without feeling cheered by his manly and resolute bearing. Right behind him comes Judge Wilkin, a little bent by years, perhaps, but with the same kindly glance in his blue eyes, and the same gentleness of bearing which years ago endeared him to every heart.

And now, in quick succession, come Col. Crooks, J. W. Willis and C. D. O'Brien. They are all good Democrats and have fought the battles of their party hand-in-hand. They are men who cannot be dismayed, and they are, each and every of them, leaders born.

While watching them go by, I hear the rattle of chains and the clatter of horses' hoofs, and I turn just in time to catch the flash and glare of an elegant equipage in which are seated Mrs. Reginald Du Puy and her pretty younger sister, Miss Greve. They lean back luxuriously, and are holding sunshades in their hands, the horses are trotting at a fast pace, and it is but a fleeting vision; then they are gone. But a moment afterwards Miss Borden drives by in her well-appointed victoria. The carriage stops at a retail shop lower down, and she alights.

I believe that it was the Empress Eugenie who said that she could always tell a lady by the way in which she alighted from a vehicle. While this assertion is rather sweeping, there is not doubt of the fact that an attentive observer can detect the grace of a lady to the manner born.

While pausing a moment at the corner, I see speeding towards me the rockaway of Mrs. Kirby Barnum and the victoria of Mrs. Theodore Sendmeier. They are nearly abreast, and not far behind is a T-cart containing Harry Foster and his young wife.

And now I am bewildered by the procession of vehicles. Here comes the big white horse of General Sibley. But the sturdy old general is not with his rosey-cheeked little grandchildren, who crowd the vehicle. Then comes Ex-Governor Ramsey in a buggy, Mrs. W. H. Lightuer and her children in a rockaway and Mrs. Corlies in a victoria.

I turn about just in time to see Judge Brisbin and his golden-haired adopted daughter coming up the street hand-in-hand. It is May and December in verity, and the sight is a charming one. The Judge clings to the good, old fashion in attire and courtliness, and looks as though he had just stepped out of a picture of one of the conservative members of the F. F. V.

And now come another pair—sometimes referred to as Damon and Pythias—Johnny Merriam and Willis Hopson. Their afternoon promenade is from Jackson Street to Wabasha Street, and they are inseparable. A little farther on I meet Byrd Hewitt coming up the street at a good swinging pace, and shortly afterwards, his brother Walter in a hansom. There is this peculiarity about these brothers. One never rides, the other never walks.

As I pass the Manheimer Block, I observe issuing from the entrance two well-known men. The first is tall and magnificently developed. As he steps across the sidewalk one cannot but admire his regal bearing and athletic movement. He gets into a buggy and drives rapidly off. The other gentlemen is tall and stout, a very giant in physical proportions. He pauses irresolutely for a moment at the entrance, then starts down the street at a good round pace, dragging a slight cane on the pavement. The first is Dr. Hutchinson; the second E. V. Smalley, the able editor of the *Northwest Magazine*.

As I pass on my way I meet at nearly every step men whose names are almost household words—men prominent in business and the professions—and ladies by the score whose names appear in every report of social festivities. Here, for instance are Messrs. Envin and Wellington, the well-known criminal lawyers, Gen. R. W. Johnson, Dr. Murphy, Dr. Stone, Major Bates, Mr. Charles Carroll Macknbin and Ge. W. H. Sanborn—they come in such quick succession that it is almost impossible to get them all down.

Not many of them are mere strollers, as myself, but whether bent upon business or pleasure, you will see them on Third Street at some time of the day. If you go down a little further, to the corner of Jackson Street, you will have even a better opportunity of viewing the celebrities. You will doubtless see Governor Merriam's two-horse road-wagon waiting for him at the door of the Merchants' Bank, and the governor inside holding audience to the innumerable people waiting to see him; you will see the crowd of lawyers and politicians who affect the Merchants' Hotel as a gathering place; in short, you will see pretty nearly all there is to be seen.

Some day I will take a point of espionage at some favorable locality and make an exact report of everything which passes before my mental and actual vision—and I can assure you, with such opportunities, this will be by no means little.

Kellogg Boulevard (old Third Street) under construction, February 23, 1931. The area below the bank was once known as Second Street. After the construction of Kellogg Boulevard old Second Street ceased to exist. *Minnesota Historical Society.*

Chapter Six

Downtown Saint Paul:
The Twentieth Century

On Sunday, December 12, 1915 the St. Paul Pioneer Press *featured a lengthy article under the headline "What a Christmas Shopper Found on a Visit to Sixth Street's Shops," a guided tour, in effect, of the great stores of old Sixth Street, and of all the merchandise one could purchase therein during the 1915 Christmas season. From the Minnesota Phonograph Company, "at the very top of business Sixth Street," to Schuneman and Evans, the last door into which our anonymous shopper of 85 years ago was to turn (the article appeared without a byline, though it would seem safe to guess that its author was female), "What a Christmas Shopper Found" was a detailed and unremitting account of all the "stuff" that one could buy on only one of downtown St. Paul's great shopping streets, and served to dramatically demonstrate how, within the space of just 75 years, St. Paul had been transformed from a tiny, backward wilderness settlement (whose retail offerings amounted to little more than Pigs Eye Parrant's watered down, overpriced jugs of whiskey), into one of the great capitalist dynamos of the Upper Midwest.*

While it could be wished that "What a Christmas Shopper Found" had included more physical description of Sixth Street and its environs, and that it had shown, perhaps, a slightly more "personal touch," we are indebted to its anonymous author for introducing us to the shops (and in many cases to the proprietors) of old Sixth Street, as well, of course, as to the extraordinary variety of their "stuff."

What A Christmas Shopper Found on a Visit to Sixth Street's Shops

BY AN ANONYMOUS LADY

An especially good place from which to start a busy day is the Minnesota Phonograph Company's store at the very top of business Sixth Street. It is a wonderful place in which to do a lot of your Christmas shopping. You can buy either a Victor or an Edison machine for a sum beginning at $15, and as for new records for the old machine—they are supplied to meet the needs and tastes of every one. There is a special list of records for this season, in English and in German—one double-disk record of the Westminster Chimes holds the very heart of Christmas. Especially for children is Eugene Field's "Jest Fore Christmas," together with two more Field poems. Lovers of the voice of John McCormack will want his superb rendition of Adeste Fideles this month. "O Little Town of Bethlehem" leads a group of Christmas carols beautifully sung by a chorus of mixed voices. There are a number of records from Handel's "Messiah," including a truly remarkable one by Arthur Middleton, "Why Do the Nations." A most unusual record is listed as "Christmas Symphony" by "Uncle Fritz and the Children's Orchestra," which includes talking children at a piano and children's toy instruments. It is unique and a record which will be played over and over without cessation. There are many records you will want—the difficulty is not of selection, but of number. And if you want a new and also extraordinary dance record, get "Ragging the Scale," a fox trot. It is a musical oddity in which the scale contrives to be a tune—a fascinating, infectious, keep-on-dancing tune.

I've always felt that a nice, fat little bank account would be the most welcome Christmas remembrance I could have, and if I knew any one who seemed inclined to gratify my desire in that direction, I should send that one in to Mr. Mellenthin of the Peoples Bank of St. Paul, on the corner of Sixth and Wabasha. He will talk enthusiastically of the pretty little folding check book as a charming gift for a lady—of the Christmas joys of a 4% savings account, showing you the little round savings bank you get when a savings amount of one dollar or more is opened in your name. The Peoples Bank is an infant institution in St. Paul, but is growing at a typical St. Paul rate, having increased its original size seven times in its seventeen months of life.

My stay in the gray and violet tearoom known as the "Violet Way," at 52 East Sixth, was too brief to tell me more than that the management believes in goods backed by personality, for the things sold for holiday remembrances are all known by the name of the maker, Mrs. Baldwin's fruit cake and mincemeat, Miss Burns' marmalades and Miss Borup's candies those names being guarantees of quality in all of us.

Victor Ekholm, 62 East Sixth, has all the other furs you may want to see, but what I am most interested in is his bear. It sounds rather a coarse, harsh fur, but nothing could be softer and silkier than a set of Russian silver bear, which is a real silver in color, with just a faint hint of the classroom brown closer to the skin. A set known as golden bear takes actual golden lights in the sunshine and is only faintly tipped with white.

Just sixteen years ago, the firm of Keljik Bros., 64 East Sixth, came into existence, and today is the largest exclusive Oriental rug store in America. There isn't any sort or size of Oriental rug you can't buy there, and speaking of size, Mr. Keljik says the largest one he ever sold was an Ispeban rug from Constantinople, which weighed 410 pounds, the price of which he preferred not to tell at all. That needn't frighten the person who desires a rug as a Christmas gift. Some of them are not particularly costly, although there is very little limit what a fine

Sixth Street, looking west from Robert. Picture from *Northwest Magazine*, December, 1892. *Minnesota Historical Society.*

rug may cost. I learned one thing in my talk with Mr. Keljik, and that is that the word "antique" in connection with Oriental rugs does not necessarily mean old. It is really a trade term, and refers to quality only, as beauty of dye, quality of wool and other points of value in a rug. A rug of many years of existence and possessing those qualities is not antique, but a rug finished last month which has them is entitled to that designation.

Crossing Minnesota Street brought me to the St. Paul Trunk and Bag Co., where Miss O'Brien showed me Christmas enough for every one. I wanted to purchase the store entire, but all my list would exhaust the interesting things I saw. There are newly imported Scotch steamer rugs, soft and softly-colored, and if you know of any one who needs a going-away bag—there are real crepe and Gladstone bags in a size fitted to a woman's needs and strength that are luxurious to look upon. There is a special sort of purse to carry in a muff and you may buy for a party age girl a pussy willow taffeta Paradise bag—which means a bag of soft tan silk, covered with a whole aviary of jewel-like birds, parrots and peacocks and orioles—all the same size. Speaking of size—fitted into a leather case is a glass topped percolator coffee pot, in which just one cup of coffee can be made, which, cased with its alcohol lamp is just seven inches in height and costs $12.

By the time this goes to press, doubtless the counters of J. George Smith's candy fairyland will be crowded with things I did not see, for few days pass that do not leave them something altogether novel and altogether charming. All these things are constantly changing and there seems little use in describing the pretty things of one day when the next will find a new lot in their places. In metal, silk and paper are the containers—boxes and baskets and hampers—with loads of things that look like anything but the nests for sugary deliciousness that they are. S. George Smith makes a specialty of delivery. In either of the Twin Cities your box of chocolates, though only a pound in weight, will be delivered to you free of charge. Carefully packed in double boxes and with each place in its own frilly cup. Smith's Dollar Chocolate Dreams or an assortment of Smith's famous Family Sweets at half the price will be sent for you to any reachable place in the world you may select.

The T. V. Morean Co., 114 Fast Sixth Street, wants to sell you Flint River pecans for your dinner table and holiday greeting cards for your friends, but their real interest is in seeing that every one that has any need for glasses has his eyes fitted with the new Crooks' lens. This is an invention of Sir. William Crooks of the X ray fame, and is a chemical glass of a scarcely perceptible wine tint which shuts out all ultra violet rays, these being harmful to the eye. I saw lorgnettes galore in a show case. If you make your own sweets and sometimes have trouble getting them just right, buy from the Morean company a candy thermometer and do yourself really professional credit.

To come back up Sixth on the other side! Had a splendidly interesting time on the south side, and in my first stop on the north it seemed that the interest wasn't going to diminish.

In the office of the St. Paul Gas Light Co., I met enthusiasm itself in the form of Mr. Ash. Of course, the big white enamel gas range which won the gold medal at the Panama exhibit generates enthusiasm of its own self, and to any woman who saw the electric bulb which lights the interior of one of its four ovens the sigh which greets the ultimate would come. Its cost? One hundred and fifty dollars. Now a practical electric stove can be purchased for $8, and included with it are a tea kettle, frying pan, stew pen and master, but the food they cook will only serve a small girl and her dolls, for the stove itself measures 11 x 15 inches. It's going to make many little girls happy and teach them much in addition.

If the bride be without a maid, she may serve her beloved his favorite breakfast, pancakes, without absenting herself from his side or filling her sitting room with smoke if some one gives her the new electric griddle, made of a composition metal which does not smoke and to which the cakes won't stick. If he prefers toast, she can have a toaster which automatically turns the slices, saving her from scorched finger tips. It also provides a place on which the coffee may be kept hot.

Electricity seems to be woman's particular servitor, for aside from all the devices by which it saves her labor, there is a set, comprising hair dryer, curler and waver, guaranteed to help her be beautiful to Edison, a suffragist.

Directly as I entered the big department store of Mannheimer Bros., at Eighth and Robert, I saw a purple dog. Not a cow—but a dog. It has brilliants for eyes and a pearl pendant from its golden collar. Why a purple dog? I don't know, and I went immediately up-elevator to escape the haunting question. I met a French skating blouse of white washable satin with chiffon sleeves. It has moleskin collar, belt and buttons, is meant for wear on the artificial ice rinks which are usurping the dance floors in Eastern hotels and cafes. Worn with it should be white kid boots with fur tops to match, and I hope Saint Paul opens its indoor skating rink soon. That blouse is near the entrance to The Little Gray Shop Around the Corner, but you won't recognize it as gray from the jumbled rainbow it contains. Small novelties from every country are gathered here. Ask to see the New England floor candlestick when you go there; it dates to the days of our Puritan ancestors.

A wide stretch of time; but only a few feet of space separate the last mentioned articles from the French Room, where negligees predominate, and these in modes of tomorrow. The very newest thing in negligee trimming is white swansdown. A becoming jacket of shell pink brocade is lined with Georgette crepe and bound with swansdown. There couldn't be a better gift for a luxury-loving lady. There's a kimono of Ombre Georgete crepe in gray, embroidered in gray iris, which is just as beautiful and probably more practical. A negligee is one of the few garments permissible as a gift, and I hope some one thinks of me when in that French room. Just outside it are lovely things for babies, and the toy shop on the same floor.

Sixth and Minnesota, c. 1935. *Minnesota Historical Society.*

So many things I saw were for the use and adornment of women only that I asked to see articles of interest to men when I went into Bullard Bros. show at 95 East Sixth. The newest and most useful of these is an auto cigar lighter, a vest pocket contrivance of silver in which a steel wheel against carborendum ignites an orange-colored cord. Any man, motorist or not, would value it for another use. Army men wear wristwatches and Mr. Bullard expects their use to widen—though slowly. If he travels there is a folding clock, which, when closed, resembles a cigarette case, and after this I was shown something only men buy, for their own use but not their own adornment. It is a new wedding ring of gold—very narrow and hand-carved in orange blossoms. For from $20 to $550 her Christmas gift may be the new flexible bracelet, made of gold, faced in platinum and set in diamonds and sapphires. A totally unadorned little platinum watch to be worn on a wrist band of black grosgrain ribbon is $300. In pretty cases come sets of veil and hat pins to match, and the prices of these seem to be anything you like. For the giver of household treasures there is some truly wonderful iridescent glass, the most beautiful thing in wine glasses I ever saw.

Looking north down **Robert Street** during the **Christmas season, c. mid-1920s. Note** the policeman at center and his stop and go sign.
Minnesota Historical Society. **Photo by C. P. Gibson.**

Mr. Bullard seems in the way of bringing peace fame to St. Paul. He has a letter from the Women's Peace Society, of which Jane Addams is president, congratulating him upon his design for a peace seal and promising him an early decision upon its adoption as their official emblem. It is a small disk bearing the word "Peace," between the point of an olive wreath which encloses an embossed plow and pruning hook. The little seal, a thin disk of copper in a green finish with a mucilaged black, is really beautiful and adds wonderfully to the appearance of a letter.

Mr. Bullard also says they have been much surprised at the unusual sale of fine diamonds they have made this season. Although diamonds are high in price and will probably be higher people are investing freely and want fine pieces.

The first question I asked in the jewelry store of E. A. Brown & Co., 87 East Sixth, was as to the real reason for the continued vogue for platinum settings. It is that platinum, with the proper alloy, is so much stronger than gold that it permits of the construction of much lighter lines and consequent greater grace and delicacy of settings. Few things could be more graceful, however, than a solid gold frame I saw for the picture of the dearest one and nothing could exceed in delicacy the fine gold link chain of the Add-a-pearl necklace. At an initial cost of $5, you may buy a chain centered by five pearls for the wee girl. Always a charming ornament, and if you add a pearl or two each birthday or Christmas, by the time she makes her debut she will have the heart's adored of every woman a real pearl necklace, which will also be a constant reminder of the love which sunned her youth.

There is only one place where more money can be spent in a given time than in a jeweler's, and that is in a furrier's. The firm of F. Albrecht & Son, Sixth and Minnesota streets, shipped out $12,000 worth of furs the day before I visited their Fur Shop, "and you couldn't hardly notice it at all." One can hardly appreciate that there are so many rare and costly furs until you wander as I did through a whole storeful of nature's fur treasures that represent the height of luxurious warmth and softness. Take for instance, just one kind of fur—the foxes. Why, I gloried in fox for almost an hour, genuine silver fox, Arctic white fox, natural blue ox, red, taupe, gray, blues, London

smoke, ash rose and pointed fox, as well as many other shades. And here's a tip. American women are this year to have a chance at the favorite fur of the European women of fashions—The Canadian Fisher. It is the largest of the sable family, ranging from a grisly brown to a dark, deep rich brownish shade in color, of a soft, silky texture—and it's a durable fur, too. On account of the war and the consequent lack of demand in the European fashion centers, Canadian Fisher can now be had at about one-third the cost of a year ago. For my own tastes, nothing—not even the royal ermine or the Imperial Russian Crown Sable—can be more beautiful than the Golden German Fitch—though the paler tints of this Russian Fitch are equally popular. Speaking of coats, I saw an order going through for a Twin City woman's coat—Alaskan seal, sable trimmed, to cost her $3,800. I saw a model trying on good, warm, stylish motor coats in sable squirrel, ringtail, leopard, raccoon and moleskin—just the thing for a woman who loves winter motoring. Men's motor coats, too, in beaver and raccoon. The last coat I snuggled into was of Hudson seal (seal-dyed muskrat), which is preferred by many to the genuine sealskin. It seemed to me for beauty, luxuriousness and style, to be fit for a queen.

There was juvenile week in the St. Paul Book and Stationery Co., at 55-59 East Sixth. Fostered by the Y. M. C. A., the schools and some ministers revealed a book display for youngsters from the Mother Goose age, up through fairy tales and Boy Scout books to college stories—everything any child could or should have is featured. Speaking of Mother Goose, there is a wonderful new edition at $2. The illustrations of which, with the accompanying verses can be purchased separately, framed or unframed. These pictures, in costume, composition and coloring, have the spirit of the new valuable early editions of babyhood's classic.

The store invites you to "browse," and you do. There are tables for every classification under which a book may come.

Far back in the store I found the calendars and booklets, Christmas cards and the rest of it. I never expected to see so many varieties of calendars. Calendars of cartoons, calendars every standard author (the Dickens one is notable), a satirical calendar or two, one addressed to the housewife especially and containing 365 desserts, and a calendar of Burgess Bedtime Stories, an ideal gift for an imagination-tired mother. There never were so many calendars in one place before. And paper dolls, what little girl would enjoy a Christmas with no paper dolls in it?

St. Paul Book and Stationary Co., 55-59 East Sixth Street, c. 1906–1908. *Minnesota Historical Society.* **Photo by C. P. Gibson.**

The most conservative place in town, I truly believe, is the store of R. W. Bonyea Piano Co. at 53 East Sixth. It handles no make of piano less than forty-five years old, which makes, of course, for reliability. There isn't any make of piano, past or present, of which Mr. Bonyea can't sell you, and if I know anything at all of pianos and wanted to include one in my Christmas benefactions, there isn't any one I'd rather go to than Mr. Bonyea. Incidentally there's a thriving little circulating library in the back of that store where you can get all of the newest books.

Miss Berkheimer, 49 E. Sixth, looked up from fondling a wee jade elephant, which means luck, to say that plumes can't properly reappear until the vogue of small hats for all occasions is over. "Becomingness is more than made," says Miss

Berkeimer, "but always in the mode there is the hat becoming," and she knows. A hat she especially fancies has its pendant veil held loose from the face, yet firmly where it belongs by a collar fur matching the trimming of the hat. I saw lots of things in her shop that aren't hats.

There are corsage flowers whose centers are a tiny powder puff and in whose loops of ribbon wee mirrors are pocketed, a dainty and useful fancy, and there are two mesh bags of literally unique design. Oddest concern I've seen yet is the corsage bracelet in whose clasp flowers, natural or artificial, may be held on the arm. I know that anklet bouquets are vogue in some circles in New York, but the arm bouquet seems to me to be more apt to please St. Paul.

Match the bathrobe to big breakfast and go to the Chaix company, Sixth and Cedar, for a waffle bath robe. No, I'm serious, that's what they call it and the slippers to match. It's washable and comes in lots of colors. Go and see it. While you're there, ask to see a vestogram. I refrain from the pun—it's a black ribbon decorated with a monogram slide of metal and worn straight or diagonally across a vest. Probably you put a watch on one end of it.

In the Sixth Street Store I found the last and best thing in midwinter millinery—jet hats. Most of them are all black—a very few are combined with bright color and one especially lovely thing effectively combines the brilliancy of its jet shape with cloudy black tulle and wee wings. Jet is especially popular because of its universal becomingness and the vivacity it seems to add to the face beneath it. Fox appears more in trimmings than in entire hats, and in combination with dull gold lace there is nothing more attractive. A hat of moleskin, rose color and gold lace—it sounds almost as good as it looks. There were many novel things for trimmings shown me—all so pretty, notably a goura butterfly and a couple of purple ostrich thistles. All sorts of things are made into flowers and stickouts. There's a rifle bird, this last a real bird, not made at all. It's a perfect thing for a street hat and though I never saw one before I hope I will again.

Of all the thoughtful little things I ever met, the after-9 P. M. street car schedule pasted inside the door of the cigar and confectionery shop of Philip Claus at Sixth and Wabasha is about the nicest. You

Parade on West Sixth Street, looking east from St. Peter, 1908. Visible in this photo are: The entrance to the Cathedral Rectory (left foreground), Schuneman and Evans Department Store (at Sixth and Wabasha), and the Sherman Block. At the extreme right is a corner of the old Grand Opera House. *Minnesota Historical Society.* **Photo by C. P. Gibson.**

Sixth Street at Market, August 29, 1932. Note the traffic signals in foreground and at far right. *Minnesota Historical Society.* **Photo by Kenneth M. Wright.**

get courtesy and careful service in this place always, and that makes all the nicer the good things to eat you can buy. I had a Claus luncheonette at a table while I wanted for my box of pomegranates and kumquats to be packed. Just now nearly all the fruit comes from California, next month it is from Florida. If you know California, you know Mission figs—plump, sundried fruit that is not pressed, but its natural shape and whose dull purple skin looks as if it had been rolled in powdered sugar. All California uses them for cooking purposes, but Claus' is the first place west of the coast in which I've ever seen them, and I've asked for them, too. A combination gumdrop and marshmallow sounds weird, but it is good, and I added to my purchase a box of imported English taffee. I've read about taffee in every English book that contains a child's character and it's as good and as English as it sounds.

Schuneman and Evans is the last doorway into which I turn. I went downstairs to the basement here, on my way stopping to investigate a pile of gay color, which proved to be chopsticks, in celluloid, to be used as hair ornaments. A pair in jade green in black hair—I would like to wear them. Handkerchiefs in every variety, bewildering numbers of handkerchiefs. I never saw so many of Santa Claus' standby gathered together before. Every attribute a man can have of size, quality, color and decoration. I didn't even try to look at all of them. There is a very fine china shop in the basement of this store, and I went to see its holiday offerings. A salad set of blue English porcelain, made by Josiah Wedgewood & Sons, which has an embossed white border, is utterly unique, very beautiful and very expensive. A dinner service in ivory tinted earthenware, from the same pottery, was quite unlike the usual thing and could be used with striking effect in a Jacobean dining room. It isn't expensive.

Have you seen the glass baking dishes? They are quite attractive and need no fancy container to look well on a dining table. To me their chief charm is that through their transparent sides you can see the condition of food as it cooks. It's a find to give to an ardent housewife.

Front page of *St. Paul Pioneer Press* announces the capture of Alvin Karpis, May 2, 1936. *Ramsey County Historical Society.*

In 1969 Alvin ("Old Creepy") Karpis was released from prison after serving 33 years for his part in the famous Hamm kidnapping case. Shortly thereafter, he began to dictate his memoirs to a writer named Bill Trent, an account of his life and crimes which was published as the Alvin Karpis Story in 1971. The Alvin Karpis Story was not, as its introduction warns us, "a nice book." It was, in fact, an "icy, brutal" one, a remorseless account of Karpis' crimes and atrocities, which begins with the start of his criminal career at the age of ten (this was when he stole his first gun; Karpis claims that he knew he was going to be a criminal from that day on) and takes us up to his arrest in St. Paul in 1936, the city which had been his refuge during the years of the infamous O'Conner System, that notorious "understanding" between the nation's gangsters and the St. Paul police department, whereby the city all but invited the country's most notorious crooks to come to town for a vacation from the law, just so long it was understood that they were to commit no crimes while within the city limits, and would liberally spend the money that they had stolen in other cities during the course of their relaxing respite from life on the run.

The favorite St. Paul hangout of Alvin Karpis during these years was a place called the Green Lantern, a Wabasha Street speakeasy which used a cigar store as a front and whose owner, Harry Sawyer, did "all kinds of favors for the Karpis-Barker gang." The Green Lantern was Alvin Karpis' "personal headquarters" and, as he relates in the following excerpt from The Alvin Karpis Story , a place where on any given night you could find "as complete a gathering of criminals as could be found anywhere in the United States."

The Green Lantern

BY ALVIN KARPIS, WITH BILL TRENT

Of all the Midwest United States cities, the one that I knew best was St. Paul, and it was a crook's haven. Every criminal of any importance in the 1930s made his home at one time or another in St. Paul. If you were looking for a guy you hadn't seen for a few months, you usually thought of two places—prison or St. Paul. If he wasn't locked up in one, he was probably hanging out in the other. St. Paul was a good spot for both pleasure and business. You could relax in its joints and speakeasies without any fear of arrest, and when you were planning a score, you could have your pick of all the top men at all the top crimes.

I didn't ever deal directly with the police and politicians who made St. Paul so congenial. I didn't have to. I was friendly with the middlemen, the guys who handled payoffs and negotiated relations between the crooks and the city, and I left it to them to pass the word and the money back and forth. The two most important guys I knew were Harry Sawyer and Sack Peifer, and they swung a lot of weight.

Sawyer and Peifer were in some ways rivals. They had similar contacts at City Hall and police headquarters and they had the same interest in beating people out of their money. But they operated differently. Peifer was involved in the rackets and Sawyer wasn't. Ordinary crooks in those days were guys who pulled jobs at random, bank stickups, burglaries, heists of different kinds. Rackets guys, on the other hand, were organized and monopolized activities like prostitution, drug traffic, bookmaking, and rum running. Peifer tended more to rackets operations, while Sawyer was a freelance boss, but both of them cooperated in keeping St. Paul safe from stickup men like me.

Peifer owned a club called the Hollyhocks. It was a glamor spot, and Peifer used it as his headquarters for runing the slot machine business and his other interests. I preferred Harry Sawyer's club. It was called the Green Lantern and used a cigar store as a front on Wabasha Avenue. Out back it was set up with booths where you could order the best beer in town—in fact the only beer that, in those Prohibition days, hadn't had the alcohol taken out of it at the breweries.

Harry Sawyer with wife Gladys. *Ramsey County Historical Society.*

287

Sawyer ran the Green Lantern like a host at a great party, and I liked the way he handled himself. He certainly did all kinds of favors for the Karpis-Barker Gang. Sawyer was the guy who tipped us off about the raid from the cops after old Dunlop blew the whistle on us. Sawyer also passed on the word when the Minnesota Bureau of Apprehension wanted us to go easy on our cigarette thefts. That was the time we'd gone in heavily for stealing cigarettes, and the bureau told Sawyer to warn us that unless we stopped it would post an armed guard in every wholesale cigarette spot in the state. We appreciated the advice and got out of the cigarette business. We appreciated, too, Sawyer's role as our personal banker. Whenever we scored on a bank job, we would put a chunk of the money in Sawyer's hands for our savings. We knew from experience that it was safer with him than it would have been in a regular bank.

The Green Lantern was always my personal headquarters in St. Paul. I knew everyone in the place, and if I didn't, Sawyer would introduce me. Everybody had the same things in common—stealing, killing, and looting. Everybody had traveled to the same places—McAlester, Hutchinson, and Lansing. It was every day of the week like a perpetual party.

The greatest blowout Sawyer threw in the place, in my experience, was on New Year's Eve, 1932. If the cops had decided to grab everybody who went in and out of the Green Lantern that night, there would have been no crime spree of 1932 and 1933. Most of the guys greeted the arrival of 1932 with Sawyer's booze, but I didn't drink. I ate Sawyer's hard-boiled eggs and sent out to McCormick's Restaurant for coffee and just sat back and watched the show.

It would have taken me months, maybe years, to meet all the people I ran into there. I didn't know it at the time, but I would do business with many of them over the next few years.

There was probably never before as complete a gathering of criminals in one room in the United States as there was in the Green Lantern that night. There were escapees from every major U.S. penitentiary. I was dazzled. There were Tommy Holden and Francis Keating, two escapees from Leavenworth. They had taken a fall in a $90,000 mail train caper in Evergreen Park, Illinois. And Phil Courtney.

Gus Winkler was there. He was on the Syndicate's execution squad and he'd knocked off dozens of guys. He worked with Fred Burke, Johnny Moore, Shotgun George Zeigler, and Crane-neck Nugent, none of whom, to my surprise, were Italians. Everybody figured the Italians were the executioners. This was not so. Harvey Bailey was there too. He was suspected of being in the Denver Mint robbery and of robbing a bank in Lincoln, Nebraska. He was believed to have earned himself a cool two million on those capers.

For a kid like me, it was great stuff. Rogues Gallery, or Hall of Fame. It depended on your point of view. But how could you not be impressed by Big Homer Wilson, who had been robbing banks for years and never had a fingerprint taken anywhere? Tommy Cannon was another phenomenally lucky robber who had never been made. Then there was Tom Philbin, the slot-machine kingpin, and Tommy Banks and Kid Cann, out of Minneapolis, who ran alcohol and booze and had the gambling in Excelsior.

The later it got, the more the place jumped. There was so much goddamn noise at midnight that Sawyer had to yell out for quiet. He had the radio on and wanted to hear Ben Pollack's orchestra play "Auld Lang Syne." Everybody got pretty sloshed, and at one point Frank Nash, a Leavenworth escapee, left to go to another party. At 8 a.m., he was back. Even when he was bombed, he always managed to look dignified. He'd always make sure, for instance, that his toupee was on straight. Anyway, he came running in with his overcoat pulled up around his neck and ran into Harvey Bailey, who was upset, to say the least.

"What bastard did this to me?" Bailey screamed, holding a shoe in his hand. He had taken off his shoes and gone to bed for a few hours and, while he was sleeping, somebody had nailed one of his big shoes to the floor. He'd had a hell of a job getting it loose. "You think that's something?" Nash growled. He opened his coat and his tie was cut off an inch below the knot. "Which one of you bastards did that?"

Since Freddie and Doc and I spent so much time living in and around St. Paul and since we worked so closely with Sawyer and Peifer on various jobs, it was inevitable that we'd get dragged into the city's politics, even if it was on a minor level. We felt obliged to contribute something to keep the crooked

Alvin Karpis arrives in St. Paul after his arrest in the Hamm Kidnapping case,
1936. *Ramsey County Historical Society.*

guys in office because, as Peifer explained to us, we partly responsible for strengthening the anticrime reform element in the city.

There was a growing reform movement reacting to the city's corruption, and they used the murder of Arthur Dunlop as a prime example that St. Paul was a crime capital. The Dunlop murder was a particularly messy job, and though Peifer and his men handled it, it was linked with Freddie and me and others who were getting to be notorious stickup men. Given the entire situation, it was only fair, as Peifer pointed out to us, that we contribute something to blocking the reformers. Fortunately, Peifer only asked us for money, not muscle, and we gave gladly. But, at first, even the cash didn't help. In the election Peifer was concerned about, the election of 1932, a reformer named Mahoney was elected mayor, and he instantly demoted the chief of police and the chief of detectives. At that point Freddie and I decided St. Paul would not be healthy and made up our minds to leave the city and operate in another part of the Midwest for a few months. Peifer wasn't discouraged. He began planning for the following year's elections in Minneapolis. He and his cronies had a number of schemes, including the organization of a massive crime wave in the area that would discredit the reformers and their administration.

Freddie and I were busy with our own personal crime wave, and we didn't make another contribution to Peifer's plans until the Minneapolis election, when he again asked for money to back a candidate who was in the bag. We anted up some cash, and this time Peifer and his contacts came through. Peifer's man won. Now the fix was to be in Minneapolis. It was possible to buy off anyone as long as you came up with enough dough.

A man of almost unprecedented achievement, Gordon Parks, composer, writer, filmmaker, photographer for Life magazine, was only 16 years old when, in 1928, he moved from Kansas to St. Paul following his mother's death. He soon found himself on the streets of the Twin Cities (after being kicked out of his sister's house, he would often take all-night rides on the streetcars back and forth between Minneapolis and St. Paul just to stay out of the cold), and then working at a succession of jobs (janitor, railway porter, piano player at a brothel, professional basketball player) in which he struggled against the racism and poverty so endemic in the society of his day.

In the following excerpts from his autobiography, A Choice of Weapons, Gordon Parks tells us the story of two of those jobs, both of which he held in downtown St. Paul. One was as a waiter at the exclusive Minnesota Club (a most traditional job for a young black man of that time), and the other as a fashion photographer at Frank Murphy's, about as untraditional a job for a young black man as would then have been imaginable.

The Minnesota Club, at Fourth and Washington, 1929. *Ramsey County Historical Society.*

The Minnesota Club

BY GORDON PARKS

The world inside the Minnesota Club was one of spacious rooms with high-beamed ceilings, of thick carpeting, of master and servant, of expensive wines and liquors, of elegant table settings and Epicurean tastes. Influential men like Frank Kellogg, Justice Pierce Butler and Jim Hill of the Great Northern Railway sat about smoking long cigars and ornate pipes in the overstuffed high-back chairs of the mahogany-paneled library. And I, dressed in a suit of blue tails, white tie and striped red vest, would stand near them discreetly listening to their confidential talk of financial deals, court decisions, their wives and children, boats, politics, women, the Stock Exchange—and the weather. To most of them, I was invisible and unhearing, a sort of dark ectoplasm that only materialized when their fingers snapped for service. I used to stand at the door and take their coats; and the camel's hair and the velvet-collared chesterfields felt good to my callused hands. Their suits were well cut and well pressed, their oxfords and grained brogues discreetly shined. Their faces looked scrubbed; their hair was always neatly trimmed and smelled of barber's soap and bay rum.

In time I got to know all their mannerisms. The way Senator Kellogg's teeth clipped his cigars intrigued me. He measured and bit in one quick motion. And I, timing that motion perfectly, would have the match lit; then I would nearly gag from the smoke as he puffed away. And Justice Butler's slumping in one of the mammoth leather chairs, his legs crossed and stretched out, his chin resting on his clasped hands, was, I thought, a picture of grace.

There was always the aroma of good food. The great silver platters of roast pheasant, duck and guinea hen banked with wild rice, the huge buttered steaks, served on planks of wood and garnished with steaming vegetables, the spicy cakes, rum sauces, ices and creamy desserts kept my appetite at its peak. And after such dinners, when the great sitting room filled with pipe and cigar smoke, I went about serving little toasted cakes and brandy. I was never hungry during those days.

There was a lot an unlettered black boy from Kansas could learn here. And what I learned I tucked deep inside, determined meanwhile to put each lesson into use whenever I could. I began to read more, slipping newspapers, novels and books of poetry from the club library. And soon a whole new world was opening up, one that would have been impossible to imagine back in Kansas.

One day I beard Justice Butler complain to another member, "I'll be damned if I can remember his name. He wrote *Arrowsmith*." And, before the other man could reply, I gulped and said, "Pardon, sir—if you don't mind—it's Sinclair Lewis."

"Lewis, Sinclair Lewis, that's it." And he went on speaking. I thought, without ever realizing where the name had come from. But a few days later he handed me a small package. "It's for you," he said. I tore off the paper. It was a first edition of Edith Wharton's *The Age of Innocence*, dating back to 1920. I thanked him warmly. That book would always have a very special meaning for me. And I told him so. The rest of that week I walked around school with it, showing it to my friends.

Frank Murphy's

by GORDON PARKS

Vogue was one of the magazines' well-to-do passengers left on the train. I used to study the luxurious fashion photographs on its pages and the uncommon names of the photographers who took them—Steichen, Blumenfeld, Horst, Beaton, Hoyningen-Huene. How lucky they were, I thought. Day dreaming once, I printed my name under a Steichen portrait of Katharine Cornell. And my imagination assured me that it looked quite natural there.

No one could accuse me of being unaggressive now. I went to every large department store in the Twin Cities asking for a chance to photograph their merchandise. The manager of John Thomas, a large women's store in Minneapolis, seemed astonished when I approached him. Looking at me curiously he said, "But our photography is all done out in New York." Then he turned from me without another word.

But I kept trying, coming finally to Frank Murphy's, the most fashionable store in St. Paul. Frank Murphy had all but walked me out the door when his wife, a handsome woman with a shock of black hair, spoke to her husband. "What does he want, Frank?" He gestured hopelessly. "To photograph fashions." She was waiting on a customer but she looked me over and said, "Well, maybe he can." Frank Murphy looked back at his wife as though she had lost her wits. "But, darling . . ."

"Wait for me, young man. I'll be with you in a minute," she said. And by now I was as bewildered as her husband. For, aggressive as I was, I wasn't prepared for such a triumph. "Wait around; she'll talk to you," Frank Murphy said helplessly.

After her customer left she turned to me. "Have you any samples of your work to show me?" she asked.

"No, I'm sorry."

"Why do you want to photograph fashion?"

"Because I know I can. That's all."

"Well, our clothes are photographed out east"—my spirits sank—"but I'm willing to give you a chance. I think it would be fun." She thought for a moment. "Can you be here tomorrow evening, right after we close? I'll have the models and dresses ready."

"Oh sure. Yes, ma'am, I'll be here right on the dot," I said anxiously.

"All right." She was turning to another customer. We'll be here waiting for you."

The ease and quickness of her decision stunned me. If I went on my regular run I would be in Chicago the next evening. what's more, I suddenly realized I didn't even have lighting equipment or a camera suitable for fashion photography. But that evening I had Sally call the commissary and say that I was ill. Then I hurried to Harvey Goldstein and told him about my assignment and he became as jittery as I, rushing about finding the necessary lamps, bulbs, films and camera. We were both exhausted late that night after he had assembled the equipment and showed me how to use it.

The dresses and models were beautiful. And Mrs. Murphy seemed just as excited as I was about the whole thing. She went around buttoning the girls into the lovely evening dresses she had selected. And Frank Murphy stood by, watching us with a quizzical and skeptical eye. The models had more enthusiasm than talent; but they too were helpful and held the long, tiring poses I demanded of them. My lighting, inspired by the pictures I had so often studied in the pages of *Vogue*, wasn't at all bad. The biggest problem came when the models appeared on the ground glass upside-down. Harvey hadn't warned me about this. And I went through the four-hour sitting with the awful feeling that there was something cock-eyed about the lens or the camera. But I bluffed it through without anyone's being aware of my nervousness. And, when we were finished, Mrs. Murphy, obviously impressed with the way I had lighted and posed the models, asked me if I would like to continue shooting sports clothes at the country club the next day. I couldn't have been happier; and it must have shown on my face, for she bade me goodnight with a smile of deep satisfaction.

The big blow fell at exactly two o'clock the next morning when I developed the film. My wife was asleep when she heard the moaning and my head bumping against the kitchen wall. "What's the trouble?" she asked through the outer door. "My life is ruined! Your life is ruined! The whole damned world is ruined!" I screamed, throwing open the room to her.

She stood, her hair up in curlers, bulky with our new child, looking at me in pity. "What's the trouble?" I sat down dejectedly. "I've double-exposed every damned picture but one. After all that work—all that work. I can't face that woman tomorrow. I just can't face her."

"How'd it happen?" she asked.

"Those damned holders. I didn't turn the black side out after I exposed the film."

We were silent for what seemed like an age, sitting there in the dim light of the kitchen. I had been given my big chance and had muffed it. "Goddamnit! Goddamnit! Goddamnit! Goddamnit!" I kept groaning. "Why the hell did this have to happen to me!"

"I'd blow up the good one, and show it to her," my wife suggested as she went off to bed. I sat for an hour before her suggestion sank in. Then I made a huge enlargement of the only good negative. It was elegantly framed and standing on an easel at the entrance to the country club when Mrs. Murphy arrived with the models the next afternoon. "My dear boy," she exclaimed, "it's absolutely beautiful. Where are the others? I just can't wait to see them."

I was tempted to lie. "But a woman like this deserves the truth-no matter what," I said to myself sadly. So I told the truth. "Forget it'" she said cheerfully; "we've got more work to do." My heart lightened instantly. "But," she warned, "no more of those nasty double exposures." The next week my photographs were shown throughout her store and in all the front windows. And I must have walked up and down that street a hundred times that first night, feeling good every time someone stopped to look at one of them.

Great Northern Railroad Stewards in St. Paul Winter Carnival Parade, 1941. *Minnesota Historical Society.*

When the war with Japan came to an end on Tuesday, August 14, 1945, the people of St. Paul—just like people all over the country—headed downtown (where else?) to celebrate. In downtown St. Paul the throng of celebrants gathered so rapidly and in such great numbers—especially at the corner of Seventh and Wabasha—that at one point the police had to be called in to protect Willard Vinitsky, that corner's veteran St. Paul Dispatch and Pioneer Press newspaper vendor, who was so overwhelmed by the thousands of celebrants that he sold out his first bundle of 500 Peace Extras only twelve minutes after they hit the streets!

On the following morning, Elliott Tarbell of the St Paul Pioneer Press *told the story of VJ Day, undoubtedly the greatest day in the history of the city, and certainly the occasion of the greatest celebration to ever take place downtown. His article, which originally appeared under the headline, "Jubilant Throng Hails Peace: Impromptu Parades, Hail of Confetti Give City Carnival Air," is reprinted here with the permission of the* St. Paul Pioneer Press.

V J Day celebrants, August 14, 1945. *Minneapolis Public Library.* Mpls. Collection.

VJ Day

by Elliott Tarbell

Ting! Ting! Ting! Ting! Ting!

The frenzied tinkling of the bells on press association teletype machines in St. Paul newspaper and radio offices signaled the "flash" bulletin just after 6 p.m. Tuesday that marked the end of the most horrible war in history and launched St. Paulites on a victory celebration that will continue through today for almost all the city's residents.

For federal government workers and state employees the holiday will run for two days because President Truman proclaimed a two-day holiday for federal employees and the governor followed suit by granting two days off for the state's workers.

City and county employees also are receiving holidays as will those from the Wilder Charities building.

For a few minutes after the first radio announcements were barked over the air and the first newspaper extras hit the streets, the crowds were calm. There was little of wild rejoicing at first, just relieved smiles as the people absorbed the news for which they had been waiting so long.

Many of them, let out of work an hour or more earlier, had been waiting downtown expectantly for the announcement that the peace which had been shattered for America back on that fateful Dec. 7, 1941 had come back all over the world.

After the first shock of the announcement that IT WAS TRUE AT LAST wore off, the crowd began to "thaw out" and the carnival spirit took over.

A group of servicemen clambered atop a parked automobile at Seventh and Wabasha and opened a quart bottle of whisky with lusty whoops. The laughing crowd cheered, automobile horns began honking, accompanied by the shouts of the crowd.

The Seventh and Wabasha corner was the center of the loop demonstration.

A jalopy occupied by some teen-age youths started circling around the block. Other cars followed. In no time the cars joining this impromptu parade were too many for a single line, and drivers started circling the block two abreast to the constantly increasing din from their horns and shouts from gay celebrants loosening up to the spirit of the occasion more as each minute passed.

As soon as word was flashed out that President Truman had announced Japan's acceptance of the surrender terms, all on-sale liquor establishments in the city closed—to remain so for 24 hours.

But before they locked their doors, they had been packed with expectant celebrants waiting for the signal to let off the pent-up urge of several days of anxious waiting through false peace reports, atomic bombings and alarms that the Japs might be trying a last bit of trickery.

Before the off-sale liquor stores closed, crowds of customers jammed the establishments and frantic clerks grabbed the nearest bottle on the shelf and sold it.

Within an hour or so the din was general over the loop with merrymakers parading their cars through the streets with an abandon that ignored completely all the lean years of rationed gasoline and tires.

The autocade soon was four abreast in some places and attempts of a few drivers to proceed in orderly fashion according to traffic rules were futile. Typifying the jammed traffic was the experience of a *Pioneer Press* photographer who had to take half an hour to drive from North St. Paul to the *Pioneer Press and Dispatch* building on Fourth Street.

And as the celebrants circled giddily around block after block they were showered with confetti, torn-up bits of newspapers, ticker tape and anything else that persons leaning out of office windows found convenient to toss at them.

Many of the celebrants went hungry in their merrymaking. Most of the eating places in the Loop locked their doors and hung out "closed" signs as soon as the surrender was announced. The few that remained open were well filled with jubilant, milling crowds, who seemed to care little whether or not they ate anyway.

But there was a solemn side, as well, in the observance.

Churches throughout the city were thrown open to those who wished to come in to pray. Within an hour or so after the surrender announcement thousands had flocked to the churches to offer prayers of thanksgiving—thanksgiving that the war was over, thanksgiving for many of them that sons and brothers and husbands were finished with their shooting war.

At the Cathedral 2,000 persons assembled in an impromptu thanksgiving service conducted by Father George E. Ryan and other Cathedral clergymen.

Patrons in movie houses received the tensely awaited announcement of Japanese surrender with suppressed emotion.

As the film flickered and the manager stepped onto the stage in one theater, one woman in the audience gasped and said, "The war's over," in a hoarse whisper heard over the whole theater.

Brief whistles, cheers and clapping followed the terse message and the crowd rose automatically to sing the national anthem.

One mother wept silently and as an elderly man walked down the aisle his voice broke in the anthem he was singing huskily.

A half dozen left the movie to join the joyous crowds on the street, but the majority settled back in their chairs to see the remainder of the show.

We all remember Bridgeman's. No trip downtown—whether you were going shopping, or to the movies, or even to your doctor or dentist appointment at the Lowry Medical Arts building—was ever complete unless it was capped off by a double chocolate malt or a banana split at Bridgeman's, that once "immensely popular" restaurant and ice cream parlor at 33 West Seventh Street in downtown St. Paul.

In the following pieces we get two completely different perspectives on Bridgeman's, one from that of a teenager who was black (Evelyn Fairbanks), and one from that of a teenager who was white (Don Del Fiaco). Don Del Fiaco's piece originally appeared in the November 3, 1980 edition of the St. Paul Dispatch. *Evelyn Fairbanks' is excerpted from her book,* Days of Rondo.

Bridgeman's

BY DON DEL FIACCO

It went down easily—like a hot fudge sundae.

Softened by time and abuse, it vanished without a burp or a tear amidst rich, smooth and sweet newness. The heavy cream of the St. Paul Loop clearly was whipped.

The Bridgeman's Ice Cream Parlor & Restaurant at 33 W. Seventh St. melted away a few weeks ago with little notice. A meeting place and hangout for young people for four decades, it was forsaken and unrespected at the end.

Once immensely popular, Bridgeman's was closed mainly because of the "age of the building" and the pedestrian "traffic shift" towards classy Town Square, a company official said in a short story on a *Dispatch* business page. The firm, he said, may open a store in the skyway system.

But another light on what once was a little white way has blinked off. And the dreariness of a small section of a brightening business district intensifies.

The western edge of Downtown around St. Peter Street was for many years a lively playground burning with post-pubescent passion. And Bridgeman's, so white and gleaming, was its sizzling core.

There are, of course, many memories, pleasant and painful.

"Chico," the establishment's husky, fearless manager, clobbered three teen-age boys, including me, in the nearby Orpheum Theater alley late one summer afternoon in the late 1940s. And there was "Tutti-Frutti," a gorgeous and snooty counter girl who dispensed many favors, but never favors to her masculine big spenders.

Bridgeman's often was the first stop on evening tours which included restless visits to the Original Coney Island and the White Castle lot at West Seventh and Auditorium Streets.

Lads swaggering in their coolness argued loudly over banana splits, triple treats and double malts. Cigarette smoke curled over empty tulip glasses as eyes followed young women employees scampering through a maze of counters.

"Put a lot of nuts on it, will ya?"

"Gimme a couple of cherries. I just love cherries."

"I guess you don't want a tip, huh?"

"What're you doin' after you get through work tonight? Want to go for a ride?"

"My boyfriend's pickin' me up."

"You don't know what you're missing. Catch you later."

A crowd lines up in front of the **RKO Orpheum Theater** for a showing of *The Golden Horde*, starring Ann Blyth and David Farrar, October 6, 1951. The Orpheum was located on Seventh Street between Wabasha and St. Peter. Note another downtown landmark, Bridgeman's, at the end of the block. *Minnesota Historical Society.* Photo by *St. Paul Dispatch-Pioneer Press.*

And so, guys in athletic and leather jackets left dime tips near soggy napkins and giggled out battered white doors into nights offering few surprises. Waitresses smiled tolerantly and weakly at waves from outside windows smeared by fingers.

Eagerly in quest of romantic conquests, the noisy group would check "the action" around the jukebox at Coney Island, harass the male and female carhops at the White Castle and race their jalopies east on Seventh.

Challenges and insults were screamed from cars roaring at the speedway's Wabasha Street starting line. Women waiting for buses ignored invitations to enter shiny vehicles with wide whitewalls.

The White Castle was demolished several years ago. The track has been narrowed to a wide path, and buildings tower at the finish line.

The corners are rather quiet now as city planners contemplate the future of blocks neglected and abandoned.

Large signs on the waxed windows of empty Bridgeman's read: "Closed. Visit Our New Ice Cream Parlour & Restaurant at 4650 Robert Trail. Thank You For Your Patronage."

Being Black in St. Paul

by Evelyn Fairbanks

Most of us were working and when we tried to spend our money for recreation, we found that we were limited there, too. Some of the places, such as Walgreen's drugstore on Seventh and Wabasha, did not openly deny service; they just waited on us last at the lunch counter. We may have only wanted Cokes, but by the time they took our orders, we asked for a full meal. When we saw the waitress bringing the food, we would get up and walk out, leaving the restaurant with a full meal to throw away because someone had told us that the cooks spit in the food when they didn't want to serve you.

Other places, like Bridgeman's soda fountain in downtown St. Paul, flatly refused service. When I was a junior in high school, eight or nine of us started going to Bridgeman's after school and sitting at the counter. The restaurant was very busy that day, and as the waitresses passes us they said, "We don't serve Negroes in here." Our response was, "We know it." We sat there for an hour, not being served and very satisfied that we were affecting their profits for the day. Finally one day the manager called the police. The police told the manager that all of us were acting within our legal rights. The manager could not bar us from the premises since the business was open to the public, but he did have the right to refuse service to us. And since we had the legal right to be there as long as we didn't disturb the peace, there was nothing the police could or would do.

We didn't have the political savvy to notify the press for support. Nor did we have any idea that young blacks throughout the country shared our resentments—and our anger, which would remain unnoticed by most of the white society until the "surprise" riots of the 1960s. So we continued our sit-in, as the technique was later called, until the manager decided it was more profitable to serve us and take a chance on offending the other customers than it was to have us occupy from eight to fifteen stools (we had picked up followers) during the rush hour.

The victory was without reward. By the time we were able to eat the ice cream, we had made enemies of the ones who were serving it. And since we had the old fear of people spitting in our food, we left Bridgeman's for the younger students coming behind us who had not angered the soda jerks.

The Strand and the Riviera theaters on Wabasha, looking south toward Seventh Street, c. 1941. Also visible (at right) are the St. Francis Hotel, Walgreen's and Schuneman's. *Minnesota Historical Society.*

In 1958 Gareth Hiebert (Oliver Towne) was persuaded by his many readers and friends to gather together, "under book covers," a collection of his columns from the St. Paul Dispatch *on the subject of, as he states in the collection's preface, "the lives and fortunes, buildings and streets of St. Paul as it looked to me in the beginning of the second half of the twentieth century." That book,* St. Paul is My Beat, *and Mr. Hiebert's subsequent book,* Once Upon a Towne, *constitute nothing less than a hymn to the city of St. Paul, a prose poem, really, which captures St. Paul in all of its many moods and aspects during the last of the glory days of its downtown. We are greatly indebted to Mr. Hiebert for allowing us to reprint these wonderful columns. They are without a doubt some of the finest writing that has ever been done about downtown St. Paul.*

Portrait of a City

BY OLIVER TOWNE

Viewed from a distance, my town is a pyramiding, jagged line of buildings—red brick, gray, salmon-colored, streaked by weather and smudged from smoke and grit.

By day, the panes of thousands of windows reflect the sun and by night gleam as pin points of light that go out one by one as if touched by an unseen hand, until the skyline is only a dark hulk in the moonlight.

Close up, the city is lines of cars darting in and out of threading traffic lines; it is the people who pour out of the buildings at noonday, who form a glut of humanity at Seventh and Wabasha, who jostle each other amid a rustle of packages on the buses that weave out of the Loop at 5 p.m.

The city is the cop on the beat at Ninth and St. Peter at 1 a.m., the children crawling over the slides and swings on a school playground in the sunshine of a warm, spring day.

It is the lonely switchmen in the railroad yards, talking their own language with lanterns, and it is the rising moan of the siren from the ambulance, the fire engine or police car.

The city is the smoky convention hall and the slam-bang din of music from a dance ball on West Seventh on Saturday night, where a bride and groom dash out to their car amid a shower of rice and cheers.

My town is the magnificent swell of a church choir's hymn on Sunday morning.

This town is a blend of the old and new, both in people and architecture. The quicksand of the rollicking river town it was more than a century ago has solidified into a firm foundation of grace and poise.

Out of it all has come a personality called St. Paul.

St. Paul is my beat. From the fashionable houses set back behind trim yards on Edgcumbe hill and Lake Phalen's shores to the dim recesses hiding shabby, dingy shacks on the West Side flats and the cul-de-sacs of Lowertown.

In the pinking dawn when the sun's rays shoot up the Mississippi out of the east to the gray of dusk when the pinheads of red, white, green and blue lights garland the hills.

At 9 a.m. at Fourth and Wabasha when the Minnesota Mutual Life chimes announce the day's work has begun; and at 5 p.m. when, as you cross the bridges toward home, the chimes ring out a mellow farewell that rolls across the jagged tops of the skyline and carry far up and down the valley.

Day or night, the city is my beat. To roam at will, scour and prowl, examine and study, note and report, from the vantage points.

Neon and Night
Silence and Seasons

Sometimes the city is confusion in my mind and sometimes the pictures sort themselves out, like postcards on a rack.

The charm and old lace qualities of places like Irvine park and Park Place, Summit Ave. and the Crocus Hill district.

The harshness of the city at Seventh and Wabasha, Fourth and Robert, and Seventh and Robert when the noon-hour surge of humanity pours relentlessly across the intersections.

The feeling of loneliness as you plod against a cold wind and driving snow up Broadway in the lower loop and see the melancholia of a neighborhood that is dying.

The drama and excitement that flashes out of the loop in neon when you get a first look at the galaxy of light and hulking, skyline buildings from the ridge of Summit park at night.

The tomblike silence as you prowl the bowels of the city, in the telephone tunnels, at Fifth and St. Peter, and try to realize that just 20 feet above your head a city is moving.

Foggy mornings when the dirty, gray shroud drapes the tops of the First National Bank and City Hall and the haze, gray blue, with a touch of the smell of burning leaves, that falls across the West Side hill and loop on a warm October evening.

The First National Bank. *Randy Jeans.*

Sundays in the park, Como Zoo, the seals "ooking" at feeding time to a crowd of youngsters, marked by bobbing balloons and trails of popcorn.

The carnival atmosphere of University Ave. at night, with the strings of lights etching the rows of used car lots, a smorgasbord of shiny paint and metal machines.

And at dusk you stand with the river watchers along the railing on Kellogg Blvd. and look back at the blocks of window lights, the silhouettes of office buildings. And, like a reigning monarch, behind those the Capitol dome, bathed in white.

Then you look down river, your face caught in the beam of a towboat spotlight for an instant. And the city, all around, becomes a person.

Spring comes to the city in ways that a country boy might not understand.

Like the morning in April when you leave for the coffee break around the corner and discover you don't need to wear a topcoat.

And the stenographers suddenly look prettier than they did yesterday.

The atmosphere in the 12th floor office, which seemed so cozy against the whining, cold wind, is stuffy and close and somebody opens a window in desperation.

And the electricians who appear to begin measuring and computing for the installation of a new window cooler.

On Wabasha, you see the first gent wearing a tropical worsted suit.

And a bank teller yawning over the dollar bills.

The ladies who sit from the opening tick to the closing tape at Jamieson & Co. stock brokerage office, wearing their new spring hats. And they remind you of Madame La Farge who knit as the guillotine fell in France.

The heady perfume of the florists' shops, open to the passing throng. And the man who looks up at the Twin City Federal sign on Sixth and Robert and opens his tie and shirt collar as the temperature flashes: 65.

And the old garbage and tin cans, covered by winter's snow, are exposed in slovenly sunshine along the river bank just below the Wabasha Street Bridge, along squatters row.

A glimpse of the first river towboats, gleaming white, moored at Lambert landing. And a fretful tug shoves a barge loaded with coal under the Wabasha Street span, two youngsters leaning over the rail to watch it pass—enchanted.

Kellogg Mall at 12:15 p.m., coats and blankets spread out on the still brown grass, dusty from winter's dirt and the wind's deposit of fine dirt.

The frantic surge as the office workers rush pellmell for the mall railing, to look out at the river and down the valley. As if they couldn't get there fast enough, or something would keep them away.

The smell of a department store basement, an aromatic rainbow of cottons, rayons, hardware goods—or what is it that provides that distinctive flavor?

And one of my favorites, gasoline dripping from the nozzle in a filling station.

The musty, cool odors of age that creep out of old, brown stones along Ramsey and the near Loop.

View of downtown St. Paul from the Hamm's tower, c. 1940's. *Minnesota Historical Society*. Paul Schuler.

The sterile smell of antiseptics, tinged with something akin to chloroform, when you walk into Ancker Hospital receiving room.

The contrasting sweetness of roses wafting from the open door-way of a floral shop.

Frying onions and roast beef gravy in an all-night cafe on University or Payne. Bacon and eggs crackling on the griddle at 7 a.m.

The combination of rubber and grease in a garage.

You associate these aromas and smells with the city, with places and things, buildings, stores, events and incidents. Once you have associated them with something or some place in your life, the two are forever inseparable.

For me, nothing quite captures the feel of a city, dynamic and restless, fast-moving and awesome as the smell of ink and newsprint, pouring off the presses as they roll newspapers into the dawn.

This is the stuff of "five-star finals," the reporters dashing into the office ahead of a deadline, this is life and death, violence on a street corner, humor, crime in the shadows, smoke-filled halls—a cross section of the city reflected on a white band rushing between rollers—savored in a smell.

The smell of the city.

Bridge to a City

The Wabasha Street Bridge is a curving, shivering, not especially grand span of steel and wood. On winter's coldest days, the whining wind pummels the pedestrians with icy fists; yet in summer, when the tar is sticky on the paving, the breeze is cool.

And it is an experience to approach the downtown giants in the morning by foot over the bridge, and to leave it the same way at dusk. There is a perspective, not only of the city, but the day itself, that is missed by the citizenry who arrive in cars and buses, deposited in packs on the Loop corners.

Did You Ever Smell A City?

Walk the streets, picking out the aromas, odors that mix into a city like the people and the buildings.

Stroll at Eleventh and Minnesota about midnight when the mouth-watering aroma of fresh bread scents the night air, pouring out of the nearby bakery, lights blazing.

Or stand, fascinated, in front of the little spice shop on Sixth, drinking in the exotic smells, the cosmopolitan odors of the world.

And the brisk, interesting aroma of roasting coffee on Fifth near Minnesota.

The distinctive blends you can call the "dime store" aroma—a gamut of brewing coffee, chocolate, perfumes, scented soaps, the salted nuts popping.

The clean smell along soap counters in a drug store and the pungent odor of the disinfectant used on the Union depot concourse tile by the automatic washer that drones through the nearly empty place at 1 a.m.

Walking the streets behind cafe kitchens, exhaust fans exuding evidence of French-fried potatoes, steaks, hamburgers.

The luring flavor of chocolate, rich-smelling, as you pass a candy store.

Candyland, on Wabasha since 1932. *Randy Jeans.*

Stale beer odors seeping out of a tavern on a hot, summer's night and the brief nauseating gusts of sewer gas, spiraling out of some storm sewer holes on a winter's evening.

The piercing, unforgettable smell of leather in a luggage shop or the row of shoe stores along E. Seventh. The warm fragrance of buttered popcorn, mixed with the smell of washed, cool air, pouring out the entrances to movie houses.

The smell of hot asphalt at noon at Fourth and Robert and the indescribable "city" scent of rain falling on searing pavements, kicking up puffs of dust and jets of steam.

You walk the city streets, savoring these aromas—exciting, harsh, but associated with tempo and traffic, people and stores.

Diesel and gasoline exhaust fumes on Robert, hot paint odors stifing the nose sometimes when it drifts across the west bank of the river.

The strangely contrasting country smell of grain, running from spouts into freight cars and barges at the river's edge near Upper Levee road.

The Story Of Two Alleys

It is easy to neglect the romance of something so prosaic as an ordinary alley.

Yet in this city there are at least two alleys which have more dignity in history than many a thoroughfare of grandeur.

And it is strange that in searching out one alley I ran into the story of the second.

It is quite probable that thousands who have stepped over its old, worn bricks have never stopped to think much about Mayall Alley. The very fact that it has a name is unusual. Derived from a St. Paul family of the same name, Mayall Alley has the sound of something a little British, of foggy nights and carriages rolling over the cobbles.

I will have to walk it on a foggy night sometime to find out if this is true. But when I went up to look it over the other day, Mayall basked in sunlight.

It cuts a path, somewhat diagonally, through an oddly shaped block bounded by W. Seventh, Ninth, Auditorium and St. Peter.

Therein is its great popularity. For the alley is a shortcut into the area of St. Joseph's hospital and surrounding neighborhood, on the fringe of the Loop.

The second Union Depot, built in 1923. *Ramsey County Historical Society.*

But more than that. Mayall is a passage into the Loop from that landmark that faces it from across Ninth—Old Assumption Catholic Church. And of all the feet that have tramped on Mayall in four score and 10 years, the majority have been going to or returning from Assumption.

Mayall, if you hunt for it on Seventh, is easy to miss. But if you walk up Seventh just beyond St. Peter you will come to an alley. Turn and you are in Mayall.

By workday, a busy place near Seventh, with trucks backing and filling, loading and unloading, and littered with debris. This is the debris of commerce, usually stuffed by nightfall into incineration or refuse cans. Most of it, anyway.

On Sundays, though, the trucks are gone and the place given over to pedestrian traffic. And the place is a little depressing as are all alleys which look on the wrong ends of buildings.

If you saunter up Mayall you will find that the twin spires of Assumption Church dominate the shadows and the view—always up there ahead.

Near Ninth, and to your left, is a huge parking lot—raised above the alley level and bordered by long stone blocks. These suggest they might once have been foundations of long demolished buildings, but I have no proof.

I recommend that any tours along Mayall be made in daylight since, at night, it takes on a rather eerie and foreboding look, conjuring up suggestions of all sorts of violence. Yet this may be all imaginary.

So I left Mayall and went up to the Public Works department to examine old plat maps for evidence of Mayall's historic past. It has been there a long time—dating back to the 1860s—but there is nothing on the maps to show that houses or shops ever faced it. And it remains a pleasant, well-traveled idiosyncrasy of the city's Loop.

It was while poring over the old plat maps that I discovered the second alley—and with it an important clue for historians who have been trying to locate traces of one of the city's most important pioneer trails—Territorial Road, second only to St. Anthony Trail.

The only segment of Territorial Road, that "super highway" of 1840-50, still popularly known is in the Midway district. It begins abruptly at the Minnesota Transfer tracks and runs into southeast Minneapolis.

How it meandered east into downtown St. Paul has been a mystery. All traces seemed to have been obliterated by progress.

But there is still a little piece of it in the Hamline District—in an alley winding as a crooked diagonal line through the block bordered by Blair, Van Buren, Wheeler and Aldine.

It will undoubtedly come as a surprise to those residents whose garbage cans line the alley to know that the lane is descended of such aristocracy. But that is old Territorial Road, plainly marked on the original plat maps.

Time and the Public Works department have covered over the remnants of the trail with asphalt and dirt, but the youngsters who live in the houses backing on it could do worse than listen, in the still of the night, for the creaking of the old wagons that once bumped down that alley. And who knows what they might find buried far below the surface?

For it will take the imagination of a child to see the alley as something else. When I drove through it one day recently, it looked like an alley—nothing more, try as I did to feel the impact of driving over history.

They Call It "Jackson Street"

Jackson Street has a strange allure.

From Kellogg north to Eighth, the street has reminded me of a well-bred gentleman on his uppers who wears threadbare, but expensive, attire with dignity.

There is that faint, musty odor of antiquity and "better days" in the atmosphere along Jackson, yet the strange sensation of faded grandeur and high drama lurks just in the shadows of the rough, brick alleys.

It has lived its four score and ten and long ago gave up trying to anchor the Lower Loop with any semblance of the glitter you find on Wabasha, Robert or St. Peter.

In retrospect, Jackson has played three roles in

Jackson Street Mashers

Jackson Street, even in some of the coldest of days, is infested with mashers—impudent roues who leer at every lady who passes them, as though Respectability ne'er wore petticoats. They keep within bounds, which precludes all possibility of arrest, but I hear there is some talk among ladies of organizing a horse-whipping club and giving some of the boldest a lesson.

Speaking of mashing, women often invite the attention of men of the stripe I have referred to by their careless conduct in public, especially when two or three of them get together. They laugh and giggle and display their hosiery in such a manner as to challenge insult. It is not an infallible rule, but as a general thing the lady who conducts herself with dignity on the street will not be insulted.

The Eye, 1890

---

its long span. It has been a gay street of commerce, hotels and cafes. And Jackson has been a misery street of lost week-ends, poverty and wobbly-gaited men whose blank stares were as bare as the empty show cases behind plate glass windows into which they looked.

And now, the wheels of commerce hum on Jackson again and, like Jericho, some of the old walls are tumbling down to make way for parking lot after parking lot and quite a few people think it is a mighty good thing for Jackson to be so accommodating. Which it probably is.

Within ten years the Jackson street I stroll down may be part of that "gay dog" past. But it still holds magic for anyone with a slight imagination.

You start at Kellogg. And there's the old Hale Building, solid from Kellogg to Fourth and to look at, it speaks of at least 70 years.

At one end, on Fourth, there used to be Sam Eady's Cigar Shop, and down toward the other end was Froderwell's Cafe. Upstairs was Than's Barbecue (now up on Fourth), a place I well remember myself for ribs and fried chicken at 2 a.m. after the last edition of the *Pioneer Press* had "gone to bed."

And during prohibition, a battery of speakeasies were said to line the building. You can stand today in Novotny's Gun Shop, one of the old timers still doing business, and look across the street at the block-long parking lot.

There, at Kellogg, was where the fabulous Merchants Hotel rose majestically, the "home away from home" of politicians, railroad executives. They used to say that if you stood at the bar of the Merchants at noon, you would see every railroad official in the city by the end of the hour.

Almost as colorful, or more so, were the two blocks on Jackson from Sixth to Eighth. In the days of the early 1900's, when Seventh and Robert was the busiest corner in town and Wabasha was on the outskirts, the Liberty Hotel on Seventh, just off Jackson, was one of the keystones of that Seventh and Jackson intersection.

And across the street was the Stees Block, on Jackson, now leveled for a parking lot. Directly opposite on Jackson, the old Foley Hotel, later the Junior and now the Jackson. Floan & Leveros and the Hub stores made up part of the remaining coterie of business firms.

And the brightest place was down a few doors on the right side of Seventh, going east. This was the old Star Theater, where the "Lady in Blue" flounced while young hearts beat in quick time, and first-line burlesque flowered.

I was talking to Angus Cameron the other day. He ran the old Liberty Hotel in the 1910 decade. It was a three-story building, entrance on Seventh, located just where the Emporium now stands.

"It was a fine place," says Mr. Cameron. "The Frederic Hotel was the first in the city to have hot and cold running water in every room. And we were the second."

Angus had the sole concession to solicit hotel business on the steamboats and he regularly sent his manager to Hastings by train to meet the vessels and ride into St. Paul, taking hotel reservations en route.

Newsmen occupied two tables in the cafe. And Angus remembered some of the names: Ed Hosking, Mex Sloan, Bill Sailer, Bill Bowers, Vic Smalley and Henry Lund, now Midway Civic Club secretary.

Across at the Stees Block a story to remember about the Old International Hotel. It happened when efforts were being made to move the State Capitol from St. Paul to St. Peter. Joe Rolette, with bill in pocket, was lured into an upstairs room and so entertained that it was three days-past the deadline for new legislation-before he found his way to the Capitol. And it never was moved.

And one can't forget the Poodle Dog bar. It stands now near the Jackson Hotel. But in the early 1900s, the bar was next to the Liberty. Tom Tobin owned it and his wife kept a kennel of French poodles. A few were always in the window and that's how the place got to be called the Poodle Dog.

The bar is still one of the picturesque places on Jackson. In the basement, says the bartender, are the remnants of the "Blue Room," where reportedly a select order of gay blades, called the Blue Pencil Club, met regularly and feted the burlesque dancers from the Star around the corner.

A touch of the old era is the sawdust still used on the herringbone tiled barroom floor. You can go on and on down Jackson, past old Rockaway's Café— one of the finest in the city—which was housed where the surplus store now does business. And the original Merchants National Bank Building, on the northeast corner of Fifth and Jackson.

That which I have described of old Jackson is difficult to fit into the present. But there all of the color has not washed away.

It is still the queen street to a host of pensioners and derelicts whose world seldom extends beyond Jackson.

And it's an avenue where you will meet such characters as "Yashko" John, Shine Meyers and Ed Wood, the Indian Fighter.

Morrie, the newsboy, claims Jackson as his business property and his voice trills up and down the street day and night.

They roll up the sidewalks on Jackson among the latest in the city and unroll them among the earliest.

And it's the boast of a loyal Jacksonian that a blade of grass has never had time to grow there.

Star And Garter On Seventh Street

It's been a long time since a burlesque queen snapped a garter from the runway of a St. Paul theater. Nowadays, the only strip tease on Seventh Street

Habitués of the Luckenheimer Saloon, at Eighth and Jackson, 1908. Note the spittoon at the feet of the man at center. *Minnesota Historical Society.*

takes place on Monday mornings when they dress the mannequins in the show windows.

But this has not always been the state of affairs in the city, to which a great many sober and serious gents in their 60s and 70s will agree.

As a point of historic record, St. Paul, from 1885 to roughly 1920, held the title of the Northwest's burlesque capital.

And while the Metropolitan and old Orpheum had their enthusiastic patrons, there is generally unanimous agreement that between Minsky's in New York and San Francisco's Market Street, the most famous "burlesque" house in the nation was once the old Star Theater at 170 E. Seventh.

This was burlesque that the present crewcut generation might not understand or appreciate. Because when the Star was shining, bathing suits still came well below the knees. And a sight of Dolly Gray or Lena LaCouvier in pink tights was enough to bulge the eyes of the baldheaded rows.

Nor did anybody ever come away with that "unwashed feeling."

The old Star has been snuffed out and you will no longer see its marquee just around the corner on Jackson. Yet it is still there, much of it, behind the shell of the old Minnesota Furniture Store.

When the theater (it was the State movie house at the last) was sold a few years ago, Harry Schumeister just expanded his furniture shop into that area, thus accounting for the present exterior facade.

It was there that I went one recent afternoon to recreate a picture in the shutaway dressing rooms, the eerie runway under the old theater section and the backstage, now a storeroom.

Mr. Schumeister's son, Melvin; who never enjoyed his father's good fortune of being next door to the Star, guided this tour into the past, with the aid of a flashlight. He, too, has been smitten by the forgotten glamour.

Through his eyes I saw the Star, as it was, 35 feet wide, with wooden-type seats and draped friezes along either wall.

And just behind what is now plate glass window was the lobby and the buzzer system that connected with a bell in Ernest Jackson's saloon at Seventh and Sibley. So that during the 10-minute intermission, the patrons could slake parched throats and still make it back in plenty of time for the curtain.

Somewhere on one wall were neatly-written signs which were duplicated in the programs and said reassuringly: "This house is disinfected to the satisfaction of the management. We invite complaints of any incivility or inattention."

In the theater's heart the floor used to angle down about five feet and there was still room for the horseshoe runway where those dancing legs displayed "cheesecake" a la 1900 to the gaping faces.

The floor has been leveled now—100 loads of dirt between it and the slanting cement surface below.

The old stage archway, with raised gold leaf designs, is still there, a wreath of empty light sockets. And behind that the stage floor, where in 1908 the Williams' Ideal Extravaganza Company, billed as the "Best Drilled and Liveliest Chorus in Burlesque" pranced and hoofed it in front of the incandescent's white heat.

And where, too, Buzz Bainbridge's players and wrestlers and boxers with national acclaim tumbled and fought. Battling Nelson and the rest.

So we left the stage then and went down into the bowels of the old Star, in the inky black, stifling hot from the heat pipes, musty smelling. Melvin Schumeister leading the way, his flashlight beam fanning left and right, probing for remnants of the "good old days."

We walked, heads bent, down the old runway, which the girls used to return backstage after they had gone through their paces on the horseshoe above.

And in the dressing rooms, under the stage, were an old oval mirror, and an oak wood bench, with arch back, circa 1900, which was obviously a stage prop.

"This is a find," said Mel. "I didn't even know it was here, cached away in a corner of one of the rooms."

And in the silence and shadows, the ghosts of titian-haired and blonde beauties, high-button shoes on demure feet, came out of the damp walls.

I could see Ellen Lester, who played "Her Highness," the pride of the regiment in "Blaze Away," primping in front of the mirror.

Or the girls of the front line tucking curls under their street hats before making a dash for Carlings downtown cafe or Rockaways restaurant with their "Stage Door Johnnies" who always waited, flowers in hand.

And Frank Fowler emoting in front of the mirror. While upstairs the chorus sang "Lady Leads the Band," a high-spirited ditty of martial note.

Perhaps the chuckles and guffaws from the audience, faintly through the walls, as they watched Cunningham and Fowley, the song and dance comedians.

J. C. Van Roo, the show's manager, pacing nervously after counting the house upstairs. And Joe Oppenheimer, proprietor and manager of the theater, peeking around the edge of the decorated asbestos curtain.

Then Mel snapped off the flashlight that had played across the old bench and mirror. And the images bleated back into the dark recesses.

And it was just a set of empty rooms again, bare and depressing in the gloom.

I asked Harry Schumeister later about the "Lady in Blue."

"There was a lady of the blue garter," he said. "Maybe she was the one. I can't recall her name. But there was another, Dolly Gray. A beautiful girl. She could have gone out with any man in town."

"She used to come back," he said, "in later years, just to see the scenes of her former glory. She was an old woman then, of faded beauty and it was a little sad to see her."

Just as it is a little sad to think of what the Star was once and now is no longer-on the gay street that has faded, too, like Dolly Gray.

They Call It "Proud Street"

It is a proud street and important. You begin just beyond the limits of West St. Paul and follow it past the rows of new houses, buildings, cafes, stores.

They call it the Main Street of West St. Paul. And, when it breaks down the long hill to Concord, the wide, handsome thoroughfare bends through the flats like an artery, the veins branching off into industrial and historic neighborhoods.

And, when it crosses the Mississippi, it goes on the finest bridge in the city.

From Fourth to Fifth, it is called the "Wall Street" of St. Paul and beyond that a canyon of merchandising. And it ends, not in humility but grandeur, on the edge of the Capitol Approach.

The name they gave it: Robert Street.

Coursing over its wide pavement each 24 hours is commerce on the move-trucks of livestock, heading south; trucks of goods, heading north and west.

The tallest building between Chicago and Denver-the First National-stands on one of its corners.

In the banks and investment houses lining its curbs are transacted more millions of dollars worth of financial business each day than on any other street in the city. On another corner stands a picturesque, landmark hotel of political and entertainment history, the Ryan.

At Seventh street intersection, Robert forms the retail hub of the lower half of the Loop, objective each day of thousands who shop; transfer point for buses in four directions; where, on that corner, the chic and well-dressed women of the city hear the sounds of the country in the caterwauling cry of livestock in trucks, waiting for the lights to change.

It was on Robert, at Kellogg, in the ancient, now gone U.S. Hotel—last of the colorful flophouses—that Jesse James and his gang rendezvoused for the Northfield bank robbery back in the 1870s.

If Robert has been a street of finance, it has been a lane of good eating—sometimes fancy, but also catering to the mass of humanity.

Strung out into 100 years, Robert has sustained millions, in over-alls and top hats and tails.

And it's still a potpourri of food-corned beef and cabbage, Italian, Chinese, prime ribs and ham staring at you through the window. You can eat cafeteria style or on white tablecloths.

Or sit at the counter on a stool at 3 A.M. and listen to the chatter of night-timers and early risers.

If Robert is a street of finance and food, a thoroughfare where brightly-decorated show windows beckon the shopper's pocket-book, it is also a street for all of us. You can buy a bauble for a quarter on one side and spend a fortune for diamonds on the other.

Robert is a gay street still and, at noon, it moves the thousands of hungry stenographers, executives, clerks and businessmen in a sluggish stream, absorbing them in shops and eateries.

For an hour and more they throng the walks, glancing hastily at the two flashing time-and-temperature signs—a special service for Robert Street patrons.

You can walk Robert between 11 a.m. and 2 p.m. and big names of the city and state fall off your lips in a stream.

It is the street of "My Friend Louie" and Morrie, the newsboy, and an assortment of other interesting people. Of Robert it can be said the street has daily loyal habitués.

Yet if you stood on one corner and canvassed the passing throng at noon, I doubt that many would know or even think about the man after whom the street was named.

Louis Robert.

He is part of the history of the street because he knew it better than its most devoted disciples.

Robert was his street and, unlike so many other avenues of the city, which are named for people who could just as well have had their names on a hundred others.

Robert was 23, big, blond, French, with wide shoulders and rippling muscles and piercing blue eyes when he came to the roistering settlement in 1844.

Because of his eyes the Indians with whom he traded later called him: "Istahonhon," which meant "very strong eyes."

It was Louis Robert who established the first trading post at Jackson Street and the river and later established other trading posts at Belle Elaine, St. Peter, Nicollet, Redwood Falls and other towns.

And this keen-witted Frenchman furthered his business and bought the "Time and Tide," a steamboat, for $20 so he'd have a ship to carry his furs to St. Louis.

His fortunes increased and he acquired four other steamboats, including the "Jeanette Robert," named after his daughter, and the "Grey Eagle," a noted river boat commanded by Capt. Edwin Bell.

And his operations always centered on Robert Street. The city's first frame house was built for him near Robert and the river, by his friend, carpenter Charles Bazille.

And in later years, his home was at Eighth and Robert where, day or night, famous Indian chiefs walked in the dusty street to his door and paid him their respects-names like Chaska, Shakopee, Little Crow and Wabasha.

As he watched, Robert's city and street flourished. And he with it. At one time he owned most of Robert Street from the bluffs on the north to the river.

He was prophetic about his street. When William Pitt Murray showed him how to sign his name on an important document, he gave him a piece of land on a swamp with a creek running through it.

"But it will be worth money some day," he said.

That land is the site today of The Golden Rule, Seventh and Robert.

General C. C. Andrews, in his book on St. Paul, said of Louis Robert: "As long as the city shall stand, the name of Louis Robert will be preserved. He was chief among its families and the city is his monument." The general might have added his "street."

For if a street were ever the symbol of its namesake, Robert street—busy, nervous, ambitious, successful, creator of wealth, wages, purveyor of goods, keen, but kind, brisk, but not brusque—is like the man, Louis Robert.

A runaway horse and cart is stopped by police at Third and Robert, 1942. *Minnesota Historical Society.* Photo by *St. Paul Dispatch.*

Seventh and Wabasha, the heart of downtown St. Paul, on a summer's night, September 2, 1952. Note that *Son of Paleface*, with Bob Hope, was showing at the Paramount and *The Big Sky*, with Kirk Douglas, was showing at the Orpheum. *Minnesota Historical Society*. **Photo by *St. Paul Pioneer Press*.**

Seventh And Wabasha

We are told that when the boys in service during World War II and again in the Korean conflict requested pictures of St. Paul, the place they wanted to see most was Seventh and Wabasha.

Other corners and intersections in the city may have a claim to fame, but Seventh and Wabasha has long been a favorite.

In each 24 hours, it plays a variety of roles and is the stage for untold real life dramas.

"Meet me at Seventh and Wabasha" is like saying in New York City, "I'll See You Under the Biltmore Clock." And, standing apart from the rest, we have often watched boy meet girl, or girl meet boy, give each other an embarrassed embrace and then walk off arm in arm.

In the morning, spewing off buses, masses of people crisscross the street, in more orderly fashion, now that they have installed traffic signals on the corners. At mid-afternoon, boys and girls with school books under their arms, some wearing the cadet uniforms of Cretin, St. Thomas Academy, St. Paul Academy and Breck, throng the corners waiting for buses. They are replaced a little later by the clerks, stenographers, shopping housewives, businessmen and overalled laborers swinging empty lunch boxes. The day's tensions, lining their faces, are starting to fade.

But it's at night, when the lights come up and the theater marquees flash their wares, that the corner wears its crown jauntily.

The dressed-up men with their dressed-up dates; the newsie calling out the headlines; cabs whisking around the corner; happy anticipation of the night's entertainment at 7 p.m.; and wistful farewells as friends part again to board separate buses at 11 p.m.

These are the dazzling hours when Seventh and Wabasha is at its animated best, the kind of corner where, on VJ-Day a girl stood on her head in the center of the intersection, and not long ago a man set off a chain of laughter by carrying a sack with a goose neck dangling out of it.

You can hock your watch and buy a mandolin and play snooker pool and stand, mouth watering, in front of the cafe in the Hamm Building where a huge turkey, dripping with juice, turns over and over on a spit.

The only "original Coney Island" hot dog in this part of the country is sold on St. Peter, and also haircuts, and rare curios and hand-painted knickknacks.

You will meet people of a thousand stories, bending their backs over counters in tiny restaurants where, if you sit long enough, the smell of fried food seeps into your clothes.

And if you want your eating plush, with night club blue lights, you can get it on St. Peter, too, in the section I mention.

And while they may not have the advertising techniques of the shops on lower St. Peter, you pick out some picturesque titles, like the "Wide Awake Shoe Repair."

A fellow once told me, too, that the pock marks in the bricks on one building were made by tommy gun bullets in the gangster days of the 1930s.

You can buy groceries and get a hotel room and take a bus—at the new Greyhound Terminal—to any place in the world, from St. Peter Street.

And to stand on the corner of Ninth and St. Peter any hour of the 24 is a study in humanity—lushes on their way to the tiny rooming houses on the fringes of the district, farm boys in for the weekend, youths wearing high-heeled boots and ten-gallon hats, longhaired "city slickers" gesturing effeminately, nurses hurrying from the hospitals in the neighborhood-anxious to get into the more mundane section of the Loop.

Old Nell still limps her way to the corner at 9 A.M. and stands watching the passing throng.

At mid-afternoon, if you come down from Exchange, you can still be in danger of being hit by a drunk listing to port and staggering to starboard.

And who is the little man with the battered bowler hat and worn overcoat who steps briskly up the street with some musty looking books under his arm?

Sundays, upper St. Peter is almost the only place in the Loop where you can still buy the makings of a Sunday night supper of cold cuts, cheese, and pickles—or buy a quart of milk and a pint of ice cream.

And if you browse through the store, bearing the name St. Vincent de Paul, or meander in the place that stacks a thousand—seemingly—items of merchandise on shelves like an old trading post, you will be surprised what you might find.

By night St. Peter, in the shadows, is a place to distrust. Here you can still lose your wallet to a strong-arming purse snatcher and be mugged in a doorway.

And this is no distinction, but it was on St. Peter, about 11 P.M., just beyond Ninth, where I saw a woman sitting on the hood of a parked car, drinking a can of beer and eating a hamburger.

The human procession that lurched past her never took a second look. Only on St. Peter would that happen.

"Dream" Street Is St. Peter

There's still a little color and personality left on old St. Peter Street, if you walk it by day and night, from Sixth Street and on up to Exchange.

Oh, it's not the "dream" street that it was, in the days when the things that went on were a sneering mockery to its pious name. But the thoroughfare still has its eccentricities.

You see a lot of strange people and window-shop odd places from Sixth to Exchange on St. Peter.

You can eat your way into the gout and drink your way into oblivion on St. Peter, in that section to which I refer.

And you can get your laundry done at one of the few Chinese laundries left in town and watch Poy Moy count and figure on his Chinese board.

Hats Off! The Seven Corner Drug Store Is Passing!

Sam, the news vendor at Seven Corners, pressed his face against the plate glass windows and stared a minute through the empty show-case into the bare room beyond.

"First time in 76 years it's been closed," he said. "Seems like you just figured there'd always be a drugstore here."

The way he kept looking it was as if he half expected some magic spell to suddenly whisk the lipstick and seltzer ads back into the show window, the pretty girl on the poster demonstrating a sunburn lotion, a placard dish of ice cream, topped by a strawberry.

The Seven Corners Drugstore is gone. Oldest in the city, starting in 1880. And Sam can't bring it back again-not with all the wishing he does.

There is a void on that once bustling corner that the shopkeepers can't get used to, not in a few days. Nor, for that matter, can the thousands of persons whose paths crisscross on the spot where the front door stands.

For that has been the streetcar and bus transfer point for the city's legions—where east brushed shoulders with west, north nodded to south. The Seven Corners Drugstore was the place everybody waited in that mass exchange.

In winter, the crush of people just inside the door at 5 p.m. was like a mob scene, with one self-appointed wayfarer acting as lookout.

"Here comes the St. Clair car," the shout would ring through the store. And for a few minutes a rush of cold, biting air swept in through the open door as the St. Clair riders filed outside.

And in summer (remember how cool the marble counter felt to the touch on a stifling afternoon?) the Seven Corners Drugstore was a refuge of shade between streetcars. Where you could sit down in the wire-backed chairs, as Joe Nemo remembers it, and revel in the best bittersweet chocolate sundae west of Chicago.

And the old magazine racks—thumbed over by countless hands. Most popular free reading room in town, especially when the Selby-Lake cars were stalled in the tunnel up a few blocks and you had to kill time.

Some days you had to elbow through the "waiting room" to get up to the cigar counter for a package of gum.

But the Seven Corners Drugstore was a wonderful place when you ran out of shaving cream, toothpaste, cigarettes or razor blades.

Folks came to rely on it the way they do an old easy chair, or a favorite pair of slippers.

To each of the millions whose steps took them in and out of the store in 76 years, the place holds a special memory.

"The Seven Corners Drugstore? Let me tell you about the incident I remember it for," says one man.

"This happened nearly 40 years ago. My wife and I were living up on Sixth Street. She was expecting our first child. One night she called—I was working nights then—and said I better come home right away. So I did and hired a cab and we drove to the hospital. But it was a false alarm. She went home.

"Next night she called. I went home, but not quite so fast. And we didn't go to Ancker Hospital in a cab. No sir. We walked down the hill, climbed on the stools in the Seven Corners Drugstore and had a leisurely ice cream soda. Then we got on the streetcar and went to the hospital. I'll never forget that drugstore."

It was the anchor of the Moore Block, in more illustrious years the medical center of the city. S. H. Reeves, it was, who opened up on the corner in 1880, then came Henry McCall, former city councilman, and after him, I believe, Ed Seiberlich and at the end Edmund Oelke.

It was a stepping stone for Mr. Seiberlich, who went on to become president of Northwestern Drug Co. And during his reign one peculiar thing. For 19 years, day or night, when you walked into the place, there was one of the Kulisheck boys on duty. Maybe it was Joe, Art or Adolph. But the last name behind the counter was Kulisheck.

I guess not even the rumors could convince the people on the Corners that the drugstore would close.

"I came here years ago," says Mario Nardi who runs a cafe next to the old drugstore. "If you ever told me I'd see the day when that place would be empty I would have said you were crazy."

And there's something a little forlorn about watching Sam, the news vendor on the corner for 14 years, standing there in silent mourning, trying in vain as he peers through the window, to bring back time.

Chameleon on Fourth Street

If ever they reevaluate the Seven Wonders of the World—and I think it's about time—I'll cast a ballot for the St. Paul Auditorium.

While there may be a few grains of excessive civic vanity in that remark, I'd say the Auditorium is far more remarkable than the Leaning Tower of Pisa or the Taj Mahal. And because it is like so many other obvious things in the city which we pass every day without seeing, few bother to understand its wonders.

Its secret is not in a pile of brick and mortar; nor architectural beauty. The secret is in its ability to change like a chameleon. In fact the Auditorium is more changeable than Minnesota weather and certainly more so than a woman's mind.

In its 30 years, the modern Auditorium has been just about everything to everybody.

It has been a suave night club, with bars and revolving tables of delicacies.

And it has been turned into a three-ring circus.

The Auditorium has been a giant, blue-draped, hushed mortuary for the funeral directors convention and the same night rocked with cheers of 3,000 hockey-mad spectators.

It is the only building in the world through which an entire parade passes—the Winter Carnival Grand Parade.

When 5,000 delegates to the Farmers Union Grain Terminal Association meeting sat down to eat their dinner in the arena during December 1957, the Auditorium recorded another milestone—the largest mass sitdown feeding in American convention history.

And for unusual roles, nobody who was there will ever forget the night of the Brown & Bigelow anniversary party a few years ago when the arena was turned into an Arizona ranch and thousands of two-inch steaks were charcoaled over open pits right on the spot.

The Auditorium is the only building in the nation where you can hold a complete convention of elaborate size without going outside. The State Medical Association proves it by registering delegates in the lobby, putting up its exhibits in the arena, eating in Stem Hall and scheduling complete clinics in the theater section.

The secret, as I said, is the ability to change-and fast. Gypsy Rose Lee could take lessons.

In auditorium manager Ed Furni's memory, the night of Jan. 18, 1958, was a stirring example. "That day we had figure skating all morning in the arena, speed skating in the afternoon and a Minnesota hockey game at night. Over in the theater, there were two performances of an old-time barn dance in the afternoon, a jazz concert in the evening—and while all these things were going on, the Home-A-Rama show was setting up in the basement Exhibition Hall."

Another spectacular sleight of hand takes place about Shrine Circus time.

It goes like this: On Saturday night, there's high school hockey in the arena; next day—Sunday—the Lakers play basketball in the same arena; that night a professional hockey game is on. Meanwhile, in the basement, elements of the Shrine Circus are pouring in, ready to create a three-ring circus in the arena by the next afternoon.

Right here, Ed explains, is a gimmick peculiar only to the Auditorium—a portable basketball floor, underside coated with waterproofing, which is placed on top of the arena ice for the basketball game, then removed by evening. And for the circus, the ice is melted and the floor dried so they can begin pouring circus sawdust on the bare terrazzo floor.

On the weekend of the annual Christmas Choral Pageant, the Auditorium arena does another Houdini. On the Saturday night before the pageant, there's a hockey game. Then the entire arena is revamped as a Christmas scene and expanded to seat 12,000 persons. No sooner is the pageant ended than crews wreck the setting and prepare the arena for 5,000 delegates to a farm meeting next morning.

The fortunate fact that the Auditorium is really about a half dozen buildings under a single roof is one answer to the riddle of this most unusual of America's civic structures. For instance, it is arranged so that at any time both the arena and exhibition hall basement can be hooked together.

You merely lift concrete slabs out of the arena floor and, presto, you have uncovered big stairways to the basement.

How much St. Paul owes the Auditorium can be put this way:

Without its existence just the way it is, there would be no International Festival of Nations, no Pops Ice Revue; the Winter Carnival Grand Parade finale would be a freezing flop and Convention business would dry to a trickle.

Considering the chances of confusion in these quick changes, it is amazing things seldom snarl.

The St. Paul Auditorium, on West Fifth Street looking east from Franklin (now Auditorium) Street, c. 1920s. *Minnesota Historical Society.* Photo by C. P. Gibson.

The only case Ed recalls was when the Queen for a Day TV show was produced in the theater.

An engineering convention was on at the same time in the arena.

Well, eager women, not always ladies, formed lines clear around the building. And in their pushy way, they got a little mixed up on directions-so that quite a few found themselves ushered into a symposium on engineering stresses and strains instead of Queen for a Day.

Romance on Market Row

Things aren't the way they used to be on City Market "row," they told me back in 1958. I didn't argue. You don't argue with Simon Goldish and O. E. (Jack) Nelson. Simon is 82 and Jack is 81 and they are the only ones left on market row along Jackson Street who remember it all—64 years on the market.

"All right," I said, "things aren't the way they used to be—but how were they?"

Simon looked at Iack. Jack looked out of the window of Simon's little office. My gaze followed his-across to the market row sheds, lined with parked cars, at the flower sellers.

His eyes paused a moment inside Simon's shed, surveying the crates of big, red tomatoes, baskets of onions, lettuce, oranges, sacks of potatoes. He sniffed the delicious and yet faintly earthly aroma of fresh vegetables and fruit. Like spring.

It was a tennis match, when they began to tell me. The two trading story for story, bouncing off my ears.

Simon told how it was when the market was on Third Street and you were late if you began romancing 180-pound sacks of potatoes around at 2 a.m. And a half century ago Bill Cooney used to signal the day's start by letting out a war whoop that woke all the guests in the nearby Merchants Hotel, so that they had to silence him.

While Simon was gathering his breath, Jack chimed in, naming names that have threaded through market history—Jack Reilly, and the peddlers, Dobson and Lipschultz and poor Mar Pfeffer who jumped to his death one morning from a room in the Hotel St. Paul.

And the La Nasas and "California" Joe Insera.

The grapefruit was unknown and Schoch's grocery finally agreed to take a few, which they dis-

played around the upstairs railing in the store. And a lady from Summit Ave. called and asked how you cook them. They bad a phrase then: "If corn grew on Seventh Street, would Schoch stock it?"

Those were the days—in the early 1900s—when the finest onions in the Northwest grew in the fields near Afton, Minn., on the St. Croix, and in the winter the entire city ate only two crates of tomatoes because they were a summertime food.

And five barrels of head lettuce from New Orleans took care of the city's needs for a week.

"It seems like only yesterday—but it really was 1897—when I sold 27 carloads of Concord grapes in one day," said Simon. "You could sell a carload of spinach off the sidewalk within a matter of hours and now you can't give it away."

"You'd work all day, six days a week and come down on Sundays," said Jack. "And you could stand on the street, on top of cases of fresh strawberries and sell them so fast it made your head swim. And keep an eye out for somebody stealing them from the edge of the pile."

Simon remembered the first time he saw a Washington apple and a navel orange. They were exotic fruits in St. Paul—reserved for the best tables in the best homes, hotels and clubs.

Ramsey county was a cucumber center, with as many as 12 carloads a day going out to Chicago, Boston and Philadelphia.

There were those summer mornings when the flood of fresh green groceries glutted the sheds in the new Jackson Row and grocers loaded up like gluttons after the long winter's famine.

Long before dawn the sheds were sold out and the truck gardeners climbed back on their wagons and went back to harvest more.

You piled and haggled and perspired on steaming August mornings and froze and got chilblains loading and unloading freight cars of oranges and lemons in winter's blizzards. The icy winds blew snow into your shed and the coal stove in the little office never quite kept up with the cold.

"One morning I loaded 450 cases of strawberries between 2 and 5:30 a.m.," said Simon. "But those were days when you hired a wagon, team and driver for $110 a month—any time of the day or night he was on call. "Do you remember the apple parades in 1920?" said Jack, pointing to a picture on the wall.

It showed wagons loaded with apples, carrying homemade signs: "Solomon said: 'Comfort me with apples'," "Oh, you pippin," and "Eat apples 24 hours a day."

Then something happened. Suburbia snuffed out the little truck gardens and sons no longer wanted to work small plots for a pittance when jobs in the city paid so much more. So the huge truck garden emerged as a full-grown business; somebody invented frozen foods; no longer did the city rely on what grew around it.

And, one by one the old-timers dropped back in the frantic pace to keep up with ever-increasing carloads of fruits and vegetables that poured in—12 months a year—from around the world.

So now only Simon and Jack are left from the old guard that once made up the "most cosmopolitan row" in the city.

"I think I hated it all the time," said Simon. "These 64 years. Who would work like a slave in a business like this?"

"I loved it," said Jack. "Like you did. Or you wouldn't be here."

They were arguing about whether they loved it or hated it when I left. But I had my answer. I knew how things used to be on the City market.

And how they're not like that anymore.

History Hotel

Some persons, riding into the Loop just after sunrise, view it as a massive castle on the Rhine, rising out of the morning mist.

The well traveled may see in it at once the opulent luxury of the Metropole in Brussels, the Grand National in Lucerne. With the bay windows, iron grillwork around the little balconies, chimneys dotting the roof, once spiraling wisps of smoke from the ornate fireplace in the high-ceilinged rooms.

The fireplaces are now merely decorative, the chimneys long cool. Yet Phil Lawrence, present manager of the Ryan Hotel at Sixth and Robert—it is the Ryan about which I am speaking—recalls when it was a chore of the bellmen to carry buckets of coal and wood to the rooms with fireplaces.

Stand in the famous old Ryan bar, at the rear of the building, and look at your image in the massive,

The Ryan Hotel, at Sixth and Robert. *Ramsey County Historical Society.*

mahogany-trimmed mirror, and somebody will mention the legend of John L. Sullivan who cracked it with his mighty fist on a dare. The legend is fact and I last heard the story from one who was there, the late Earl Jones, a waiter who became a fixture in the Ryan himself before a hit-run driver cut off his life in the 80s a few years ago.

Which story also was recalled a year or so ago when a boxing ring was set up in the marble-pillared lobby and Del Flanagan worked out each noon before at least two of his matches. About where Mary Garden sang impromptu opera.

Those pillars, by the way, are not real marble, but synthetic covering, installed by Italian artists who imitated the real McCoy down to realistic cracks in the surface.

If your imagination needs exciting, walk up the wide staircase covered by deep carpeting, lined by heavy, oak banisters, and you achieve the same feeling of grandeur—on the same steps that President Grover Cleveland must have felt in 1887, or some of those in attendance at the banquet in 1888 marking Bishop John Ireland's elevation to archbishop, or, perhaps the night they honored James J. Hill in 1893 upon the completion of the Great Northern Railway to the Pacific coast.

I got the feeling of the Ryan's magnificent role in St. Paul hostelry history the other day. I sat at a business luncheon in one of the private dining rooms over some of catering manager Harry Keeney's lentil soup and prime ribs, served on heavy dinner service, and looked out of the window through the crimson drapes. I was almost surprised to see motorcars instead of horse-drawn carriages and drays clattering on the street below.

As I looked around the room, at the marble-framed fireplace, I remembered from my own experience an evening I once spent there as the guest of some swashbuckling Montana livestockmen who'd ridden in on the annual fall parade of sheep trains and were celebrating the harvest.

And other evenings, election nights, when the same dining rooms were turned into party victory quarters and the faithful Came by to pay homage to their champions of the ballot boxes.

Receptions long before my time when the actresses and actors, famed singers and European royalty held "court" on the mezzanine.

What I am trying to say is that between some point in the Alleghenies and San Francisco, I doubt that there ever was or still is a hotel like the Ryan, which has kept neck and neck with progress without losing the almost vanished charm of the great hotels that flourished between 1885 when it was built and the early 1900s.

Though telephone operators and cashier may work under 1959-style drop ceilings in the lobby, and the new elevator is the last word in modernism, the seasoned atmosphere of the Ryan has not been lost. Just kept up by its present owners, Yale and Harry Johnson, who recognize that age can be a useful trademark, not a handicap.

The existence of the Ryan is due to a gentleman, Dennis Ryan, a mining magnate, who built the six stories-plus lobby in 1885. There is debate about who signed No. 1 on the register for the first of the 300 rooms. Some sources say it was Ryan himself.

But another lists General James Heaton Baker of Mankato.

Dennis Ryan set a tradition of good eating which has followed the Ryan all the days of its life. He opened with a banquet too long to detail, but there were such viands as Kennebec Salmon, larded sweetbreads, teal duck, champagne jelly, tenderloin of beef, spring lamb, green turtle soup, washed down with vins de Pasto, de Graves, cardinal punch and finally French coffee.

All this was served in what is now the Marquette Ballroom, which has been the later setting for some of the most fabulous affairs of city and state.

Adding a fillip to the first banquet was the fact that it was served on some $10,000 worth of specially-kilned Limoges China, pieces of which were stored in the hotel vault until a few years ago, but used only five times. They since have been disposed of.

The Ryan's reputation for setting a good table has never been in doubt since. There are, presently flourishing, five eateries, more than in any hotel in this part of the country. And one has a choice between linen and gleaming silverware with menu to match or the sandwich bar toward the rear where the corned beef sandwich is a talking piece. Its Sunday smorgasbord matches the rare items Dennis Ryan's chefs prepared in 1885.

A chill may run up your spine when you learn that, just before World War II, there was serious talk of tearing asunder those three-foot thick walls in favor of a parking lot.

For those old walls, which would spin many a story if they could talk, daily perform yeoman service in providing lodging for the night.

Punch at the Ryan

The Ryan Hotel, whose roman pillars in the lobby have looked at many a piece of history being made since the 1880s, a few years back witnessed the punch being put back into boxing in St. Paul.

What was billed as the best free noon-hour show in town was staged in the Ryan by the principals in a big boxing event.

The lads worked out in a huge ring, erected in the center of the Ryan lobby. And they played to a standing room crowd only during the week—mainly because if you sat down in the easy chairs you couldn't see.

I went around to see the spectacle and it was a good thing I got there before the fight began. The sports in town had just about filled the lobby and spectators were draped up the wide staircase leading to the mezzanine.

The lobby of the Ryan Hotel, 1938. *Minnesota Historical Society*. Photo by Kenneth Wright.

A fellow standing next to me said be estimated the crowd at about 500—including cigars.

"Madam Schumann-Heink didn't draw like this back when she was at the Ryan," said the fellow. 'And neither did Mary Garden."

"Of course they weren't sparring in a ring wearing tights either," I said.

Kid Gavilan, the Cuban fighter, came through the crowd then. He was a dazzling success in a red, white and blue robe. The Kid nodded and bowed and climbed into the ring.

"He oughta have the title," said a man behind me.

Jim Hegerle, the Kid's sparring partner, marched in about then.

These noontime sparring matches were a little confusing.

Wednesday's principals changed partners for the Ryan exhibitions, so that Mr. Hegerle punched with Mr. Gavilan and Del Flanagan traded fists with Tommy Swan. In the Auditorium they were reversed so that it came cut Mr. Gavilan fighting Mr. Flanagan in the main event and Mr. Hegerle and Mr. Swan in the preliminary.

But I guess everybody knows that.

Well, Harry (Doe) Adams, veteran St. Paul fight trainer, got into the ring then, called "time" and Gavilan and Hegerle went to work. They looked to me like they were standing still until I discovered I was watching a pillar instead of the sparring. So I moved around to the other side to get a better look at the play.

Mr. Gavilan put on a good performance. So did Mr. Hegerle. Their gloves powed together, Mr. Gavilan took time out to lecture the crowd about scenery in Cuba. Mr. Hegerle waved to a few friends in the audience; then they began slamming each other again.

Crowd reaction was varied. One fellow kept bobbing his head with the fighters. Another lit the cork end of a cigarette and everybody acted polite and applauded only at the end of a round.

By this time the Ryan lobby was like an old-time, smoke-filled gym, or, as someone said: "Mayhem Manor." Harry Adams came over and said it reminded him a lot of the Rose Room gym in the Hamm Building many years ago.

"These exhibitions are really bringing boxing back to St. Paul," he said. "I mean these here in the Ryan. This is real promotion and it's going over big. Look at the mob. Last Sunday, the boys worked out in the Marquette room upstairs and 400 paid a quarter to watch. Now if that isn't enthusiasm."

I could see the sight was warming Harry's fighting heart. He's been in the boxing business 40 years now. Billy Light, My Sullivan, Chancy Retzlaff and Jack Gibbons were some of the boxers in his training history.

Jack Raleigh, the fight promoter, stood on the fringe of the crowd. He looked like his name was "Happy."

It was Jack's idea to build up enthusiasm for boxing matches by holding sparring sessions in the Ryan lobby.

"This ought to be a good one Wednesday night," he said. "The gate is a whopper right now. I think we can do $45,000."

Mr. Gavilan and Mr. Hegerle had ceased their bickering in the ring and Gavilan went into his dance and rope skipping.

"We give him about 45 minutes and then Flanagan comes on with Swan for the same kind of workout," said Jack.

I don't think the Ryan guests from out of town were quite sure whether they were in a hotel or Madison Square Garden with beds.

I remember one fellow who was trying to check out at the cashier's cage. Every time he started to write a check for the tab, the crowd surged against him, jerking the pen in his hand.

Finally he squeezed himself up against the counter, reached for his wallet and took out some cash.

As he eased his way toward the door, I thought I heard him say, "It was a great fight, Ma! I won."

East Seventh Street, looking east toward Minnesota and Robert, Christmas Eve, 1949. *Minnesota Historical Society.* Photo by *St. Paul Dispatch-Pioneer Press.*

Christmas Eve In The City

Along about 4:30 p.m. the lights begin to come on and a strange quiet muffles the city with the dusk.

And if you go up one of the seven hills of St. Paul and watch and listen, you feel the stillness of the city below on Christmas Eve. Even in the chilly wind the warmth of this one night will rise off the forests of buildings.

In the now dim, almost empty aisles of the department stores on Wabasha and Robert, the fever of the weeks before has subsided. The white covers have been drawn over the confusion of the counters. Only the echoes of the shoppers' frenzy, the employees' parties at the end still ring faintly.

The people have long ago left the Loop. In place of the 5 p.m. rush hour, the last trickle of the stream of humanity rides out on buses and cars, leaving only rows of parking meters like picket fences. The Minnesota Mutual chimes play to an empty house at 5 p.m.

There are gay, bright lights in the city tonight, but not from the flashing neon of the cafes and bars, night clubs or taverns. These, too, are dark. For tonight the lights belong to Christmas—to the lighted trees, shining out of mansion and hovel alike. Of decorations swinging in the night wind, spotlights bathing church steeples, which point like beacons into the darkness.

There is music in the city, too. For this night—at least it is not rock 'n' roll or the discordant jangle of the music of an era or a generation. It is the music of the ages, rising in a crescendo from an organ in a church, from voices gathered around a piano, playing out of the radio in the cab that prowls the streets, on the desk of the hotel night clerk.

It is the tune that the patrolman hums to himself as he walks his beat along Jackson Street and the nun recalls from her childhood as she keeps her vigil in the corridors of St. Joseph's Hospital.

And the soft caroling down the halls of Ancker Hospital drowns out the cries of anguish in the receiving room and the moan of the siren at the back door.

You hear it, too, reverberating through the vaulted Union Depot concourse, played by the organ set in the center, a perfect background for the happy shouts of friends and families in arm-in-arm reunion at Gate 11 or 12 or 18. And down in the trainshed, in the half light of the limited's locomotive cab, the engineer opens his lunchbox and takes out a cold sandwich and whistles a Christmas tune as he recalls Christmas eves of his boyhood.

And I wonder if the pilot of the plane, winging across the city for a landing, imagines himself as something like a Santa Claus, bringing human gifts to people waiting in the terminal? Or does he sing "Jingle Bells" to himself?

And so you stand there on one of the seven hills of St. Paul and look across it on Christmas eve. Then you think how it is with some of the people hidden behind those lights.

There's Casey, the cab driver, taking people to midnight church services, and you know he won't have to spend Christmas in his lonely room. You wonder which of the many invitations to dinner he accepted—those that were phoned in to you.

You remember another lonely man, Father George Skluzacek, chaplain at the Carmelite Convent at Lake Demontreville, and remember the care with which the Guild of Catholic Women packed his gifts while you watched a week ago. "He is one of our special people," they said.

For just a minute you think about Mrs. Gladys Weins, alone tonight at 1641 S. Concord, who took her widow's mite and turned it into Christmas cards for hundreds of men and women in prisons. And you remember the story you heard yesterday about Wilhelm Rande, Norwegian seafarer and artist, who brought his wife and 16-year-old daughter to the city and about the hopes he has that this will be the promised city for a 61-year-old artist, yet the dwindling cash in his pocket was not enough to buy them much of a Christmas for their little apartment. So their only friend in tile city, a guy named Al Smith, took what little he had and gave it to them.

You'd like to look in, too, on the bare apartments and tattered houses and see the looks on the faces of all the children who will know Christmas is for them, too, because of the generosity of the city. A lot of those lights out there tonight are halos being worn.

You have a thought, too, for a little girl named Shannon Neagle, who was 9 and didn't quite live to see the city tonight. Her funeral was yesterday. But the gift she left is as wonderful as any that will be given this year. Her illness created a bond of friendship among the families who live in Windward Heights No.2. They learned the joy of unselfishness.

Suddenly, standing there on the hill you know that word the key to the way it is in the city tonight.

It is mirrored in the judge who will forsake his own Christmas dinner tomorrow to eat with the prisoners in the City Workhouse and talk with each of them.

It is the stranger you meet on the street corner tonight, who wishes you a "Merry Christmas" instead of passing without recognition. The cop who buys the transient a cup of coffee and finds him a bed at the Union Gospel Mission.

And so you walk back into the city, with only one regret. It is like this in the city only once a year.

A car passes and the driver leans out and shouts: "Merry Christmas!"

"Merry Christmas!" you shout back. And it's meant for everybody

Photo courtesy of Patricia Hampl

Patricia Hampl is one of the finest writers I know of, one of those writers (Jonathan Raban is another) whose talents are so transcendent that whenever I have occasion to read them I invariably find myself wondering how many limbs, or digits (or, in some moment of extreme Faustian envy and madness, souls) I'd be willing to give up in order to in even one instance be able to approximate the subtle felicities of their prose.

When I recently reread Ms. Hampl's wonderful book, A Romantic Education, *I was thrilled to find that she had on two occasions written about her memories of downtown: once about having lunch with her Aunt Lillian in Dayton's Skyroom in downtown Minneapolis; and once about a series of shopping sprees in which she had indulged herself while on lunch break in downtown St. Paul. We're extremely fortunate that St. Paul has produced a writer as good as Patricia Hampl. We're lucky as hell that at least on this one occasion she chose to write about our two downtowns.*

Lunch

BY PATRICIA HAMPL

I wandered through department stores behind my dreamy, yet purposeful aunt, stalking with her the expanding rudiments of style, hunting down what gorgeousness we could, stopping only for lunch in the Sky Room of Dayton's Department Store. There, on the twelfth floor, high above the pile of merchandise nearer to heaven, we would take our time over lunch because, Aunt Lillian said, we had been working hard.

We sat at a table, a rounded banquette holding us and our purchases. The bags and boxes always had their own segment of the upholstered seat, as if they constituted a third person. Aunt Lillian encouraged me to order from the full luncheon menu, citing again the morning's hard work.

"Do I have to eat my creamed onions?" I once asked sullenly. There was the brief, puzzled pause of the childless woman, far enough removed from riding her over a ten-year period that she found the question unanswerable at first, the kind of abstruse problem only mathematicians or Eastern religions bothered with. When she recognized it as a child's challenge to authority, she still could not quite play the game. She gave what, at the time, I considered the most eccentric possible answer. "You mustn't eat," she said, "what you don't like." Mustn't. Not the aristocratic spirit of my grandmother's dasn't. Mustn't. Another duty style demanded. Fantastic. "But," my aunt added, "creamed onions are an elegant vegetable."

This was the first appearance on my horizon of what I later learned were critical standards. I looked down at my plate, at the despised onions pooled next to the acceptable Salisbury steak and the luminous round of mashed potato with its volcanic depression glowing with melted butter. The onions were different, just slightly different now. It wasn't just me and the creamed onions anymore in our wordless stand-off. Now it was me, the creamed onions, and the creamed onions' reputation. I did not eat them; I did not give in so easily. But it was something new—how I, because I did not like creamed onions, must not eat them . . . and yet they were elegant. Beauty was not, after all, in the eye of the beholder, not just any beholder. The way of style, of beauty, was not an easy road, not just a matter of opinion. There were givens. Here was authority greater than the parental one I had known. Aunt Lillian might not care about my relation to creamed onions qua creamed onions (unlike my mother who propped me up in front of congealing breakfasts in a test of wills), but, about the place of creamed onions in the world, my aunt was firm. They ceased to be domestic and began to be cultural.

In the afternoon we continued our shopping. I was logy and listless, sated from lunch, and I drooped against posts or curled up in chairs in the fitting rooms or in the model living rooms Aunt Lillian always visited, drifting by the mock-ups like a spy taking her notes. On the rare occasions my brother came with us, the afternoons were torture. He was worn out by then, listless from the heavy lunch—his only reason for coming along—and he lacked my passion for style. Once, when his whining had gotten him nowhere and Aunt Lillian stepped up her pace, adding Bedding and Towels to his troubles, he sat down on a chair in Better Dresses and simply wept, the tears of boredom gushing down his cheeks.

But I was happy and followed my aunt wherever she went. The whole enterprise suggests entombment, I suppose: we arrived at 9 a.m. when the store opened, checked our coats in a locker in the ladies' lounge, and methodically covered every inch of the

View of downtown St. Paul looking north from Wabasha, near Sixth, 1973. Dayton's is at right. Young Quinlan is at center. *Minnesota Historical Society.* **Photo by Eugene D. Becker.**

largest department store in Minneapolis until, at 5:30 p.m., we retrieved our coats, and departed to the sound of some loudly clanging clear-out bell, from a door already locked to incoming customers, which was opened by a custodian leaning on a large broom, smoking a cigarette, waiting to begin his sweep. Uncle Bill waited outside at the curb in his Buick, ready to hear of our day.

Aunt Lillian always shopped in Minneapolis, another essential facet of her otherness, her glamour.

Another indication of her wealth certainly, for in some strange algebra of my own, I felt that Minneapolis, being bigger than St. Paul, must cost more. In my own family shopping in Minneapolis was frowned upon: "You make your money in St. Paul, you spend it here; why go to Minneapolis?" But this only heightened the charm of our shopping trips, of Aunt Lillian, of any affectation at all. Even then, I had become a firm believer in the greater greenness of faraway grasses.

We ate "on the desk," marking the copy and leaving our greasy fingerprints on the porous paper. But the lunch hour itself we each spent as we wanted, not eating, but on break. Some people read; others, caught in the tireless embrace of words, quietly worked the crossword puzzle. One man prepared his weekly column on stamp collecting for the Sunday paper. Another plugged in his blender which he'd brought from home and he whirred up health drinks that were cottony with bran flakes. I, however, shopped. At least on the two nights of the week, Monday and Thursday, that the downtown stores were open at night.

I seemed to be the only one in the stores, the merchandise and the bored clerks with their arms propped on the showcases positioned there for me alone, the solitary shopper of the night. I lost paycheck after paycheck to the soft fantasy of fashion on those nights, while my comrades stayed safely on the desk, reading their spy novels, working their crosswords, checking the box scores, arguing politics (Eugene McCarthy was running for the Democratic nomination, and on my days off I went clean for Gene—I was clean anyway—and knocked on doors in Wisconsin towns where a primary was held.) They stayed on the desk, saving their money. But I threaded my way through the maze of boutiques that cleverly, phonily, evoked the color and brio of a street bazaar, although every cash register was wired to the single credit department above. I knew and didn't care. I spent and spent.

I bought homely, mismatched things; sometimes, they were breathtakingy expensive and my mother gasped when I came home and I modeled them for her. "You went there?" she said, gesturing to the black bag of a deadly elegant little shop, appalled at my audacity. Sometimes I almost cackled with greed at how cheap I'd gotten a rumpled wool skin at the bottom of a basement clearance table. I seemed to have no taste or common sense, no ruling principle. I bought absurd things I never wore or wore only as a kind of penance (you bought it, now you wear it). It occurred to me that I didn't have Aunt Lillian's knack and was devoid of taste.

But the whole enterprise was too dreamlike and compulsive to have anything to do with taste. I see the vacant, ungrasping faces of the evening clerks of Dayton's, not eager, not even interested, in my money. And there I am, rushing and crazed, careening through the aisles in my forty-five minutes, frantic to make a purchase. I scrambled in and out of my clothes three or four times a night in different fitting rooms, exhausted and steamy by the time I got back to the newspaper.

All I knew was that some gnawing hunger abated briefly when I left Better Blouses clutching the smooth beige bag lit from within by a silk shirt that was possibly perfect. I've sometimes thought it was the bag alone I was after: the evidence of purchasing power, the badge of the consumer. Maybe it was, partly. The bags of great department stores and, even more, those of elegant small shops seem to me the seizable emblems of those aloof, intractable places. Like Dexter Green in Fitzgerald's "Winter Dreams," maybe I "wanted not association with glittering things and glittering people," but, as he did, "the glittering things themselves."

But it was more than the crisp bag, and more than the object within it. It was the elevated sphere of the perfect that I sought, away from the grimy newsroom and what had turned out, to my snobbish sorrow, not to be a glamorous occupation after all, but a dispirited tending of wire-service machines and the tedious grammar work that wasn't much different from the sentence diagramming I'd done in third grade. I bought stupidly, things that either didn't fit or didn't suit me, and depleted my salary so that at the end of six months I had nothing at all, because I wasn't buying clothes. I was after the abstract.

I was always the last person back at the desk after the lunch hour, the next wad of copy already laid at my place where I left my welter of soft copy pencils. Nobody ever complained.

I was the mascot. Or maybe, after all their years and all their economies, they understood. "Well," one of them would say as I rushed in, "and what did you get tonight?" They all paused briefly, and smiled, and said it was pretty, whatever bright rag I pulled out of my smooth bag.

Mickey's. *Randy Jeans.*

Mickey's Diner is an institution. It's sat forever on its corner at Ninth and St. Peter, and even though everything around it has completely changed (its corner was changing in a particularly dramatic fashion when the following article first appeared in the May, 1989 issue of Mpls/St. Paul magazine; at that time Mickey's was sitting next to the huge hole in the ground that would soon be home to the St. Paul Companies building), its status was undoubtedly best summed up by Rose, the waitress, when she told Tim Brady (the author of that article, and the gentleman to whom we are indebted for the rights to reprint it in these pages) that "Mickey's is still the same place."

Mickey's

by Tim Brady

It's early Thursday morning in St. Paul, and while the city's other institutions are just rubbing the sleep from their eyes, Mickey's Diner has long since showered and shaved. For 50 years, 24 hours a day, 365 days a year, this wheel-less railroad car has chugged smoothly in place, fueled by the good urban grease of its Sputnik burgers, French fries and Potatoes O'Brian.

Everyone knows Mickey's. It's sat forever in red-and-gold splendor on the corner of 9th and St. Peter streets, like some swollen wurst baffled in ketchup and mustard. Out-of-town rubes point it out to their kids at tournament time. Julio Iglesias recently offered Mickey's patrons an impromptu serenade. They've shot music videos on its doorstep. And the National Register of Historic Places has given the diner its pax vobiscum. Mickey's remains unimpressed: It's got to live here.

"I suppose this place is a testament to my lack of imagination," says Eric Mattson. "What you see is pretty much what you get."

Mattson is the owner of Mickey's and the son of one of its cofounders. He first worked here as a kid peeling potatoes and took over Mickey's in 1970 when his father died. (He also owns another Mickey's on West 7th Street, open since 1969.)

Bert Mattson and David "Mickey" Crimmins opened the doors to the restaurant in the late 1930s in the midst of a fad. It was the dawn of the age of superhighways and air travel, and trains looked more and more like iron-wheeled dinosaurs speeding through the countryside. Yet people had a hankering for the shoulder-to-shoulder ambiance of a dining car. Diners started springing up all over the country, and you could get 'em to go at the Jerry O'Mahoney Company in Elizabeth, N.J. Crimmins and Mattson ordered theirs in 1937. "It's a prefab structure," Eric Mattson says. "Delivered to St. Paul by rail in 1938. It was never a genuine dining car."

Mickey's exterior is a blend of porcelain and stainless steel that "hasn't been painted in 50 years," Mattson says. Inside, a counter runs three-quarters of the joint's length, then stops for a huddle of booths.

In this age of kitsch and nostalgia, when every suburban shopping mall from here to Los Angeles has its imitation greasy spoon, it's good to know the real thing still exists in the heart of St. Paul. Real diners have neighbors like Mickey's neighbors: the Greyhound bus terminal and the check cashing store across the street. The guy on the stool beside you has never been to Edina, let alone the Ediner, and there's a Chinese chef who doesn't know a word of English pouring coffee for the customers.

The waitresses at Mickey's don't have to be coached to offer a sassy patter. When Mary Kiritschenko leans into the counter at Mickey's and asks what you need, you're looking at the genuine article. No one at Mickey's can tell you exactly how long he or she has worked at the diner, but Mary admits to a tenure that stretches to double digits. She manages the place and works the smokers section to the right of the register as you walk in. Rose Erdes is at the fry stove and covers the nonsmokers.

"You got to talk to Rose if you want to find out about this place," Mary says. Then she proceeds to tell you all about Mickey's. The big hole in the ground next door where the St. Paul Companies are expanding actually is going to be the diner's new lounge area, she says. Drunks, she tells you, are known here as "dehorns," though she refuses to offer any etymology for the word. Mickey's hasn't changed a bit over the years, she says, "though the people inside might be wearing out.

"But you gotta talk to Rose if you really want to find out about the place."

Mary is lean, quick, dark-haired and dark-eyed, and when she tells you she's knocked a few unruly patrons off the stools, you believe her. Rose, on the other hand, looks like your great aunt digesting a particularly powerful sermon. When you tamp out your cigarette and move three seats down the counter to Rose's section, it's like moving across a state line, except Mary's call for an order of Potatoes O'Brian (yes, spell that with an A) still rings loud and clear.

Rose has had two stints at Mickey's, the first one beginning 44 years ago. She says she remembers a time when the bus station across the street teemed with sailors coming home from the war. She also remembers a time when St. Paul didn't hop in its car and head to Woodbury every night at 5 o'clock. "Mickey's is the same place," she says. "Everything around it has changed."

Mickey's entertains a shifting clientele. The cabbies and bus drivers come in at 4 and 5 for a pre-shift jolt of caffeine. The breakfast crew begins to trail in sometime thereafter and lingers through the morning. At noon, a few more suits mix in with the regulars. There's another coffee crowd late in the afternoon, and then it's strays for suppers, early and late, until the apres-bartime crowd comes in.

The customers are a melange of city types, ranging at the counter from the heavy-metal street kid with six earrings and a clanging leather jacket to little old ladies cool in cat glasses and hats that scream, "Proudly purchased in 1962." Out-of-towners visiting relatives in the neighborhood hospitals drop in too, as do parents with kids in the nearby juvenile center. Tasseled loafers are few and far between.

Those who come feed on all-day breakfasts, Mulligan stew and those triple-decker Sputnik Burgers, which were born during the space race in 1957 and have continued to drip on your chin through the Mercury program, moon landings and shuttle disasters. They're still called Sputniks.

"Mickey's just doesn't change that much," Mattson says. Though once again the city is transforming around it. When that big hole in the ground that Mary likes to think of as Mickey's new lounge actually is filled with several stories of insurance company, Mickey's will look more and more like a little bus waiting for the light to change on St. Peter.

Don't bet that it moves in the next 50 years.

William Hoffman wrote four books about growing up on St. Paul's West Side, among them, Those Were the Days *and* West Side Story II. *In the following two excerpts from* West Side Story II, *William Hoffman first tells the story of "Downtown on a Saturday," and then of his boyhood career "Selling Newspapers" in downtown St. Paul. In both pieces, Mr. Hoffman provides us with a fascinating window on the world of downtown St. Paul in the 1920s. We're grateful, indeed, for the opportunity to reprint them in the pages of* Downtown.

Downtown On a Saturday

BY WILLIAM HOFFMAN

For West Siders, Saturday was a day to go downtown—where else! Downtown was a twenty-minute walk from any point in the West Side. Either you walked across the Robert or Wabasha Street Bridge, or you took the Hamline South Robert Street or South St. Paul streetcars for a nickel. No one took the streetcar unless it was an emergency, and spending a nickel to ride when one could walk was seen as profligacy. Besides, it was the Sabbath, upon which day it was forbidden to do any riding, and even the few atheists and other unbelievers did not ride—although perhaps, for other reasons.

Downtown, of course, was not the downtown of today, and without intending to deprecate the efforts of today's Chamber of Commerce, it was an exciting place to spend most of your Saturday. It was a place filled with crowds of buyers and window-shoppers from all over town. There was a mixture of little stores that were worth going into, and even a penny could get you something worthwhile. A nickel would get you into a movie, buy you a half pound of peanut butter kisses or chocolate fudge (with nuts), or a "trephe" hot dog and a big cold glass of Hires Root Beer for another five cents.

The Golden Rule "lounge" was a good place to meet your friends and plan a tour for the rest of the day, or provided a place just to take your shoes off to rest. The dime stores were filled with customers, most of them buying and a few shoplifting. They were genuine "five and ten cent" stores, and it wasn't until the Neisner chain came into town between Woolworth's and Kresges that we saw another kind of sign auguring the distant future; it read, "5, 10, and 25 cents." With a nickel and wursht sandwich from home, you could easily spend a whole day at the Alahambra or Unique Theatre.

Today, between some desultory and non-disciplined efforts at dieting, my Ruth will bring me home some chocolate fudge from our leading candy stores no less. But she knows, and I know that it doesn't have the same taste my ten cent store "chawzeri" had. It just isn't the same, what with the cream and butter and genuine chocolate. Even with my penuriousness, I would gladly pay more for my nickel "chawzeri." Maybe the trouble is that today's fudge-makers do their work in a sterile kitchen with rubber gloves and esoteric formulas.

One of the busiest blocks downtown was between Fifth and Sixth on Wabasha Street. On the one side, which drew the heaviest crowds, was Berde's Butcher Shop and Yale Johnson's Fruit Store. It was no simple matter getting in or getting out, and since there were no deliveries, people flowed out jostling each other and carrying bags tucked up to their chins. The elder Berde was a familiar figure, with bands across his chest, and Yale Johnson was in

Seventh Street, looking east from Wabasha. C. 1922. *Ramsey County Historical Society*

there pitching with the rest of his crew (on their way to becoming doctors and lawyers), wearing the same berry-smeared apron and a big cigar in his mouth. Years later, a rash of small fruit and vegetable stores blossomed out along the length of Wabasha, but none ever had the volume or the real flavor of Johnson's.

Several women's shoe stores, selling low priced shoes were also on the same block, and the names of our friends who worked as "shoe dogs" are legion. They will all remember working under great stress

and an admonition hanging over their heads like the sword of Damocles—"let no customer pass." You didn't dare let a customer get away, and if it looked that way, you had to pass that harried and harassed person to another salesman, usually the manager or his assistant who, hearing the strident cry of "number *33*" manned the pass at Thermopylae. (That customer shall not pass!) Purses, shoelaces and stockings provided extra commission money, but woe to the "shoe dog" who didn't produce. You just had to learn and to believe that if you persevered, any shoe could fit anyone—it was just a matter of pushing, squeezing, shoving, cajoling, sweat, and sweet talk. And there is good reason to believe that more than one desperate shoe dog might have considered even minor (or major) foot surgery for an obstinate customer. Thom McAnn Shoe Store was on the corner of Sixth and Wabasha, and it was there I purchased my first pair of white shoes for three dollars and thirty cents, "none higher."

On another occasion, writing about shoes and some "shoe dogs" who became doctors, I referred to Mintz's Shoe Store on Fairfield, which was, of course, closed on Saturdays, but opened on Sundays. There were two long tables for "specials." Specials meant all lefts and all rights (and never the twain shall meet). Bargain hunters, of necessity, did the best they could to match a left with a right, but it was little less than a miracle if this ever happened. Buyers had to accommodate themselves to ill-fitting shoes and could be identified throughout childhood and adolescence by a bunion on the big toe caused by a right shoe worn on the left foot and a left on the right—the Mintz syndrome! I wrote at that time that some of today's prominent and able physicians probably still had these bunions after all these years.

Not to be forgotten, and literally and physically tucked away in a hallway between Fifth and Sixth, was the Courtesy Newsstand operated by Harry Fredkove. Harry carried newspapers from all over the world, including the *Daily Forward*. There was a special nook in the back for "dirty" magazines, which weren't very dirty by today's standards; but it was an exciting and intriguing hole in the wall. In later years, Harry merged with Crist's Book Shop (or vice-versa), which was joined to his newsstand. If you remember Harry, you will remember his fast gait down the street, beating the palm of one hand with a rolled up newspaper he carried in the other.

The library was always our favorite oasis on Saturdays; it was cool no matter how hot the weather was outside, and there were always some of your friends there, constantly being "hushed up" by the harassed librarians. In the vocally loud and volatile families of which we were all a part, whispering was a strange phenomenon forced upon us only in a library. It remains a beautiful building and one part of it, the Hill Library, must forever be associated with

Mr. Donald Singerman who imparted to so many of us a love for books.

There was the Emporium, Schuneman-Mannheimers, and most important, on the way home, Davini's Confectionery Store, where some of my younger contemporaries finally succumbed to a ham on bun sandwich for a nickel. No matter how tempted, I stuck to the cheese with lots of mustard, and one fine day, when I found a quarter in the street, lingered (but not without guilt) over a chocolate malt. For a total of twenty-five cents—including the cheese sandwich—I could have rented a room for the night at the U.S. Hotel across the street. Legend has it that the Jesse James gang rode out through the archway leading from the U.S. Hotel's courtyard into Robert Street. If you had ever seen the inside of a room at the U.S. Hotel, you could easily believe that the James gang, having stayed overnight, were really fleeing from the hotel to a find a better place, and that the Northfield fiasco was just because the gang hadn't had a good night's rest trying to compete for some room with the multitude of bed bugs and cockroaches.

Reminiscing about downtown on a Saturday brings to mind (with Charlotte Kogen's help) a number of fur stores and their proprietors. It would really be a cavalier treatment of the downtown if they were left out. The history of St. Paul was, in part, written by fur traders and merchants who made St. Paul the center of the fur industry. Even at this time of your life you should remember your history lessons and stories of the squeaking ox-carts loaded with furs.

Joe Getzug had a shop in the Degree of Honor Building, and a colleague who came later (not a landsman!), Paul Glemaker, operated the fashionable Glemaker Furs. I. Rosen, the bachelor of all the furriers, was located near George Devitt's Restaurant, and a few doors away Meyer Nemer and Dave Krupp had their establishment. Max Kogen Furs and Joe Gerschgow provided two additional opportunities to bargain. Between Cedar and Minnesota, Rosen-Engelson boasted of lavish display rooms, and just across the way, Mandel Furs catered to fur buyers and was followed by John W. Thomas, who later occupied the same building. Then there was Joe Tischler and still another establishment nearby, Eva Hope Furs. A. M. Miller & Sons (Max and Sam) were long-time furriers between Minnesota and Robert Streets, just opposite Tatkin Furs. Albrecht's Furs was also on Sixth

The Emporium, Seventh and Robert, April 15, 1948. *Minnesota Historical Society.* Photo by *St. Paul Dispatch-Pioneer Press.*

Street. H. Harris originally opened as a fur coat man-ufacturer, but later went on to cloth coats.

They were all a fascinating breed of men in one of the most competitive fields in industry, and many, including their highly temperamental employees, were creative designers with a great flair for fashion and quality. It was not uncommon for a worker to aspire to own his own place, and so it happened many a time. Wasn't this, after all, the dream of America!

Apropos of furs, there was a time when every West Side woman wanted a muskrat coat. They were not cheap, but the gals simply had to have one. In the early Thirties a gang of muskrat thieves prowled the Robert Street Bridge and the streets leading to the bridge, brazenly wrestling away the coats away from their owners until the police mounted "operation muskrat." There was some suspicion that the threat-ened owners of the muskrat coats would rather have parted with their virtue (if given a choice).

Oh, it was fun to go downtown on Saturday, long before progress and downtown renovation stole our happy haunts away. Bring back, please, Maceys, Husch Brothers, Bannons, the Robert Street Market, and Politz's Hat Store ($1.99 to $2.99 for a hat), and please bring back Davini's and Port Arthur's Chow Mein and "Maish" Marks selling papers on 4th and Robert.

Alas, it is all lost to us forever!

Selling Newspapers

Joe Moss was in town last year, and I had the pleasure of his company for a few days. A lot of people will remember Joe Moss as the man who was in charge of newspaper street circulation for the *St. Paul Daily News*. If you ever sold papers, more than likely it was Joe Moss who threw the papers at you in the old mail room next to the noisy presses.

You would line up in front of the window, calling out your corner—Fifth and Wabasha, Winnecke Doer, Fifth and Cedar, and so on. On the other side of the window, Joe would pick up a stack of newspapers, and in one swift, deft and powerful motion, propel your papers, with cannon speed, into your outstretched arms. If you were small (and it seemed that everyone was), the force of the papers—we called them "sheets"—would just about bowl you over. There was no sympathy in the mail room. It was each kid for himself, and everybody was anxious to be out on the street as quickly as possible. If you were lucky, you could peddle a few sheets on the way to your own corner before that special piece of turf was taken over by its owner. If you were caught, you had to "buy back." If you were stronger and faster, you might get away with it.

During the week, the morning "pink" edition and the afternoon "whites," or home edition, were sold by the older kids and men who were no longer in school; they manned the streets until the rest of us got out of school and hitched rides to get to the window by three-thirty, at which time, the street edition was available. On Saturdays, once being Bar-Mitzved, most of the kids occupied their corners from nine in the morning until about six in the evening, through rain, snow, cold, the heat, and illness. Being sick enough to be away from your corner meant you were ready to meet your maker or were—at the very least—paralyzed!

Although it is Joe I began to write about, there were other street circulators—all colorful characters. There was Bill Smith (one of the first) and, of course, Riggy and Louie Menook for the *Dispatch and Pioneer Press* (the green sheets). Mogie Bernstein, "King of the Newsboys," always on the go and hatless no matter what the weather, succeeded Tommy Moss (Joe's brother), whose untimely and early death left many of us saddened.

All of these men were hustlers themselves; they were not at all averse to tucking papers under their arms and hawking them on the streets to perk up street circulation and earn a few extra dimes. Like the younger newsboys who sold for them, their voices were even more raucous and carried a sense of compelling urgency, even when the crisis existed only in their minds and empty pockets. They shoved their papers, folded in half at harried customers, to keep anyone from getting a free and quick look at the headlines, and they expected a nickel (at least) for a two-cent paper. Woe be to the poor creatures who waited for their change; they were stared down with a hateful eye that said, "Go sue me." The closest approximation is the New York taxi driver whom you fail to tip adequately. For all that, however, they were highly principled men who had learned the hard way how to cope with an environment in which nothing was free. Yet any moocher could get to them, because they were never as tough as they appeared.

The evening edition of the *Dispatch* was green and the *St. Paul Daily News*, pink. There was always a running battle of sorts among the street circulators to promote their own wares. Some of the busier corners had two newsboys—one selling the *Dispatch* and the other the *Daily News*. If one was prudent (and hungry), you might convince Joe or Louie that you should peddle both papers instead of having two kids competing with each other on the same corner. Each circulator, in those instances, insisted that his paper be carried on the outside for visibility. It worked as long as you were able to scout in advance a quick visit from either Joe or Louie. For example, if you saw Joe coming, you made sure you were showing "pink," and if Louie was making the rounds, you hastily shifted colors. If you saw both coming, the better part of valor (and survival) prompted a quick retreat into the alley or some other sanctuary. Do not believe for a moment that any one of us was fooling anyone, but so it went. And if either one pursued the matter a bit further by inquiring solicitously as to your disappearance from the corner, the obvious answer, of course, was that you had to relieve yourself. With tongue in cheek it might be said that all of the newsboys, at least in this respect, belonged to a special group of their "peers."

Riggy, who was Louie's sidekick and partner, was a particularly loveable fellow. The story has it that Louie was Riggy's fight manager at one time, or was it the other way around? I can't remember. They were inseparable, and you seldom saw one without the other. Riggy was an easy mark for anyone who touched him for a "loan," and I don't ever recall him getting angry. He always had a smile and carried on with an admiration for all the world. His compatriot, Louie, who always had a stogy in a corner of his mouth, was, and is, a long time dabbler in stocks, and at one time or another did well.

For quite some time the *Dispatch* street circulation office was in a dingy little building in the middle of the block on Minnesota Street, and after six o'clock, you checked in there with your returns. Joe Moss's check-in room was on the second floor of the *Daily News* office, long since taken over and occupied by the *St. Paul Dispatch and Pioneer Press*. You trudged up the stairs with a pocket full (or less than full) of pennies and nickels and paid Joe and his assistant one and one-fourth pennies for each two-cent paper you sold. You had to be lucky and have received some tips over and above the two cents to come home with much money at all. There were the good days and some that were mighty slim.

On the better days, you might stop off at Davini's, between Third and Fourth Street on Robert, and buy a cheese sandwich on a bun for a nickel. Others bought ham sandwiches for the same price. The ham eaters, I wanted to believe, would ultimately be "shtroophed" (punished) for their terrible indiscretion, but it seems that they never were and grew up like the rest of us. You could splurge and get a slice of lemon or chocolate pie for another nickel, but that required further deliberation and some soul searching.

I do not play with the word "deliberation" in this instance. I had a good corner on Fifth and Wabasha that I shared with Gordy Ukes, who also had a stogy in his mouth most of the time. On a good afternoon after school, I sometimes made as much as 85 cents or even more if a special "extra" came out. Even with 85 cents, spending as much as a dime at Davini's represented a large percentage of total earnings. Believe me, one didn't do that lightly except for the few who never seemed to care like the rest of us—and wound up millionaires, or close to it! It goes to show something, but even as a professor I can't be sure, even today, what exactly it went to show.

There were many "extras," like the Dempsey-Tunney battle, the Lindbergh kidnapping, a local murder here and there, Babe Ruth hitting four in a row. Since some of these events occurred before radio, the more enterprising newsboys "boojacked." I do not know where that term came from, but it referred to papers being hawked in the neighborhoods, and, of course, at a higher price. It was usually the older guys who got out in the neighborhoods for a quick killing, and although there were many more who did so, I recall, at this moment, fellows by the name of "Cockeye" McGregor, "Tots and Gersh" Herman, Foley Edelman, and Puggy Lande.

You may remember another means of communication before there was a Super Heterodyne Radio in your house. The *Dispatch* had an electric score board projecting out in the street. The batter was identified by the flashing of a light, and his progress was recorded by lights on a simulated diamond-shaped ball field. No one, having been part of the huge crowds milling in the street below, could ever forget the almost indescribable thrill of watching the lights flash 1st, 2nd, 3rd, and home for the greatest of all—Babe Ruth, himself.

The newsboys came and went during the decades and ultimately disappeared from the streets forever; they grew up on the streets fighting the cruel cold, the storms, the heat, and frustration especially on those days when it seemed as though no one wanted to buy a paper. They became wise early, learned what the world was really like, were afraid of nothing, and dared life. But neither the cold nor the heat bothered them nearly as much as those lean days when we came home with almost next to nothing and felt the sad despair of a mother reaching out and getting less than hoped for.

There were some other ways of earning some extra pennies and nickels. Most of us were familiar with the location of all the whore houses in town long before we understood their functional dynamics or their reason d'être. It did not take long for our naïveté to vanish. You might say we were junior pimps in a way, steering people to community resources, but truly, we never meant any denigration of the girls, nor did we think badly of them. We earned extra pennies in other ways. We "persuaded" farmers looking for rooms to let us carry their luggage, we conveyed messages between lovers, and even made arrangements for some assignations. We never told and were generally trusted. Ah, what great and titillating stories are waiting to be told!

View of downtown St. Paul from the top of Summit Avenue Hill, c. 1925. *Minnesota Historical Society.* **Northwestern Photographic studios.**

Downtown St. Paul at night, November 27, 1962. *Minnesota Historical Society.* **Photo by Kenneth Wright.**

Greg Horan is a formerly homeless person who was an editor for The Way Life Is: Street Views from Downtown St. Paul, *a free newsletter that was produced by "street writers and volunteers," all of whom, like Greg, had known the pain and indignity of trying to survive as a homeless person on the streets of downtown St. Paul. In the June, 1993 issue of* The Way Life Is, *Greg wrote an article entitled, "A Lonely Walk Toward Morning," a powerful evocation of what it actually feels like to spend a night on the streets. Greg is currently working as an advocate for homeless people for the St. Paul Area Coalition for the Homeless. "A Lonely Walk Toward Morning" is reprinted with his kind permission.*

A Lonely Walk Toward Morning

by Greg Horan

I find myself alone, broken, and homeless. It's a cool evening in September. It is windy and I'm afraid it's going to rain. The clock strikes twelve. My legs feel sore and rubbery. I need a place to sit down. Sometimes I look to buildings with a large doorway. Hiding in parked cars, or sleeping on grates, or finding a bench hidden away from view. These are all bad options, but they must be considered. I choose a bench hidden from view—I hope.

The dark is your friend because it helps hide you. The dark is also your enemy, because it hides stalkers. You sit down. You put your legs up on the bench to restore circulation. After a few days of being on the streets your legs begin to bloat. They feel like anchors. The swelling and discoloring become notable after a week on the streets. I sit on the bench for an hour. Suddenly I hear a sound. A group of young men approach with a radio. I've heard about them at the mission—beating up homeless people for small change and a laugh. I crawl to my feet. I walk toward the light—a Super America. I suddenly have a sharp pain and I know I need to go to the bathroom. I struggle as quickly as I can to Super America. I enter and search out the bathroom. Locked. Oh no. I hope someone gets out fast. A policeman glances at me with suspicion. Finally, the bathroom door opens.

I leave Super America and return to the streets. I do the alley routine. I see two drunks beating up an old man for a bottle of cheap wine.

It's 2:30 and I'm dead tired. I see a parking garage with below-ground ramps. It's warmer below ground. I'm tired of walking and I need sleep badly. I take a chance.

I go along a stairway where no one can see. The cement is cold. It is full with oil and grease. It is my home for tonight.

I fall asleep. The next thing I feel is pain. Is it a nightmare? No, it's a security guard kicking my back and neck. I move quickly to leave but my legs are slowed by pain.

I figure it's about 5 o'clock now and I feel raindrops. I have a-buck-seventy-five to my name. I see Mickey's Diner. My back and neck really hurt. I wish I could see a doctor, but I settle for a cup of coffee.

I see a girl sleeping in the doorway of Joseph's Coat. I enter Mickey's and it's time to go to the bathroom downstairs.

I drink coffee until 7:00 and walk around waiting for the Dorothy Day Center to open. I'm wet, cold and tired.

The feeling of being hunted, stalked, and of being on the outside of society are feelings of the night. You are treated like a criminal for being poor. In fact, the criminal is treated better than a homeless person. He's given a warm place to stay, a warm meal, and rights that a person who is poor does not have.

A man curses at me as I walk toward the Dorothy Day Center, which opens at 8 o'clock. I see Ann Harris and Suzanne. They smile and say hello. A new day begins although I am tired from the last. Today I search for a new home and a bed not made of cold cement. I'm waiting for a new day, a warm smile, and a new dream. But I'm afraid only darkness awaits me

Rights and Permissions

The editor wishes to thank the following individuals and publishers for their permission to use copyrighted materials:

"People and Places in Old Saint Paul," by Alice Montfort Dunn with James Taylor Dunn, originally appeared in *Minnesota History*, Spring 1952. It is reprinted, along with additional materials provided by Mr. Dunn, by permission of James Taylor Dunn.

"Memories of Early St. Paul: Perilous Escape from Fire Down Eighty-foot Bluff," by Mrs. George R. Becker with George A. Rea, originally appeared in the Fall 1973 issue of *Ramsey County History*. It is reprinted by permission of the Ramsey County Historical Society.

"The Green Lantern," by Alvin Karpis with Bill Trent, originally appeared in *The Alvin Karpis Story*, Coward McCann Geoghegan, in 1971. It is reprinted by permission of the Putnam Publishing Company.

"The Minnesota Club," by Gordon Parks, is excerpted from *A Choice of Weapons*, Harpers, 1965. It is reprinted by permission of Harper, Collins Publishers.

"VJ Day," by Elliott Tarbell, originally appeared in the August 15, 1945 issue of the *St. Paul Pioneer Press*. It is reprinted with their permission.

"Bridgeman's," by Don Del Fiaco, originally appeared in the November 13, 1980 issue of the *St. Paul Dispatch*. It is reprinted by permission of the *St. Paul Pioneer Press*.

"Being Black in St. Paul," by Evelyn Fairbanks, originally appeared in *The Days of Rondo*, Minnesota Historical Society Press, 1980. It is reprinted by permission of the Minnesota Historical Society and the author.

"Portrait of a City," by Oliver Towne, originally appeared as parts of two books, *St. Paul is My Beat*, North Central Publishing Co., 1958, and *Once Upon a Towne*, North Central Publishing Co., 1959. It is reprinted by permission of the author.

"Lunch," by Patricia Hampl, originally appeared in two separate sections of *A Romantic Education*, Houghton, Mifflin, 1981. It is reprinted by permission of the author.

"Mickey's Diner," by Tim Brady, originally appeared in the May, 1989 issue of *Mpls/St. Paul* magazine. It is reprinted by permission of the author.

"A Lonely Walk Toward Morning," by Greg Horan, originally appeared in *The Way Life Is: Street Views from Downtown St. Paul*. It is reprinted by permission of the author.

"The Difference Between Then and Now," by Brenda Ueland, originally appeared in *Me*, G. P. Putnam's Sons, 1939. It is reprinted by permission of the author's daughter and the Schubert Club.

"Bridge Square," by Joseph W. Zalusky, originally appeared in *Hennepin History*, Summer 1961. It is reprinted by permission of the Hennepin County Historical Society.

"The West Hotel and the Hostesses' Receptions and Balls," by Loring M. Staples, originally appeared as part of *The West Hotel Story, 1884-1940: Memories of Past Splendor,* Carlson Printing Company, 1979. It is reprinted by permission of his family.

"When Washington Avenue was the Great White Way," by Beatrice Morosco, originally appeared in the Summer 1972 issue of *Hennepin History*. It is reprinted by permission of the Hennepin County Historical Society.

"The Last Trolley Ride," by Joseph W. Zalusky, originally appeared in the Spring 1970 issue of *Hennepin History*. It is reprinted by permission of the Hennepin County Historical Society.

"Fourth Street, Was it Heaven?," by Bradley Morison, originally appeared in *Sunlight on Your Doorstep: The Minneapolis Tribune's First Hundred Years*, 1867-1967, Ross & Haines, 1966. It is reprinted by permission of the *Star Tribune*.

"Grandma's House," by Cedric Adams, originally appeared in the August 10, 1958, and the April 7, 1957 editions of the *Minneapolis Tribune*. It is reprinted by permission of the *Star Tribune*.

"Foshay's Folly," by James Parsons, originally appeared in the March, 1966 issue of the *Twin Citian*. It is reprinted by permission of the author.

"The Battle of the Nylons," by James Gray, originally appeared in *You Can Get it at Dayton's*, 1962. It is reprinted by permission of the Dayton Hudson Corporation.

"Last Call: The Twilight of the Gateway," by David Rosheim, originally appeared as part of *The Other Minnepolis: or The Rise and Fall of the Gateway, the Old Minneapolis Skid Row*, Andromeda Press, 1978. It is reprinted by permission of the author.

"The City that had Gone Indoors," by Jonathan Raban, originally appeared as parts of *Old Glory*, Simon and Schuster, 1981. It is reprinted by permission of the author.

"Keep Harmon Open," by Brian R. Hammond, originally appeared in *Keep Harmon Open: An Urban Homesteader's Journal*, Lowry Hill, 1978. It is reprinted by permission of the author.

"Murray's—The Age of Elegance," by Garrison Keillor, originally appeared in *Time* magazine. It is reprinted by permission of the author. © Copyright 1997 by Garrison Keillor.

•Every effort has been made to secure permissions for publication of all contributions to this volume from authors and publishers. In those rare instances where no response has been forthcoming, it is assumed that all rights rest in the public domain.

Biographical Notes

Cedric Adams was a WCCO radio personality and a columnist for the *Minneapolis Star*. It is said that at the time of his death, in 1961, that he may well have been the most well-known man in Minnesota.

David Anderson is a bookseller from Stillwater, Minnesota. He is the editor of *Quotations from Chairman Calvin*, and *Before the Dome: Baseball in Minnesota When the Grass Was Real*.

Mrs. George R. Becker was the daughter of August Mueller, owner of a tailor shop that in 1870 became the victim of one of the worst fires in the history of downtown St. Paul. She told the story of that fire, with the assistance of George A. Rea, in *Ramsey County History* in 1973.

Willie Bingstad was a former street person and downtown "resident" at the time he wrote about his days on the streets of downtown Minneapolis for the *Twin Citian* in 1967.

J. W. Bond was a writer who visited St. Paul in 1850. He was the author of *Minnesota and its Resources*.

Henry Broderick was the author of *I Remember Minneapolis*.

Tim Brady is a writer who lives in St. Paul, Minnesota. He has written for *Mpls/St. Paul* magazine and other publications.

Edward Conant was born in Portland, Maine and came to Minneapolis as a boy of seven in 1870. He worked as a secretary to T. B. Walker and as a purchasing agent for Thomas Lowry. He was a member of the *Minnesota Historical Society*, the Hennepin County Historical Society, the Minnesota Territorial Pioneers and the Sons of the American Revolution.

Don Del Fiaco was a columnist for the *St. Paul Dispatch*.

Alice Montfort Dunn, whose father was the owner of the old Windsor Hotel, grew up in downtown St. Paul. Her son, James Taylor Dunn, who helped her compile her memories of the early days of the city for *Minnesota History*, is the author of *The St. Croix*, and served for many years as chief librarian of the Minnesota Historical Society.

Evelyn Fairbanks is the author of *The Days of Rondo*.

Paul Ferrell moved from the backwoods of Michigan to Minneapolis, where he eventually became a Washington Avenue businessman. He was the author of *Michigan Mossback*.

James Gray was the author of many books, including *You Can Get it at Dayton's, Pine, Stream and Prairie*, and *Open Wide the Door*.

Henry Griffith was the author of *Minneapolis: The New Sawdust Town*. He was born in Minneapolis in 1882, and during the course of his long life was associated with many of the most famous and influential figures of the Minneapolis of his day.

Brian R. Hammond is a former resident of the downtown neighborhood of Harmon Place. He is the author of *Keep Harmon Open: An Urban Homesteader's Journal*, and is currently at work on a novel.

Dave Hill was an ex-con, "career eccentric," and prominent Minneapolis writer.

Patricia Hampl is the author of *Women Before the Aquarium, Virgin Time, A Romantic Education*, and other books. She is a graduate of the Iowa Writer's Workshop and the recipient of a Houghton Mifflin Literary Fellowship Award.

William Hoffman was the author of *West Side Story II, Those Were the Days, Tales of Hoffman*, and *Mendel*. He taught at Macalester College for many years.

Greg Horan is a formerly homeless person who edited and wrote for the magazine, *The Way Life Is: Street Views from Downtown St. Paul.* He is currently working for the St. Paul Area Coalition for the Homeless.

Garrison Keillor is the host of "The Prairie Home Companion" radio program. He is the author of *Lake Wobegon Days, Happy to Be Here* and other books.

Alvin Karpis was one of the most notorious criminals in America during the 1930s, and in 1936 was sentenced to 33 years in prison for his part in the famous Hamm kidnapping case. Upon his release from prison in 1969 he dictated his memoirs to a writer named Bill Trent. They were published as *The Alvin Karpis Story* in 1971.

Bradley Morison was for many years an editor and reporter for the Minneapolis Tribune. He was author of *Sunlight on Your Doorstep,* a history of the *Minneapolis Tribune.*

Dave Moore spent virtually his entire professional life as a broadcaster for WCCO television. He was also known for his acting ability and his love of the theater. He was author of the book, *A Member of the Family.*

Beatrice Morosco was an actress and a member of the famous theatrical family, the Moroscos. She was author of *The Restless Ones.*

Gordon Parks is a writer, musician, composer, photographer and filmmaker. He is the author of *A Choice of Weapons, Voices in the Mirror, Born Black, To Smile in Autumn: A Memoir,* and many other books.

James Parsons is a *Star Tribune* reporter of long standing.

Jonathan Raban was born in Norfolk, England in 1942. He is the author of *Old Glory, Arabia: A Journey through the Labyrinth* and other books. In 1997 he received the National Book Critics Award for general non-fiction for his book, *Bad Land.*

David Rosheim is the author of *The Other Minneapolis, or The Rise and Fall of the Gateway, the old Minneapolis Skid Row.* He lives in Maquoketa, Iowa.

A. J. Russell was a columnist for the old *Minneapolis Journal* for 45 years. He was the author of nine books, including *Fourth Street* and *One of Our First Families and Other Essays.*

E. V. Smalley was the editor of *Northwest Magazine.*

Loring M. Staples was an attorney and the author of *The West Hotel Story, 1884-1940: Memories of Past Splendor.*

Elliott Tarbell was a reporter for the *St. Paul Dispatch.*

Oliver Towne (a.k.a. Gareth Hiebert) was for many years a columnist for the *St. Paul Dispatch.* He is the author of *St. Paul is My Beat* and *Once Upon a Towne.*

Gretchen Tselos wrote for the old *Twin Citian* magazine.

Mark Twain was the author of *Life on the Mississippi, Huckleberry Finn, Tom Sawyer* and other books.

Brenda Ueland was the author of *Me, If You Want to Write* and other books.

Charles Rumford Walker was the author of *American City: A Rank-and-File History, Bread and Fire, Our Gods Are Not Born,* and *Steel: The Diary of a Furnace Worker.*

Joseph W. Zalusky served for many years as the editor of *Hennepin County History.*

Bibliography

Adams, John S., and Barbara J. VanDrasek. *Minneapolis-St. Paul: People, Places and Public Life.* Minneapolis: University of Minnesota Press, 1993.

Anderson, Chester O., ed. *Growing Up in Minnesota: Ten Writers Remember Their Childhoods.* Minneapolis: University of Minnesota Press, 1976.

Atwater, Isaac, ed. *History of the City of Minneapolis, Minnesota.* New York: Mynsel and Co., 1893.

Bennett, Edward H., with Andrew Wright Crawford. *Plan of Minneapolis.* Minneapolis: Civic Commission, 1917.

Blegen, Theodore C. *Minnesota: A History of the State.* Minneapolis: University of Minnesota Press, 1975.

Bond, J. Wesley. *Minnesota and Its Resources.* Chicago: Keen & Lee, Philadelphia: Charles Sesilver, 1857.

Borchert, John R. *America's Northern Heartland.* Minneapolis: University of Minnesota Press, 1987.

Borchert, John R., and David Gebhard, David Lanegran, and Judith A. Martin. *Legacy of Minneapolis: Preservation Amid Change.* Minneapolis: Voyageur Press, 1983.

Botkin, B. A. *Sidewalks of America.* Bobbs-Merrill, *1954.*

Bromley, Edward A., comp. *Minneapolis Portrait of the Past: A Photographic History of the Early Days of Minneapolis*: F. L. Thresher, 1890, Minneapolis: Voyageur Press, 1973.

Castle, Henry A. *History of St Paul and Vicinity: A Chronicle of Progress. 3* vol. Chicago and New York: Lewis Publishing Co. 1912.

Christianson, Theodore. *Minnesota: The Land of Sky-Tinted Waters. A History of the State and Its People.* 5 vols. Chicago: American Historical Society, 1935.

Clark, Clifford B., ed. *Minnesota in a Century of Change: The State and it's People Since 1900.* St. Paul: *Minnesota Historical Society,* 1989.

Deblinger, Paul. *Culpepper's Minneapolis and Saint Paul.* Minneapolis: Culpepper Press, 1990.

Donovan, Frank P., Jr., and Wright, Cushing F. *The First Through a Century, 1853-1953: A History of the First National Bank of St Paul.* St. Paul: Itasca Press, Webb Publishing Co., 1954.

Eaton, Leonard K. *Gateway Cities and Other Essays.* Ames: Iowa State University Press, 1989.

Empson, Donald. *The Street Where You Live: A guide to the Street Names of St Paul. St.* Paul: Witsend Press, 1975.

Ervin, Jean Adams. *The Twin Cities Perceived: A Study in Words and Drawings.* Minneapolis: The University of Minnesota Press, 1976.

Fairbanks, Evelyn. *The Days of Rondo.* St. Paul: *Minnesota Historical Society* Press, 1990.

Faue, Elizabeth. *Community of Suffering and Struggle: Women, Men and the Labor Movement in Minneapolis, 1915-1945.* Chapel Hill & London: The University of North Carolina Press, 1991.

Federal Writer's Project, Minnesota. *Minnesota: A State Guide.* (American Guide Series.) New York: Viking, 1938.

Flanagan, Barbara. *Minneapolis.* New York: St. Martins, 1973.

Flandrau, Grace. "St. Paul: The Personality of a City," in *Minnesota History,* 22:1-12 (March, 1941).

Folwell, William W. *A History of Minnesota.* 4 vols. St. Paul: *Minnesota Historical Society*, 1921-30.

Frame, Robert M., III. *James J Hill's St. Paul: A Guide to Historic Sites.* St. Paul: James Jerome Hill Reference Library, 1988.

Fridley, Russell W. "The Beginnings of St. Paul," *Gopher Historian* XIV, (Spring, 1960) pp.1-4.

Frieden, Bernard J. and Lynne B. Sagalyn. *Downtown Inc.: How America Rebuilds Cities.* Cambridge, Massachusetts:MIT Press, 1989.

Garreau, Joel. *Edge City: Life on the New Frontier.* New York: Doubleday, 1991.

Gebhard, David, and Tom Martinson. *A Guide to the Architecture of Minnesota.* Minneapolis: University of Minnesota Press, 1977.

Greater Minneapolis. Minneapolis: The Minneapolis Chamber of Commerce, January, 1958.

Griffith, Henry L. *Minneapolis, The New Sawdust Town.* [Minneapolis]: Privately Published, 1968.

Hammond, Brian R. *Keep Harmon Open: An Urban Homesteader's Journal.* Minneapolis: Lowry Hill, 1981.

Hampl, Patricia. *A Romantic Education.* Boston: Houghton Mifflin Co., 1981.

Hardman, Benedict E. *Everybody Called Him Cedric.* Minneapolis: Serendipity Press, 1970.

Hennessy, William B. *Past and Present of St Paul, Minnesota.* Chicago: S. J. Clarke Publishing Co., 1906.

Hiebert, Gareth D. *Once Upon a Towne* by Oliver Towne, pseud. [St. Paul]: North Central Pub. Co., 1959.

Hiebert, Gareth D. *Saint Paul is My Beat* by Oliver Towne, pseud [St. Paul]: North Central Pub. Co., 1958.

Hoffman, William. *West Side Story II.* North Central Pub. Co., 1981.

Howard, William W. "The City of St. Paul," *Harpers Weekly,* February 22, 1890, p.149.

Hudson, Horace B., ed. *A Half Century of Minneapolis.* Minneapolis: Hudson Publishing Co., 1908.

Hull, William H. ed. *All Hell Broke Loose.* Edina, Minnesota: privately published, 1985.

Jacob, Bernard, and Carol Morphew. *Pocket Architecture: A Walking Guide to the Architecture of Downtown Minneapolis and Downtown St Paul.* Minneapolis: Minnesota Society, American Institute of Architects, 1984: rev. ed., 1987.

Kane, Lucile M. *The Falls of St. Anthony: The Waterfall That Built Minneapolis.* St. Paul: *Minnesota Historical Society* Press, 1983.

Karpis, Alvin. *The Alvin Karpis Story. New York :* Coward McCann Geohegan, 1971.

Kaufman, Sam H. *The Skyway Cities.* Minneapolis: CSP1, *1985.*

Kunz, Virginia Brainard. *St. Paul: The First 150 Years.* St. Paul: The St. Paul Foundation, 1991.

Kunz, Virginia Brainard. *The Mississippi and St Paul.* St. Paul: *Ramsey County Historical Society,* 1987.

Kunz, Virginia Brainard. *St. Paul: A Modern Renaissance.* Northridge, Calif: Windsor Publications, 1986.

Kunz, Virginia Brainard. *St Paul: Saga of an American City.* Woodland Hills, Calif: Windsor Publications, 1977.

Kunz, Virginia Brainard. ed. *Rocky Roots: Three Walking Tours of Downtown St Paul.* St. Paul: *Ramsey County Historical Society,* 1978.

Liebling, Jerome and Don Morrison. *The Face of Minneapolis.* Minneapolis: Dillon Press, 1966.

Ludwig, Jack. "A Tale of Twin Cities," In *Holiday,* June, 1962, pp.54-63.

Mason, Karen, and Carol Lacey. *Women's History Tour of the Twin Cities.* Minneapolis: Nodin Press, 1982.

Meier, Peg. *Coffee Made Her Insane & Other Nuggets from Old Minnesota Newspapers.* Minneapolis: Neighbors Publishing, 1988.

Millett, Larry. *Lost Twin Cities,* St. Paul; *Minnesota Historical Society* Press, 1992.

Morison, Bradley L. *Sunlight On Your Doorstep: The Minneapolis Tribune's First Hundred Years. 1867-1967.* Minneapolis: Ross and Haines, 1966.

Morosco, Beatrice. *The Restless Ones: A Family History.* Minneapolis: Ross & Haines, 1963.

Neill, Edward D. *History of Ramsey County and The City of St. Paul.* Minneapolis: North Star Publishing Co., 1881.

Parks, Gordon. *A Choice of Weapons.* New York: Harper & Row, 1965.

Parsons, E. Dudley. *The Story of Minneapolis.* Minneapolis: Privately published, 1913.

Pyle, J.G. ed. *Picturesque St Paul. St.* Paul: Northwestern Photo Co. [1888]. "A Practical Guide to the Twin Cities." *Fortune Magazine* 13:4 (April 1936: 112 ff.

Roberts, Rome. *The Minnesota Merry-Go-Round, or A Diary of the Legislature of the Age:* Privately published, 1935.

Rosheim, David L. *The Other Minneapolis or the Rise and Fall of the Gateway, the Old Minneapolis Skid Row.* Maquoketa, Iowa: Andromeda Press, 1978.

Russell, Arthur J. *Fourth Street.* Privately published, 1917.

Russell, Arthur J. *One of Our First Families and a Few Other Minnesota Essays.* Minneapolis: Leonard H. Wells, 1925.

Schmid, Calvin F. *Social Saga of Two Cities: An Ecological and Statistical Study of Social Trends in Minneapolis and St Paul.* Minneapolis: Council of Social Agencies, Bureau of Social Research, 1937.

Sherman, John K. *Sunday Best.* Minneapolis: Ross and Haines, Inc. 1963.

Shutter, Marion D. ed. *History of Minneapolis, Gateway to the Northwest. 3* vols. Chicago and Minneapolis: S.J. Clarke Publishing), 1923.

Smalley, E. V. "Progressive Minneapolis," *Northwest Magazine,* February 1895, p 21.

Staples, Loring M. *The West Hotel Story, 1884-1940: Memories of Past Splendor.* Minneapolis: Carlson Printing Co., 1979.

Stevens, John H. *Personal Recollections of Minnesota and It's People, and Early History of Minneapolis.* Minneapolis: Privately published, 1890.

Stipanovich, Joseph. *City of Lakes: An Illustrated History of Minneapolis.* Woodland Hills, Calif: Windsor Publications, 1982.

Swanson, Roy W. *The Minnesota Book of Days.* St. Paul: [Author], 1949.

Thayer, Steve. *Saint Mudd: A Novel of Gangsters and Saints.* Washington DC: Pilot Grove Press, 1988.

Ueland, Brenda. *Me.* New York: G. P. Putnam's Sons, 1939.

Walker, Charles Rumford. *American City: A Rank-and-File History.* New York: Farrar Rinchart, 1937.

Whiting, Frank M. *Minnesota Theater: From Old Fort Snelling To The Guthrie.* St. Paul: Pogo Press, 1988.

Whyte, William H. *City: Rediscovering The Center.* New York: Doubleday, 1988.

Williams, J. Fletcher. *A History of St Paul to 1875.* St. Paul: *Minnesota Historical Society,* 1876: Borealis Books, 1983.

Writer's Program. *Minneapolis: The Story of a City.* Minneapolis: Minneapolis Board of Education and Minnesota Department of Education, 1940. New York: AMS Press, 1948.

Index